AF519880

Encyclopaedia of Information Technology and Communication Science

Encyclopaedia of
Information Technology
and
Communication Science

Volume 1

David Park

ANMOL PUBLICATIONS PVT. LTD.
NEW DELHI - 110 002 (INDIA)

ANMOL PUBLICATIONS PVT. LTD.
H.O.: 4374/4B, Ansari Road, Darya Ganj,
New Delhi - 110 002 (India)
B.O.: No. 1015, Ist Main Road, BSK IIIrd Stage
IIIrd Phase, IIIrd Block,
Bangalore - 560 085 (India)
Visit us at: www.anmolpublication.com

Encyclopaedia of Information Technology and Communication Science
© Reserved

First Published, 2007

ISBN 978-81-261-3374-1 (Set)

[Responsibility for the facts stated, opinions expressed, conclusions reached and plagiarism, if any, in these volumes is entirely that of the Editor. The Publisher bears no responsibility for them, whatsoever.]

PRINTED IN INDIA

Printed at Mehra Offset Press Delhi.

Contents

Preface

In today's world communication science and information technology are rapidly growing fields of study, research and development that is cutting across many traditional boundaries. This encyclopaedia titled "Encyclopaedia of Information Technology and Communication Science" is really very unique in terms of coverage, scope, elaboration, usefulness and futuristic perspective. It will provide readers with a user-friendly approach towards acquainting themselves with various select traditional and newly emerging fields of world communication science and information technology. Everyday we see that these sciences and technologies have varied fields of study, which are always growing. To understand the applications and usefulness of these sciences, we need to explain at least one of its fields, such as Multimedia, for example. Multimedia science is a relatively new discipline, and there is currently no consensus on a precise definition of what this science actually is.

Information as a concept bears a diversity of meanings, from everyday usage to technical settings. Generally speaking, the concept of information is closely related to notions of constraint, communication, control, data, form, instruction, knowledge, meaning, mental stimulus, pattern, perception, and representation. Many people speak about the Information Age as the advent of the Knowledge Age or knowledge society, the information society, and information technologies, and even though informatics, information science and computer science are often in the spotlight, the word "information" is often used without careful consideration of the various meanings it has acquired. As with other industrial processes, commercial IT has moved in all respects from a custom, craft-based industry where the product was tailored to fit the customer; to multi-use components taken off the shelf to find the best-fit in any situation. Mass-production has greatly reduced costs and IT is available to the smallest company or one-man band — or school-kid. LEO was hardware tailored for a single client. Today, Intel Pentium and compatible chips are standard and become parts of other components which are combined as needed. One individual change of note was the freeing of computers and removable storage from protected, air-filtered environments. Microsoft and IBM at various times have been influential enough to impose order on IT and the resultant standardisations allowed specialist software to flourish.

Software is available off the shelf: apart from Microsoft Office or IBM Lotus Notes, there are also specialist packages for payroll and personnel management, account maintenance and customer management, to name a few. These are highly specialised and intricate components of larger environments, but they rely upon common conventions and interfaces. Data storage has also standardised. Relational databases are developed by different suppliers to common formats and conventions. Common file formats can be shared by large main-frames and desk-top personal computers, allowing online, real-time input and validation. In parallel, software development has fragmented. There are still specialist technicians, but these increasingly use standardised methodologies where outcomes are predictable and accessible. At the other end of the scale, any office manager can dabble in spreadsheets or databases and obtain acceptable results.

This encyclopaedia titled "Encyclopaedia of Information Technology and Communication Science" is of great contemporary relevance. It will serve as a reference book on the said subject and tends to acquaint readers with both in-depth and extensive knowledge of the subject concerned. This "Encyclopaedia of Information Technology and Communication Science" is a unique initiative to provide the most comprehensive coverage to the subject area in question. This encyclopedia mainly focuses on the following areas: Introduction to Information Technology & Communication Science; Multimedia Information Graphics, Design & Printing; Computer Programming and Hardware Systems; Internet, E-mail, Network System and Computer Security; Music Science and Technology; Audio Visual Technology, Photography and Design; Elements of Advanced Communication System; Mobile Phone and Mobile Computing; and Speech Recoginition Tools and Technologies.

—Editor

1

Introduction to Information Technology & Communication Science

Significance of Information Technology

Information technology (IT) is a manifestation of public and private investment in science and engineering (S&E) that is enabling broad and significant changes in society. Many observers (Drucker 1999; Alberts and Papp 1997; Castells 1996; Freeman, Soete, and Efendioglu 1995; Kranzberg 1989) compare the rapid development and expansion of IT to the industrial revolution in terms of its potential scope and impact on society. Few other modern advances in technology have had the capacity to affect so fundamentally the way people work, live, learn, and govern themselves. As with the industrial revolution, both the time and direction of many of the changes are difficult to predict. The relationship between IT and S&E has two aspects. In addition to being a product of S&E, IT is enabling changes in S&E. IT has become an important part of the overall U.S. investment in research and development (R&D) and affects how R&D is conducted in all disciplines. For example, scientists and engineers make extensive use of computer modeling and simulation and large shared databases; advances in networking facilitate global collaboration in research and product development; and IT producers employ scientists and engineers, implement the results of academic research, and conduct significant amounts of applied R&D. IT also influences the pipeline for S&E through its effects on the demand for people with technical skills and through its use in education at all levels. This chapter addresses IT as a leading example of the effects of investment in S&E on society and focuses on IT as a major force underlying changes in the S&E enterprise. A complete discussion of the impact of IT on society and the economy is beyond the scope of this chapter because IT has become integrated into nearly all aspects of society, from entertainment to national security. Moreover, in recent years, other government publications (Council of Economic Advisers 2001; U.S. Department of Commerce (DOC) 2000a,b) have begun to cover important aspects of the digital economy. References and notes in this chapter direct the reader to some of these other more detailed sources. The chapter begins with a description of trends in IT and then discusses some major implications of IT, including effects on the economy and the general public. Finally, it discusses the effects of IT on elements of the S&E system, including R&D, innovation processes, higher education, and the IT workforce.

Information

Information as a concept bears a diversity of meanings, from everyday usage to technical settings. Generally speaking, the concept of information is closely related to notions of constraint, communication, control, data, form, instruction, knowledge, meaning, mental stimulus, pattern, perception, and representation. Many people speak about the Information Age as the advent of the Knowledge Age or knowledge society, the information society, and information technologies, and even though informatics, information science and computer science are often in the spotlight, the word "information" is often used without careful consideration of the various meanings it has acquired.

Measuring Information Entropy

The view of information as a message came into prominence with the publication in 1948 of an influential paper by Claude Shannon, "A Mathematical Theory of Communication." This paper provides the foundations of information theory and endows the word *information* not only with a technical meaning but also a measure. If the sending device is equally likely to send any one of a set of *N* messages, then the preferred measure of "the information produced when one message is chosen from the set" is the base two logarithm of *N* (This measure is called self-information). In this paper, Shannon continues:

> *The choice of a logarithmic base corresponds to the choice of a unit for measuring information. If the base 2 is used the resulting units may be called binary digits, or more briefly bits, a word suggested by J.W. Tukey. A device with two stable positions, such as a relay or a flip-flop circuit, can store one bit of information. N such devices can store N bits...* [The Bell System Technical Journal, Vol. 27, p. 379, (July 1948).]

A complementary way of measuring information is provided by Algorithmic information theory. In brief, this measures the information content of a list of symbols based on how predictable they are, or more specifically how easy it is to generate the list. The sequence below would have a very low algorithmic information measurement since it is a very predictable pattern, and as the pattern continues the measurement would not change. Shannon information would give the same information measurement for each symbol, since they are statistically random, and each new symbol would increase the measurement. It is important to recognise the limitations of Shannon's work from the perspective of human meaning. When referring to the meaning content of a message Shannon noted *"Frequently the messages have meaning"... these semantic aspects of communication are irrelevant to the engineering problem. The significant aspect is that the actual message is one selected from a set of possible messages"* (emphasis in original). In Information Theory signals are part of a process, not a substance, they do something, they do not contain any specific meaning. Combining Algorithmic information theory and Information Theory we can conclude that the most random signal contains the most information as it can be interpreted in any way and cannot be compressed. Micheal Reddy noted that *"signals" of the mathematical theory are "patterns that can be exchanged". There is no message contained in the signal, the signals covey the ability to select from a set of possible messages."* In information theory "the system must be designed to operate for each possible selection, not just the one which will actually be chosen since this is unknown at the time of design.

Information as a Message

Information is the state of a system of interest (curiosity). Message is the information materialized. Information is a quality of a message that is sent from a sender to one or more receivers. Information is always *about* something (size of a parameter, occurrence of an event, ...). Viewed in this manner, information does not have to be accurate. It may be a truth or a lie, or just the sound of a kiss. Even a disruptive noise used to inhibit the flow of communication and create misunderstanding would in this view be a form of information. However, generally speaking, the *amount* of information in the received message increases the more accurate the message is. This model assumes there is a definite sender and at least one receiver. Many refinements of the model assume the existence of a common language understood by the sender and at least one of the receivers. An important variation identifies information as that which would be communicated by a message if it were sent from a sender to a receiver capable of understanding the message. However, in requiring the existence of a definite sender, the "information as a message" model does not attach any significance to the idea that information is something that can be extracted from an environment, e.g., through observation, reading or measurement. Information is a term with many meanings depending on context, but is as a rule closely related to such concepts as meaning, knowledge, instruction, communication, representation, and mental stimulus. Simply stated, Information is a message received and understood. In terms of data, it can be defined as a collection of facts from which conclusions may be drawn. There are many other aspects of information since it is the knowledge acquired through study or experience or instruction. But overall, information is the result of processing, manipulating and organizing data in a way that adds to the knowledge of the person receiving it. Communication theory is a numerical measure of the uncertainty of an outcome, for example, we can say that "the signal contained thousands of bits of information". Communication theory tends to use the concept of information entropy, generally attributed to C.E. Shannon. Another form of information is the Fisher information, a concept of R.A. Fisher.

This is used in application of statistics to estimation theory and to science in general. Fisher information is thought of as the amount of information that a message carries about an unobservable parameter. It can be computed from knowledge of the likelihood function defining the system. For example, with a normal likelihood function, the Fisher information is the reciprocal of the variance of the law. In the absence of knowledge of the likelihood law, the Fisher information may be computed from normally distributed score data as the reciprocal of their second moment. Even though information and data are often used interchangeably, they are actually very different. Data is a set of unrelated information, and as such is of no use till it is properly evaluated. Upon evaluation, once there is some significant relation between data, and they show some relevance, then it is converted into information. Now this same data can be used for different purposes. Thus, till the data convey some information, they are not useful.

Information as a Pattern

Information is any represented pattern. This view assumes neither accuracy nor directly communicating parties, but instead assumes a separation between an object and its representation, as well as the involvement of someone capable of understanding this relationship. This view seems therefore to require a conscious mind. Consider the following example: economic statistics represent an economy, however inaccurately. What are commonly referred to as data in computing, statistics, and other fields, are forms of information in this sense. The electro-magnetic patterns in a computer network and connected devices are related to something other than the pattern itself, such as text to be displayed and keyboard input. Signals, signs, and symbols are also in this category. On the other hand, according to semiotics, data is symbols with certain syntax and information is data with a certain semantic. Painting and drawing contain information to the extent that they represent something such as an assortment of objects on a table, a profile, or a landscape. In other words, when a pattern of something is transposed to a pattern of something else, the latter is information. This type of information still assumes some involvement of conscious mind, of either the entity constructing the representation, or the entity interpreting it. If you accept that information can be defined merely as a pattern, does it not follow that neither utility nor meaning are necessary components of information?

Surely a distinction must be made between raw unprocessed data and information which possesses utility, value or some quantum of meaning. Information may indeed be characterised as a pattern; it is a necessary condition, but not sufficient. For example a telephone book follows a specific pattern: name, address, telephone number. An individual entry does not become "informative" in some sense unless and until it possesses some degree of utility, value or meaning. For example, someone might look up a girlfriend's number, might order a take away etc. The vast majority of numbers will never be construed as "information" in any meaningful sense. The gap between data and information is only closed by a behavioural bridge whereby some value, utility or meaning is added to transform mere data or pattern into information. When one constructs a representation of an object, one can selectively extract from the object (sampling) or use a system of signs to replace (encoding), or both. The sampling and encoding result in representation. An example of the former is a "sample" of a product; an example of the latter is "verbal description" of a product. Both contain information of the product, however inaccurate. When one interprets representation, one can predict a broader pattern from a limited number of observations (inference) or understand the relation between patterns of two different things (decoding). One example of the former is to sip a soup to know if it is spoiled; an example of the latter is examining footprints to determine the animal and its condition. In both cases, information sources are not constructed or presented by some "sender" of information. To repeat, information in this sense does not assume direct communication, but it assumes involvement of some conscious mind. Regardless, information is dependent upon, but usually unrelated to and separate from, the medium or media used to express it. In other words, the position of a theoretical series of bits, or even the output once interpreted by a computer or similar device, is unimportant, except when someone or something is present to interpret the information. Therefore, a quantity of information is totally distinct from its medium.

Information as an Influence Which Leads to a Transformation

Information is any type of pattern that influences the formation or transformation of other patterns. In this sense, there is no need for a conscious mind to perceive, much less appreciate, the pattern. Consider, for example, DNA. The sequence of nucleotides is a pattern that influences the formation and development of an organism without any need for a conscious mind. Systems theory at times seems to refer to information in this sense, assuming information does not necessarily involve any conscious mind, and patterns circulating (due to feedback) in the system can be called information. In other words, it can be said that information in this sense is something potentially perceived as representation, though not created or presented for that purpose. When Marshall McLuhan speaks of media and their effects on human cultures, he refers to the structure of artifacts that in turn shape our behaviors and mindsets. Also, pheromones are often said to be "information" in this sense. In 2003, J.D. Bekenstein claimed there is a growing trend in physics to define the physical world as being made of information itself (and thus information is defined in this way).

Information as Sensory Input

Often information is viewed as a type of input to an organism or designed device. Inputs are of two kinds. Some inputs are important to the function of the organism (for example, food) or device (energy) by themselves. In his book *Sensory Ecology,* Dusenbery called these causal inputs. Other inputs (information) are important only because they are associated with causal inputs and can be used to predict the occurrence of a causal input at a later time (and perhaps another place). Some information is important because of association with other information but eventually there must be a connection to a causal input. In practice, information is usually carried by weak stimuli that must be detected by specialized sensory systems and amplified by energy inputs before they can be functional to the organism or device. For example, light is often a causal input to plants but provides information to animals. The colored light reflected from a flower is too weak to do much photosynthetic work but the visual system of the bee detects it and the bee's nervous system uses the information to guide the bee to the flower, where the bee often finds nectar or pollen, which are causal inputs, serving a nutritional function.

Information is any type of sensory input. When an organism with a nervous system receives an input, it transforms the input into an electrical signal. This is regarded information by some. The idea of representation is still relevant, but in a slightly different manner. That is, while abstract painting does not represent anything concretely, when the viewer sees the painting, it is nevertheless transformed into electrical signals that create a representation of the painting. Defined this way, information does not have to be related to truth, communication, or representation of an object. Entertainment in general is not intended to be informative. Music, the performing arts, amusement parks, works of fiction and so on are thus forms of information in this sense, but they are not forms of information according to the previous definitions above. Consider another example: food supplies both nutrition and taste for those who eat it. If information is equated to sensory input, then nutrition is not information but taste is.

Etymology

According to the Oxford English Dictionary, the earliest historical meaning of the word *information* in English was the act of *informing*, or giving form or shape to the mind, as in education, instruction, or training. A quote from 1387: "Five books come down from heaven for information of mankind." It was also used for an *item* of training, *e.g.* a particular instruction. "Melibee had heard the great skills and reasons of Dame Prudence, and her wise informations and techniques." (1386)

The English word was apparently derived by adding the common "noun of action" ending "*-ation*" (descended through French from Latin "*-tio*") to the earlier verb *to inform*, in the sense of to give form to the mind, to discipline, instruct, teach: "Men so wise should go and inform their kings." (1330) *Inform* itself comes (via French) from the Latin verb *informare*, to give form to, to form an idea of. Furthermore, Latin itself already even contained the word *informatio* meaning concept or idea, but the extent to which this may have influenced the development of the word *information* in English is unclear. As a final note, the ancient Greek word for *form* was eidos, and this word was famously used in a technical philosophical sense by Plato (and later Aristotle) to denote the ideal identity or essence of something (see The Forms).

Information as a Property in Physics

Information has a well defined meaning in physics. Examples of this include the phenomenon of quantum entanglement where particles can interact without reference to their separation or the speed of light. Information itself cannot travel faster than light even if the information is transmitted indirectly. This could lead to the fact that all attempts at physically observing a particle with an "entangled" relationship to another are slowed down, even though the particles are not connected in any other way other than by the information they carry. Another link is demonstrated by the Maxwell's demon thought experiment. In this experiment, a direct relationship between information and another physical property, entropy, is demonstrated. A consequence is that it is impossible to destroy information without increasing the entropy of a system; in practical terms this often means generating heat. Thus, in the study of logic gates, the theoretical lower bound of thermal energy released by an *AND gate* is more than for the *NOT gate* (because information is destroyed in an *AND gate* and simply converted in a *NOT gate*). Physical information is of particular importance in the theory of quantum computers.

Information is Not Data

The words, *information* and *data*, are used interchangeably in many contexts. This may lead to their confusion. However, they are not synonyms. Often data is defined as raw facts while information is processed data. Another distinction that is made is that information is the things that we know and data is the representation of the information. As an example, we may be thinking about a favorite niece's age, who is four. We would tend to represent that with Arabic numerals (4), but we could represent it using Roman numerals (IV), or any other way we agree on. The information has not changed in each case, although the data has. Note that we tend to think of information in terms of declarative knowledge. That is, the facts we know such as a temperature, an age, etc. Information can also be skills and things we know how to do, which is called procedural knowledge. An important consequence of this distinction is that information has meaning (i.e. can inform), while data does not. Computers work with data (representations) and not information (meanings). This is why a computer will calculate the average employee number even though it is meaningless. Note that one person's information may be another's data depending on whether the recipient understand the data (or its context).

Also, when someone (or some*thing*, such as a computer system) is given a fact, it may only be data, but when they make sense of (or interpret) it, often by bringing it together with other facts, it may become information. Information is usually thought of as, in a strict sense, a subset of data. However, sometimes the reverse interpretation can be taken (such as describing data as "raw information"). Data may also have a more specific sense in some fields (e.g.: referring to a certain type or set of *information* used in that context). When used pragmatically in everyday speech, it usually specifically refers to collections of numbers, or, in a wider sense, to any content not of relevance or interest to the speaker, or not (yet) understood by the speaker themselves in particular.

Data is unstructured, lacks context and may not be relevant to the recipient. When data is correctly organized, filtered and presented with context it can become information because it then has "value" to the recipient. Data which is not information (i.e.: has not yet informed or been given a context) is often called raw data.

Information as Records

Records are a specialized form of information. Essentially records are information produced as by-products of business activities or transactions or consciously as a record of such activities or transactions and retained because of their value. Primarily the value is as evidence of the activities of the organization but they may also be retained for their informational value. Sound Records management ensures that the integrity of records is preserved for as long as they are required. The international standard on Records management, ISO 15489, defines records as "information created, received, and maintained as evidence and information by an organization or person, in pursuance of legal obligations or in the transaction of business". The International Committee on Archives (ICA) Committee on electronic records defined a record as, "a specific piece of recorded information generated, collected or received in the initiation, conduct or completion of an activity and that comprises sufficient content, context and structure to provide proof or evidence of that activity". Records may be retained because of their business value, as part of the Corporate memory of the organization or to meet legal, fiscal or accountability requirements imposed on the organization. Willis (2005) expressed the view that sound management of business records and information delivered "...six key requirements for good Corporate governance ... transparency; accountability; due process; compliance; meeting statutory and common law requirements; and security of personal and corporate information.

Non-Cellular Wireless Communication Systems

People always wanted to communicate and their demands grew with the possibilities offered by technology. Nowadays, modern technology enables mobile communications in many situations. An important component in mobile communications are non-cellular wireless communication systems for short distances. Wireless communication systems can be roughly divided into two categories: cellular and non-cellular systems. In cellular systems the area to be covered is divided in a number of cells. All communication in a cell goes via a single base-station located in that cell. Hand-over protocols and connections between base-stations enable roaming over cell borders. The consequence of this concept is that both an infrastructure and a complex protocol are required.

Non-cellular systems form another category of wireless communication systems for which no infrastructure is required. In this sense the complete system itself is mobile. This thesis deals with systems providing short distance, multi-access, ad-hoc based, point to point communication links. Shortly, we focus on "non-cellular wireless communication systems". Applications can primarily be found as indoor data communication systems as illustrated. As this figure only shows a number of properties of the target communication system, the main properties are listed below:

- Non-cellular systems do not require an infrastructure. Our target system is a non-cellular communication system for short distances.
- Multi-access enables several simultaneous communication links.
- Random-access, this term is in this context defined as the ability of users to initiate a communication link at any arbitrary moment.
- Digital data-communication links Although not completely clear from the picture, the target system is a digital communication system. Applications can be both data-links and (via a speech-coder) speech-links.

This thesis addresses the different aspects of the realization trajectory of such communication systems. Explaining a design methodology by using a concrete design example has the advantage of exactly showing where "difficult" points can be found. For this reason, the design trajectory of a communication system referred to as *wissce* is used to illustrate the proposed design methodology. Concerning such a communication system, a number of sales-points exist. For instance the net data-speed should be high enough to enable reasonable data-transmission speeds. A user would like to have this speed as high as possible, there are however technical limitations. In our system we will therefore use as a constraint a minimum speed of 64 kbit/s which is equal to a single ISDN channel. Another issue is reliability: In most situations a user should be able to initiate a communication link. During communication, the bit error rate (*ber*) has to be acceptable. Other points would be that a user can initiate a transmission link at any arbitrary moment. Also a user does not like long synchronization times or the requirement to install an expensive infrastructure. The possibility to take the system itself and use it at another place would be beneficial. For transmission speed reasons it is also important to provide duplex connections. In this way transmission and reception at the same time becomes possible. The user's wishes are addressed in more detail in chapter 5 where they will be used as a basis to find a system specification.

Geographic Information System

A geographic information system (GIS), or more commonly referred to as a geospatial information system is a system for capturing, storing, analyzing and managing data and associated attributes which are spatially referenced to the earth. In the strictest sense, it is a computer system capable of integrating, storing, editing, analyzing, sharing, and displaying geographically-referenced information. In a more generic sense, GIS is a tool that allows users to create interactive queries (user created searches), analyze the spatial information, edit data, and present the results of all these operations. Geographic information science is the science underlying the applications and systems, taught as a degree program by several universities. Geographic information system technology can be used for scientific investigations, resource management, asset management, Environmental Impact Assessment, Urban planning, cartography, criminology, history, sales, marketing, and route planning.

For example, a GIS might allow emergency planners to easily calculate emergency response times in the event of a natural disaster, a GIS might be used to find wetlands that need protection from pollution, or a GIS can be used by a company to find new potential customers similar to the ones they already have and project sales due to expanding into that market.

Techniques Used in GIS

Data Creation

Modern GIS technologies use digital information, for which various digitized data creation methods are used. The most common method of data creation is digitization, where a hardcopy map or survey plan is transferred into a digital medium through the use of a computer-aided drafting (CAD) program, and georeferencing capabilities.

Relating Information from Different Sources

If you could relate information about the rainfall of your state to aerial photographs of your county, you might be able to tell which wetlands dry up at certain times of the year. A GIS, which can use information from many different sources in many different forms, can help with such analyses. The primary requirement for the source data consists of knowing the locations for the variables. Location may be annotated by x, y, and z coordinates of longitude, latitude, and elevation, or by other geocode systems like ZIP Codes or by highway mile markers. Any variable that can be located spatially can be fed into a GIS. Several computer databases that can be directly entered into a GIS are being produced by government agencies and non-government organizations. Different kinds of data in map form can be entered into a GIS.

A GIS can also convert existing digital information, which may not yet be in map form, into forms it can recognize and use. For example, digital satellite images generated through remote sensing can be analyzed to produce a map-like layer of digital information about vegetative covers. Another fairly developed resource for naming GIS objects is the Getty Thesaurus of Geographic Names (GTGN), which is a structured vocabulary containing around 1,000,000 names and other information about places.

Likewise, census or hydrologic tabular data can be converted to map-like form, serving as layers of thematic information in a GIS.

Data Representation

GIS data represents real world objects (roads, land use, elevation) with digital data. Real world objects can be divided into two abstractions: discrete objects (a house) and continuous fields (rain fall amount or elevation). There are two broad methods used to store data in a GIS for both abstractions: Raster and Vector.

Raster

Raster data type consists of rows and columns of cells where in each cell is stored a single value. Most often, raster data are images (raster images), but besides just color, the value recorded for each cell may be a discrete value, such as land use, a continuous value, such as rainfall, or a null value if no data is available. While a raster cell stores a single value, it can be extended by using raster bands to represent RGB (red, green, blue) colors, colormaps (a mapping between a thematic code and RGB value), or an extended attribute table with one row for each unique cell value. The resolution of the raster dataset is its cell width in ground units. For example, in a LIDAR raster image, each cell may be a pixel that represents an area of 3 meters by 3 meters. Usually cells represent square areas of the ground, but other shapes can also be used.

Vector

Vector data type uses geometries such as points, lines (series of point coordinates), or polygons, also called areas (shapes bounded by lines), to represent objects. Examples include property boundaries for a housing subdivision represented as polygons and well locations represented as points. Vector features can be made to respect spatial integrity through the application of topology rules such as 'polygons must not overlap'. Vector data can also be used to represent continuously varying phenomena. Contour lines and triangulated irregular networks (TIN) are used to represent elevation or other continuously changing values. TINs record values at point locations, which are connected by lines to form an irregular mesh of triangles. The face of the triangles represent the terrain surface.

History of Development

On the walls of caves near Lascaux, France, Cro-Magnon hunters drew pictures of the animals they hunted at 35,000 years ago. Associated with the animal drawings are track lines and tallies thought to depict migration routes. While simplistic in comparison to modern technologies, these early records mimic the two-element structure of modern geographic information systems, an image associated with attribute information. Possibly the earliest use of the geographic method, in 1854 John Snow depicted a cholera outbreak in London using points to represent the locations of individual cases. His study of the distribution of cholera led to the source of the disease, a contaminated water pump within the heart of the outbreak. While the basic elements of topology and theme existed previously in cartography, the John Snow map was unique, using cartographic methods to depict clusters of a geographically dependent phenomena for the first time.

The early 20th century saw the development of "photo lithography" where maps were separated into layers. Computer hardware development spurred by nuclear weapon research would lead to general purpose computer "mapping" applications by the early 1960s. The year 1964 saw the development of the world's first true operational GIS in Ottawa, Ontario by the federal Department of Energy, Mines, and Resources. Developed by Roger Tomlinson, it was called "Canadian Geographic Information Systems" (CGIS) and was used to store, analyse, and manipulate data collected for the Canada Land Inventory (CLI)—an initiative to determine the land capability for rural Canada by mapping information about soils, agriculture, recreation, wildlife, waterfowl, forestry, and land use at a scale of 1:250,000. A rating classification factor was also added to permit analysis. CGIS was the world's first "system" and was an improvement over "mapping" applications as it provided capabilities for overlay, measurement, and digitizing/scanning. It supported a national coordinate system that spanned the continent, coded lines as "arcs" having a true embedded topology, and it stored the attribute and locational information in separate files. As a result of this, Tomlinson has become known as the "father of GIS." CGIS lasted into the 1990s and built the largest digital land resource database in Canada. It was developed as a mainframe based system in support of federal and provincial resource planning and management. Its strength was continent-wide analysis of complex data sets. The CGIS was never available in a commercial form. Its initial development and success stimulated various commercial mapping applications being sold by vendors such as ESRI, MapInfo, Intergraph and CARIS to successfully incorporate many of the CGIS features, combining the first generation approach to separation of spatial and attribute information with a second generation approach to organizing attribute data into database structures. The 1980s and 1990s industry growth were spurred on by the growing use of GIS on Unix workstations and the personal computer. By the end of the 20th century, the rapid growth in various systems had been consolidated and standardized on relatively few platforms and users were beginning to export the concept of viewing GIS data over the Internet, requiring data format and transfer standards. More recently, there is a growing flavor of free, open source GIS packages such as GRASS GIS and Quantum GIS which run on a range of operating systems and can be customised to perform specific tasks.

Merits and Demerits

There are advantages and disadvantages to using a raster or vector data model to represent reality. Raster datasets record a value for all points in the area covered which may require more storage space than representing data in a vector format that can store data only where needed. Raster data also allows easy implementation of overlay operations, which are more difficult with vector data. Vector data can be displayed as vector graphics used on traditional maps, whereas raster data will appear as an image that may have a blocky appearance for object boundaries. Vector data can be a lot easier to register, scale, and reproject. This can make it much simpler to combine vector layers from different sources.

Non-spatial Data

Additional non-spatial data can also be stored besides the spatial data represented by the coordinates of a vector geometry or the position of a raster cell. In vector data, the additional data are attributes of the object. For example, a forest inventory polygon may also have an identifier value and information about tree species. In raster data the cell value can store attribute information, but it can also be used as an identifier that can relate to records in another table.

Data Capture

Data capture—entering information into the system—consumes much of the time of GIS practitioners. There are a variety of methods used to enter data into a GIS where it is stored in a digital format. Existing data printed on paper or PET film maps can be digitized or scanned to produce digital data. A digitizer produces vector data as an operator traces points, lines, and polygon boundaries from a map. Scanning a map results in raster data that could be further processed to produce vector data. Survey data can be directly entered into a GIS from digital data collection systems on survey instruments. Positions from a Global Positioning System (GPS), another survey tool, can also be directly entered into a GIS.

Remotely sensed data also plays an important role in data collection and consist of sensors attached to a platform. Sensors include cameras, digital scanners and LIDAR, while platforms usually consist of aircraft and satellites. The majority of digital data currently comes from photo interpretation of aerial photographs. Soft copy workstations are used to digitize features directly from stereo pairs of digital photographs. These systems allow data to be captured in 2 and 3 dimensions, with elevations measured directly from a stereo pair using principles of photogrammetry. Currently, analog aerial photos are scanned before being entered into a soft copy system, but as high quality digital cameras become cheaper this step will be skipped.

Satellite remote sensing provides another important source of spatial data. Here satellites use different sensor packages to passively measure the reflectance from parts of the electromagnetic spectrum or radio waves that were sent out from an active sensor such as radar. Remote sensing collects raster data that can be further processed to identify objects and classes of interest, such as land cover. When data is captured, the user should consider if the data should be captured with either a relative accuracy or absolute accuracy, since this could not only influence how information will be interpreted but also the cost of data capture. In addition to collecting and entering spatial data, attribute data is also entered into a GIS. For vector data, this includes additional information about the objects represented in the system. After entering data into a GIS, the data usually requires editing, to remove errors, or further processing. For vector data it must be made "topologically correct" before it can be used for some advanced analysis. For example, in a road network, lines must connect with nodes at an intersection. Errors such as undershoots and overshoots must also be removed. For scanned maps, blemishes on the source map may need to be removed from the resulting raster. For example, a fleck of dirt might connect two lines that should not be connected.

Projections, Coordinate Systems and Registration

A property ownership map and a soils map might show data at different scales. Map information in a GIS must be manipulated so that it registers, or fits, with information gathered from other maps. Before the digital data can be analyzed, they may have to undergo other manipulations—projection and coordinate conversions, for example—that integrate them into a GIS. The earth can be represented by various models, each of which may provide a different set of coordinates (e.g., latitude, longitude, elevation) for any given point on the earth's surface. The simplest model is to assume the earth is a perfect sphere. As more measurements of the earth have accumulated, the models of the earth have become more sophisticated and more accurate. In fact, there are models that apply to different areas of the earth to provide increased accuracy (e.g., North American Datum, 1927 - NAD27 - works well in North America, but not in Europe). *Projection* is a fundamental component of map making. A projection is a mathematical means of transferring information from a model of the Earth, which represents a three-dimensional curved surface, to a two-dimensional medium—paper or a computer screen. Different projections are used for different types of maps because each projection particularly suits certain uses. For example, a projection that accurately represents the shapes of the continents will distort their relative sizes. Since much of the information in a GIS comes from existing maps, a GIS uses the processing power of the computer to transform digital information, gathered from sources with different projections and/or different coordinate systems, to a common projection and coordinate system.

Raster-to-Vector Translation

Data restructuring can be performed by a GIS to convert data into different formats. For example, a GIS may be used to convert a satellite image map to a vector structure by generating lines around all cells with the same classification, while determining the cell spatial relationships, such as adjacency or inclusion. More advanced data processing can occur with image processing, a technique developed in the late 1960s by NASA and the private sector to provide contrast enhancement, false colour rendering and a variety of other techniques including use of two dimensional Fourier transforms. Since digital data are collected and stored in various ways, the two data sources may not be entirely compatible. So a GIS must be able to convert geographic data from one structure to another.

Spatial Analysis with GIS

Data Modeling

It is difficult to relate wetlands maps to rainfall amounts recorded at different points such as airports, television stations, and high schools. A GIS, however, can be used to depict two- and three-dimensional characteristics of the Earth's surface, subsurface, and atmosphere from information points. For example, a GIS can quickly generate a map with isopleth or contour lines that indicate differing amounts of rainfall. Such a map can be thought of as a rainfall contour map. Many sophisticated methods can estimate the characteristics of surfaces from a limited number of point measurements. A two-dimensional contour map created from the surface modeling of rainfall point measurements may be overlaid and analyzed with any other map in a GIS covering the same area.

Additionally, from a series of three-dimensional points, or digital elevation model, isopleth lines representing elevation contours can be generated, along with slope analysis, shaded relief, and other elevation products. Watersheds can be easily defined for any given reach, by computing all of the areas contiguous and uphill from any given point of interest. Similarly, an expected thalweg of where surface water would want to travel in intermittent and permanent streams can be computed from elevation data in the GIS.

Cartographic Modeling

The term "cartographic modeling" was (probably) coined by Dana Tomlin in his PhD dissertation and later in his book which has the term in the title. Cartographic modeling refers to a process where several thematic layers of the same area are produced, processed, and analyzed. Tomlin used raster layers, but the overlay method (see below) can be used more generally. Operations on map layers can be combined into algorithms, and eventually into simulation or optimization models.

Networks

If all the factories near a wetland were accidentally to release chemicals into the river at the same time, how long would it take for a damaging amount of pollutant to enter the wetland reserve? A GIS can simulate the routing of materials along a linear network. Values such as slope, speed limit, or pipe diameter can be incorporated into network modelling in order to represent the flow of the phenomenon more accurately. Network modelling is commonly employed in transportation planning, hydrology modelling, and infrastructure modelling.

Map Overlay

The combination of two separate spatial datasets (points, lines or polygons) to create a new output vector dataset. These overlays are similar to mathematical Venn diagram overlays. A union overlay combines the geographic features and attribute tables of both inputs into a single new output. An intersect overlay defines the area where both inputs overlap and retains a set of attribute fields for each. A symmetric difference overlay defines an output area that includes the total area of both inputs except for the overlapping area.

Data extraction is a GIS process similar to vector overlay, though it can be used in either vector or raster data analysis. Rather than combining the properties and features of both datasets, data extraction involves using a "clip" or "mask" to extract the features of one dataset that fall within the spatial extent of another dataset.

In raster data analysis, the overlay of datasets is accomplished through a process known as "local operation on multiple rasters" or "map algebra," through a function that combines the values of each raster's matrix. This function may weigh some inputs more than others through use of an "index model" that reflects the influence of various factors upon a geographic phenomenon.

Topological Modeling

In the past years, were there any gas stations or factories operating next to the swamp? Any within two miles and uphill from the swamp? A GIS can recognize and analyze the spatial relationships that exist within digitally stored spatial data. These topological relationships allow complex spatial modelling and analysis to be performed. Topological relationships between geometric entities traditionally include adjacency (what adjoins what), containment (what encloses what), and proximity (how close something is to something else).

Automated Cartography

Digital cartography and GIS both encode spatial relationships in structured formal representations. GIS is used in digital cartography modeling as a (semi) automated process of making maps, so called Automated Cartography. In practice, it can be a subset of a GIS, within which it is equivalent to the stage of visualization, since in most cases not all of the GIS functionality is used. Cartographic products can be either in a digital or in a hardcopy format. Powerful analysis techniques with different data representation can produce high-quality maps within a short time period. The main problem in Automated Cartography is to use a single set of data to produce multiple products at a variety of scales, a technique known as Generalization.

Geostatistics

Using Geostatistics to predict fields from points. Point pattern analysis. A way of looking at the statistical properties of spatial data. What makes it unique from other kinds of statistics is the use of graph theory and matrix algebra to reduce the number of parameters in the data being analyzed. This is necessary because it is actually the second-order properties of the GIS data that need analyzing. When we measure any phenomena, our observation methods dictate the accuracy of any subsequent analysis. Whether our study is concerned with the nature of traffic patterns in an urban core, or with the analysis of weather patterns over the Pacific, there will always contain a variable or a degree of precision which escapes our measurement; this is determined directly by the scale and distribution of our data collection, or survey methods. In order to apply statistical relevance to spatial analysis, an 'average' must be determined so that points, or gradients, outside of any immediate measurement may be included as to their predicted behavior. Limitations in statistics and data collection mean that it is impossible to directly measure a continuum without the inferential methods of analysis, of which, several forms of interpolation are used in order to predict the behavior of particles and locations not directly measured. Interpolation is the process by which a surface is created, usually a raster dataset, through the input of data collected at a number of sample points. There are several forms of interpolation, each which treats the data differently, depending on the properties of the dataset. In comparing interpolation methods, the first consideration should be whether or not the source data will change (exact or approximate). Next is whether the method is subjective, a human interpretation, or objective. Then there is the nature of transitions between points: are they abrupt or gradual. Finally, there is whether a method is global (it uses the entire dataset to form the model), or local where an algorithm is repeated for a small section of terrain.

Digital Elevation Models (DEM), Digital terrain models (DTM), Triangulated irregular networks (TIN), Edge finding algorithms, Theissen Polygons, Fourier analysis, Weighted moving averages, Inverse Distance Weighted, Moving averages, Kriging, Spline, Trend surface analysis.

Regionalized Variable Theory

Spatial Autocorrelation Principle: Data collected at any position will have a greater similarity to, or influence on, those locations within its immediate vicinity.

Geocoding

Geocoding is calculating spatial locations (X,Y coordinates) from street addresses. A reference theme is required to geocode individual addresses, such as a road centerline file with address ranges. The individual address locations are interpolated, or estimated, by examining address ranges along a road segment. These are usually provided in the form of a table or database. The GIS will then place a dot approximately where that address belongs along the segment of centerline. For example, an address point of 500 will be at the midpoint of a line segment that starts with address 1 and ends with address 1000. Geocoding can also be applied against actual parcel data, typically from municipal tax maps. In this case, the result of the geocoding will be an actually positioned space as opposed to an interpolated point. It should be noted that there are several (potentially dangerous) caveats that are often overlooked when using interpolation. See the full entry for Geocoding for more information. Various algorithms are used to help with address matching when the spellings of addresses differ.

Address information that a particular entity or organization has data on, such as the post office, may not entirely match the reference theme. There could be variations in street name spelling, community name, etc. Consequently, the user generally has the ability to make matching criteria more stringent, or to relax those parameters so that more addresses will be mapped. Care must be taken to review the results so as not to erroneously map addresses incorrectly due to overzealous matching parameters.

Reverse Geocoding

Reverse geocoding is the process of returning an estimated street address number as it relates to a given coordinate. For example, a user can click on a road centerline theme (thus providing a coordinate) and have information returned that reflects the estimated house number. This house number is interpolated from a range assigned to that road segment. If the user clicks at the midpoint of a segment that starts with address 1 and ends with 100, the returned value will be somewhere near 50. Note that reverse geocoding does not return actual addresses, only estimates of what should be there based on the predetermined range.

Data Output and Cartography

Cartography is the design and production of maps, or visual representations of spatial data. The vast majority of modern cartography is done with the help of computers, usually using a GIS. Most GIS software gives the user substantial control over the appearance of the data.

Cartographic work serves two major functions: *First,* it produces graphics on the screen or on paper that convey the results of analysis to the people who make decisions about resources. Wall maps and other graphics can be generated, allowing the viewer to visualize and thereby understand the results of analyses or simulations of potential events. Web Map Servers facilitate distribution of generated maps via the web technology. *Second,* other database information can be generated for further analysis or use. A list of all addresses within 1 mile of a toxic spill for instance.

Graphic Display Techniques

Traditional maps are abstractions of the real world, a sampling of important elements portrayed on a sheet of paper with symbols to represent physical objects. People who use maps must interpret these symbols. Topographic maps show the shape of land surface with contour lines; the actual shape of the land can be seen only in the mind's eye. Today, graphic display techniques such as shading based on altitude in a GIS can make relationships among map elements visible, heightening one's ability to extract and analyze information. For example, two types of data were combined in a GIS to produce a perspective view of a portion of San Mateo County, California.

- The digital elevation model, consisting of surface elevations recorded on a 30-meter horizontal grid, shows high elevations as white and low elevation as black.
- The accompanying Landsat Thematic Mapper image shows a false-color infrared image looking down at the same area in 30-meter pixels, or picture elements, for the same coordinate points, pixel by pixel, as the elevation information.

A GIS was used to register and combine the two images to render the three-dimensional perspective view looking down the San Andreas Fault, using the Thematic Mapper image pixels, but shaded using the elevation of the landforms. The GIS display depends on the viewing point of the observer and time of day of the display, to properly render the shadows created by the sun's rays at that latitude, longitude, and time of day.

Spatial ETL

Spatial ETL tools provide the data processing functionality of traditional Extract, Transform, Load (ETL) software, but with a primary focus on the ability to manage spatial data. They provide GIS users with the ability to translate data between different standards and proprietary formats, whilst geometrically transforming the data en-route.

GIS Software

GIS software is the main method through which geographic data is accessed, transferred, transformed, overlaid, processed and displayed. Various software form integral components of this interface to GIS data. There are numerous commercial, open source and even shareware products that fill these roles. Commercial software is mostly used in industry with ESRI being the leader, while government and military departments often use custom software, open source products, such as GRASS, or more specialized products. The public and small organizations generally use free GIS readers, rapidly expanding online resources or shareware.

Originally up to the late 1990's, when GIS data was mostly based on large computers and used to maintain internal records, software was a stand-alone product. However with increased access to the internet and networks and demand for distributed geographic data grew, GIS software gradually changed its entire outlook to the delivery of data over a network. GIS software is now usually marketed as combination of various interoperable applications and API's.

Geodatabases

The overall functionality as well as the very vast capabilities of GIS technology itself have grown enormously with the creation of the geodatabase. This can best be described as the latest data format to be made available in ESRI GIS software. On the surface the data appears to be the same as it did when shapefiles were the primary file type. The difference notably lies behind the scenes. Shapefiles (still functional) use. shp as one of the five sub-files that comprise one shapefile. The. shp portion of the shapefile is where the spatial component of the data is stored, and the. dbf portion is where the attribute data is stored.

The geodatabase is based on a Microsoft Access format, thus enabling end users to apply and execute different operations to the data. With geodatabases, functionality and shared capability in data editing between vector and raster data are alike. The geodatabase enables raster data to be handled as vector data. Although vector data still possesses more options in an editing process, simple. tif, geotif,.and. mrsid files when contained in a geodatabase can be displayed and edited.

The geodatabase emerged with the release of ArcGIS 8.X and now includes both personal and enterprise geodatabases. ArcGIS 9.2 added "file" geodatabses.

Data Creation

GIS processing software is used for the task preparing data for use within a GIS. This transforms the raw or legacy geographic data into a format usable by GIS products. For example an aerial photograph may need to be stretched (orthorectified) so that its pixels align with longitude and latitude gradations (or what ever grid is needed). This can be distinguished from the transformations done within GIS analysis software by the fact that these changes are permanent, more complex and time consuming. This a specialized high-end type of software is generally used by person skilled in photogrammetry and / or GIS processing aspects of computer science. In addition, AutoCAD, normally used for draughts of engineering projects, can be configured for the editing of vector maps, and has some products that have migrating towards GIS use. It is especially useful as it has strong support for digitization. Raw geographic data can be edited in many standard database and spreadsheet applications and in some cases a text editor may be used as long as care is taken to properly format data. Examples are OrthoEngine and ArcEditor

Statistical

GIS statistical software uses standard database queries to retrieve data and analyse data for decision making. For example, it can be used to determine how many persons of an income of greater than 60,000 live in a given street block. The data is sometimes referenced with postal/zip codes and street locations rather than with geodetic data. This is used by computer scientists and statisticians with CS skills, with an objective of characterizing an area for marketing or governing decisions. Standard DBMS can be used or specialized GIS statistical software. These are many times setup on servers so that they can be queried with web-browsers. Examples are MySQL or ArcSDE.

Management and Analysis

GIS analysis software takes GIS data and overlays or otherwise combines it so that the data can be visually analysed. It can output a detailed map, image or movie used to communicate an idea or concept with respect to a region of interest. This is usually used by persons who are trained in cartography, geography or a GIS professional as this type of application is complex and takes some time to master. The software performs transformation on raster and vector data sometimes of differing datums, grid system, or reference system, into one coherent image. It can also analyse changes over time within a region. This software is central to the professional analysis and presentation of GIS data. Examples include the ArcGIS family of ESRI GIS applications (which replaced ESRI's older Arc/INFO), XMap and GRASS.

Readers

GIS readers are applications, usually free, that are distributed to allow the public to easily view maps created via a GIS, as well as view GIS-managed data. By definition, they usually allow very little if any editing of the map or underlying map data. Readers can be normal standalone applications that need to be installed locally, though they generally then connect to data servers over the Internet to access the relevant information. Readers can also be included as an embedded application within a web page, obviating the need for local installation. Readers are designed to be relatively simple and easy to use, tending to emphasize global coverage, visible light raster data and accessible vector data. Google Earth, ArcReader and GeoPDF are examples.

Web API

This is the evolution of the scripts that were common with most early GIS systems. An application programming interface is a set of subroutines (organized as object oriented programming) designed to perform a specific task. GIS API's are designed to manage GIS data for its delivery to a web browser client from a GIS server. They are accessed with commonly used scripting language such as VBA or javascript. They are used to build a server system for the delivery of GIS that is to made available over an intranet or publicly over the internet.

Open-Source GIS Software

Most requirements that can be set for a GIS can be satisfied with free or open-source software. Recently an international foundation (OSGeo) was started to support and build the highest-quality open source geospatial software. With the broad use of non-proprietary and open data formats such as the Shape File format for vector data and the Geotiff format for raster data, as well as the adoption of Open Geospatial Consortium (OGC) protocols such as Web Mapping Service (WMS) and Web Feature Service (WFS), development of open source software continues to evolve, especially for web and web service oriented applications. Well-known open source GIS software includes GRASS GIS, Quantum GIS, MapServer, GDAL/OGR, PostGIS, uDig, OpenJUMP, gvSIG, and others.

Mobile Transfer

While not strictly a GIS application, there are applications that take GIS data and format and transfer that data in a scaled down, limitation-aware manner to PDA and GPS Receiver devices so they can be used for field applications.

The Future of GIS

Many disciplines can benefit from GIS technology. An active GIS market has resulted in lower costs and continual improvements in the hardware and software components of GIS. These developments will, in turn, result in a much wider use of the technology throughout science, government, business, and industry, with applications including real estate, public health, crime mapping, national defense, sustainable development, natural resources, transportation and logistics. GIS is also diverging into location-based services (LBS). LBS allows GPS enabled mobile devices to display their location in relation to fixed assets (nearest restaurant, gas station, fire hydrant), mobile assets (friends, children, police car) or to relay their position back to a central server for display or other processing. These services continue to develop with the increased integration of GPS functionality with increasingly powerful mobile electronics (cell phones, PDA's, laptops).

OGC Standards

Open Geospatial Consortium (OGC) in short is an international industry consortium of 333 companies, government agencies and universities participating in a consensus process to develop publicly available geoprocessing specifications. Open interfaces and protocols defined by OpenGIS Specifications support interoperable solutions that "geo-enable" the Web, wireless and location-based services, and mainstream IT, and empower technology developers to make complex spatial information and services accessible and useful with all kinds of applications. GIS products are broken down by the OGC into two categories, based on how completely and accurately the software follows the OGC specifications. *Compliant Products* are software products that comply to OGC's OpenGIS® Specifications. When a product has been tested and certified as compliant through the OGC Testing Program, the product is automatically registered as "compliant" on this site.

Implementing Products are software products that implement OpenGIS Specifications but have not yet passed a compliance test. Compliance tests are not available for all specifications. Developers can register their products as implementing draft or approved specifications, though OGC reserves the right to review and verify each entry.

Web Mapping

Google Maps is different from other web map servers (like MapQuest, Yahoo! Maps, or Rand McNally) because Google Maps exposes an API that enables users to associate attributes with interactive maps. This is in effect a GIS. However Google Maps is largely "point" oriented and other than using different point markers, you have to click on the markers to get the metadata.

Global Change and Climate History Program

Maps have traditionally been used to explore the Earth and to exploit its resources. GIS technology, as an expansion of cartographic science, has enhanced the efficiency and analytic power of traditional mapping. Now, as the scientific community recognizes the environmental consequences of human activity, GIS technology is becoming an essential tool in the effort to understand the process of global change. Various map and satellite information sources can combine in modes that simulate the interactions of complex natural systems.

Through a function known as visualization, a GIS can be used to produce images - not just maps, but drawings, animations, and other cartographic products. These images allow researchers to view their subjects in ways that literally never have been seen before. The images often are equally helpful in conveying the technical concepts of GIS study-subjects to non-scientists.

Adding the Dimension of Time

The condition of the Earth's surface, atmosphere, and subsurface can be examined by feeding satellite data into a GIS. GIS technology gives researchers the ability to examine the variations in Earth processes over days, months, and years.

As an example, the changes in vegetation vigor through a growing season can be animated to determine when drought was most extensive in a particular region. The resulting graphic, known as a normalized vegetation index, represents a rough measure of plant health. Working with two variables over time would then allow researchers to detect regional differences in the lag between a decline in rainfall and its effect on vegetation.

GIS technology and the availability of digital data on regional and global scales enable such analyses. The satellite sensor output used to generate a vegetation graphic is produced by the Advanced Very High Resolution Radiometer (AVHRR). This sensor system detects the amounts of energy reflected from the Earth's surface across various bands of the spectrum for surface areas of about 1 square kilometer. The satellite sensor produces images of a particular location on the Earth twice a day. AVHRR is only one of many sensor systems used for Earth surface analysis. More sensors will follow, generating ever greater amounts of data. GIS and related technology will help greatly in the management and analysis of these large volumes of data, allowing for better understanding of terrestrial processes and better management of human activities to maintain world economic vitality and environmental quality. In addition to the integration of time in environmental studies, GIS is also being explored for its ability to track and model the progress of humans throughout their daily routines.

A concrete example of progress in this area is the recent release of time-specific population data by the US Census. In this data set, the populations of cities are shown for daytime and evening hours highlighting the pattern of concentration and dispersion generated by North American commuting patterns. The manipulation and generation of data required to produce this data would not have been possible without GIS. Using models to project the data held by a GIS forward in time have enabled planners to test policy decisions. These systems are known as Spatial Decision Support Systems

Understanding GPS Technology

Trying to figure out where you are is probably one of humankind's oldest problems. Navigation and positioning are crucial to so many activities and yet the process has always been quite cumbersome and inexact. In the earliest days mankind used the stars to navigate. Early instruments also sited the stars to determine position. The science of horology began in part because navigation depended on precise timing the movement of the stars. Over the years all kinds of technologies have tried to simplify the task but every one has had some disadvantage.

Finally, the U.S. Department of Defense decided that the military had to have a precise form of worldwide positioning. Fortunately they had the deep pockets it took to build something really good. The result is the Global Positioning System, a system that's changed navigation forever. The Global Positioning System (GPS) is a worldwide radio-navigation system formed from a constellation of 24 satellites and their ground stations. GPS uses these "man-made stars" as reference points to calculate positions accurate to a matter of meters. In fact, with advanced forms of GPS you can make measurements to better than a centimeter! In a sense it's like giving every square meter on the planet a unique address. GPS receivers have been miniaturized to just a few integrated circuits and so are becoming very economical. And that makes the technology accessible to virtually everyone. These days GPS is finding its way into cars, boats, planes, construction equipment, movie making gear, farm machinery, even laptop computers. Soon GPS will become almost as basic as the cell telephone. In fact, GPS technology is being used now in cell phones to implement the emergency ('911') location system.

How GPS Works

Here's how GPS works in six logical steps:

1. The basis of GPS is "triangulation" from satellites.
2. To "triangulate," a GPS receiver measures distance using the travel time of radio signals.
3. To measure travel time, GPS needs very accurate timing which it achieves with some tricks.
4. Along with distance, you need to know exactly where the satellites are in space. High orbits and careful monitoring are the secret.
5. You must correct for any delays the signal experiences as it travels through the atmosphere.
6. Finally (for us), you can now obtain the precise time from the GPS satellites.

We'll explain each of these points in subsequent sections.

Improbable as it may seem, the whole idea behind GPS is to use satellites in space as reference points for locations here on earth. That's right, by very, very accurately measuring our distance from three satellites we can "triangulate" our position anywhere on earth. Forget for a moment how our receiver measures this distance. We'll get to that later. First consider how distance measurements from three satellites can pinpoint you in space.

Triangulation

- Position is calculated from distance measurements (ranges) to satellites.
- Mathematically we need four satellite ranges to determine exact position.
- Three ranges are enough if we reject ridiculous answers or use other tricks.
- Another range is required for technical reasons to be discussed later.

The Geometry

Suppose we measure our distance from a satellite and find it to be 10,000 miles.

Knowing that we're 10,000 miles from a particular satellite narrows down all the possible locations we could be in the whole universe to the surface of a sphere that is centered on this satellite and has a radius of 10,000 miles Next, say we measure our distance to a second satellite and find out that it's 11,000 miles away. That tells us that we're not only on the first sphere but we're also on a sphere that's 11,000 miles from the second satellite. Or in other words, we're somewhere on the circle where these two spheres intersect. If we then make a measurement from a third satellite and find that we're 12,000 miles from that one, that narrows our position down even further, to the two points where the 12,000 mile sphere cuts through the circle that's the intersection of the first two spheres.

So by ranging from three satellites we can narrow our position to just two points in space. This arrangement of satellites is also called a "constellation". To decide which one is our true location we could make a fourth measurement. But usually one of the two points is a ridiculous answer (either too far from Earth or moving at an impossible velocity) and can be rejected without a measurement. A fourth measurement does come in very handy for another reason however, but we'll tell you about that later. Next we'll see how the system measures distances to satellites.

Distance Measuring

1. Distance to a satellite is determined by measuring how long a radio signal takes to reach us from that satellite.
2. To make the measurement we assume that both the satellite and our receiver are generating the same pseudo-random codes at exactly the same time.
3. By comparing how late the satellite's pseudo-random code appears compared to our receiver's code, we determine how long it took to reach us.
4. Multiply that travel time by the speed of light and you've got distance.

We saw in the last section that a position is calculated from distance measurements to at least three satellites. But how can you measure the distance to something that's floating around in space? We do it by timing how long it takes for a signal sent from the satellite to arrive at our receiver.

The Math

In a sense, the whole thing boils down to those "velocity times travel time" math problems we did in high school. Remember the old: "If a car goes 60 miles per hour for two hours, how far does it travel?"

Velocity (60 mph) x Time (2 hours) = Distance (120 miles)

In the case of GPS we're measuring a radio signal so the velocity is going to be the speed of light or roughly 186,000 miles per second.

The problem is measuring the travel time. The timing problem is tricky. First, the times are going to be awfully short. If a satellite were right overhead the travel time would be something like 0.06 seconds. So we're going to need some really precise clocks. We'll talk about those soon. But assuming we have precise clocks, how do we measure travel time? To explain it let's use a goofy analogy. Suppose there was a way to get both the satellite and the receiver to start playing "Stairway to Heaven" at precisely 12 noon. If sound could reach us from space then standing at the receiver we'd hear two versions of the 'Stairway to Heaven', one from our receiver and one from the satellite.

These two versions would be out of sync. The version coming from the satellite would be a little delayed because it had to travel more than 11,000 miles. If we wanted to see just how delayed the satellite's version was, we could start delaying the receiver's version until they fell into perfect sync. The amount we have to shift back the receiver's version is equal to the travel time of the satellite's version. So we just multiply that time times the speed of light and voila! we've got our distance to the satellite.

That's basically how GPS works. Only instead of 'Stairway to Heaven' the satellites and receivers use something called a "Pseudo Random Code" - which is probably quicker to sing than 'Stairway to Heaven'.

Random Code

The Pseudo Random Code (PRC) is a fundamental part of GPS. Physically it's just a very complicated digital code, or in other words, a complicated sequence of "on" and "off" pulses. The signal is so complicated that it almost looks like random electrical noise. Hence the name "Pseudo-Random." There are several good reasons for that complexity: First, the complex pattern helps make sure that the receiver doesn't accidentally sync up to some other signal. The patterns are so complex that it's highly unlikely that a stray signal will have exactly the same shape.

Since each satellite has its own unique Pseudo-Random Code this complexity also guarantees that the receiver won't accidentally pick up another satellite's signal. So all the satellites can use the same frequency without jamming each other. And it makes it more difficult for a hostile force to jam the system. In fact the Pseudo Random Code gives the Department of Defense a way to control access to the system. But there's another reason for the complexity of the Pseudo Random Code, a reason that's crucial to making GPS economical. The codes make it possible to use "information theory" to "amplify" the GPS signal. And that's why GPS receivers don't need big satellite dishes to receive the GPS signals. We glossed over one point in our silly 'Stairway to Heaven' analogy. It assumes that we can guarantee that both the satellite and the receiver start generating their codes at exactly the same time. But how do we make sure everybody is perfectly synced? Stay tuned and see.

Timing

Achieving Perfect Timing

1. Accurate timing is the key to measuring distance to satellites.
2. Satellites are accurate because they have atomic clocks on board.
3. Receiver clocks don't have to be too accurate because an extra satellite range measurement can remove errors

Discussion

If measuring the travel time of a radio signal is the key to GPS, then our stop watches had better be darn good, because if their timing is off by just a thousandth of a second, at the speed of light, that translates into almost 200 miles of error! On the satellite side, timing is almost perfect because they have incredibly precise atomic clocks on board. But what about our receivers here on the ground? Remember that both the satellite and the receiver need to be able to precisely synchronize their pseudo-random codes to make the system work. (to review this point click here) If our receivers needed atomic clocks (which cost upwards of $50K to $100K) GPS would be a lame duck technology. Nobody could afford it.

Luckily the designers of GPS came up with a brilliant little trick that lets us get by with much less accurate clocks in our receivers. This trick is one of the key elements of GPS and as an added side benefit it means that every GPS receiver is essentially an atomic-accuracy clock. The secret to perfect timing is to make an extra satellite measurement. That's right, if three perfect measurements can locate a point in 3-dimensional space, then four imperfect measurements can do the same thing.

Extra Measurement Cures Timing Offset

If our receiver's clocks were perfect, then all our satellite ranges would intersect at a single point (which is our position). But with imperfect clocks, a fourth measurement, done as a cross-check, will NOT intersect with the first three. So the receiver's computer says "Uh-oh! there is a discrepancy in my measurements. I must not be perfectly synced with universal time." Since any offset from universal time will affect all of our measurements, the receiver looks for a single correction factor that it can subtract from all its timing measurements that would cause them all to intersect at a single point. That correction brings the receiver's clock back into sync with universal time, and bingo! — you've got atomic accuracy time right in the palm of your hand.

Once it has that correction it applies to all the rest of its measurements and now we've got precise positioning. One consequence of this principle is that any decent

GPS receiver will need to have at least four channels so that it can make the four measurements simultaneously. With the pseudo-random code as a rock solid timing sync pulse, and this extra measurement trick to get us perfectly synced to universal time, we have got everything we need to measure our distance to a satellite in space. But for the triangulation to work we not only need to know distance, we also need to know exactly where the satellites are. In the next section we'll see how we accomplish that.

Satellite Tracking

- GPS satellites are so high up their orbits are very predictable.
- To use the satellites as references for range measurements we need to know exactly where they are.
- Minor variations in their orbits are measured by the Department of Defense.
- The error information is sent to the satellites, to be transmitted along with the timing signals.

Discussion

Thus far we've been assuming that we know where the GPS satellites are so we can use them as reference points. But how do we know exactly where they are? After all they're floating around 11,000 miles up in space. That 11,000 mile altitude is actually a benefit in this case, because something that high is well clear of the atmosphere. And that means it will orbit according to very simple mathematics. The Air Force has injected each GPS satellite into a very precise orbit, according to the GPS master plan. On the ground all GPS receivers have an almanac programmed into their computers that tells them where in the sky each satellite is, moment by moment. The basic orbits are quite exact but just to make things perfect the GPS satellites are constantly monitored by the Department of Defense. They use very precise radar to check each satellite's exact altitude, position and speed. The errors they're checking for are called "ephemeris errors" because they affect the satellite's orbit or "ephemeris."

These errors are caused by gravitational pulls from the moon and sun and by the pressure of solar radiation on the satellites. The errors are usually very slight but if you want great accuracy they must be taken into account. Once the Department of Defense has measured a satellite's exact position, they relay that information back up to the satellite itself. The satellite then includes this new corrected position information in the timing signals it's broadcasting. So a GPS signal is more than just pseudo-random code for timing purposes.

It also contains a navigation message with ephemeris information as well. With perfect timing and the satellite's exact position you'd think we'd be ready to make perfect position calculations. But there's trouble afoot.

Handling Errors

1. The earth's ionosphere and atmosphere cause delays in the GPS signal that translate into position errors. See a summary of error sources.
2. Some errors can be factored out using mathematics and modeling.
3. The configuration of the satellites in the sky can magnify other errors.
4. Differential GPS can eliminate almost all error.

Up to now we've been treating the calculations that go into GPS very abstractly, as if the whole thing were happening in a vacuum. But in the real world there are lots of things that can happen to a GPS signal that will make its life less than mathematically perfect. To get the most out of the system, a good GPS receiver needs to take a wide variety of possible errors into account. Here's what they've got to deal with. First, one of the basic assumptions we've been using is not exactly true. We've been saying that you calculate distance to a satellite by multiplying a signal's travel time by the speed of light. But the speed of light is only constant in a vacuum.

As a GPS signal passes through the charged particles of the ionosphere and then through the water vapor in the troposphere it gets slowed down a bit, and this creates the same kind of error as bad clocks. There are a couple of ways to minimize this kind of error. For one thing we can predict what a typical delay might be on a typical day. This is called modeling and it helps but, of course, atmospheric conditions are rarely exactly typical. Another way to get a handle on these atmosphere-induced errors is to compare the relative speeds of two different signals. This "dual frequency" measurement is very sophisticated and is only possible with advanced receivers. Trouble for the GPS signal doesn't end when it gets down to the ground. The signal may bounce off various local obstructions before it gets to our receiver. This is called multi-path error and is similar to the ghosting you might see on a TV. Good receivers use sophisticated signal rejection techniques to minimize this problem. Trouble for the GPS signal doesn't end when it gets down to the ground. The signal may bounce off various local obstructions before it gets to our receiver. This is called multi-path error and is similar to the ghosting you might see on a TV. Good receivers use sophisticated signal rejection techniques to minimize this problem.

Satellite Errors

Even though the satellites are very sophisticated they do account for some tiny errors in the system. The atomic clocks they use are very, very precise but they're not perfect. Minute discrepancies can occur, and these translate into travel time measurement errors. And even though the satellites positions are constantly monitored, they can't be watched every second. So slight position or "ephemeris" errors can sneak in between monitoring times. Basic geometry itself can magnify these other errors with a principle called "Geometric Dilution of Precision" or GDOP. It sounds complicated but the principle is quite simple. There are usually more satellites available than a receiver needs to fix a position, so the receiver picks a few and ignores the rest. If it picks satellites that are close together in the sky the intersecting circles that define a position will cross at very shallow angles. That increases the gray area or error margin around a position. If it picks satellites that are widely separated the circles intersect at almost right angles and that minimizes the error region. Good receivers determine which satellites will give the lowest GDOP.

Timekeeping

Bringing Precise Time to the World

Although GPS is well-known for navigation, tracking, and mapping, it's also used to disseminate precise time, time intervals, and frequency. Time is a powerful commodity, and exact time is more powerful still. Knowing that a group of timed events is perfectly synchronized is often very important. GPS makes the job of synchronizing our clocks easy and reliable. There are three fundamental ways we use time. As a universal marker, time tells us when things happened or when they will. As a way to synchronize people, events, even other types of signals, time helps keep the world on schedule. And as a way to tell how long things last, time provides and accurate, unambiguous sense of duration.

GPS satellites carry highly accurate atomic clocks. And in order for the system to work, our GPS receivers here on the ground synchronize themselves to these clocks. That means that every GPS receiver is, in essence, an atomic accuracy clock. Astronomers, power companies, computer networks, communications systems, banks, and radio and television stations can benefit from this precise timing. One investment banking firm uses GPS to guarantee their transactions are recorded simultaneously at all offices around the world. And a major Pacific Northwest utility company makes sure their power is distributed at just the right time along their thousands of miles of transmission lines. Beagle Software offers the Star Sync product which sets any Windows computer to the GPS clock and can serve as a time source for computers on a network. We hope you've enjoyed our brief discussion about the technology behind GPS.

Telecom Milestones

The Groundbreaking Decade - Major Developments in the Hong Kong Telecom Industry in the Past 10 Years (30 June 2003)

Milestones of Telecommunications in Hong Kong

Year	Milestones
1871	Submarine telegraph cables were landed in Hong Kong at Telegraph Bay in Pokfulam.

1873 • Eastern Extension Australia and China Telegraph Company was formed and operated links from Madras, to Darwin, Singapore, Saigon, Hong Kong and Shanghai.

1877 • Telephone was introduced in Hong Kong, one year after Alexander Graham Bell patented his invention.

1882 • First public telephone service was introduced into Hong Kong by Oriental Telephone and Electric Company which later became China and Japan Telephone and Electric Company.

1905 • Cable was laid across Victoria Harbour to extend telephone services to Kowloon.

1925 • China and Japan Telephone and Electric Company was taken over by the newly formed Hong Kong Telephone Company Limited (HKTC). Hong Kong Government granted HKTC the sole right to supply and operate telephone services in Hong Kong for a period of 50 years commencing 1 July.

1931 • Telephone service between Hong Kong and Guangzhou was launched

1954 • Leased telegraph circuits were in operation between Hong Kong and overseas administrations.

1962 • Franchised licence was granted to Cable & Wireless Limited to provide external telephone and telegraph circuits and services until 31 December 1987.

1968 • Hong Kong Government extended HKTC's franchise for a further period of 20 years with effect from 1 July 1975.

1971 • First public radio paging service was introduced in Hong Kong by Apollo Telephone Answering Services Limited.

1976 • International Direct Dialing (IDD) was introduced.

1981 • Optical fibre cables were deployed in the local telephone network by HKTC.

• An exclusive licence with expiry in 2006, covering the provision of a range of external telecommunications circuits and services, was granted to Cable and Wireless (Hong Kong) Limited.

1984 • First public mobile radiotelephone service using NAMTS (NEC Advance Mobile Telephone System) was introduced by Communication Services Limited (CSL), a wholly owned subsidiary company of HKTC.

• Chinatel was granted a licence to operate a public car telephone (Comvik) system.

- Hutchison Telephone Company Limited was granted a licence to operate an AMPS cellular radiotelephone network.

1985
- The interconnection charge for public mobile radiotelephone service was set at 7 cents per minute.

1987
- CSL was granted a licence to operate a TACS cellular radiotelephone network. The network was called UNITACS.

1988
- Hutchison Telephone Company Limited was granted a licence to operate the second TACS cellular radiotelephone network.
- Hong Kong Telecommunications Limited formed by merger of Hong Kong Telephone Company Limited and Cable and Wireless (Hong Kong) Limited.
- Asia Satellite Telecommunications Company Limited (AsiaSat) was formed and was the first local and Asia's privately owned satellite operator.

1989
- Chinatel was renamed as Pacific Link Communications Limited and the subscribers were offered a deal to change over to a new ETACS cellular radiotelephone network.

1990
- The Hong Kong Telecommunications Limited was restructured to four wholly-owned operating companies: Hong Kong Telephone Company Limited, Hong Kong Telecom International Limited (formerly Cable and Wireless (Hong Kong) Limited), Hong Kong Telecom CSL Limited and Computasia Limited.
- The first satellite of AsiaSat (AsiaSat 1) was launched in April.

1991
- The interconnection charges for public mobile radiotelephone services and for value added services were revised to 9 cents per minute.

1992
- Telepoint (CT2) services were launched by Hutchison Paging Company Limited and Chevalier (Telepoint) Limited in March and April respectively.
- The first Frequency Coordination Agreement between Hong Kong and Guangdong was signed in May.
- Pacific Link launched its Digital-AMPS mobile telephone service in October.
- SmartCom Limited was awarded a licence to operate GSM network.
- The number of paging customers exceeded 1 million.

1993
- Hong Kong's local telephone network was fully digitalised.
- SmartCom Limited (later became SmarTone Mobile Communications Limited) launched its GSM system in January.
- Pacific TeleLink Limited launched its CT2 service in March.
- Wharf Cable Limited was granted an exclusive cable television licence in June to operate cable television services in Hong Kong for 3 years.

- The Office of the Telecommunications Authority (OFTA) was established on 1 July.
- Hong Kong Telecom CSL launched its GSM service in July.
- TA took over the control of telephone numbers.

1994
- Fixed telephone exchange lines exceeded 3 million.
- The number of paging customers peaked in December.

1995
- Telephone numbers were changed from 7 to 8 digits on 1 January.
- Following the expiry of HKTC's franchise on 30 June, HKTC and three new companies (New World Telephone Limited, New T&T Hong Kong Limited and Hutchison Communications Limited) were licensed to provide local fixed telecommunication services on a competitive basis.
- Hutchison Telephone launched its GSM and CDMA service in June and October respectively.

1996
- Six licences were issued in September for provision of personal communication services (PCS). The licensees were: Hutchison Telephone Company Limited, Mandarin Communications Limited, New World PCS Limited, Pacific Link Communications Limited, P Plus Communications Limited and Peoples Telephone Company Limited.
- All CT-2 networks were shut down and public CT-2 services were terminated.
- New T&T launched its direct exchange line service (DEL) to business customers in October.
- New World Telephone offered DEL services to business and residential customers in January & November respectively.
- HKTC launched the first integrated services digital network (ISDN) in Hong Kong in October, offering commercial ISDN basic rate interface (BRI) and primary rate interface (PRI).
- The first Calling Number Display (CND) service was introduced in HKTC's fixed network in December.
- Mobile phone subscribers exceeded 1 million.

1997
- Full portability of telephone numbers was achieved for fixed telephone services in January.
- Direct exchange line services were available to business and residential customers from Hutchison Communications in January.
- Peoples Telephone Company Limited launched its PCS in January.
- New World and Hutchison joined the competition in the PCS market in March.

- **First licence for provision of Virtual Private Network Services was issued to BT (Hong Kong) Limited in May.**
- **P Plus Communications and Mandarin Communications launched their PCS in June.**
- **Pacific Link launched its PCS in July.**
- **Calling Name Display (CNAMD) service was introduced in mid-October.**
- **Hong Kong Telecom CSL Limited acquired Pacific Link Communications Limited in December. The acquisition included the digital cellular phone services (D-Amps), PCS (GSM1800) and radio paging services.**
- **Mobile phone subscribers exceeded 2 million.**

1998

- **First licence for provision of International Simple Resale (ISR) for Fax and Data Services was issued to City Telecom (HK) Limited in January.**
- **P Plus Communications Limited, one of the six PCS operators, was acquired by SmarTone Telecommunications Holdings Limited in March**
- **In March, after lengthy negotiation with the Government, Hong Kong Telecom International surrendered its exclusive licence for provision of certain external telecommunication circuits and services eight years earlier than the scheduled expiry in 2006 in return for a cash compensation of HK$6.7 billion.**
- **Analogue mobile phone service was completely phased out. Mobile service began fully digitalised.**
- **The Hong Kong Telecommunications Equipment Evaluation and Certification (HKTEC) Scheme was launched in September.**

1999

- **The external telecommunications services market was liberalised with effect from 1 January. External telecommunications services operators were allowed to refile traffic through Hong Kong between locations at the distant ends of Category A routes (routes include those over which it would be possible for genuine price competition to occur through direct ISR connection, indirect routing through refiling, direct physical connection through competitive external gateway facilities or such connection indirectly established via transit arrangements).**
- **Mobile Number Portability was implemented on 1 March.**
- **In August, Hong Kong reached an agreement with Australia, Singapore and Chinese Taipei on implementation of APEC TEL MRA Phase I Procedures which facilitates mutual recognition of test reports.**
- **The number of Internet dial-up customers exceeded 1 million in August.**

- The number of mobile phone subscribers exceeded 3 million in February and surpassed the number of fixed telephone lines in November.

2000
- In January, the telecommunications market was fully liberalised after the liberalisation of the external facility-based market. Five licences for local fixed telecommunication network services using wireless means, twelve satellite-based external FTNS licences and four cable-based external FTNS licences were issued. Hong Kong Cable TV was issued a licence to provide telecommunications services over its hybrid fibre coaxial cable (HFC) networks.
- Mobile phone subscribers exceeded 4 million in January.
- Hong Kong Broadband Network Limited, one of the five wireless local fixed network licensees, launched its services in February.
- The number of Internet dial-up customers exceeded 2 million in April.
- The Telecommunication (Amendment) Ordinance 2000 was passed by the Legislative Council in June. Major amendments include enhancing the competition safeguards for the telecommunications industry, improving the interconnection and access to land and buildings for the establishment of telecommunications equipment for the telecommunications operators, streamlining the licensing framework to respond more flexibly to market development and providing powers to the TA on certain technical matters (e.g. numbering plan and technical standards).
- In June, AsiaSat was awarded a licence to launch and operate a satellite (AsiaSat 4) carrying the four Broadcasting Satellite Service (BSS) channels assigned to Hong Kong.
- Pacific Century CyberWorks acquired Cable & Wireless HKT in August (Hong Kong Telecommunications Limited changed its name to Cable & Wireless HKT Limited in July 1999).
- Mobile phone subscribers exceeded 5 million in October.
- In November, a new Frequency Coordination Agreement was signed between Hong Kong and Guangdong on procedures and standards for coordinating terrestrial radiocommunications services in the frequency band from 30 MHz to 40 GHz
- Cable-based external FTNS operator Level 3 Communications Limited announced that the first leg of its pan-Asia submarine cable system was landed in Hong Kong in November.

2001
- Cable-based external FTNS operator Asia Global Crossing Hong Kong Limited announced that its submarine cable "East Asia Crossing" had landed in Hong Kong in January.

- Cable-based external FTNS operator China Unicom International Limited had completed its overland cable between Hong Kong and mainland China and launched services in the first quarter.
- Asia Pacific Cable Network 2 landed in Hong Kong in February. It will connect the Mainland China, Hong Kong, Japan, Korea, Malaysia, Philippines, Singapore and Taiwan.
- A new automatic direction-finding system to monitor radio channels and locate sources of interference in and around Hong Kong was installed in the Radio Monitoring Unit of OFTA.
- Broadband Internet customers exceeded 0.44 million in March, representing a five-fold increase within one year.
- The Telecommunications (Carrier Licences) Regulation was brought into effect on 1 April, introducing a more effective and efficient licensing regime for carrier licence.
- Mobile phone subscribers exceeded 5.5 million in April, representing an 80% penetration of the population.
- The Telecommunications (Amendment) Ordinance 2001 was enacted by the Legislative Council in May. The major amendment is to empower the Secretary for Information Technology and Broadcasting and the TA to conduct auctions or tenders for the use of spectrum. Such provision is necessary for the licensing of third generation mobile services (3G) and future exercises involving auctions or tenders.
- The C2C submarine cable network landed at Chung Hom Kok in July. The submarine link will connect Hong Kong, Philippines, Taiwan and Singapore.
- Licensing for third generation mobile service was completed in October with the award of licences to four successful bidders: Hong Kong CSL Limited, Hutchison 3G HK Limited, SmarTone 3G Limited and SUNDAY 3G (Hong Kong) Limited. In accordance with the 3G regulatory framework, the network licensees are required to open up at least 30 per cent of their capacity for use by non-affiliated Mobile Virtual Network Operators (MVNO) and/or content and service providers.
- Inter-operator Short Message Service was launched by all six mobile network operators in December, allowing a customer to send short message to other customers even they are in different networks.
- In December, the capacity of external telecommunications facilities, namely the cable and satellite systems, recorded a tremendous increase over the year from 18 Gbps to 235 Gbps. The increase in bandwidth was mainly attributed to the new submarine cable capacity brought in Hong Kong by

the cable-based external FTNS operators.

2002

- In January, the TA announced details on the implementation of the policy to fully liberalize the FTNS market from 1 January 2003 with no pre-set limit on the number of licences to be issued.
- In March, the number of broadband Internet customers reached 716,000, representing more than 10% of population.
- Asia's first Mutlimedia Messaging Services (MMS) was launched in Hong Kong by Hong Kong CSL in April.
- In June, the Billing and Metering Integrity Scheme was announced by the TA. Operators will be required to comply with the billing and metering integrity standards and requirements by 1 January, 2003.
- Hong Kong was ranked top of the Mobile/Internet index rankings by the International Telecommunication Union (ITU) in its report - "Internet for a Mobile Generation" released in September 2002.
- In October, the Class Licence for In-Building Telecommunications System was introduced. It was the first class licence created after the introduction of the class licence system into the telecommunications regulatory regime by the Telecommunication (Amendment) Ordinance 2000.
- Inter-operator Multi-media Messaging Service was launched by mobile network operators in December, allowing customers to send multi-media messages to customers in different networks.

2003

- The telecommunications market was fully liberalised. Further competition was introduced with more fixed telecommunication operators licensed to provide services from January 2003.
- The number of broadband Internet customers exceeded one million in January.
- In January, the Class Licence for the provision of Public Wireless Local Area Network (LAN) Services was introduced. The Class Licence will provide a streamlined licensing regime for operators to run public wireless LAN services without the need for individual licence application or approval.
- In April, the AsiaSat 4 satellite which carries the four Broadcasting Satellite Service (BSS) channels assigned to Hong Kong was successfully launched. The transponders on board the satellite may be used to provide telecommunications and broadcasting coverage across the Asia region.
- In September, the number of broadband Internet customers reached 1.16 million and exceeded that of dial-up Internet customers.

- The penetration rate of mobile subscribers exceeded 100%, attributing to the increase of usage of pre-paid SIM cards.

2004
- Hutchison 3G HK Limited launched the first Third Generation Mobile (3G) service in Hong Kong in January.
- APT Satellite Company Limited launched APSTAR V in June, the seventh satellite licensed by Hong Kong.
- The government announced in July that Type II interconnection obligation at exchange level would be fully withdrawn by 30 June 2008. In the run up to 30 June 2008, the withdrawal would be implemented on a building-by-building basis and apply to buildings already connected to at least two self-built customer access networks.
- As of September 2004, broadband Internet customer accounts exceeded 1.4 million while the household broadband penetration rate was very close to 59%.
- In September, mobile phone subscribers exceeded 8 million, representing a 117% penetration of the population.
- The government decided in November to grant the nine incumbent GSM and PCS licensees providing 2G mobile services new Mobile Carrier Licences for a period of 15 years after the expiry of their existing licences between 2005 and 2006.
- Hong Kong Broadband Network Limited announced a plan in November to launch the high speed symmetric 100Mbps and 1000 Mbps residential broadband services.
- Smartone 3G Limited and Hong Kong CSL Limited launched their 3G services in December.

2005
- In January, OFTA introduced a framework under which quality of service (QoS) information on residential broadband Internet service will be available to consumers for making informed choices.
- OFTA announced its decision in January to lift the prior - approval requirement on PCCW-HKT Telephone Limited's prices via the issue of a new Fixed Carrier Licence, shifting from the *ex ante* to the *ex post* regulation approach. The lifting of the prior-approval requirement has given the company greater flexibility in responding to market competition.
- APT Satellite Company Limited launched APSTAR VI in April, the eighth satellite licensed by Hong Kong.
- The Telecommunications (Telecommunications Apparatus) (Exemption from Licensing) (Amendment) Order came into effect on 15 April. The

Order expanded and updated the telecommunications apparatus exempted from licensing to reflect technological advancement and market situation.

- PCCW Limited purchased a majority share of SUNDAY Communications Limited in June.
- SUNDAY 3G (Hong Kong) Limited launched its 3G services in June.

2006

- A Class Licence for Citizen Band Radio was created in January to facilitate public use of the radio operating in the 26.96-27.41MHz band for recreational and other communications purposes.
- A new Services-Based Operator (SBO) Licence for the provision of Internet Protocol (IP) telephony services was introduced in January.
- China Mobile (Hong Kong) Limited acquired China Resources Peoples Telephone Company Limited in March and renamed it to China Mobile Peoples Telephone Company Limited.
- A joint venture company, CSL New World Mobility Limited was created in April to own two mobile telephone operators, New World PCS Limited and Hong Kong CSL Limited.
- The first High-Speed Downlink Packet Access (HSDPA) mobile broadband network that provides a data speed of 1.8Mbps with full coverage in Hong Kong was launched in June.
- The number of 3G subscribers exceeded 1 million in July.
- A class licensing regime to regulate the resellers of telecommunications services was introduced in September.
- The number of households covered by at least two self-built customer access networks increased to 76% of the total number of households in October.
- The ITU TELECOM WORLD 2006 was held in Hong Kong in December. This is the first time since its inauguration in 1971 that an ITU TELECOM WORLD event is held outside Geneva.

Information-Seeking Perspective

The perspective on information seeking taken in this book has its roots in the work of scholars in information science, psychology, education, communications, and computer science. The perspective emerges from three beliefs about human existence: Life is active, analog, and accumulative. The active view of life implies that we learn by "bumping into the environment." This experiential and biological view was expressed in the learning philosophy of John Dewey and the psychological theory of Jean Piaget. Our actions may be classified as reactive or proactive. Reactions require perceptive inputs of information and relatively rapid recall of information from memory.

We perceive the situation at hand through our senses and determine our reactions according to existing mental models. Proactions are guided by plans, employ outputs of information (e.g., trial balloons) and active information gathering (e.g., hypothesis testing), and require synthesis of information. The balance between reactive and proactive actions is determined by individual characteristics such as age or experience and by the stability and organisation of the environment. Thus, highly organised social and political environments allow those who have experience to manipulate more information in imaginative and reflective ways to plan their actions. The information society and its highly organised work environments demand highly developed personal information infrastructures to guide its members' many intellectual and physical actions. Life as an analog process means that it is continuous and periodic. The continuity of individual lives implies that information incessantly flows from the environment, regardless of how we are able to process and store it. This continuity forces us to develop mental and physical apertures as part of our personal information infrastructures so that we can control information flow. Periodicity describes the "ups and downs" of our physiological, psychological, and spiritual lives. These periods are both internally determined and influenced by the environment, and they affect our abilities to seek, accept, and process information.

Life as accumulation is a corollary of continuity in that it is difficult or impossible for us to selectively and purposely forget the effects of information we have processed during our lives. As information affects our knowledge structures, these structures are extended, reinforced, or altered. This accretional process not only broadens our understanding of the world but also bolsters our biases and affects our subsequent expectations. This belief implies that organisation of our information resources is critical to effective future actions and that we must not only control the amount of information but also must create evaluative filters to minimise inaccurate or low-quality information.

Life requires us to plan and execute actions (actions can be mental activities as well as physical). To do so, we need to have plausible mental models (understandings) of the world. To have such mental models, we need information - anything with the potential to change a mental state (Belkin, 1978). Thus, information seeking is a process driven by life itself. More specifically, information seeking is a process driven by humans' needs for information so that they can interact with the environment. This view of information seeking has paralleled developments in our thinking about psychology, sociology, and technology.

Rather than focusing exclusively on the representation, storage, and systematic retrieval of information or on information systems, the current view of information seeking emphasises communication and the needs, characteristics, and actions of information seekers (Dervin & Nilan, 1986). This focus has followed the development of cognitive psychology, which goes beyond the stimulus-response (input-output) constraints of behavioral psychology to examine human cognitive processes. It has been reinforced by developments in communications and computing technology and their attendant problems related to acceptance, behavioral changes, and potential abuse. As discussed in the previous chapter, these developments have led to more interactions among people and systems.

Information-Seeking Process

The information-seeking process is both systematic and opportunistic. The degree to which a search exhibits algorithms, heuristics, and serendipity depends on the strategic decisions that the information seeker makes and how the information-seeking factors interact as the search progresses. The information-seeking process is composed of a set of subprocesses. Information seeking begins with the recognition and acceptance of the problem and continues until the problem is resolved or abandoned. In the figure, the likelihood of a subprocess calling another subprocess is represented crudely by three types of arcs. Bold, solid arcs represent the most likely (default) transitions from one subprocess to another; dashed arcs represent high-probability transitions; and solid arcs represent low-transition probabilities. These subprocesses may default to phases or steps in a sequential algorithm, but they are better considered as functions or activity modules that may be called into action recursively at any time, that may be continuously active (types of sentinels or demons), that are temporarily frozen while others proceed, and that may make calls to other subprocess. Thus, the information-seeking process can proceed along parallel lines of progress and take advantage of opportunities arising from intermediate or random results. The degree to which the information-seeking process deviates from a top-down, sequential default provides a basis for characterising browsing and analytical search, and the number of iterations (cycles) per unit time serves as a gross measure of interactivity.

Recognise and Accept an Information Problem

Recognising and accepting an information problem can be internally motivated (e.g., curiosity about the details of immediate thought) or externally motivated (e.g., a teacher asking a question or making an assignment). The problem may be characterised as a gap (Dervin, 1977), a visceral need (Taylor, 1962), an anomaly (Belkin, 1980), as a defect in a mental model, or as an unstable collection of noumenal clouds, but it is manifested as a resource demand on the perceptual or memory systems - the person becomes "aware" of the problem. At this point, the problem may be suppressed or accepted. Suppression is influenced by setting and the information seeker's judgment about the immediate costs (physical and mental) of initiating the search (e.g., "This is not worth the effort; I'll worry about this later"). If the information seeker judges the situation to be appropriate, he or she will accept the problem and begin to define it for the search. Acceptance is influenced by knowledge about the task domain, by the setting, by knowledge of search systems, and by the information seeker's confidence in his or her personal information infrastructure. Recognition and acceptance are typically ignored by system designers, as they are viewed as user specific and thus uncontrollable. However, systems that invite interaction and support satisfying engagement lead users to accept information problems more readily. Attention to this subprocess also rein-forces the users' control and volition in any intellectual activity. Problem acceptance initiates problem definition.

Define and Understand the Problem

Problem definition is a critical step in the information-seeking process. This subprocess remains active as long as the information seeking progresses.

To understand and define a problem, it must be limited, labeled, and a form or frame for the answer determined. The problem may be limited by identifying related knowledge or similar problems or by listing what specific knowledge is not, related. Concepts, words, phrases, events, or people related to the problem can be listed and grouped into categories that serve as the basis for assigning labels and problem statements (giving names to noumenal clouds). This process represents what Taylor called the *conscious need.* The information seeker may hypothesise what the answer will be but at least creates an expectation of what the answer will "look like," for example, will be a date, a fact, a route, an idea, an interpretation, or an expression. An expectation of the physical form of the answer (e.g., texts with tables, an image with an annotation, ideas shaped from interactions with various people and documents) may emerge that, in turn, strongly influences the selection of a search system. These expectations about outcomes ultimately guide (and bias) action. The limiting, labeling, and framing of solution properties lead to the articulation of an information-seeking task, what Taylor referred to as the *formalised need.* While defining the problem, the information seeker represents the problem internally as a task with properties that allow progress to be judged and then determines a general strategy to use for subsequent steps.

Choose a Search System

Choosing a search system is dependent on the information seeker's previous experience with the task domain, the scope of his or her personal information infrastructure, and the expectations about the answer that may have been formed while defining the problem and the task. Domain knowledge is a powerful variable in selecting a search system and focusing the search. Experts in a domain have experience with the primary search systems specific to the domain. Economists in our studies were able to make spontaneous judgments about whether information required for assigned information problems was likely to be found in one or another journal. Likewise, attorneys were readily able to determine whether information in their assigned searches would be found in case law, statutes, or treatises. In both these cases, some professional intermediaries who regularly conducted searches in these domains were also able to predict where relevant information could be found (Marchionini, et al., 1993).

The information seeker's personal information infrastructure is dependent on past experience with information problems in general, their general cognitive abilities, and experience with particular systems. It is well known that information seekers prefer colleagues or human sources to formal sources and then proximate sources of information and easy-to-use systems. These preferences are powerful factors in information seeking and reflect natural human efforts to minimise costs, especially to seek the path of least cognitive resistance (Marchionini, 1987). Naive information seekers have default search systems that they turn to for many tasks. For example, Marchionini (1989c) found that high school students used books and encyclopedias as default sources for a variety of information problems. When experienced information seekers are faced with tasks in foreign domains, they often seek general background information in reference systems that can help refine the problem and point them to primary search systems. Given the constraints of domain knowledge, general cognitive conditions, and previous search experience, information seekers try to map the search task onto one or more search systems.

The mapping process takes into consideration the type of task (e.g., complexity, specificity of answer) and the characteristics of available or familiar search systems. In practice, information seekers consult several search systems as they move toward solutions to their problems. For example, in libraries, information seekers may ask a reference librarian where to begin searching, or they may consult an index or a card catalog and eventually one or more journal or book primary sources. As electronic search systems and network access proliferate, more and more potential sources will become available to information seekers. It is becoming increasingly important to use secondary or *n*-ary systems to limit the time and effort spent locating and using primary systems. With a few exceptions, today's electronic systems are specific to one or two particular levels of search (e.g., bibliographic records) rather than providing a common interface to many levels of systems. For example, there are expert systems that emulate a reference service, thousands of online bibliographic databases, and hundreds of online or CD-ROM full-text databases. Filtering, ordering, and selecting the collection of sources become increasingly important to mapping tasks onto search systems.

Formulate a Query

Query formulation involves matching understanding of the task with the system selected. In many cases, the first query formulation identifies an entry point to the search system and is followed by browsing and/or query reformulations. Query formulation requires two kinds of mappings: a semantic mapping of the information seeker's vocabulary used to articulate the task onto the system's vocabulary used to gain access to the content, and an action mapping of the strategies and tactics that the information seeker deems best to forward the task to the rules and features that the system interface allows. Semantic mapping is similar to moving from Taylor's formalised need to the compromised need (1962) and is highly influenced by earlier mappings from the sensation (visceral need) that forces attention to a problem (conscious need) and the mappings while defining the problem from fuzzy noumena and general concepts into specific terms and concept classes (formalised need). In general, this mapping takes as its domain the entire set of identifiers (possible expressions) available to an individual information seeker and the complete set of identifiers (recognizable expressions) available to a system as its range.

The mapping function most commonly takes words (rather than phrases or concepts) associated with the task onto the set of words that serve as entry points (indexed words or con-trolled vocabulary) to the system content. For static search systems such as books, the information seeker has total control (and responsibility) for the mapping and tries to match words or phrases from the task statement itself (or terms related to them), with words or phrases in the title, index, table of contents, headings, list of keywords, and text. For dynamic search systems such as people, the intelligence of both parties can be applied to enrich the mapping function, as the controlled vocabulary of a human is both large (in fact, is the same as the entire content vocabulary) and more associationally connected. Thus, experts in a domain not only know more terms that directly relate to the information seeker's query formulation, but they also can add additional terms and interact with the information seeker to clarify and verify the query. In the case of professional intermediaries, the process of formulating a query is part of the reference interview and has been shown to be an important determinant of intermediary performance.

In the case of electronic search systems, the query formulation is partially dynamic and system designers have used a wide range of techniques to assist the information seeker. Such techniques include expert system intermediaries (Croft & Thompson, 1987; Marcus, 1983), online suggestions (Meadow, 1988), query-by-example (Zloof, 1977), dynamic queries (Shneiderman, 1992), and hypertext (Croft & Turtle, 1989; Frisse, 1988; Marchionini & Shneiderman, 1988). An electronic system may have a strictly controlled vocabulary (e.g., field names in a database) or a full-text vocabulary (e.g., inverted file), each clearly affecting the cardinality of the set of items retrieved as a result of applying a mapping. The problem of representing concepts in document sets is fundamental to information science and is considered from several perspectives in subsequent chapters. Action mappings lake possible sets of actions to the inputs that a search system can recognise.

If semantic mappings are thought of as "what" or declarative in nature, then action mappings are "how" or procedural in nature. Just as a search system limits the vocabulary that an information seeker may use in query formulation, search systems also limit how queries may be expressed. For example, humans recognise spoken or written expressions, but books do not, and electronic systems so far can recognise only a few expressions. Electronic systems may support Boolean expressions and provide a special syntax for how they may be formed. Electronic systems may allow users to enter any terms they wish, offer a menu that specifies all possible terms, or provide traversable links among various partitions of the database. At even more detailed levels, the system demands that users specify terms or previous sets using explicit characters, cases, or punctuation. Marchionini (1992) argued that electronic systems made many of their greatest contributions to information seeking at the query formulation phase. These advances have been significant in the area of action mappings thus far, in that electronic systems provide a much broader range of ways to articulate queries, even though these ways are spread across different systems rather than being generally available in a single system at the discretion of the information seeker. Progress in augmenting information seekers' mapping of task vocabulary to system vocabulary has been more difficult, but human-computer dialogues and machine inferencing have yielded promising directions for aiding semantic mappings.

Examine Results

Executing a query results in a response from the search system. This response is an intermediate outcome and must be examined by the information seeker to assess progress toward completing the information-seeking task. This examination is dependent on the quantity, type, and format of the response and involves judgments about the relevance of information contained in the response. Responses are provided by information systems in units specific to the type of database, for example, numeric values, bibliographic records, fixed-length fields, entire documents, specific images, or verbal expositions on a topic. A response to a query may contain zero, one, a few, or many of these units, often referred to as *hits*.

The information problem and the user's personal information infrastructure determine the information seeker's expectations about the number of units required to complete a task, although these expectations often change as the information seeking progresses. For example, information seekers typically expect zero or one hit when searching a card catalog for a specific title, and zero, one, or many for a query about a topic (subject search). Users of print encyclopedias typically expect, to find zero, one, or a few articles on a topic and may be quite surprised to find hundreds of hits when using a full-text electronic encyclopedia for the same topic.

A significant difference in printed and full-text electronic encyclopedias is that electronic systems often retrieve many articles, thus requiring another major decision in the examination of results (Marchionini, 1989c). When multiple hits are returned, they are usually presented as a set made up of document surrogates such as titles, bibliographic records, or descriptive identifiers. The way in which these sets are organised and presented affects how information seekers examine individual units, make relevance judgments, and decide what steps to take next.

In a library, a set of catalog cards on a broad topic are ordered alphabetically according to the main entry for that document. In a set of bibliographic records retrieved from an online search system, the items are often ordered in chronological order, beginning with the most recent. In more advanced electronic retrieval systems, items may be ranked according to query-term frequencies. In hypertext systems, explicit links to other units and implicit links such as next page, previous unit, or index lookups are provided by the database designer. The ordering of resultant sets becomes more important as the size of the set increases, and the ability to manipulate orderings of sets of items is recommended for all electronic search systems. The propensity of electronic systems to report large sets of documents significantly affects the examination of results subprocess, complicating the decision making associated with selecting relevant items of information.

The information seeker must judge the relevance of individual retrieved units with respect to the information-seeking task at hand. Relevance is a central theme of information science and has been considered from both theoretical and practical perspectives. Cooper (1971) defined logical relevance as a formal basis for evaluation of retrieval systems, and Wilson (1973) described situational relevance as dependent on the particular information problem at hand. Situational relevance is more specific to the relevance judgments that information seekers make as they examine intermediate results of search (see Saracevic, 1976, for a review of the literature related to relevance in information science and the April 1994 issue of the *Journal of the American Society for Information Science* for a series of articles). From a practical perspective, relevance serves as the main criterion for computing performance measures such as recall and precision.

From an information seeker's perspective, relevance may be considered as the decision about what action to take next in the information-seeking process. Alter-natives include terminate search because the goal has been achieved; pursue the document more fully, that is, examine it again or more exhaustively; pursue the document later, that is, note its existence and location and continue examining other results; pursue implications of the document to the continuation of search (e.g., identify terms to use in subsequent queries); and continue examining other results in this iteration, formulate a new query, or redefine the problem; reject the document completely and continue examining results; or reject the document and stop seeking information without completing the task. Note that the examine-results subprocess.

The examination of specific items for relevance is obviously affected by the type (primary, secondary, numeric, graphic, textual) and the quantity (number of units or documents) of information in the retrieved set. For small sets of results, items can be scanned quickly, browsed systematically, or inspected comprehensively. For large sets of results, the set may be reduced by reformulating the query, or semantically related surrogates (e.g., titles, abstracts, thumbnail images) can be scanned to identify those that suggest a more comprehensive relevance assessment. Marchionini and his colleagues argued that information seekers are willing to scan substantial sets of textual or graphic documents if they are given appropriate display and control mechanisms (Liebscher & Marchionini, 1988; Marchionini, 1989c).

As with query formulation, electronic systems have made substantial progress in supporting the examination of results. Ranked output and alternative orderings of output offer substantial advantages to experienced information seekers because they assist in managing large result sets. Examination is also aided by display techniques such as highlighting query words in retrieved documents, presenting different levels of organisational details (e.g., table of contents and full text - Egan et al., 1989), fisheye views that cluster potentially relevant items in a spatially ordered manner (Purnas, 1986), and high-resolution graphic views of information in hierarchical displays (e.g., Card, Robertson. & Mackinlay, 1991).

Execute Search

Execution of the physical actions to query an information source is driven by the information seeker's mental model of the search system. Execution is based on the semantic and action mappings developed while formulating the query. Looking something up requires actions like articulating a question verbally, picking up a volume, or pressing a key. For a card catalog, execution may entail selecting proper drawers and using alphabetical ordering rules; for an online database, execution may entail typing the query and sending it with a special keypress (e.g., return); for a hypertext, execution may entail browsing the database by following the links provided by the author. Communication and computing technology has greatly affected how searches are executed (and consequently if or when they are executed), by altering the physical actions necessary. Phone calls, telefacsimiles, and electronic mail make the execution of a search with a human search system much more feasible, and electronic networks allow direct queries of remote collections from a home or office. Although interfaces for these devices are often complicated and frustrating, the effects of performing information-seeking tasks in physically proximate space cannot be overestimated. Search execution is one of the most obvious changes wrought by electronic environments, as information seekers per-form many fewer physical actions at workstations than they do in libraries or offices.

Reflect/Iterate/Stop

An information search is seldom completed with only a single query and retrieved set. More often, the initial retrieved set serves as feedback for further query formulations and executions. Deciding when and how to iterate requires an assessment of the information-seeking process itself, how it relates to accepting the problem and the expected effort, and how well the extracted information maps onto the task. Monitoring the progress of information seeking is crucial to browsing strategies that are highly interactive and opportunistic. Determination of a stopping function may depend on external functions like setting or search system or on internal functions like motivation, task-domain knowledge, and information-seeking ability. Stopping decisions in full-text electronic systems are more complex because retrieval is both physically easier and yields more robust outcomes.

Extract Information

There is an inextricable relationship between judging information to be relevant and extracting it for all or part of the problem's solution. Assessments about relevance cause information extraction actions to be taken, although information can be relevant to the problem but not fully meet the conditions of the task's goal. If a retrieved document is judged relevant, the information seeker may choose to continue assessing its relevance by extracting and saving information or to defer extraction and continue examining results. In the latter case, the document will eventually be reexamined, and a revised relevance assessment made based on what other documents were added to the relevant list and what events the information seeker experienced since the previous relevance judgment. To extract information, an information seeker applies skills such as reading, scanning, listening, classifying, copying, and storing information.

In the case of secondary databases, extraction may entail copying or printing bibliographic citations to facilitate retrieval of actual documents. In the case of verbal questions to human experts, listening skills, clarification requests or restatements of the information in one's own words aid in extracting the information relevant to the task. In full-text systems, basic reading skills, scanning skills, use of structural features such as headings and outlines, and jumping from section to section aid in extracting relevant information. As information is extracted, it is manipulated and integrated into the information seeker's knowledge of the domain.

As more information is extracted and stored, new items may not be as relevant as they would have been before other items were manipulated and integrated. Information extraction often includes some physical action such as copying onto paper or another medium and saving those copies in larger structures according to well-defined organisational rules.

For electronic systems, some of the techniques for ordering and display mentioned in the previous section on examination help users by allowing them to cut and paste items easily, including the contextual components that may appear in other windows on the screen. Thus, saving a section outline from a table of contents, the paragraphs around the most relevant information, and a path or query statement that retrieved the document all can be extracted and aggregated easily. Electronic tools for cutting and pasting already offer substantial advantages for extracting information from texts, static and moving images, and sound.

Summary of Subprocesses

The information-seeking process is dynamic and action oriented. The concurrent activation of some subprocesses is not captured. Because these subprocesses are controlled by the information seeker, they most often take heuristic or opportunistic paths according to skills and experience.

These paths depend on ongoing judgments about the costs and benefits of the progress being made, redefinements of the task goals, and relevance judgments about the retrieved information. Electronic search systems have had a substantial impact on several of the subprocesses, especially the query formulation and examination of result subprocesses. Highly interactive search systems and full-text databases have begun to blur the boundaries separating the subprocesses and tend to decrease the linearity of their progression. The information-seeking framework is composed of factors that affect information-seeking behavior and this dynamic, information seeker-centered pro-cess. In the chapters ahead we will examine more specifically how electronic environments affect information seeking and the information seeker. In the next chapter we revisit the information seeker and consider the building blocks for personal information infrastructures.

Compressing Digital Information

Data compression techniques are not special to multimedia. They are simply a much more urgent requirement than in most other areas of application. The benefits of data compression have always been obvious. If a message can be compressed one hundred times, it can be transmitted in one-hundredth of the time, or transmitted at the same speed through a channel with one-hundredth of the bandwidth, and it can be stored in one-hundredth of the volume of the original. Of course, the message will make sense only if it can be successfully decompressed when it reaches the user. Although this analysis is not strictly accurate—there is always a compression/decompression overhead of about 5 per cent-the benefits and potential cost savings are substantial and compression techniques have been a major field of development from the time of the very earliest digital databases. Although a full analysis of compression techniques is beyond the scope of this book, it is important to emphasise that a large number of proprietary compression schemes are now available, most conforming to underlying world standards established and internationally agreed in the early 1990s.

While we will not dwell on the technicality of such schemes, compression is of such great significance in the development of digital media, it is important to touch on some key ideas.

Compression by Redundancy

One of the most important approaches to compression is to exploit the inherent redundancies in information. The simplest example of redundancy is to imagine a personnel record held in a computer system. If you use 'M' and 'F' to denote male or female in the gender field of the record, you require eight bits of data to represent either character. If you decide to replace the characters with an agreed, fixed-length one-bit code, you immediately achieve an eight to one compression of the gender field. This kind of simple redundancy occurs widely in databases and a significant level of compression can thereby be achieved through little more than an exercise of common sense and ingenuity. In the case of images, considerable redundancy can be found simply by locating pans of the image that are the same.

The basic technique is called run length coding and works by replacing a long run of unchanging data by the shortest possible code. For example, imagine a television picture, one-third of which is showing a uniformly blue sky. In digital terms, the sky would normally require about 0.4 megabytes of data. However, a massive compression can be achieved by creating a relatively short code of just a few bytes which effectively tells the computer that 'the next 400,000 bytes will be blue'. The short code would then be acted on just before display to produce the appropriate number of blue pixels to represent the sky. This concept underlies a technique for compressing video which has become vitally important in multimedia.

The basic idea is extended, however, to keep track of a constantly changing picture and to detect only those elements in it which change. Typically, for example, a modern compression scheme will work from a sequence of 'reference frames' throughout the video sequence. These reference frames are encoded in their entirety. The only additional information stored is the video information that changes between each of the consecutive frames. The rest is thrown away.

The most widely used compression schemes based on this process discard well over 90 per cent of the original video information and still manage to reconstruct good quality footage. In cases where there is plenty of fast action such as sports coverage, however, such compression schemes are placed under real pressure simply because they cannot keep up with the levels of change taking place between reference frames. Although they are constantly being refined, the basic approach of compression through throwing information away — known picturesquely as 'lossy' compression—is obviously fundamentally limited. You can never throw away more than everything and once you are discarding over 95 per cent of the original video information, you are touching the limits of what can be regenerated—at acceptable quality — from so little underlying data.

For all its obvious limitations, however, lossy compression now dominates media development in all sectors where compression is important and is commonly applied in a format called MPEG (after a team called the Motion Picture Experts Group) which has effectively become the world standard for video compression schemes. Audio compression can also be achieved by identifying acceptable levels of redundancy and stripping them out. For example, digitising an analogue sound signal requires the repeated sampling of the analogue waveform. The value of the different levels arising from each of the samplings are turned into a bit code. Reproducing a smooth waveform in digital code requires a very high rate of sampling every second, particularly if the wave is complex with many different component frequencies.

However, because the wave is being represented by discrete sampling operations, the digital representation will be a 'stepped' shape rather than a continuous smooth curve. The more samples taken, the smoother and less stepped the representation will be and the better quality of the sound. One way, therefore, of reducing the digital data is simply to reduce the number of samples taken. This works but quickly leads to reduced quality. Practical compression techniques try to cut the data with the minimum effect on quality. Most serious work has focused on improving pulse code modulation (PCM)—the basic method of breaking a waveform into discrete elements for digitisation—and on the transmission of the bit codes that measure the value of the waveform. An important variation known as adaptive differential pulse code modulation (ADPCM) is today widely used as the basic compression standard for much CD media development.

Data compression is so vital to the future of information media that considerable international efforts have been made to create global standards governing the way in which compression is handled. The standards administered by the International Standards Organisation (ISO) will eventually form the basis of all multimedia video communications services and publishing covering Integrated Services Digital Network (ISDN), satellite and terrestrial broadcast systems, local area networks and storage media such as magnetic hard disc, optical disc and digital audio tape (DAT). Each of the standards initiatives seek a common method of compression based on the discrete cosine transform (DCT) process which will ultimately assist the process of authoring multimedia for a range of different platforms and help to building underlying inter-platform compatibilities. Although we will not examine the technical aspects of these standards, it is important to identify briefly the most important initiatives.

There are three. First, there is a standard that applies specifically to videoconferencing. It is called H.261 (or, sometimes, px64) and has been formulated by the European Commissions Consultative Committee on International Telephony and Telegraphy (CCITT). It came into force as an international standard during 1991. Second is the Joint Photographic Experts Group (JPEG) which has now created a standard for compressing still images (although it can also be used for video). The third is called the Motion Picture Experts Group (MPEG). As its name suggests, MPEG defines a standard for coding moving images and associated audio.

The Consumer Market Emerges

And it would have remained that simple if something quite unexpected had not have taken place in the early 1990s. With the benefit of hindsight, it should not have seemed so unexpected. After all, the market focus of CD-ROM had always been based on a simple logic. Access to CD-ROM titles demands elaborate computer hardware. So the market can exist only where such hardware is relatively commonplace. As we have seen, when CD-ROM first appeared in 1985, desktop computers were largely confined to informational professionals and academics. Not surprisingly, therefore, the first customers for CD-ROM technology were librarians and academic researchers. Within a few years-as computing became cheaper and marginally more friendly-PCs became increasingly common on the desks of business executives. This launched the corporate sector of the CD-ROM market-place. As computing became still cheaper and ever more accessible, it should have come as no surprise to see a market in homes emerging for consumer CD-ROM products. In fact, it seemed to come like a bolt from the blue. Suddenly, the Western world woke up to the fact that millions of powerful desktop computers were being purchased for use in homes. The PC was on its way to becoming a consumer appliance. Perhaps one of the chief reasons why this came as such a shock to many observers was because a new generation of special CD-ROM appliances designed specifically for consumer use was supposed to be taking the ground that PCs were inheriting.

The smokescreen created by the marketing hype surrounding them had taken a great many eyes off the ball. To understand this important strand of development, we have to step back to the mid-1980s and the emergence of CD-ROM as an expensive, arcane, computeresque technology. Indeed, to distinguish it from the consumer appliances that followed, we will refer to CD-ROMs accessed by computers that look like computers as. PC CD-ROM.

Even as Philips and Sony were releasing the first PC CD-ROM drives and the world was scratching its head and wondering what to do with them, a deeper, long-term strategy was already being formulated to bring CD-ROM into our living rooms. At the time, with only a few thousand drives in use anywhere in the world, it was an audacious concept. How could CD-ROM possibly be construed as a mass market medium when it was still struggling to be born as a highly technical, vertical market product? For Philips, however, the evolution of CD-ROM from its origins in CD-audio was part of a vital process of evolving a long-term commercialisation of the underlying technology. They had built CD-audio for the consumer market and after a slow start it had become the biggest consumer electronics success since the television. Then came CD-ROM, based on a consumer technology but reinterpreted as a professional information product. The next step was to reformulate CD-ROM and revisit the potentially lucrative consumer market. The path was therefore clean an entertainment product was evolved into a professional product which in turn was to be evolved into an entertainment product again. Philips wanted to build a virtuous circle and make a small fortune by establishing CD technology as the most pervasive entertainment and information medium the world had ever seen-at least, since the creation of the printed page.

Philips' strategy for achieving this was based on one very good and one very bad idea. The very good idea was to create a computer capable of playing CD-ROM tides that was disguised to look like a domestic appliance, as easy to operate as an electric kettle. The very bad idea was to imagine that such an appliance would be used by a nuclear family to share a rich, interactive experience together in front of their television screen in the living room. The evolved form of CD-ROM which Philips developed is called compact disc interactive (CD-I). Physically, it is a neatly designed black box which racks well with the usual hi-fi and video paraphernalia in many living rooms. The fact that the box contains a combined multimedia computer and CD-ROM drive is cunningly disguised and the device is simply positioned as a multimedia entertainment appliance. From a marketing point of view, of course, that positioning is anything but simple, as Philips found early on when it tried to explain to an uncomprehending audience what 'interactivity' and 'multimedia' meant. In other words, while simple in concept, the process of communicating the product offering in terms the market could understand was a challenging — and as yet largely unsolved-problem, one that was to cripple the early take-up of CD-I players.

Because it is aimed at the living room, CD-I is designed to offer the kind of multimedia experience best suited to a living-room environment. In other words, CD-I's operating system (known as RTOS-real time operating system) is optimised to deliver a highly televisual form of multimedia best viewed from middle distance, rich with sound and images and capable of emulating the syntax of television-like programming. The hardware is designed, of course, to play back via a conventional domestic television while interaction with the software is governed not by a keyboard but by a simple, infra-red remote control device. Although a control of this kind limits the intensity of the interactivity, it perfectly suits the traditional approach to controlling television and ether media experiences in the living room.

The history of CD-I's efforts in the consumer market is salutary. Other emulators such as Commodore with its CDTV system and 3DO with a consumer CD-ROM 'black box' technology boasting 'a quantum leap in graphics performance', all ran into the same brick wall. Although the detailed analysis is complex, the bottomline is simple. On the whole, consumers want to do two closely connected things in front of their television screen: relax and have fun. In other words, early CD-I titles -largely funded by Philips because few other content or development companies would risk investment in the new system-which aimed to provide rich, interactive cultural and educational experiences were simply barking up the wrong tree. Tides like *The Russia of the Czars* and *Treasures of the Smithsonian,* beautifully produced as they were, were too much hard work for the average consumers. And since software inevitably sells hardware,

Philips rapidly found themselves unable to sell CD-I readily much beyond that eternal, mad band of early adopters who seem to buy any new consumer electronics technology that comes to market.

The acid reality of the market-place caused Philips to revamp its software development strategy and it is worth noting two things immediately. First, at the early stages of establishing any new consumer multimedia system it is ultimately software development strategy that determines the future of the related hardware. Consumers understand the hardware offering via the software. Which is just another way of saying that technology does not sell. What sells is the application of technology-what it can do for us and the benefits it can deliver in our lives. The second key point is that when a proprietary technology like CD-I is trying to establish an installed base, the hardware originators cannot shirk getting involved in shaping and driving the software strategy. The reason is self-evident. Few software developers or publishers are likely to be so utterly confident of a new platform that they will invest heavily in developing software for it without some cast-iron guarantees about the growth of an installed base of users -which is jargon for the emergence of a decent number of customers. No such guarantees can ever be given so, most times, the hardware companies have to bite the bullet and fund software development. Philips bit the bullet right through with CD-I and not only funded but also embraced software development as a new strategic strand in its core business. But recognising the realities of the market meant casting aside the former emphasis on worthy interactive titles and turning instead to mainstream entertainment. This meant two main themes: games and movies.

Distribution Nightmare

As this book is written, a growing realisation is dawning that the consumer CD-ROM market is heading towards considerable crisis. There is a heavy irony in this because the awareness of impending disaster is emerging just as the market appears to be rocketing in size. The statistics-albeit US ones-speak for themselves. At the end of 1993, the US market generated by sales through direct and retail channels and bundled OEM (original equipment manufacturer) deals between publishers and hardware vendors, was worth about $200 million. A year later, the market had topped $650 million. By the end of 1995 it had touched $1.5 billion. Apart from the sheer pace and magnitude of the growth, there are two very important factors hidden in the statistics.

First, the number of units reaching the market through sales to consumers now vastly outstrips the number being given away free as titles bundled with hardware purchases. In 1995, such bundles represented about 35 per cent of all units reaching the US market. Two years earlier, the figure had been around 70 per cent. This is highly significant because it appears to indicate a crucial underlying trend. Instead of getting CD-ROM tides free with hardware, consumers are purchasing titles themselves, presumably because of a specific, strong interest in them. In other words, market demand has arrived and instead of title publishers pushing their titles at consumers through giveaways, they are beginning to feel the welcome effect of consumers coming in off the street keen at last to buy their products.

Second, although the figure has declined somewhat since 1993, around 40 per cent of the sales are generated by content-based tides. In other words, info- and edutainment is a large sector of the market with games a comparable but by no means dominant category. This is good news for the mainstream publishing community unfamiliar with games industry culture and-coupled with spectacular market growth-has played an important part in the rapid expansion in the number of titles being issued. In 1994, for example, as the market more than trebled in size within a single year, developers and publishers rushed to meet the rising tide of demand with a vast number of new titles. At the end of 1993, fewer than 400 CD-ROM titles with true consumer market orientation were available worldwide. Twelve months later the number had swollen to around 3,000. Since then, not only has the raw number of titles continued to increase but also development budgets have soared as publishers have struggled to distinguish their offerings with every more spectacular visual effects, ever more tightly packed content and ever more big name film actors to 'star' in their productions. But market growth, and the publishing frenzy it provoked, seems to contain the seeds of its own destruction.

The avalanche of new titles has created a massive log jam in retail distribution channels. Shelf space is at a premium. In the United States, where the market is most advanced, even the most committed CD-ROM retailers are stocking only 300-400 titles and, from retailer to retailer, they tend to be the same 300-400 titles. In other words, the vast majority of new products are failing to get retail exposure. None of this is surprising. The market-place has simply expanded faster than the retail infrastructure for handling it. This is not the contradiction in terms it seems, simply because it is not retail distribution alone that is permitting market growth. Bundling-despite the decline in its influence-and direct distribution are both still major components. But the slow growth of retail support is a major inhibitor and a serious problem for publishers and developers alike.

European Markets Emerge

Virtually everything we have stated so far about the consumer market has related to events in the United States and for good reason. The shift in the centre of gravity of PC CD-ROM publishing first emerged most emphatically and obviously in the United States and while the US market differs substantially in structure, culture and metabolism from Europe, it is nonetheless a useful laboratory for studying the underlying processes of change soon to sweep through European markets. To get a sense of just how emphatic the shift in the States was, consider the proportion of the total PC CD-ROM population that was in US homes in the early 1990s. In 1991, a mere 4 per cent of all drives were in homes. By the end of 1993, the number had leapt to 60 per cent and reached 70 per cent a year later.

In Europe, the same pattern began to emerge in 1994. This was the year when the consumer PC CD-ROM market arrived-at least in terms of the numbers of CD-ROM drives in European homes. In 1993, for example about 80,000 UK homes had PC CD-ROM drives. At the end of 1994, the installed base had soared to 500,000 and at the end of 1995 stood at around 1.7 million-a twenty times increase in two years! In Germany, the picture was even more dramatic: 127,000 drives rising to 1.1 million at the end of 1994 and jumping again to 3.1 million at the end of 1995. The pattern in France was 87,000 rising to 400,000 and then to 1.4 million at the end of 1995. This colossal growth, however, disguised a key factor in the metabolism of the market. While hardware purchases soared, CD-ROM software sales remained modest and patchy.

In particular, it was evident that the possession of CD-ROM drives no longer implied their use. In 1995 in the hottest European market, Germany, for example, 38 per cent of all CD-ROM homes possessed no discs at all. In France the figure was 13 per cent and in the UK 15 per cent. This apparently extraordinary finding has a simple explanation. As PCs increasingly have CD-ROM drives routinely built-in, buyers of PCs are getting hold of drives without being primarily interested in using them. Their principal motivation is to own a PC. This is radically different from the position only a few months previously when drives were purchased as a deliberate act, driven by real and specific interest in CD-ROM. The reason why the German percentage is so high is because in the German PC market aggressive hardware vendors such as Vorbis and Escom have made special efforts to bundle cheap CD-ROM drives with PCs to create ultra low cost, multifeatured packages.

All this says one very clear thing about any analysis of the European and, by implication, US markets. The link between the installed base of drives and a title market is weakening. The possession of the technology no longer implies its use. For Europe, in particular, this means that the huge rise in the drive population should not be taken to imply automatically a comparably large emerging title market. Indeed, in 1995, the realities were bleak for European multimedia publishers. In the UK, an average good selling edutainment or infotainment title was selling around 5,000 copies. One or two bestsellers were reaching about 20,000. In Germany, the country with by far the biggest and fastest growing population of CD-ROM drives, the picture was little different. Of around 1,700 titles available in German (both indigenous German language titles and English language imports), only 4 per cent sold more than 20,000 copies. About 6 per cent sold between 10,000 and 20,000. and 13 per cent between 5,000 and 10,000. This left over 75 per cent of titles selling 5,000 copies or fewer.

The real problem that these numbers imply is that the economics of selling fully featured CD-ROM titles into individual national markets does average levels of sale quoted above do not even allow their direct costs of production, let alone overheads. There is an exception, of course. The economics do not work but they do European publishers. They can work for US companies who have already amortised most of their costs over domestic sales of their titles. For them, the European market is in excellent opportunity to escape the congestion of US distribution channels and the grief it is causing and mop up profit in Europe. The fact that this a taking place is indicated for all to see by export figures for the US consumer industry as a whole. In 1994, 24 per cent of the value of the US market was generated by export sales-mainly to Europe. Up to the mid-year of 1995, the figure had leapt to nearly 40 per cent. And in 1994, the 24 per cent was of a market of around $650 million. In 1995, assuming the percentage persisted to the year end, the 40 per cent was a substantial slice of a cake probably worth around $1.6 billion. It is no coincidence that in 1995 Encarta was the only information CD-ROM to feature in the top twenty bestsellers in the UK alongside of a wealth of games titles. Encarta, in fifth place, was a bestseller because it was for the first time localised to its market. The UK, for the first time, had a UK edition. This is in important straw in the wind. Not only are US publishers increasing exploiting the European market, they are also taking it seriously. In other words, they are not merely seeking to shift a few additional units. They are investing in localising and reculturing their products in order to leverage them across the diversity of European national requirements and tastes. This is strong medicine for European publishers.

Already faced with a fragmented market, unviably low unit sales-except for a few hits-and an embryonic and diffident distribution infrastructure, they are in danger of being swept away by the big battalions from the United States. The only credible answer is for European publishers to rapidly develop pan-European strategies. This means a range of partnerships and alliances aimed at cross-leveraging rides with appropriate levels of sensitive localisation and reculturing. The European multimedia industries must work together in a realistic fusion of co-operation and competition in order to maintain a grip on the future of their own market-place. The UK polisher, Dorling Kindersley, has already demonstrated how well co-publishing models can work in the multimedia business and it is now increasing important for others to follow its brilliant lead.

Commercialising a Web Site

If a site is successful in staking out its franchise and creating a constituency of long-term users of the site, how can it turn its promising position into one that generates substantial revenues? One thing is sure, it will need to do this quickly because the cost of entry for those aiming to build substantial and effective Web publishing operations is no longer modest. There was once a view that the attraction of the Web was the cheapness of being there. A few thousand dollars could buy the hardware, software and connection to get a server linked to the Internet This is still true: it does cost only a few thousand dollars-so long as you do not plan to do anything significant with the Web presence that you have created. A powerful site capable of building a substantial constituency-and retaining it -needs major upfront investment and, just as important, substantial ongoing investment to keep the site fresh, dynamic and on the leading edge of Web technology and functionality. The best commercial sites currently operating have dollar budgets well into eight figures per annum and-like making a movie, computer game or multimedia CD-ROM title-there is effectively no limit to what can be spent. So, with the cost on entry soaring, the pressure on revenue generation is increasingly intense.

The first understanding that site owners must have-whatever media culture they come from-is that to stand any chance of profitability, sites will almost certainly need multiple sources of revenue. This is a familiar idea, for example, to magazine companies but a strange and largely alien one, say, for book publishers. However, it is crucial, particularly in these early pioneering years, because no one yet fully understands where the main emphasis in revenue generation will ultimately come from. Until this becomes clearer, everyone trying to make money from costly Web presences must look for revenue from every possible source. That is why today's operators of Web shopping malls are likely to fail-because they have committed their business model to attracting visitors to their sites and then commercialising those visits via a single form of revenue generation. Of course, business models are never blunt instruments and there will, in practice, be many variations but multiplicity is a vital key in searching for ways of making the Web viable. There are at least four major paradigms for revenue generation-others, no doubt, will emerge:

- Conducting transactions
- Selling links
- Selling content
- Selling advertising

Conducting Transactions

A third key revenue stream is based on offering Web constituencies the opportunity to conduct transactions online. This has been the great hope of the consumer online networks for over a decade. It is no accident that Prodigy, for example, is partly owned by US retailing giant Sears. The original concept was that having won a large base of subscribers, Prodigy could turn into a huge, home shopping environment in which billions of dollars of business would be transacted by merchants, each of whom would pay Prodigy a small slice of the action. In fact, by 1993, electronic shopping barely accounted for 2 per cent of Prodigy's revenues. The other proprietaries have had similar success.

The mood is changing, however, and the belief is growing that as serious volumes of users emerge, home shopping will come into its inheritance as one of the major revenue generators of the online industry. With the Web expanding rapidly, opportunities for this kind of trade appear to be exploding. Analysts and forecasters are falling over themselves to predict the sheer size of the emerging market-place. Depending on who you listen to, the market could be worth anything from $6 billion to $300 billion by the turn of the century—a sure indication that no one really knows. The sense so far among home shopping specialists is that if the virtual shops and malls are built, the customers will come. Even if they do come, of course, it is worth remembering for the sake of perspective that even the most optimistic estimates of the market look tiny compared to real world shopping. The retail grocery market in the United States alone is currently worth half a trillion dollars per annum.

The reality of home shopping on proprietary services has been that the opportunities to shop have been limited to relatively few suppliers who have offered a largely unappealing shopping experience. Indeed, it is questionable whether any true shopping experience can be delivered online—replete with its essential elements of entertainment, serendipity and socialising. Probably the best that can be offered is a reliable buying experience majoring on the fact that online shops can offer limitless shelf space with comprehensive range of products. They are also best at selling commodities rather than products with varied values and benefits. Because of this, online is a good place to offer access to large catalogues of media and software products which can be ordered online and fulfilled by conventional channels. It is not surprising, therefore, that in surveys of those online shoppers that could be found in the United States in 1995, 48 per it tended to buy computer software and 34 per cent purchased entertainment products, especially music CDs and, to a much lesser extent, books and videos. Most (about 74 per cent) cited convenience as the main reason shopping online. Strikingly, only a minority favoured specially created shopping mall sites to make purchases with nearly 70 per cent tending to conduct transactions at single sites which provided a transactional facility a strand of their offering.

This suggests a powerful idea about shopping online. The fact that services on single sites are most popular may suggest that online shopping forks best when the transaction facility is placed close to the point of interest that drives the impulse to buy. To understand this idea better, consider a simple example. One of the earliest pioneers of Web sites among record companies was US label Geffen. Today at the Geffen site you surf through a range of attractive pages that tell you more than most want to know about Geffen artists and recordings, all colourfully and complete with sound samples. Strategically placed among pages are buttons with the words 'I want this CD now!' written on them. Not surprisingly, the buttons occur next to some of the most persuasive descriptions of latest album releases. By clicking the button, the user is instantly hyperlinked to another site run by a direct mail CD specialist CD Now which has created a massive CD shopping presence on the Web. The link does not simply take the user to the front door of CD Now's shop, it takes them directly to that location within CD Now where can place an order for the album they have just been reading about. In other words, the impulse to buy has been commercialised by Geffen (and, incidentally, by CD Now) at the very moment the impulse is generated.

This is a powerful model for the future of online shopping because it places shopping, like advertising, in close proximity to content. Indeed, just as we argued for advertising, online shopping may be best expressed as a strand within content, contextualised and supporting the content experience.

Currently, online shopping remains in its infancy and faces particular problems on the Web. Most obvious is the issue of security on the Web and the lack of effective electronic payment mechanisms that will allow customers both to place an order and pay for the goods in a single, safe and reliable transaction. Proprietary networks have never had this problem because all data moving through their networks pass exclusively through their own infrastructures and, thanks to established subscriber management systems, consolidating online purchases within normal billing mechanisms is a simple process. On the Web, by contrast, concern about secure payment is probably the single most important factor inhibiting the growth of Web commerce. We will consider security and payment mechanisms briefly later but for now we need only note that—despite the depth of concern that is evident among Web users—trustworthy technical solutions are rapidly emerging which will provide a small number of dominant standards by sometime in 1997 which will spark rapid and sustained growth in Web commerce during 1998 and beyond.

As a revenue—generating option, however, transactions look like a strong possibility for the medium-term future. The potential, as with advertising, is based upon the creation by distinctive and successful sites of established constituencies. Just as advertisers will pay for access to such constituencies, so will merchants with offerings appropriate to the demographic of the constituency.

Selling Links

Once a site has established its franchise and built a constituency it is able to influence that constituency in important ways. Most important for proprietors of related but non-competing sites, is the possibility of gaining traffic from the 'hot' site by persuading the site owner to point its constituency at them. So far, this kind of hotlinking is usually agreed on a largely reciprocal basis but once sites have established themselves as successful and well used, they can drive much harder bargains. To some extent, the desire to generate revenue from hotlinking must be balanced with the need to add value to one site by providing links to others of related interest. Such linking is a key feature in determining a site's attractiveness and it would be ill judged to sacrifice good linking possibilities simply because a she is unable to generate revenue from the link destinations.

More interesting than one successful site merely generating hard cash by trading its constituency by selling links is the possibility of agreeing deals with paid-for sites to get preferential access terms for constituents. Proprietors of premium sites or premium areas within sites will be inclined to give substantial discounts in return for a guaranteed flow of traffic. Meantime, site owners can offer an even more attractive package for access to their own sites by, perhaps, making a subscription charge that includes free access to a number of otherwise paid-for sites. In other words, this kind of deal allows major Web sites to become packagers of other sites, offering a low-cost point of entry to a range of content and service experiences which, paid for individually, would amount to a substantial monthly cost. The key building block, however, is the ownership of a constituency which, either through raw size or valuable demographic focus, can be readily traded with others.

The Changing Face of the Web

The conversion of the Web from being an arena for a few computer enthusiasts to a vast, sprawling environment filled with the bustle of commercial activity is not merely based on underpinnings such as security and payment mechanisms. The subjective experience of individuals using the Web is crucial to the pace and character of its future development.

Most times today the Web still seems a silent, infuriatingly slow and confusing place to visit. In fact, it is often such a dispiriting experience to surf the Web, it seems incredible that there is such widespread talk of the Web's creation as being almost on an equal footing in terms of global significance with the invention of digital computing. Is it really going to such a revolutionary impact on our lives? The answer is yes, in time, while the mainstream revolution is still-as this book is written-a (very) few years away, the seeds of revolution are everywhere to be seen. In coming years, the Web is going to change out of all recognition so far as the experience of existing, Webwise users are concerned. And by looking is about to happen for some of us we can get a sense for the kind of place the Web will soon become for all of us.

An important straw in the wind is the launch early in 1995 by Seattle-Progressive Networks of RealAudio, a software package available free from its Web site. In the first year following its launch, nearly a million copies of the client software were distributed free and over 100 Web sites were offering RealAudio content. RealAudio works by compressing segments of an audio stream and sending it packet by packet from the server to the client computer. As the packets arrive they are buffered in the client memory, decompressed and then played back as soon as the buffer is full as a stream of sound. During playback, the buffering process continues to give the effect of a continuous stream. So far, quality on an ordinary dial-up connection at 14.4 kbs is, in radio broadcasting terms, a little below AM and in long continuous streams it is possible to hear occasional blips in the flow as each buffered segment is accessed. But it is a dramatically different experience from the traditional lengthy process of downloading files and playing them offline.

One of the earliest applications of RealAudio has been radio 'broadcasting'. From RealAudio's site you can access 24-hour Internet radio, which is based on the hourly output of news from ABC. The transmission is updated every hour and the previous 24 hours of programming is stored at the site. This means that what you hear is never more than a maximum of one hour later than its actual broadcast time and that you have access to all the news broadcast during the day in a true on-demand fashion. Clearly, this is still far from a real-time experience but the effect is almost as satisfying-particularly for European ears tuned in to the world of transatlantic radio, for the first time. Elsewhere, music retailers and bands are also showing interest in the technology. The Rolling Stones are already making extensive use of RealAudio samples at their Voodoo Lounge site with unreleased extracts from some of their tours while elsewhere vendors are offering a try-before-you-buy option for cyberspace music shoppers.

Other RealAudio sites have quickly emerged including popular Korean songs from a site in Seoul, NTT-AD radio in Tokyo, Fox FM radio from Melbourne and scores of music, radio and magazine related sites based in North America. The only European-sites so far are a Swedish national radio station, the Wildpark from Berlin, a fortune-telling service from London and radio services from the Open University at Milton Keynes in the UK and from a site in Milan, Italy. Later in 1995, RealAudio was joined by a seemingly more powerful competitor which holds the prospect of real-time multimedia on the Web. US software specialist Xing Technology Corporation has announced a new generation of server software that promises to deliver real-time audio and video to ordinary dial-up users.

For a lucky few, real-time video and audio are already there. The only drawback is that you need an ultra-fast connection to the fastest backbones of the Net in order to get the bandwidth you need. Very few people, for example, have the benefit of links to the US M-bone (an experimental multicast backbone system) or access to expensive high speed links such as T-lines. Xing claims it is going to change this situation dramatically with a new compression-based technology which will operate over conventional telephone lines. Xing's new product is called Streamworks.

Compatible with most existing Web browsers, it works over standard TCP/IP networks including, of course, the Internet itself. The engine driving Streamworks is a software implementation of MPEG which makes it possible to draw both video and audio from a server in real-time, allowing true on-demand access to multimedia content. The technology has already been proved in private business applications using fast lines. NBC's Desktop Video and Reuters Financial Television, for example, both use the underlying server technology but send the data streams over private, fast

TCP/IP networks to their customers. The real breakthrough lies in the fact that the Streamworks implementation is designed for the World Wide Web and the considerably lower access speeds which commonly prevail. According to Xing, using an associated compression package in the server software, good quality audio can be delivered via an ordinary dial-up connection to the Internet via a 14.4 kbs modem.

High quality audio is available through 28.8 kbs modems. With ISDN links Streamworks can, of course, do much better. Using the full 128 kbs available from two ISDN channels, Xing says that Stream-works can deliver in real-time, quarter screen video at 30 frames per second. Presumably frame speed can be traded against window size, enabling a window to be used where there is little fast action in the video being delivered. All that client computers need is Xing decompression software, which will soon be widely downloadable from a number of Web sites. With this in place, users will be able to use their browsers to access Streamworks wherever they emerge.

Early interest-not surprisingly-is coming radio stations. Radio Data Group-a subsidiary of EZ Communications, a US operator based in Washington State with 21 stations serving 8 national markets in its portfolio-has been the first to move. It has signed a deal with Xing to put live radio on the Web right away. The first stations to go live will be KMPS and KZOK serving the Seattle area. Michael Rau, president of Radio Data, reports that setting up an Internet broadcasting operation is straightforward and cheap'. The operation of software is very simple, much like the operation of a radio receiver,' Rau explains. 'When a hypertext link is selected, the radio station programme is instantly available and is the same programme material that is being broadcast at the time. It is not an audio file that needs downloading.... The operation is as simple as turning on a radio and selecting a station.'

Other radio companies are sure to follow but it is clear that non-traditional broadcasters may soon be setting up Xing sites too. So long as they have access to content, set-up costs are comparatively modest. At the time of writing, Xing's server software costs between $3,500 and $6,500 and is easy to configure and use. Client software can be downloaded free from Xing's own Web site. Registration-which buys full technical support and upgrade offers-currently costs a mere $29. RealAudio and Streamworks are just examples. Many other systems like them are emerging and the trend is towards better, faster, cheaper 'good enough' multimedia. These developments are facets of the revolution now to reshape our experience of the Web.

Elsewhere, three dimensional are also fast arriving. Virtual Reality Modelling Language (VRML), for example, is cheating the bandwidth restrictions of conventional dial-up access, enabling Web sites to create interactive 3D environments which can be accessed by dial-up connections. Here bandwidth limitations are thwarted by an ingenious technique which makes the client computer do the grunt work. In other words, only low resolution instructions are sent over the network. When these are received by a VRML compliant browser, the client computer builds the virtual world and provides the interactivity which generates the 3D application. Worlds Inc., for example, the US software company acquired in 1995 by UK media group, Pearson, has used an enhanced form of VRML to create a remarkable real-time chat environment that features 3D rooms and visual representations (known as avatars) of other simultaneous users of the system. Perhaps most intriguing of all is the emergence of a new object-oriented programming language from Sun Microsystems, called Java. Java is a terse, secure, machine independent language which will increasingly be supported by major Web browsers. Sun has its own Java browser called HotJava but Netscape has also incorporated the technology in its new version of Navigator, ensuring that Java becomes a widely accessible language for most Web users.

Java's fascination lies in its ability to send entire applications over the Net in compact bundles of code called applets (a contraction of the word 'application'). This makes it possible to send not only data but also an entire added value package containing, says data and analysis and manipulation software to a Java compliant browser. In practical terms, Java effectively reshapes the potential of Web sites making them capable of delivering any application from a 3D animation sequence to support text in a Web document to a complete wordprocessing or spreadsheet application. It is also possible to continuously update an applet as it runs on a client machine. This makes it possible to stream real-time data like a conventional wire feed of news or financial information. If it can be written in Java it can be sent as an applet. Because Java is machine independent, target computers need only a simple Java viewer installed to gain access to whatever the applets contain. It is this reader technology which will soon be available in millions of browsers worldwide. There are three important points about all of this remarkable development activity. First, we need to keep our feet on the ground.

Java has a long way to go before it becomes a language in which applications can be built quickly and cheaply. All the other multimedia and 3D bells and whistles are compelling and seductive but cost money. At a time when the Web is still generating only modest revenues for its commercial pioneers, building all-singing, all-dancing sites is a big roll of the dice. Annual budgets are today increasingly numbered in millions, even tens of millions of dollars to build and maintain leading edge sites. While the power to transform the Web experience is being delivered fast, its use has to be wedded to the economic limitations of existing Web business models. Second, and despite this cautionary note, the Web is clearly in the process of being transformed and our experience of it today is no guide to what it will be like in only a year's time.

In other words, if we are building a Web strategy now — aside from economic housekeeping issues-it must not reflect the capabilities of the Web as it is today. We have to look ahead at the interactive, multimedia future. Third, we need to understand this transformation as something which both changes the possible uses of the Web and the audience of users. Once the Web ceases to be the slow and silent place it is today and comes to life with sound, images and real-time interactivities which can be accessed via plain old telephone lines, it will attract an ever-widening demographic of users. Tomorrow's Web is truly everyone's Web.

This is the ultimate, impossible question but one worth asking in spite of it being unanswerable. The immediate issue, of course, is who is asking because the answer will differ with differing agendas. We will examine some answers for only two communities: the world of content owners and originators-those who will ultimately drive the future offerings of the media industry in the new age — and the world of ordinary users and experiences of media content. Each sit at extreme ends of a complex value chain. For commercial players, a key question will be where they sit in that value chain and how they should move to wield influence over those sectors most crucial to their own competitive advantage in whatever markets they target. The recipients of the outpourings of the media industry — digital or otherwise — have an equally pressing issue to confront. Where and how should they spend their media dollar? What product or, increasingly, which experience will most satisfy their needs? Ultimately, their decisions determine the future of the entire media industry and, within it, who will flourish and prosper and who will go to the wall. As this suggests, digital media are not at heart a technological issue.

This may be a curious thought with which to conclude a study of digital media, especially one which has offered so much commentary about technology. Nonetheless, it is a point worth making. In any consideration of digital media, we must, of course, focus on technology and its varied promises. However, we must never lose sight of a vital fact. It is people who design digital media systems and it is people who use them. This has quite simple implications. Designers, developers and publishers of digital media offerings need to make a careful and accurate analysis of the human needs that their products are meant to address. Then they must translate their analysis into effective interface and product design.

Although simple in essence, this notion is difficult to implement. True mastery of design and development in digital media-particularly in multimedia -demands more than an incremental change in existing established skills. It requires a genuine transformation or, perhaps, convergence. In the creation of effective digital products and services the professions of information scientist, designer, computer programmer, systems analyst, film maker, financier, and publisher must somehow be drawn together, either in a single extraordinary person or into a well-managed and effective creative team. By doing this we may begin to see products that people will want to buy and use. We need to remember that however dazzling the technology may become, someone must be there to pay the bill.

Digital media, like any technological advance, can be driven forward only by commercial success. This means addressing and meeting the needs of the people who will part with money for the products created for them. Ultimately, therefore, the real issue in digital media is not technology but the paying customer.

REFERENCES

Angus J. Kennedy, *The Internet: The Rough Guide*, London: Rough Guides, 1999, pp. 502.

Bill Gates, *The Road Ahead*, Viking, 1996, pp.332,.

Brian Austin, *Using the Internet*, Warwickshire (UK): Computer Step, 2000, pp.512.

Charles Jonscher, *WiredLife*, Bantam Press, 1999, pp.245.

Chris DiBona et al, *Open Sources: Voices from the Open Source Revolution*, Sebastopol: O'Reilly, 1999, pp.272.

Danny Goodman, *Living at Light Speed: your survival guide to life on the information superhighway*, Random House, 1995. pp.244.

David Gauntlett, *Web.Studies: Rewiring media studies for the digital age*, London: Arnold, 2000, pp.250.

David L. Farquhar, *Optimising Windows for Games, Graphics & Multimedia*, Sebastopol, CA: O'Reilly, 2000, pp.278.

Eric S. Raymond, *The Cathedral and the Bazaar: Musings on Linux and Open Source by an Accidental Revolutionary*, Sebastopol: O'Reilly, 1999, pp.268.

Ernest Ackerman and Karen Hartman, *Internet Today! Email, searching, and the World Wide Web*, Chicago & London: Franklin, Beedle & Associates, 1999, pp.302.

Esther Dyson, *Release 2.0: A design for living in the digital age*, Viking: London, 1997, pp.307.

Geoff Preston, *The Internet in Easy Steps*, Warwickshire: Computer Step, 2000, pp.384.

Gordon Graham, *The Internet: a philosophical inquiry*, Routledge, 1999, pp.179.

Jim McClellan, *The Guardian Guide to the Internet*, London: Fourth Estate, 1999, pp.448.

John Naughton, *A Brief History of the Future: The Origins of the Internet*, London: Weidenfeld & Nicolson, 1999, pp. 320.

Katie Hafner and Matthew Lyon, *Where Wizards Stay Up Late: the origins of the Internet*, Simon & Schuster, 1998, pp.304.

Kiersten Conner and Ed Krol, *The Whole Internet: The Next Generation*, Sebastopol: O'Reilly, 1999, pp.576.

Michael Price, *Windows 98 in Easy Steps*, Birmingham: Computer Step, 1999, pp.384.

Mitchell Shnier, *Dictionary of PC Hardware and Data Communications Terms*, Sebastopol (CA): O'Reilly & Associates, 1996, pp.516.

Nicholas Negroponte, *Being Digital*, Hodder & Stoughton, 1995, pp. 243.

Peter Norton and John Goodman, *Peter Norton's 'Inside the PC'*, (seventh edition) Sams, 1998, pp.721.

Rick Maybury, *Boot Up Projects: The Daily Telegraph Guide to Doing Something Useful with your Computer*, London: Orion Business Books, 2000, pp. 191.

Rick Maybury, *Boot Up: The Daily Telegraph Beginner's Guide to Computers and Computing*, London: Orion Business Books, 1999, pp. 185.

Robert Bruce Thompson & Barbara Fritchman Thompson, *PC Hardware in a Nutshell*, Sebastopol (CA): O'Reilly, pp.501.

Robert X. Cringley, *Accidental Empires*, Addison-Wesley/Viking, 2nd edition, 1996, pp.358.

Sven Birkerts, *The Gutenberg Elegies: The Fate of Reading in an Electronic Age*, Fawcett Columbine, 1994.

Tim Berners-Lee, *Weaving the Web*, London: Orion Business Books, 1999, pp.234.

Tim O'Reilley and Troy Mott, *Windows 95 in a Nutshell: A Desktop Quick Reference*, Sebastopol (CA): O'Reilly and Associates, 1998, pp.504.

2

Multimedia Information Graphics, Design & Printing

Information Graphics

Information graphics or infographics are visual representations of information, data or knowledge. These graphics are used anywhere where information needs to be explained quickly or simply, such as in signs, maps, journalism, technical writing, and education. They are also used extensively as tools by computer scientists, mathematicians, and statisticians to ease the process of developing and communicating conceptual information. They are applied in all aspects of scientific visualization.

History of Information Graphics

Early Experiments

In prehistory, early humans created the first information graphics: cave paintings and later maps. Map-making began several millennia before writing, and map at Çatalhöyük dates from around 7500 BCE. Later icons were used to keep record of cattle and stock. The Indians of Mesoamerica used imagery to depict the journeys of past generations. Illegible on their own, they served as a supportive element to memory and storytelling. In 1626 Christopher Scheiner published the *Rosa Ursina sive Sol* which used a variety of graphics to reveal his astronomical research on the sun. He used a series of images to explain the rotation of the sun over time (by tracking sunspots). In 1786, William Playfair published the first data graphs in his book The Commercial and Political Atlas. The book is filled with statistical graphs that represent the economy of 18th century England using bar charts and histograms. In 1801 Playfair introduced the first area chart in *Statistical Breviary*. James Joseph Sylvester introduced the term "graph" in 1878 and published a set of diagrams showing the relationship between chemical bonds and mathematical properties. These were also the first mathematic graphs. 1861 saw the release of a seminal information graphic on the subject of Napoleon's disastrous march on Moscow. The creator, Charles

Joseph Minard, captured four different changing variables that contributed to the failure, in a single two-dimensional image:

- the army's direction as they travelled
- the location the troops passed through
- the size of the army as troops died from hunger and wounds
- the freezing temperatures they experienced

The Development of a Visual Language in the 20th Century

In 1936 Otto Neurath introduced a system of pictographs intended to function as an international visual or picture language. Isotype included a set of stylized human figures which were the basis for the ubiquitous modern stick figures. In 1942 Isidore Isou published the Lettrist manifesto. The 1972 Munich Olympics were the venue for Otl Aicher to introduce a new set of pictograms that proved to be extremely popular, and influenced the ubiquitous modern stick figures used in public signs. Also in 1972 the Pioneer Plaque was launched into space with the Pioneer 10 probe. Inscribed into the plaque was an information graphic intended as a kind of interstellar message in a bottle, designed by Carl Sagan and Frank Drake. The message is unique in that it is intended to be understood by extraterrestrial beings who would share no common language with humans. It depicts a picture of a man and a woman standing in front of a simplified silhouette of the probe in order to give a sense of scale. It also contains a map lccating the sun relative to a number of pulsars, and a simplified depiction of the solar system, with the probe's path from earth into outer space shown with an arrow.

Elements of Information Graphics

The basic material of an information graphic is the data, information, or knowledge that the graphic presents. In the case of data, the creator may make use of automated tools such as graphing software to represent the data in the form of lines, boxes, arrows, and various symbols and pictograms. The information graphic might also feature a key which defines the visual elements in plain English. A scale and labels are also common.

Modern Uses

Today information graphics surround us in the media, in published works both pedestrian and scientific, in road signs and manuals. They illustrate information that would be unwieldy in text form, and act as a visual shorthand for everyday concepts such as stop and go. In newspapers, infographics are commonly used to show the weather, as well as maps and site plans for newsworthy events, and graphs for statistical data. Some books are almost entirely made up of information graphics, such as David Macaulay's The Way Things Work. Although they are used heavily in children's books, they are also common in scientific literature, where they are used to illustrate physical systems, especially ones that cannot be photographed (such as cutaway diagrams, astronomical diagrams, and images of microscopic or sub-microscopic systems). Modern maps, especially route maps for transit systems, use infographic techniques to integrate a variety of information, such as the conceptual layout of the transit network, transfer points, and local landmarks. Traffic signs and other public signs rely heavily on information graphics, such as stylized human figures (the ubiquitous stick figure), icons and emblems to represent concepts such as yield, caution, and the direction of traffic. Public places such as transit terminals usually have some sort of integrated "signage system" with standardized icons and stylized maps. Technical manuals make extensive use of diagrams and also common icons to highlight warnings, dangers, and standards certifications.

Modern Practitioners of Information Graphics/Design

A statistician and sculptor, Edward Tufte has written a series of highly regarded books on the subject of information graphics. Tufte also delivers lectures and workshops on a regular basis. He describes the process of incorporating many dimensions of information into a two-dimensional image as 'escaping flatland' (alluding to the 2-dimensional world of the Victorian novella *Flatland*). Nigel Holmes is an established commercial creator of what he calls "explanation graphics". His works deal not only with the visual display of information but also of knowledge-how to do things. He created graphics for *Time* magazine for 16 years, and is the author of several books on the subject. Close and strongly related to the field of information graphics, is information design. Actually, making infographics is a certain discipline within the information design world.

Types of Information Graphic

- chart
- flowchart
- histogram
- graph
- map
- diagram
- concept map
- mind map
- signage systems

Interpreting Information Graphics

Many information graphics are specialised forms of depiction that represent their content in sophisticated and often abstract ways. In order to interpret the meaning of these graphics appropriately, the viewer requires a suitable level of graphicacy. In many cases, the required graphicacy involves comprehension skills that are learned rather than innate. At a fundamental level, the skills of decoding individual graphic signs and symbols must be acquired before sense can be made of an information graphic as a whole. However, knowledge of the conventions for distributing and arranging these individual components is also necessary for the building of understanding.

Graphic Design Occupations

A number of occupations are commonly classified under the broad term of *graphic designer*. Graphic design career paths cover all ends of the creative spectrum. Many of these job descriptions overlap heavily.

Graphic art Managers

The following are positions or responsibilities and usually titles, held by experienced graphic designers in related management roles:

Creative Director

Creative directors are in charge of a creative team that produces artwork to be displayed in advertising campaigns, or on products. A creative team can consist of artists (e.g. art directors graphic designers, illustrators, photographers, copywriters, production artists) and a production staff. Creative directors initiate or inspire creative ideas and make sure that the art works include those ideas to the client's satisfaction. Creative directors usually are promoted from an art director or copywriter position. A creative directors job may also involve responsibilities usually associated with a client representative or a project manager.

Art Director

Art directors make sure that illustrators and production artists produce and complete their work on time and to the creative director or client's satisfaction. Art directors also play a major role in the development of a project by making decisions on the visual elements of the project, and by giving the final say on the selection of models, art, props, colors, and other elements. Art directors need advanced training in graphic design as they often do artwork and designing themselves. However, an art director's time may be consumed doing supervisory and administrative work.

Art Production Manager

Art production managers or traffic managers oversee the production aspect of art to improve efficiency and cost effectiveness. Art production managers supervise artists or advise the supervisors of artists. Creative directors and art directors often assume the role of art production managers, especially when production cost is not a critical concern.

Hands-on Graphic Designers

The following are positions or responsibilities, not necessarily titles, held by art directors and graphic designers:

Brand Identity Developer

Brand identity design is concerned with the visual aspects of a company or organization's brand or identity. A brand identity design is the visual element that represents how a company wants to be seen; it is the company's visual identity, and is how a company illustrates its 'image.' A company's brand identity can be represented in terms of design through a unique logo, or signage, and is then often integrated throughout all the elements of a company's materials such as business cards, stationery, packaging, media advertising, promotions, and more. Brand identity may include logo design. Brand identity development is usually a collaborative effort between creative directors, art directors, copywriters, account managers and the client.

Logo Designer

The job of a logo designer is to provide a new and innovative way to express the key message of a company through an image. Logo designers take the information given to them by the client and work, using their own creativity along with marketing strategy to find an appropriate image that their client can use to represent what they are trying to encourage, or sell, or what they are about. It is not likely that a company will specialize in logo design or have a position for a designated logo designer. Art directors and graphic designers usually perform logo designs.

Illustrator

Illustrators conceptualize and create illustrations that represent an idea or a story through two-dimensional or three-dimensional images. Illustrators may do drawings for printed materials such as books, magazines, and other publications, or for commercial products such as textiles, packaging, wrapping paper, greeting cards, calendars, stationery, and more. Illustrators use many different media, from pencil and paint to digital formatting, to prepare and create their illustrations. An illustrator consults with clients in order to determine what illustrations will best meet the story they are trying to tell, or what message they are trying to communicate. Illustrating may be a secondary skill requirement of graphic designer or a specialty skill of a freelance artist, usually known for a unique style of illustrating. Illustration may be published separately as in fine art. However, illustrations are usually inserted into page layouts for communication design in the context of graphic design professions.

Layout Artists

A layout artist deals with the structure and layout out of images and text in a pleasing format for printed media. This can include magazine work, brochures, flyers, books, CD booklets, posters, and similar formats. For magazines and similar productions, color, typeface, text formatting, graphic layout and more must be considered. Is the chosen typeface good for long term reading, or will the eyes get tired? Does that title typeface fit the feel of the rest of the article? Are the photos arranged in such a way that is pleasing to the eye, and directs the reader in the right flow or direction? These are just some of the questions a layout artist must ask themselves. Page layouts are usually done by art directors, graphic designers, production artists or a combination of those positions. Entry level layout work is often known as paste up art. Entry level layout graphic designers are often known as production artists.

Web Designer

A web designer's work could be viewed by thousands of people every day. Web designers create the pages, layout, and graphics for web pages, and play a key role in the development of a website. Web designers have the task of creating the look and feel of a website by choosing the style, and by designing attractive graphics, images, and other visual elements, and adapting them for the website's pages. Web designers also design and develop the navigation tools of a site. Web designers may make decisions regarding what content is included on a web page, where things are placed, and how the aesthetic and continuity is maintained from one screen to the next. All of this involves skill and training in computer graphics, graphic design, and in the latest in computer and web technology.

Depending on the scope of the project, web design may involve collaboration between software engineers and graphic designers. The graphic design of a website may be as simple as a page layout sketch or handling just the graphics in an HTML editor, while the advance coding is done separately by programmers. In other cases, graphic designers may be challenged to become both graphic designer and programmer in the process of web design in positions often known as web masters.

List of Graphic Design Institutions

Professional Organizations for Graphic Designers

International

- Alliance Graphique Internationale (AGI)
- International Council of Graphic Design Associations
- Society for Environmental Graphic Design

Asia-Pacific

- Australian Graphic Design Association
- Design Institute of Australia

Europe

- British Design and Art Direction
- Chartered Society of Designers (multidisciplinary-UK)
- Design Business Association (UK)

North America

- AIGA, the professional association for design in America
- The Association of Registered Graphic Designers of Ontario (RGD Ontario)
- Graphic Artists Guild
- The Graphic Alliance
- Society of Graphic Designers of Canada-GDC

South America

- Associação dos Designers Gráficos-ADG Brasil
- Asociacion de Diseñadores Gráficos de Buenos Aires-UDGBA Argentina
- Asociación de Diseñadores Gráficos de Venezuela

Schools Teaching Graphic Design

Argentina

- Facultad de Arquitectura, Diseñoy Urbanismo (FADU)

Australia

- University of Technology, Sydney
- Australian National University, Canberra School of Art
- Charles Sturt University, School of Visual and Performing Arts
- Curtin University School of Art
- Edith Cowan University (ECU) Perth School of Communications and Contemporary Arts
- Enmore Design Centre
- QANTM College
- Raffles KvB Institute
- Swinburne University

Brazil

- Escola Superior de Desenho Industrial (ESDI)

- Pontífice Universidade Católica (PUC-RJ)
- Escola de Belas Artes, São Paulo
- Faculdade de Arquitetura e Urbanismo, USP

Canada

- College of the North Atlantic
- George Brown College
- NSCAD University-Nova Scotia College of Art and Design
- OCAD-Ontario College of Art & Design
- York University/Sheridan Institute Joint Program in Design

France

- Ecole des beaux-arts de Rennes
- Ecole d'Arts de Annecy
- Ecole Nationale des Beaux Arts et Arts Appliqués Bourges

Japan

- Tokyo National University of Fine Arts and Music (Geidai)
- Tama Art University (Tamabi)
- Musashino Art University (Musabi)
- Tokyo Zokei University (Zokei)
- Joshibi University of Art and Design (Joshibi)
- Nihon University College of Art (Nichigei)

Iceland

- Listaháskólinn-Iceland Academy of the Arts

India

- Srishti School of Art, Design and Technology
- National Institute of Design
- Symbiosis Institute of Design

Portugal

- Faculdade de Belas Artes da Universidade do Porto

Singapore

- Lasalle-sia College of the Arts

- SAE Institute-Singapore Campus, Creative Media & Digital Film Programs
- Nanyang Academy of Fine Arts (NAFA)
- School of Art, Design & Media (part of NTU)

South Africa

- Inscape Design College

United Kingdom

- Central St Martins College of Art and Design
- Edinburgh College of Art
- Glasgow School of Art
- Royal College of Art
- University College Falmouth
- Plymouth University
- Bournemouth College of Art

United States

- Art Institute of Chicago
- Auburn University
- Bellevue Community College: Continuing Education
- Boston University
- California College of the Arts
- California Institute of the Arts
- Carnegie Mellon University
- Corcoran College of Art and Design
- Cranbrook Institute
- Fashion Institute of Technology
- Kent State University
- Maryland Institute College of Art
- Massachusetts College of Art
- Minneapolis College of Art and Design
- Portfolio Center
- Pratt Institute
- Rhode Island School of Design

- Rochester Institute of Technology
- Salve Regina University
- Savannah College of Art and Design
- School of the Museum of Fine Arts, Boston
- School of Visual Arts
- Tufts University
- University of Illinois at Chicago
- University of North Texas
- University of Massachusetts at Dartmouth
- University of the Pacific
- Virginia Commonwealth University
- Washington University, St. Louis
- Yale University

Typography

Typography is the art and technique of setting written subject matter in type using a combination of typefaces, point size, line length, leading (line spacing) and letter spacing. Typography is performed by typesetters, compositors, typographers, graphic artists, art directors, and clerical workers. Until the Digital Age typography was a specialized occupation. Digitization opened up typography to new generations of visual designers and lay users.

History

For the origins and evolution of typography, see the main articles History of western typography, History of typography in East Asia, and Movable type Typography traces its origins to the first punches and dies used to make seals and currency in ancient times. Typography with modular moveable metal type began in 13th-century Korea, and was developed again in mid-15th century Europe with the development of specialized techniques for casting and combining cheap copies of letterpunches in the vast quantities required to print multiple copies of texts.

Text Typography

In traditional typography, text is *composed* to create a readable, coherent, and visually satisfying whole that works invisibly, without the awareness of the reader. Even distribution with a minimum of distractions and anomalies are aimed at producing clarity and transparency. Choice of font(s) is perhaps the primary aspect of text typography—prose fiction, non-fiction, editorial, educational, religious, scientific, spiritual and commercial writing all have differing characteristics and requirements. For historic material, established text typefaces are frequently chosen according to a scheme of historical *genre* acquired by a long process of accretion, with considerable overlap between historical periods. Contemporary books are more likely to be set with state-of-the-art seriffed "text romans" or "book romans" with design values echoing present-day design arts, which are closely based on traditional models such as those of Nicolas Jenson, Francesco Griffo (a punchcutter who created the model for Aldine typefaces), and Claude Garamond. With their more specialized requirements, newspapers and magazines rely on compact, tightly-fitted text romans specially designed for the task, which offer maximum flexibility, readability and efficient use of page space. Sans serif text fonts are often used for introductory paragraphs, incidental text and whole short articles. A current fashion is to pair sans serif type for headings with a high-performance seriffed font of matching style for the text of an article. The text layout, tone or *color* of set matter, and the interplay of text with white space of the page and other graphic elements combine to impart a "feel" or "resonance" to the subject matter. With printed media typographers are also concerned with binding margins, paper selection and printing methods. Typography is modulated by Orthography and linguistics, word structures, word frequencies, morphology, phonetic constructs and linguistic syntax. Typography also is subject to specific cultural conventions. For example, in French it is customary to insert a non-breaking space before a colon (:) or semicolon (;) in a sentence, while in English it is not.

Scope

In contemporary use, the practice and study of typography is very broad, covering all aspects of letter design and application, including typesetting & typeface design; handwriting & calligraphy; graffiti; inscriptional & architectural lettering; poster design and other large scale lettering such as signage and billboards; business communications & promotional collateral; advertising; wordmarks & typographic logos (logotypes); apparel (clothing); vehicle instrument panels; kinetic typography in motion picture films and television; and as a component of industrial design—type resides on household appliances, pens and wristwatches. Since digitization typography's range of applications has become more eclectic, appearing on web pages, LCD mobile phone screens, and hand-held video games. The ubiquity of type has led typographers to coin the phrase "Type is everywhere". Typography generally follows four principles, using repetition, contrast, proximity, and alignment.

Readability and Legibility

Readability concerns how easily or comfortably a typeset text reads. Studies of readability suggest that our ability to read is based on recognition of individual glyph forms ("parallel letterwise recognition"), performed by the human brain's highly-developed shape cognition facility. Text set in lower case is found to be more readable, presumably because lower case letter structures and word shapes are more distinctive, having greater saliency with the presence of extenders (ascenders, descenders and other projecting parts). Readers cognize the upper portions of letters more than the lower portions in the recognition process. Capital letters by comparison are of uniform height and less varied in structure; this the generally accepted reason that all-capitals text is found to be less readable in tests of extended reading, causing slower reading speed and less comprehension.

Readability is compromised by letterspacing, word spacing and leading that are too tight or too loose. Generous vertical space separates lines of text, making it easier for the eye to distinguish one line from the next, or previous line. Poorly designed fonts and those that are too tightly or loosely fitted can also result in poor readability. Some typographers believe that another factor, the Bouma or overall word shape, is also very important in readability, and that parallel letterwise recognition is either wrong, less important, or not the entire picture. Studies that distinguish between the two models have favored parallel letterwise recognition, and the latter is widely accepted by cognitive psychologists. Legibility is the ease and speed with which the reader can decipher each letterform and word. This is determined by the design of individual characters and how clearly they are rendered. Legibility can be affected by choice of ink and paper colors.

Newspapers, Magazines, and Periodicals

Typography is used in all newspapers, magazines and periodicals. Headlines are often set in larger type to attract attention and are placed near the masthead. For example, USA Today uses a bold, colourful and comparatively modern style through their use of different fonts and colors; type sizes vary widely, and the newspaper name is placed on a coloured background. In contrast, New York Times use a more traditional approach with fewer colors, less font variation and more columns. Generally, every magazine, newspaper and periodical standardizes on a small collection of typefaces (fonts) to aid in the navigation of its content, to create a sense of familiarity, or create dramatic effects. Some publications such as The Guardian and The Economist, commission bespoke typefaces from a type designer, a specialist typographer who designs typefaces.

Display Typography

Typography is a potent element in graphic design, where there is less concern for readability and more potential for using type in an artistic manner. Type is combined with negative space, graphic elements and pictures, forming relationships and dialog between words and images.

Color and size of type elements are much more prevalent than in text typography. Most display typography exploits type at larger sizes, where the details of letter design are magnified. Color is used for its emotional effect in conveying the tone and nature of subject matter. Display typography encompasses posters; book covers; typographic logos and wordmarks; billboards; packaging; on-product typography;

calligraphy; graffitti; inscriptional & architectural lettering; poster design and other large scale lettering signage; business communications & promotional collateral; advertising; wordmarks & typographic logos (logotypes), and kinetic typography in motion pictures and television; vending machine displays; online & computer screen displays. The wanted poster for the assassins of Abraham Lincoln was printed with lead and woodcut type, and incorporates photography.

Inscriptional & Architectural Lettering

The history of inscriptional lettering is intimately tied to the history of writing, the evolution of letterforms, and the craft of the hand. The widespread use of the computer and various etching and sandblasting techniques today has made the hand carved monument a rarity, and the number of lettercarvers left in the States continues to dwindle. For monumental lettering to be effective it must be considered carefully in its context. Proportions of letters need to be altered as their size and distance from the viewer increases. An expert letterer gains understanding of these nuances through much practice and observation of their craft. Letters drawn by hand and for a specific project have the possibility of being richly specific and profoundly beautiful in the hand of a master. Each can also take up to an hour to carve, so it is no wonder that the automated sandblasting process has become the industry standard. To create a sandblasted letter, a rubber mat is laser cut from a computer file and glued to the stone. The sand then bites a coarse groove or channel into the exposed surface. Unfortunately, many of the computer applications which create these files and interface with the laser cutter do not have many typefaces available, and often have inferior versions of typefaces that are available. What can now be done in minutes, however, lacks the striking architecture and geometry of the chisel-cut letter which allows light to play across its distinct interior planes. Recently, there has been some rumbling in typographic circles over the proposed 9/11 memorial in New Jersey. Frederic Schwartz, the project architect, has chosen to render the names of the victims in "a familiar and easy-to-read typeface": Times New Roman. This democratic choice (the families of victims were closely involved with the design plan) could perhaps be echoing the controversial Emigre adage "People read best what they read most" in that Times is the default for many applications, but it seems to many that the choice is really a non-choice, or poor choice at best. These letterforms, originally designed for small print in newspaper setting, will be blown up to nearly four inches high.

Advertising

Typography has long been a vital part of promotional material and advertising. Designers often use typography to set a theme and mood in an advertisement; for example using bold, large text to convey a particular message to the reader. Type is often used to draw attention to a particular advertisement, combined with efficient use of color, shapes and images. Today, typography in advertising often reflects a company's brand. Fonts used in advertisements convey different messages to the reader, classical fonts are for a strong personality, while more modern fonts are for a cleaner, neutral look. Bold fonts are used for making statements and attracting attention.

Intelligent Multimedia: A Case Study

Project Description

We are developing a high-level platform for 3D and rich media virtual environments based on agent-technology, using the languages DLP, Java, and VRML. On top of this platform we have developed an scripting language STEP for specifying humanoid movements and gestures, based on dynamic logic. Our goal is to study aspects of the deployment and architecture of virtual environments as an interface to multimedia information systems. Our platform also supports embodied conversational agents, see [Eliëns et al. (2002)]. As demonstrators we have developed a distributed soccer-game prototype with intelligent autonomous avatar-embodied agents as players [Huang et al. (2002)], a humanoid animation demonstrating Tai-Chi, [Huang et al. (2002b)], avatars presenting a dialog in a mixed media presentation environment, [Eliëns et al. (2003)], a domestic agent that can be addressed in natural language, [Hildebrand et al. (2003)], an avatar reaching for objects that uses reasoning and inverse kinematics, [Huang et al. (2003d)], and an avatar conducting music, [Ruttkay et al. (2003a)]. As a student project in the Casus Practicum, we have developed a 3D presentation for INCCA, the International Network for the Conservation of Contemporary Art, in cooperation with ICN, the Dutch Cultural Heritage Institute.

Funding

Our research has been supported by two NWO projects:

- WASP — Web Agent Support Program
- RIF — Retrieval of Information in virtual worlds using Feature detectors

The combined effort of these projects led to the DLP+X3D platform and the development of the STEP language.

In addition, we have one pending proposal with Michiel Hildebrand as candidate researcher:

- (submitted) IMMEDIATE — Intelligent MultiMEDIA Transactions Environment

Cooperation

The work on *embodied conversational agents* is being done in cooperation with dr. Z. Ruttkay from CWI. The work on the *cultural heritage* application is done in cooperation with drs. T. Scholte from ICN.

Publications

Apart from publications in international conference proceedings and workshops, we have demonstrated our work on the ICT Kenniscongres 2002 in the theme *intelligent multimedia*.

In preparation is a prestigious book on *Life-like Characters*, for which we have contributed a chapter describing our platform and STEP, [Huang et al. (2003c)]. The editor of this book, Helmut Prendinger from Tokyo University, commented on our chapter: *I really have to say that your chapter is very very well done, very interesting, very comprehensive, and very readable. It says exactly the things people want to know when they are looking for some scripting language to animate their characters. Above that, your STEP system is very well motivated and nicely embedded in other strands of computer science research.*

A Brief History

Although the WASP proposal was written in 1996, long before the RIF proposal (1998), dr. Z. Huang started as a post-doc on the WASP project when the RIF project ran already for more than six months. Since we then felt that the WASP project proposal was slightly outdated, we made an effort to merge the WASP and RIF projects, by focussing on agents in 3D virtual environments which resulted in a paper presenting a taxonomy of Web agents, [Huang et al. (2000)]. However, after about a year the continuity of the RIF project was endangered due to a mutation of personnel at CWI. So, NWO was asked for permission to utilize the RIF funds for prolonging the WASP project. This was granted, provided that the research goals of the RIF project were sufficiently covered within WASP.

In the RIF project we used the blaxxun Community Server and VRML to realize information retrieval and delivery in multi-user 3D environments. Agents were then conceived as extensions on the server-side using blaxxun's native agents enriched with embedded logic. However, at the same time that the RIF project funds were transferred to WASP, the first prototype of DLP in Java became available, and we decided, somewhat radically, to drop the more low-level blaxxun technology in favor of a unified approach in DLP. Thus, we extended DLP with primitives for manipulating VRML worlds, using the Java External Authoring Interface that is part of VRML. The DLP+VRML framework proved to be surprisingly effective, as testified by the following references:

DLP+VRML

- architecture for agents in virtual environments — [Huang et al. (2001)]
- intelligent avatars in 3D virtual worlds — [Huang et al. (2001)]
- demonstrator: multi-user soccer game — [Huang et al. (2002)]

Now, the language DLP itself has quite a long history, [Eliëns (1992)]. It has also been described in [Eliëns (2000)]. As a language, DLP offers an object-oriented extension of (traditional, Edinburgh-style) Prolog, with multi-threaded objects, non-logical instance or state variables, communication by rendex-vous and (distributed) backtracking. After preliminary prototypes in C++, we focussed on an implementation in Java, to be able to use DLP for Web programming, [Visser and Eliëns (2000)]. The first Java implementation became available relatively late, but just in time to create the DLP+VRML extension when needed.

As concerns the acceptance of our approach within the Web3D community, we wish to point to the acceptance of our [Huang et al. (2002)] paper for the highly competitive international Web3D Conference 2002 (acceptance: 1 out of 13), and the acceptance of [Huang et al. (2003a)] for the Web3D 2003 Conference. More recently, we have made an effort to publish in the ECA (Embodied Conversation Agents) community, as testified by our contribution to the *Life-like Agents* book, [Huang et al. (2003c)]. We also received an invitation for the Dagstuhl seminar on *Evaluating Embodied Conversational Agents* in March 2004.

Embedding in Education: Focus on Multimedia

The *intelligent multimedia* research has a strong impact on the educational activities for the specialisation(s) Multimedia with Computer Science and Multimedia and Culture for Information Science.

In the first year students start with a general Introduction to Multimedia. This course centers around three themes: the convergence between media, platforms and delivery technology, the availability of broadband communication and its impact on the development of standards such as MPEG-4, and multimedia information retrieval as an essential ingredient of the growing multimedia information repository on the Web.

There are two follow-up courses, which are given in respectively the second and third year:

- Multimedia Authoring I — Web3D/VRML
- Multimedia Authoring II — Virtual Environments

The first of these courses deals with the technology for creating 3D scenes and worlds, whereas the second is more focused on providing intelligent services in virtual environments. Students use the DLP+VRML framework for their assignment in the second course.

In addition for Multimedia and Culture there is a Multimedia Development Casus Practicum in which the technology is applied in an assignment developed with the Dutch Cultural Heritage Institute (ICN).

For both specialisations, Multimedia and Multimedia and Culture we plan to offer a course on XML-based Multimedia Technology, to be developed by dr. Z. Huang, to make students familiar with advanced topics in XML-based information processing. As a remark, our platform does already support the use of XML and XSLT stylesheets, [Huang et al. (2003b)], and we are migrating to a DLP+X3D platform, with X3D as the XML-based successor of VRML.

Research Directions

Apart from the issues involved in the modelling and realization of embodied agents in rich media 3D environments, there are also issues with regard to the architecture and implementation of our DLP+X3D platform.

Parallelism and Synchronization

Complex humanoid gestures are of a highly parallel nature. The STEP scripting language supports a direct way of modelling parallel gestures by offering a parallel construct (*par*), which results in the simultaneous execution of (possibly compound) actions. To avoid unconstrained thread creation, the STEP engine makes use of a thread pool, containing a fixed number of threads, from which threads are allocated to actions. Once the action is finished, the thread is put back in the pool. This approach works well for most examples. However when many threads are needed, as in the conductor example (which requires approximately 60 threads), problems may occur, in particular when there are may background jobs.

Modeling and Representation

Our agent model may be characterized as a BDI-model, extended with *sensors* and *effectors* needed for the interaction in a virtual environment. The STEP scripting language has been developed to facilitate the specification of communicative acts, like gestures. However, we would also like to explore text-to-speech synthesis as an extra modality of communication. One interesting research issue is how to specify a reusable library of gestures, accommodating for differences in (personal) style. This is currently being investigated by Z. Ruttkay from CWI.

Another interesting issue is the use of inverse kinematics to grasp objects. However, when an object is not within reach, the agent has to reason about the best way to get near to the object, to be able to reach it.

Architecture and Implementation

To solve the problem of reliable timing would require not only a modification of the STEP engine, but also a rather different implementation of the DLP threads supporting the parallelism in STEP. Currently, the implementation only allows for *best effort* parallelism and does not provide the means for *deadline scheduling*.

However, it is our impression that we have reached the utmost efficiency feasible within the Java platform. Therefore we have been considering to redevelop the DLP+X3D platform in a .NET environment. An additional advantage of migrating to the .NET environment would be the possible integration of functionality such as *text-to-speech* synthesis which is not readily available in the Java environment.

Intelligent Multimedia Tutoring for Manufacturing Education

Introduction

Many of the drawbacks of traditional classroom-like training methods, namely, limited time spent on particular topics of interest to the student, limited instructor access, and difficulties in transferring lecture information to real world situations, are not unique to the manufacturing environment. In any ill-structured domain, which typically requires knowledge of multiple concepts and complex relationships, learning and instruction "cannot be compartmentalized, linear, uniperspectival, neatly hierarchical, simply analogical, or rigidly prepackaged". The desirability of new instructional media which allows students to interact with course materials in a more exploratory manner has become a dominant theme in current educational technology development. However, computer-based training already has a relatively long history and has been shown to positively influence the amount of material learned, the time taken to learn it, and the enjoyment of the learning experience (e.g.,. Furthermore, many of these training systems incorporate artificial intelligence techniques to provide deeper levels of interaction with the student. More recently, advances in putting powerful, inexpensive display systems on the desktop have led many to consider interactive multimedia solutions to the expanding demand for engaging and stimulating courseware. The sudden accessibility of high-tech graphics, animation, video and sound capabilities, and the proliferation of multimedia authoring software have made it very easy to quickly produce impressive presentations and interactive modules.

However, while typical multimedia systems for education allow users to navigate through subject-related resource material in an attractive and informative manner, "it is well known that page turning or browsing does not ensure effective learning...flashy graphics and simulations are not enough; the experience has to be authentic and relevant to the learner's life". Therefore, a current technical goal is to utilize the solid foundation of intelligent tutoring systems as a platform for a more sophisticated control of multimedia objects in a learning environment. Such programs can pose interactive problem-solving situations appropriate to the level of the student, track the student's performance, and intervene where necessary to coach the student in particular principles. Through intelligent interaction, such tutors can help guide the student through the reasoning process, giving advice, or redirecting the student's focus of attention at appropriate times. The nature of the student's errors or misunderstandings determines the type of assistance provided, and the system employs its multimedia capabilities in a manner that is most helpful to the student at the time.

One of the major challenges to be addressed is the achievement of this integration of technologies. Unfortunately, much of the multimedia authoring software available today does not provide the level of control usually needed for an intelligent tutoring system, nor does it provide easy ways to link its products to externally developed intelligent programs. Thus, the development of an integrated intelligent multimedia tutoring system can be more costly in terms of time, effort and portability than current expectations will allow. Furthermore, the application of this technology to the design of courseware in the manufacturing domain, particularly for industrial training courses, introduces additional challenging issues.

Approach

The work described in this paper emphasizes the design and implementation of intelligent multimedia tutoring modules which are intended to supplement in-house technical training courses for the Boeing Defense and Space Group. In this project, there are two complementary goals: first, to explore the research issues involved in introducing educational technology into these types of training environments. These issues include knowledge acquisition, system design and implementation, and, ultimately, testing and evaluation of the effectiveness of these materials. The second goal is to produce rapid prototypes of some of the different modules in order to demonstrate proof of concept, and to justify the further investment in supplementing and/or replacing the traditional courseware with this new modality.

Our theoretical approach begins with the traditional components of intelligent tutoring: a student model, an expert knowledge component and a tutoring module. The student model tracks the performance of the student and maintains a profile of the student's level and accomplishments at that level. This includes information about the last lesson learned, a progress check through test evaluations, and an indication of the student's experience level (e.g., novice or expert). The domain knowledge is encoded in the expert component. In our model, this knowledge is encapsulated as a "collective of experts", each of which knows about a particular small aspect of the subject matter, and is capable of presenting it in one of four presentation modes, according to the current teaching strategy. This partitioning of the domain knowledge into very small pieces provides flexibility in the construction of the lesson plans (i.e., if a short review of a certain topic is desired, using a particular presentation mode, that expert can easily be invoked without bringing in additional material). The tutoring module controls the entire training session, and can be thought of primarily as a planner. It examines the student's profile, chooses the topics, and then creates an appropriate lesson plan. This lesson plan consists of a series of goals which are attained through the services of the corresponding experts.

In addition to these three components, our model also includes a multimedia interface world, which contains the individual r ultimedia objects (movies, sound bytes, simulations, etc.) that are utilized by the domain experts, and also encompasses the objects and relationships of the metaphorical "world" inside which the tutorial session is conducted. This is an extension of the notion of microworld which is common in artificial intelligence. The preliminary system design. This first version of the system gives all control to the tutor, which must devise the plan, search for the appropriate experts, and then invoke them. A drawback of this approach, of course, is that it may not be possible to do an exhaustive search of appropriate experts each time, and, therefore, the most effective solution might not always be found.

The next evolution of this design will give more autonomy to the individual experts, requiring them to "report" their capabilities, and to compete with each other for participation in the lesson plan. This will be done through a blackboard-style architecture, where the tutor posts current information in a common data area, known as the blackboard, and the domain experts respond to this information if they are able to make a contribution to the plan. The modular design of the collective of experts should facilitate this extension to a blackboard-based system, where the tutor may just post the current teaching goals to the blackboard, and the experts then compete for the opportunity to contribute the relevant piece of knowledge in the most desirable presentation style.

Application to Industry

The general subject matter for our project is Nondestructive Inspection (NDI), which involves the detection of cracks and flaws in various airplane parts, using techniques which do not disturb or destroy the part itself. Conventional NDI methods include radiographic, ultrasonic, eddy current and penetrant inspections, and our first project is focused on the training course for Eddy Current Inspection.

This course has a number of features, which are common to other NDI training courses, and which may impact the way in which the technology can be introduced into the course curriculum. First of all, these courses are often taught in very short periods of time (e.g., two days for the Eddy Currents class), and are extremely information-intensive. Trainees who take these courses can vary in expertise from vocational high school level who are just beginning their apprenticeships, to experienced engineers who wish to review and obtain a deeper understanding of the concepts. Any session of the course may contain students from all levels of experience, and typically there is one presentation for all. There are typically theoretical as well as practical aspects to the courses, which means that the students must try to master two different modes of material. For example, in the Eddy Currents training course, the theoretical part is concerned with explaining fundamentals of electricity and magnetism as well as the particular characteristics of eddy currents, and their effects upon the materials and instruments. These concepts are often invisible, inaudible, intangible, and abstract. On the other hand, the practical side of the course requires the student to physically assemble the equipment, grasp the probe, calibrate by moving the probe over small material "standards", observe the meter movements, and listen for audio signals that may be adjunct to the meter readings. Suddenly, the student's physical perception is at the forefront of the task, and yet, he/she must also try to connect the theoretical concepts to the physical results.

Another interesting characteristic is that these short courses often do not review or test the material learned. In the case of the Eddy Currents course, the student demonstrates mastery of the subject during certification testing, which is done at intervals throughout his/her career, and which typically looks at the trainee's effectiveness at the task itself (e.g., correct detection of surface cracks under a variety of conditions), rather than a formal understanding of the underlying theory.

In the Eddy Currents course, all of the theoretical subject matter is currently presented in the traditional manner of overhead transparency presentation with occasional demonstrations using hand-built teaching aids. The practical part of the course provides students with hands-on experience of detecting cracks using a number of different probes, meters, and materials in the classroom setting. The purpose of introducing educational technology into this course is twofold: first, to explore the effectiveness of adding interactions, simulations, and animations to the presentation of the theoretical material, and second, to provide stand-alone practice sessions in which the students can review the course information as often as desired, without requiring the presence of the instructor. It is felt that such supplementary technology may increase the effectiveness of the inspection process, and may provide a product which can be disseminated to the customers of Boeing, who must also train their personnel to perform such inspections.

Two preliminary prototype modules have been developed for the Eddy Currents course on the topics of conductivity testing and surface crack inspection. In designing these modules, a major goal was to avoid simply replicating the sequential transparency-based material in a more "entertaining" fashion. An alternative approach is to lead the student through the inspection process, zooming in to details which reveal hitherto unseen aspects of the objects (e.g., material, probe, meter, etc.) by utilizing the capabilities of multimedia presentations. This technique promises to be particularly effective in the demonstrations involving electric and magnetic properties, and should allow the student to experience the theory in the context of the task itself.

In the current implementation, the emphasis has been placed on development of the multimedia interface world objects and their relationships. For example, the Conductivity Testing module needs to contain objects representing: voltmeter, different types of metals, probes, electrons, alloys, heat, etc. These objects have relationships to each other that must be identified. For example, alloy added to a metal reduces conductivity; heat treatment of the metal with alloy will increase conductivity; each of these will change the meter reading when the probe is passed over the metal. The representations for the objects and their relationships can be textual, static pictures (graphics), animations, simulations, video clips or combinations of these. From these groupings, the experts can be identified. For example, one expert which "knows" about Factors Affecting Conductivity, invokes the following sequence: probe-simulation, add-alloy-simulation, probe-simulation, add-heat-simulation, probe-simulation. The simulation permits user interaction with the objects on the screen, and is appropriate for students who are first learning about this subject. On the other hand, a more experienced student might want to review the concepts, without having to physically execute each simulation. In this case, an expert which invokes the corresponding text objects would be more appropriate. These first modules have been developed using commercial authoring software, which, unfortunately, has very little intelligent capabilities in it. This decision was taken primarily to match the software development environment available to our Boeing collaborators, and to explore the capabilities of the authoring tools. The package is excellent for developing the multimedia objects themselves, and incorporating interactions into the presentations. It also allows tests to be administered, and performs some elementary student tracking, which can be considered a primitive version of the student model.

Conclusion

Although a number of limitations of this approach have been identified, we have achieved part of our goal of producing rapid prototype materials which can be evaluated by the course instructors, and if approved, can be integrated into the current curriculum. Further extensions are planned to improve these prototypes, and to introduce increasing levels of intelligence.

Our second goal of producing stand-alone problem-solving modules will require not only the mastery of the subject matter together with a suite of more sophisticated simulations, but will need a more extensive model of how the student integrates perception and problem-solving in these inspection types of tasks. This cognitive foundation will incorporate knowledge about what is seen, how that information can be perceptually enhanced (e.g., visually and aurally), how that knowledge fits into the generation of hypotheses, what additional information and/or evidence is needed to support or rule out a hypothesis, and how to represent the student's confidence in what is seen as well as what is decided.

As our work becomes integrated into the actual courses conducted on-site at Boeing, we plan to conduct studies with the trainees to determine whether this injection of educational technology supports the goals of improved performance of the task as well as increased understanding of the theoretical underpinnings.

Information Design

Information design is the design of visual displays of data. It is defined as the art and science of preparing information so that it can be used by human beings with efficiency and effectiveness (Jacobson 2000).

In computer science and information technology, information design is sometimes a rough synonym for (but is not necessarily the same discipline as) information architecture, the design of information systems, databases, or data structures. This sense includes data modelling and process analysis.

Web Design

Web design is the design of web pages, websites and web applications using HTML, CSS, images, and other media.

Web design is in contrast with web development, which includes web server configuration, writing web applications and server security.

History

Tim Berners-Lee, the inventor of the World Wide Web, published a website in August 1991, making him also the first web designer. His first was to use hypertext with an existing email link. Early on, websites were written in basic HTML, a markup language giving websites basic structure (headings and paragraphs), and the ability to link using hypertext. This was new and different to existing forms of communication-users could easily open other pages using browsers. As the Web and web design progressed, the markup language used to make it, known as Hypertext Mark-up Language or HTML, became more complex and flexible. Features like tables, which could be used to display tabular information, were soon subverted for use as invisible layout devices. With the advent of Cascading Style Sheets (CSS), table based layout is increasingly regarded as outdated. Database integration technologies such as server-side scripting (see CGI, PHP, ASP.NET, ASP, JSP, and ColdFusion) and design standards like CSS further changed and enhanced the way the Web is made. The introduction of Macromedia Flash (now Adobe Flash) into an already interactivity-ready scene has further changed the face of the Web, giving new power to designers and media creators, and offering new interactivity features to users, often at the expense of partial search engine visibility and browser functions available to HTML.

Website Design

A website is a collection of information about a particular topic or subject. Designing a website is defined as the arrangement and creation of web pages that in turn make up a website. A web page consists of information for which the website is developed. For example, a website might be compared to a book, where each page of the book is a web page.

A website typically consists of text and images. The first page of a website is known as the Home page or Index. Some websites use what is commonly called an Enter Page. Enter pages might include a welcome message, language/region selection, or disclaimer. Each web page within a website is an HTML file which has its own URL. After each web page is created, they are typically linked together using a navigation menu composed of hyperlinks.

Once a website is completed, it must be published or uploaded in order to be viewable to the public over the internet. This is done using an FTP client. Once published, the webmaster may use a variety of techniques to increase the traffic, or hits, that the website receives. This may include submitting the website to a search engine such as Google or Yahoo, exchanging links with other websites, creating affiliations with similar websites, etc.

A relatively new technique for creating websites called Remote Scripting has allowed more dynamic use of the web without the use of Flash or other specialized plug-ins. Leading the various techniques is Ajax, although other methods are still common, as Ajax is not a fully developed standard.

Multidisciplinary Requirements

Website design crosses multiple disciplines of information systems, information technology and communication design. The website is an information system whose components are sometimes classified as front-end and back-end. The observable content (e.g. page layout, user interface, graphics, text, audio) is known as the front-end. The back-end comprises the organization and efficiency of the source code, invisible scripted functions, and the server-side components that process the output from the front-end. Depending on the size of a Web development project, it may be carried out by a multi-skilled individual (sometimes called a web master), or a project manager may oversee collaborative design between group members with specialized skills.

Issues

As in most collaborative designs, there are conflicts between differing goals and methods of web site designs. These are a few of the ongoing ones.

Lack of Collaboration in Design

In the early stages of the web, there wasn't as much collaboration between web designs and larger advertising campaigns, customer transactions, social networking, intranets and extranets as there is now. Web pages were mainly static online brochures disconnected from the larger projects.

Many web pages are still disconnected from larger projects. Special design considerations are necessary for use within these larger projects. These design considerations are often overlooked, especially in cases where there is a lack of leadership, understanding or concern for the larger project to facilitate collaboration. This often results in unhealthy competition or compromise between departments, and less than optimal use of web pages.

Liquid Versus Fixed Layouts

Programmers were the original web page designers in the early 1990s. Currently most web designers come from a graphic artist background in print, where the artist has absolute control over the size and dimensions of all aspects of the design. On the web however, the Web designer has no control over several factors, including the size of the browser window and the size and characteristics of available fonts.

Many designers compensate for this by wrapping their entire webpage in a fixed width box, essentially limiting it to an exact pixel-perfect value, which is a *fixed layout*. Some create the illusion of liquidity by building the graphics for their webpage at a size larger than any current standard monitor size. Other designers say that this is bad because it ignores the preferences of the user, who might have their browser sized a specific way that they like best. These people propose a *liquid layout*, where the size of the Web page adjusts itself based on the size of the browser window.

There is a usability reason (rather than wanting control) for why a designer may choose a more fixed layout. Studies have shown that there is usually an optimal line width in terms of readability. One rule to appear from such studies is that lines should be between 40-60 characters long, or approximately 11 words per line. But users may choose their windows size and font selection to optimize other factors more important to them.

In some cases, it is difficult to create fixed layouts which work well given the amount of content needed, and the fact that one has to try to cater for the needs of all prospective users.

Similar to liquid layout is the optional *fit to window* feature with Adobe Flash content. This is a fixed layout that optimally scales the contents of the page without changing the arrangement or text wrapping when the browser is resized.

Flash

Adobe Flash (formerly Macromedia Flash) is a proprietary, robust graphics animation/application development program used to create and deliver dynamic content, media (such as sound and video), and interactive applications over the web via the browser.

Flash is not a standard produced by a vendor-neutral standards organization like most of the core protocols and formats on the Internet. Flash is much more restrictive than the open HTML format, though, requiring a proprietary plugin to be seen, and it does not integrate with most web browser UI features like the "Back" button. However, those restrictions may be useful depending on the goals of the web site design.

Flash as a format has become very widespread on the desktop market. According to NPD study, 98% of US Web users have the Flash Player installed, with 45%-56% (depending on region) having the latest version. Numbers vary depending on the detection scheme and research demographics.

Many graphic artists use Flash because it gives them exact control over every part of the design, and anything can be animated and generally "jazzed up". Some application designers enjoy flash because it lets them create applications that don't have to be refreshed or go to a new web page every time an action occurs. Flash can use embedded fonts instead of the standard fonts installed on most computers. There are many sites which forego HTML entirely for Flash. Other sites may use Flash content combined with HTML as conservatively as gifs or jpegs would be used, but with smaller vector file sizes and the option of faster loading animations. Flash may also be used to protect content from unauthorized duplication or searching.

Flash detractors claim that Flash websites tend to be poorly designed, and often use confusing and non-standard user-interfaces. Up until recently, search engines have been unable to index Flash objects, which has prevented sites from having their contents easily found. It is possible to specify alternate content to be displayed for browsers that do not support Flash. Using alternate content also helps search engines to understand the page, and can result in much better visibility for the page. This, however, does not enable search engines to read images used in the place of text for styling purposes, nor are the vast majority of Flash websites disability accessible (for screen readers, for example) or Section 508 compliant.

The most recent incarnation of Flash's scripting language (called "actionscript", which is an ECMA language similar to JavaScript) incorporates long-awaited usability features, such as respecting the browser's font size and allowing blind users to use screen readers. Actionscript 2.0 is an Object-Oriented language, allowing the use of CSS, XML, and the design of class-based web applications.

CSS Versus Tables

Back when Netscape Navigator 4 dominated the browser market, the popular (but now deprecated) solution available for designers to lay out a Web page was by using tables. Often even simple designs for a page would require dozens of tables nested in each other. Many web templates in Dreamweaver and other WYSIWYG editors still use this technique today. Navigator 4 didn't support CSS to a useful degree, so it simply wasn't used.

After the browser wars were over, and Internet Explorer dominated the market, designers started turning towards CSS as an alternate, better means of laying out their pages. CSS proponents say that tables should only be used for tabular data, not for layout. Using CSS instead of tables also returns HTML to a semantic markup, which helps bots and search engines understand what's going on in a web page. Today, all modern Web browsers now support CSS with different degrees of limitations.

However, one of the main points against CSS is that by relying on it exclusively, control is essentially relinquished as each browser has its own quirks which result in a slightly different page display. This is especially a problem as not every browser supports the same subset of CSS rules. For designers who are used to table-based layouts, developing Web sites in CSS often becomes a matter of trying to replicate what can be done with tables, leading some to find CSS design rather cumbersome due to lack of familiarity. For example, at one time it was rather difficult to produce certain design elements, such as vertical positioning, and full-length footers in a design using absolute positions. With the abundance of CSS resources available online today, though, designing with reasonable adherence to standards involves little more than applying CSS 2.1 or CSS 3 to properly structured markup. These days most modern browsers have solved most of these quirks in CSS rendering and this has made many different CSS layouts possible. However, some people continue to use old browsers, and designers need to keep this in mind, and allow for graceful degrading of pages in older browsers. Most notable among these old browsers are Internet Explorer 5 and 5.5, which, according to some web designers, are becoming the new Netscape Navigator 4 — a block that holds the World Wide Web back from converting to CSS design.

How it Looks vs. How it Works

Since so many web developers have a graphic arts background, some may pay more attention to how a page looks, without considering how visitors are going to find the page via a search engine. Some may rely more on advertising than search engines to attract visitors to the site. On the other side of the issue, search engine optimization consultants (SEOs) obsess about how well a web site works technically and textually: how much traffic it generates via search engines, and how many sales it makes, assuming looks don't contribute to the sales. As a result, the designers and SEOs often end up in disputes where the designer wants more 'pretty' graphics, and the SEO wants lots of 'ugly' keyword-rich text, bullet lists, and text links. One could argue that this is a false dichotomy due to the possibility that a web design may integrate the two disciplines for a collaborative synergetic solution. Because some graphics serve communication purposes in addition to aesthetics, how well a site works may depend on the graphic designer's visual communication ideas as well as the SEO considerations. Another problem when using lots of graphics on a page is that download times can be greatly lengthened, often irritating the user. This has become less of a problem as the internet has evolved with high-speed internet and the use of vector graphics. This is an engineering challenge to increase bandwidth in addition to an artistic challenge to minimize graphics and graphic file sizes. This is an on-going challenge as increased bandwidth invites increased amounts of content.

Accessible Web Design

Accessible Web design is the art of creating webpages that are accessible to everyone, using any device. It is especially important so that people with disabilities-whether due to accident, disease or old age-can access the information in Web pages and be able to navigate through the website.

To be accessible, web pages and sites must conform to certain accessibility principles. These can be grouped into the following main areas:

- use semantic markup that provides a meaningful structure to the document (i.e. Web page)
- use a valid markup language that conforms to a published DTD or Schema
- provide text equivalents for any non-text components (e.g. images, multimedia)
- use hyperlinks that makes sense when read out of context. (e.g. avoid "Click Here.")
- don't use frames
- use CSS rather than HTML Tables for layout.
- author the page so that when the source code is read line-by-line by user agents (such as a screen readers) it remains intelligible. (Using tables for design will often result in information that is not.)

However, W3C permits an exception where tables for layout either make sense when linearized or an alternate version (perhaps linearized) is made available.

Dynamic Web Design

The traditional method of laying out web pages, HTML, is static. There are two ways of delivering content dynamically:

Server-Side

A web server, running special software, constructs an HTML page 'on the fly', according to the user's request and possibly other variables, such as time or stock levels.

Suitable scripting languages include:

- ASP
- ASP.NET
- ColdFusion
- JSP
- Lasso

- Perl
- PHP
- Python
- Ruby

XSLT can be used to translate data from XML format into HTML.

MySQL and PostgreSQL are popular free SQL databases, suitable for use with the above. They can be used to allow users, subject to password access if required, to update content.

Client-Side

Client-side scripting works at the user's browser, and therefore should not be used for "mission critical' work, where the user's capabilities are not known – it is more suited to adding decoration and other ephemeral content. It is most often achieved through JavaScript.

Client side DHTML can pose major problems for Web accessibility and search engine optimization. Most software designed for assisting people with disabilities, and most search engine robots do not support client side DHTML.

If a web site's menus are built with JavaScript, it is usually impossible for search engines to find the pages listed in the menus, unless an alternative navigation scheme is provided elsewhere on the page. (NOTE: By using nested lists for navigation menus, and slightly more complex, DOM-based scripts, this problem may be overcome.)

Website Planning

Before creating and uploading a website, it is important to take the time to plan exactly what is needed in the website. Thoroughly considering the audience or target market, as well as defining the purpose and deciding the content will be developed are extremely important.

Purpose

It is essential to define the purpose of the website as one of the first steps in the planning process. A purpose statement should show focus based on what the website will accomplish and what the users will get from it. A clearly defined purpose will help the rest of the planning process as the audience is identified and the content of the site is developed. Setting short and long term goals for the website will help make clear the purpose and plan for the future when expansion, modification, and improvement will take place. Also, goal-setting practices and measurable objectives should be identified to track the progress of the site and determine success.

Audience

Defining the audience is a key step in the website planning process. The audience is the group of people who are expected to visit your website – the market being targeted. These people will be viewing the website for a specific reason and it is important to know exactly what they are looking for when they visit the site. A clearly defined purpose or goal of the site as well as an understanding of what visitors want to do/feel when they come to your site will help to identify the target audience. Upon considering who is most likely to need/use the content, a list of characteristics common to the users such as:

- Audience Characteristics
- Information Preferences
- Computer Specifications
- Web Experience

Taking into account the characteristics of the audience will allow an effective website to be created that will deliver the desired content to the target audience.

Compatibility and Restrictions

Because of the market share of modern browsers (depending on your target market), the compatibility of your website with the viewers is restricted. For instance, a website that is designed for the majority of websurfers will be limited to the use of valid XHTML 1.0 Strict or older, Cascading Style Sheets Level 1, and 1024x768 display resolution. This is because Internet Explorer is not fully W3C standards compliant with the modularity of XHTML 1.1 and the majority of CSS beyond 1. A target market of more alternative browser (e.g. Firefox and Opera) users allow for more W3C compliance and thus a greater range of options for a web designer. Another restriction on webpage design is the use of different Image file formats. The majority of users can support GIF, JPEG, and PNG (with restrictions). Again Internet Explorer is the major restriction here, not fully supporting PNG's advanced transparency features, resulting in the GIF format still being the most widely used graphic file format for transparent images. Many website incompatibilities go unnoticed by the designer and unreported by the users. The only way to be certain a website will work on a particular platform is to test it on that platform.

Content

Content evaluation and organization requires that the purpose of the website be clearly defined. Collecting a list of the necessary content then organizing it according to the audience's needs is a key step in website planning. In the process of gathering the content being offered, any items that do not support the defined purpose or accomplish target audience objectives should be removed. It is a good idea to test the content and purpose on a focus group and compare the offerings to the audience needs. The next step in the process is categorizing the content and organizing it according to user needs. Each category should be named with a concise and descriptive title that will become a link on the website. Planning for the site's content ensures that the wants/needs of the target audience and the purpose of the site will be fulfilled.

Storyboarding

Storyboarding is the process of taking into account the purpose, audience and content to design the site structure that is most suitable for the website. In this process the organized and categorized content is used to develop a diagram or map. This creates a visual of how the web pages will be laid out and interconnected which helps decide how the content is portrayed. There are three main ways of diagramming the website organization:

- Linear Website Diagrams will allow the users to move in a predetermined sequence;
- Hierarchical structures (of Tree Design Website Diagrams) provide more than one path for users to take to their destination;
- Branch Design Website Diagrams allow for many interconnections between web pages.

In the process of storyboarding a record is made of the description, purpose and title of each page in the site and they are linked together according to the most effective and logical diagram type. Depending on the number of pages the website will include, methods include using pieces of paper and drawing lines to connect them or alternatively, creating the storyboard using computer software. Storyboarding can be considered like a creating a prototype for the website – a model which allows the website layout to be reviewed, resulting in suggested changes, improvements and/or enhancements. This review process increases the likelihood of success of the website. Some people refer to this as a "tree" because it branches from the main page.

Motion Graphic Design

Motion graphic design is the art of graphic design within the context of motion graphics such as film, video or computer animation. Examples include the typography and graphics you see as the titles for a film, or the spinning, three-dimensional logo at the end of a TV commercial. Although this art form has been around for decades, it has taken quantum leaps forward in recent years. If you watch much TV or see many films, you will have noticed that the graphics, the typography, and the visual effects within these mediums have become much more elaborate and sophisticated. The dramatic elevation of this art form is largely due to technology improvements. Computer programs for the film and video industry have become vastly more powerful, and more available. Probably the leading program used by motion graphic designers is Adobe After Effects, which allows you to create and modify graphics over time. Adobe After Effects is sometimes referred to as "Photoshop for film." A newcomer to the market for motion graphic design programs is Apple Computer's Motion. Motion is an inexpensive and user-friendly program that promises to hugely enlarge the ranks of motion graphic designers. A typical motion graphic designer is a person trained in traditional graphic design who has learned to integrate the elements of time and space into his/her existing skillset of design knowledge. Motion graphic designers can also come from filmmaking or animation backgrounds.

Practical Principles of Motion Graphic Design

When using a motion graphic design application, you will find its an object oriented application. Most software package works by importing media files from your computer, camera or any other data storage medium. These media files can be still images in pixel or vector format, movie sequences and audio files. Inside the application you'll create a 'new composition' with an own and independent timeline, resolution, frames-per-second and pixel size.

When creating a composition, you insert one or more of your media files. The files appear on the composition window, as well as in the timeline. Your media files work as layers which you can arrange in order (who's on top of who) and in time (where the layer begins and ends in the timeline).

Layers have properties which you can manipulate such as position (x, y and sometimes Z), scale, rotation, opacity, etc. Layers merge with each other by using transparency information provided by the alpha channel and blending modes, which change the way a layer affects the layers below. Almost all the modifiable properties can be keyframed, which means that its value can be stored at certain positions through time. And this is one of the basic principles in computer animation, the use of the computer to interpolate values between keyframes through time.

Motion Graphic Design & Digital Compositing Software Packages

- Adobe After Effects
- Autodesk Combustion / Flame / Inferno
- Apple Motion/Shake
- Pinnacle Commotion
- Eyeon Digital Fusion
- Adobe Flash

Complementary Software

Since motion graphic design is created using images and video sequences, a great complementary tool is a 3d software package. Cinema 4D is widely used for its intuitive interface, layered export to Adobe After Effects, and the additional MoGraph module, but there are also several others. Such packages can generate images or video sequences with an alpha channel, which stores all the transparency information.

Some of the applications are:

- Maxon Cinema 4D
- Autodesk 3d studio max
- Softimage XSI
- Autodesk Maya
- NewTek Lightwave
- Adobe Flash
- Adobe After Effects
- Autodesk Combustion

User Interface Design

User interface design or user interface engineering is the design of computers, gadgets, appliances, machines, mobile communication devices, software applications, and websites with the focus on the user's experience and interaction. Unlike traditional design where the goal is to make the object or application physically attractive, the goal of user interface design is to make the user's interaction experience as simple and intuitive as possible—what is often called user-centered design. Where good graphic/ industrial design is bold and eye catching, good user interface design is often subtle and invisible.

User Interface design is involved in a wide range of projects from mall kiosks to software applications to car navigation systems to e-commerce sites; all of these projects have some things in common yet also require some unique skills and knowledge. As a result, user interface designers tend to specialize in certain types of projects and have skills centered around their expertise, whether that be software design, web design, or industrial design. What all these projects have in common is, of course, the focus on how the user interacts with the device/system/application.

Processes

There are several phases and processes in the user interface design some of which are more demanded upon than others depending on the project. (note for the remainder of this section the word *system* is used to denote any project whether it is a web site, application, or device)

- Functionality requirements gathering-assembling a list of the functionality required of the system to accomplish the goals of the project and the potential needs of the users.
- User analysis-analyzation of the potential users of the system either through discussion with people who work with the users and/or the potential users themselves. Typical questions involve:
  - What would the user want the system to do?
  - How would the system fit in with the users normal workflow or daily activities?
  - How technically savvy is the user and what similar systems does the user already use?
  - What interface look & feel styles appeal to the user?
- Information architecture-development of the process and/or information flow of the system (i.e. for phone tree systems, this would be an option tree flowchart and for web sites this would be a site flow that shows the hierarchy of the pages).
- Prototyping-development of wireframes, either in the form of paper prototypes or simple interactive screens. These prototypes are stripped of all look & feel elements and most content in order to concentrate on the interface.
- Usability testing-testing of the prototypes on an actual user—often using a technique called talk aloud protocol where you ask the user to talk about their thoughts during the experience.
- Graphic Interface design-actual look & feel design of the final graphical user interface (GUI) based on the findings developed during the usability testing. This last phase is often handled separately by a graphic designer who also has knowledge in user interface design. However, some user interface designers are also proficient graphic designers.

User intrface design needs good understanding of user needs.

Art Director

The term art director, is an overall title for a variety of similar job functions in advertising, publishing, film and television, the Internet, and video games.

Publishing

In publishing, where the term originated, an art director organizes the pages of a magazine or newspaper and in consultation with an editor, chooses or designs accompanying pictures or graphics. Typically, this art director reports to the editor. At larger books or magazines, there are assistant and associate art directors that report to the art director. Many times a Design Director oversees the entire team.

Advertising

Art directors in advertising aren't necessarily the head of an art department although the title may suggest it. In modern advertising practice, they typically work in tandem with a copywriter. Together, the art director and copywriter work on a concept for commercials, print advertisements, and any other advertising medium. Individually, the art director is mostly responsible for the visual look and feel of the creative product, and the copywriter has ultimate responsibility for the product's verbal and textual content.

Both are responsible for coming up with big, effective and persuasive ideas. Depending on the competencies of each, they may share tasks that are traditionally designated for one or the other, for instance, an art director may suggest certain wording and a copywriter may suggest a certain aesthetic for a project.

The art director/copywriter tandem is overseen by a creative director. Art directors may also oversee a team of junior designers, image developers and production artists. In a smaller organization the art director may fill these roles as well. In a larger organization, art directors may oversee other art directors in a senior/junior art director relationship.

Film

An art director, in the hierarchical structure of a film art department, works directly below the production designer, and above the set designer, but on the same level as the set decorator. A large part of their duties include the administrative aspects of the art department. They are responsible for assigning tasks to personnel, keeping track of the art department budget and scheduling, as well as overall quality control. They are often also a liaison to other departments; especially the construction department. In the past, the art director title was used to denote the head of the art department (hence the Academy Award for Best Art Direction) however, the Art Directors' union felt that the title was becoming too diluted, as multiple art directors were appearing on a single show, negating the idea of one person responsible to the look of a show, and people started giving themselves the title without the approval of the union. As a result, the union decided to create the title of production designer, and created rules as to the use of the title, namely there can be only one production designer on a show, and the union must approve the use of the title. This has not translated to TV commercials, where the head of the art department is still called the art director.

Printing

The art of printing has been around since before date was actually being recorded. There is evidence that print went as far back as 6700 B.C. It is not until the form of language came about until printing was able to be dissected and further investigated. Well some people get boob jobs and others have wet vag inas.

Printing is a process for production of texts and images, typically with ink on paper using a printing press. It is often carried out as a large-scale industrial process, and is an essential part of publishing and transaction printing.

History

Block Printing in China

Woodblock printing on paper, whereby individual sheets were pressed against wooden blocks with the text and illustrations carved into them, was first recorded in China in the Tang Dynasty, although as a method for printing patterns on cloth the earliest surviving examples from China date to before 220, and from Egypt to the 6th or 7th centuries.

In the Tang Dynasty, a Chinese writer named Fenzhi first mentioned in his book "Yuan Xian San Ji" that the woodblock was used to print Buddhist scripture during the Zhenguan years (627-649 A.D.). The oldest known Chinese surviving printed work is a woodblock-printed Buddhist scripture of Wu Zetian period (684-705 A.D.); discovered in Tubofan, Xinjiang province, China in 1906, it is now stored in a calligraphy museum in Tokyo, Japan. The oldest surviving documented printed book, a copy of the Buddhist Diamond Sutra, is dated 848 AD, but a recent excavation at a Korean pagoda may have unearthed an even earlier Buddhist text dating to AD 750-751. In the modern Chinese historiography, printing is considered one of the Four Great Inventions of ancient China.

In a memorial to the throne in 1023, Northern Song Dynasty China, it recorded that the central government at that time used copperplate to print the paper money also the copper-block to print the numbers and characters on the money, nowadays we can find these shadows from the Song paper money. Later in the Jin Dynasty, people used the same but more developed technique to print paper money and formal official documents, the typical example of this kind of movable copper-block printing is a printed "check" of Jin Dynasty in the year of 1215.

Block Printing in Europe

Block printing came to Christian Europe as a method for printing on cloth, where it was common by 1300. Images printed on cloth for religious purposes could be quite large and elaborate, and when paper became relatively easily available, around 1400, the medium transferred very quickly to small woodcut religious images and playing cards printed on paper. These prints were produced in very large numbers from about 1425 onwards.

Around the mid-century, *block-books*, woodcut books with both text and images, usually carved in the same block, emerged as a cheaper alternative to manuscripts and books printed with moveable type. These were all short heavily illustrated works, the bestsellers of the day, repeated in many different block-book versions: the Ars moriendi and the Biblia pauperum were the most common. There is still some controversy among scholars as to whether their introduction preceded or, the majority view, followed the introduction of movable type, with the range of estimated dates being between about 1440-1460.

The volume of Joseph Needham's *Science and Civilization in China* dealing with Paper and printing has a chapter that suggests that "European block printers must not only have seen Chinese samples, but perhaps had been taught by missionaries or others who had learned these un-European methods from Chinese printers during their residence in China.", but this ignores the ample evidence of the actual development of uses of the process in Europe.

Movable Type Printing

Movable type allowed for a much more flexible processes than hand copying or block printing.

In East Asia

Movable type printing was first invented in 1041 by Bi Sheng in China. Sheng used clay type, which broke easily, but Wang Zhen later carved more durable type from wood.

The transition from wood type to metal type occurred during the Goryeo Dynasty of Korea and is credited to Chwe Yun-Ui.

For a description of

- the oldest surviving metal type
- early books printed with such metal type
- the oldest surviving movable metal print book printed in Korea in 1377,
- the Korean font casting process as recorded by Song Hyon in the 15th c., and
- problems due to the nature of the Chinese language

Movable type, though known in China, was not extensively used there until the European-style printing press was introduced in relatively recent times.

East Asian printing technology may possibly have diffused into Europe through the trade routes from China through India or the Arabic world, although there is no evidence. The lack of known intermediaries and profound technical differences in detail indicate that Gutenberg's invention of movable type was done independently.

In Europe

Johann Gutenberg, of the German city of Mainz, developed European printing technology in 1440, with which the classical age of printing began. Also, Johann Fust and Peter Schöffer experimented with him in Mainz. Genealogically, all modern movable type printing can be traced back to a single source, Gutenberg's printing press which he derived from the design of long known agricultural presses. East Asian style movable type printing, which was based on laborious manual rubbing and which had been scarcely used, practically died out after the introduction of European style printing in the 19th century.

Gutenberg is also credited with the introduction of an oil-based ink which was more durable than previously used water-based inks. Having worked as a professional goldsmith, Gutenberg made skillful use of the knowledge of metals he had learned as a craftsman. Gutenberg was also the first to make his type from an alloy of lead, tin, and antimony, which was critical for producing durable type that produced high-quality printed books, and proved to be more suitable for printing than the clay, wooden or bronze types used in East Asia. To create these lead types, Gutenberg used what some considered his most ingenious invention, a special matrix wherewith the moulding of new movable types with an unprecedented precision at short notice became feasible. Within a year after his B42, Gutenberg also published the first coloured prints.

Gutenberg's invention of the printing press revolutionized communication and book production leading to the spread of knowledge. Rapidly, printing spread from Germany by emigrating German printers, but also by foreign apprentices returning home. A printing press was built in Venice in 1469, and by 1500 the city had 417 printers. In 1470 Johann Heynlin set up a printing press in Paris. In 1473 Kasper Straube published the Almanach Cracoviense ad annum 1474 in Kraków. In 1476 a printing press was developed in England by William Caxton. The Italian Juan Pablos set up an imported press in Mexico City in 1539. Stephen Day was the first to build a printing press in North America at Massachusetts Bay in 1628, and helped establish the Cambridge Press.

Printing Houses

Early printing houses (near the time of Gutenberg) were run by "master printers." These printers owned shops, selected and edited manuscripts, determined the sizes of print runs, sold the works they produced, raised capital and organized distribution. Some master printing houses became the cultural centre for literati such as Erasmus.

- Early print shop apprentices: Apprentices, usually between the ages of 15 and 20, worked for master printers. Apprentices were not required to be literate, and literacy rates at the time were very low, in comparison to today. Apprentices prepared ink, dampened sheets of paper, and assisted at the press. An apprentice who wished to learn to become a compositor had to learn Latin and spend time under the supervision of a journeyman.
- Early Journeyman printers: After completing their apprenticeships, *journeyman* printers were free to roam Europe with their tools of trade and print where they journeyed to. This facilitated the spread of printing to areas that were less print-centred.
- Early Compositors: Those who set the type for printing.
- Early Pressmen: the person who ran the press. This was physically labour intensive.

The earliest-known image of a European, Gutenberg-style print shop is the *Dance of Death* by Matthias Huss, at Lyon, 1499. This image depicts a compositor standing at a compositor's case being grabbed by a skeleton. The case is raised to facilitate his work. The image also shows a pressman being grabbed by a skeleton. At the right of the printing house a bookshop is shown.

Financial Aspects

Court records from the city of Mainz document that Johannes Fust was, for some time, Gutenberg's financial backer.

By the sixteenth century jobs associated with printing were becoming increasingly specialized. Structures supporting publishers were more and more complex, leading to this division of labour. In Europe between 1500 and 1700 the role of the Master Printer was dying out and giving way to the bookseller – publisher. Printing during this period had a stronger commercial imperative than previously. Risks associated with the industry however were substantial, although dependent on the nature of the publication.

Bookseller publishers negotiated at trade fairs and at print shops. Jobbing work appeared in which printers did menial tasks in the beginning of their careers to support themselves.

1500 – 1700: Publishers developed several new methods of funding projects.

1. Cooperative associations/publication syndicates—a number of individuals shared the risks associated with printing and shared in the profit. This was pioneered by the French.

2. Subscription publishing—pioneered by the English in the early 17th century. A prospectus for a publication was drawn up by a publisher to raise funding. The prospectus was given to potential buyers who signed up for a copy. If there were not enough subscriptions the publication did not go ahead. Lists of subscribers were included in the books as endorsements. If enough people subscribed a reprint might occur. Some authors used subscription publication to bypass the publisher entirely.
3. Installment publishing—books were issued in parts until a complete book had been issued. This was not necessarily done with a fixed time period. It was an effective method of spreading cost over a period of time. It also allowed earlier returns on investment to help cover production costs of subsequent installments.

The *Mechanick Exercises*, by Joseph Moxon, in London, 1683, was said to be the first publication done in installments. [*citation needed*]

Publishing trade organizations allowed publishers to organize business concerns collectively. Systems of self-regulation occurred in these arrangements. For example, if one publisher did something to irritate other publishers he would be controlled by peer pressure. Such systems are known as cartels, and are in most countries now considered to be in restraint of trade. These arrangements helped deal with labour unrest among journeymen, who faced difficult working conditions. Brotherhoods predated unions, without the formal regulations now associated with unions.

In most cases, publishers bought the copyright in a work from the author, and made some arrangement about the possible profits. This required a substantial amount of capital in addition to the capital for the physical equipment and staff, Alternatively, an author who had sufficient money would sometimes keep the copyright himself, and simply pay the printer for the production of the book. For further developments, *see main article: copyright*

As described in *Prints and Visual Communication*, by William Ivins.

Eighteenth Century Innovations

At the end of the eighteenth century there were several remarkable innovations in the graphic techniques and those that were utilized to make their materials. Bewick developed the method of using engraving tools on the end of the wood. Senefelder discovered lithography. Blake made relief etchings.

Nineteenth Century Innovations

Early in the nineteenth century Stanhope, George E. Clymer, Koenig and others introduced new kinds of type presses, which for strength surpassed anything that had previously been known.

Modern Printing Technology

In 2006 there are approximately 30,700 printing companies in the United States, accounting for $112 billion, according to the *2006 U.S. Industry & Market Outlook* by Barnes Reports. Print jobs that move through the Internet made up 12.5% of the total U.S. Printing market last year, according to research firm InfoTrend/CAP Ventures.

Books and newspapers are printed today using the technique of offset lithography. Other common techniques include

- flexography used for packaging, labels, newspapers
- relief print, (mainly used for catalogues),
- screen printing from T-shirts to floor tiles
- rotogravure mainly used for magazines and packaging,
- inkjet used typically to print a small number of books or packaging, and also to print a variety of materials from high quality papers simulate offset printing, to floor tiles
- hot wax dye transfer
- laser printing mainly used in offices and for transactional printing (bills, bank documents).

State-of-the-art presses use to mix more printing techniques so you can have an offset machine with a flexo section for the varnishing of the product they are printing or a digital printing unit.

Gravure

For this process, the image to be printed is made up of small holes sunk into the surface of the printing plate. The cells are filled with ink and the excess is scraped off the surface, then a rubber-covered roller presses paper onto the surface of the plate and into contact with the ink in the cells. The printing plates are usually made from copper and may be produced by engraving or etching.

Gravure printing is used for long, high-quality print runs such as magazines, mail-order catalogues, packaging, and printing onto fabric and wallpaper. It is also used for printing postage stamps and decorative plastic laminates, such as kitchen worktops.

Digital Printing

Printing at home or in an office or engineering environment is subdivided into:

- small format (up to ledger size paper sheets), as used in business offices and libraries

- wide format (up to 3' or 914mm wide rolls of paper), as used in drafting and design establishments.

Some of the more common printing technologies are

- line printing — where pre-formed characters are applied to the paper by lines
- daisy wheel — where pre-formed characters are applied individually
- dot-matrix — which produces arbitrary patterns of dots with an array of printing studs
- heat transfer — like early fax machines or modern receipt printers that apply heat to special paper, which turns black to form the printed image
- blueprint — and related chemical technologies
- inkjet — including bubble-jet — where ink is sprayed onto the paper to create the desired image
- laser — where toner consisting primarily of polymer with pigment of the desired colours is melted and applied directly to the paper to create the desired image.

Vendors typically stress the total cost to operate the equipment, involving complex calculations that include all cost factors involved in the operation as well as the capital equipment costs, amortization, etc. For the most part, toner systems beat inkjet in the long run, whereas inkjets are less expensive in the initial purchase price.

Professional digital printing (using toner) primarily uses an electrical charge to transfer toner or liquid ink to the substrate it is printed on. Digital print quality has steadily improved from early color and black & white copiers to sophisticated colour digital presses like the Xerox iGen3, the Kodak Nexpress and the HP Indigo Digital Press series. The iGen3 and Nexpress use toner particles and the Indigo uses liquid ink. All three are made for small runs and variable data, and rival offset in quality. Digital offset presses are called direct imaging presses; although these receive computer files and automatically turn them into print-ready plates, they cannot insert variable data.

Small press and fanzines generally use digital printing or more rarely xerography. Prior to the introduction of cheap photocopying the use of machines such as the spirit duplicator, hectograph, and mimeograph was common.

Human-Centered Models of Information Seeking

Attention to users of information systems and consideration of their needs from a communications perspective are well represented in the literature. Dervin (1977) was particularly influential in focusing attention on users' needs through her model based on people's need to make sense of the world. The model posits that users go through three phases in making sense of the world, that is, by facing and solving their information problems. The first phase establishes the context for the information need, called the *situation.* People find a gap between what they understand and what they need in order to make sense of the current situation. These gaps are manifested by questions. The answers or hypotheses for these gaps are then used to move to the next situation. This situation-gap-use model applies to more general human conditions than information seeking but has been adopted by researchers in information science and communications as a framework for studying the information-seeking process.

Belkin and his colleagues (Belkin, 1980; Belkin, Oddy, & Brooks, 1982) constructed a model of information seeking that focuses on information seekers' anomalous states of knowledge (ASK). In this model, information seekers are concerned with a problem, but the problem itself and the information needed to solve the problem are not clearly understood. Accordingly, information seekers must go through a process of clarification to articulate a search request, with the obvious implication that search systems should support iterative and interactive dialogues with users. This model was designed to explain generally open-ended information problems and does not directly apply to fact-retrieval problems or to accretional information seeking by experts in a field. The ASK model serves as a theoretical basis for the design of highly interactive information systems.

In a much more specific context, Kuhlthau (1988) devised a model of how students search for information as part of the writing process. Her model extends to both cognitive and affective perspectives and was developed through observations and interviews with students over long periods of time. The model crosses feelings, thoughts, and actions through seven stages: task initiation, topic selection, prefocus exploration, focus formulation, information collection, search closure, and the starting of writing. The model is robust across different age groups of learners (Kuhlthau, Turock, George, & Belvin, 1990) and addresses the affective states of information seekers.

These and other models of information-seeking behavior share perspectives on information seeking as a problem-solving activity that depends on communication acts. This perspective is accepted by researchers and practitioners in information science but has only begun to influence designers and engineers who implement electronic retrieval systems. Because this perspective does parallel the user-centered philosophy dominant in human-computer interaction research, it is likely that electronic retrieval systems will eventually exhibit interfaces that support active, problem-oriented information seeking. The perspective shared by these models is also the basis for the framework developed in this chapter. Before describing the components of the framework and the processes associated with them, we offer an overview of three types of user studies that motivate and provide examples for this framework.

What is Multimedia?

It may seem odd to bother with a specific definition when we have already implied one. But multimedia is an ever present word in the language of digital media and it is worth-even briefly-making sure that when we use it we all mean the same thing.

The history of definitions of multimedia is an interesting story in itself and while we will not spend much time on it, it is worth looking back at some very early efforts just to illustrate how tough a task it once seemed. In 1990, for example, when the word was only just becoming commonplace, the Information Workstation Group's study, *Micro Multimedia,* suggested:

> Micro multimedia is multimedia supported by a microprocessor(s). It uses multiple media data types. The Information Workstation Group definition requires the presence of graphics or natural images unless Micro Cinema is present. The use of audio or numerics with text does not qualify as multimedia. The presence of text or numerics is optional. Motion is not required. Interactivity is not required... Programmed passive experiences can be multimedia... Materials excluded from micro multimedia include: television receivers where the end user can not effect [*sic*] the onboard computer programming, CD-V (linear play), programmable digital watches with graphic displays and audio alarms.

There is more, but just this sample suggests the deep and unintelligible waters it is easy to fall into when trying to be explicit about multimedia. The British magazine, *Multimedia: computing with sound and motion,* published in the same year by EMAP, apart from attempting a definition in its own title, also took a much more robust approach to defining multimedia in its first editorial:

> Multimedia is all things to all people. The name can convey a highly specific meaning or less than nothing, depending on your audience. In fact, multimedia is a singular mix of disparate technologies with overlapping applications in pursuit of a market and an identity.

This may have been true at the time but if multimedia was really in search of an identity, it is a curious irony because at the time and for some years afterwards, multimedia suffered from having rather too many of them. In their excellent evergreen *CD-I Designers' Guide* (McGraw-Hill 1992), Signe Hoffos together with Dr Graham Sharpless, Phillip Smith and Nick Lewis make this point in the course of their own struggle with definitions:

> The word multimedia has already acquired diverse meanings in various technical fields. Some computer buffs use multimedia to describe the hardware which allows computer data to be sent from one machine to another. Many audio visual specialists remember when multimedia meant presentations which combine still images from slide projectors with a soundtrack. Some software producers use the

term to describe packages which combine computer-generated text and graphics on the same screen, especially if the graphics move or there are sound effects.

Hoffos and her team eventually find at least part of the solution to defining multimedia by describing it in terms of the technology that delivers it.

Ideally, multimedia systems provide in a single box, all the hardware and software necessary to combine still and moving pictures—including video, photographic images, computer graphics and animation—with sound, text, computer-generated data and computer programs. Equally, all the information in a multimedia programme—sound, pictures, text and data—can be recorded on a single object (typically, an optical disc).

There is, of course, a final option in the definition game. Avoid tackling the issue directly and offer context instead. In his study, *The Challenge of Multimedia* (Infonortics 1992), Patrick Gibbins tries this tactic with some success, refusing to be drawn into explicit definitions and arguing that the multimedia will become clear in the context of the study. But, tempting it is to take this easier route, and true though it is that indeed support understanding, we obviously need to do our the term down more firmly. If we allow multimedia as a term shapeless and subjective, how can we ever hope to have a for understanding its implications for the information industry and the generations of information users who may (or may not) benefit from it?

A useful starting point is to go back to the 1970s to a time when computers were still huge, unfriendly devices demanding air-conditioned environments and costing millions. Even if desktop computing had not yet been invented, the term 'multimedia' was already in use. In the world of educational publishing, in particular, multimedia meant kits, typically a combination of pupils' booklets, teachers' guides, film strips, audio tapes, and photographic slides. Such products, attractively boxed and delivered to the classrooms of the early 1970s, certainly offered multiple media — text, images and sound—but each was delivered as an independent element in the package. The different media were fragmented, difficult to integrate. Welding them into a single resource for classroom teaching was a difficult task for the teachers and a confusing, unsatisfactory experience for pupils. Despite a strong commitment to resource-based teaching at the time, most schools found multimedia kits more trouble than they were worth. Most were commercial failures and publishers quietly dropped them and returned to textbooks, the monomedia which had always been the core of their business.

We could spend much time analysing the possible reasons for the failure of classroom multimedia in the 1970s. One clear reason, directly relevant to our pursuit of an identity for multimedia, concerns the way in which the different media were being presented. Although excellent in themselves, each of the elements of the multimedia kit was delivered independently. This fragmentation was, of course, unavoidable. In the mid-1970s, the technology needed to bind the individual media together simply did not exist. There was no way of combining the information in the workbooks, the sounds of the audio tape or the images of the slides and film strips. In the mid-1990s, however, the multimedia environment is dramatically different. Electronic technology provides a single medium with the power to integrate diverse types of information. So the first stage of identifying modern multimedia is to focus on its power to draw together different forms of communication, smoothly integrating them within a digital environment, and providing access to the stored information using computer systems which are fast, friendly and, above all, interactive.

We now have an identity for multimedia, a working definition against which we can measure developments and potential impacts. We can describe multimedia as follows:

> *'Multimedia' is the seamless integration of data, text, sound and images of all kinds within a single, digital information environment.*

By 'seamless' integration we mean so close an interweaving that the discrete character of the different types of individual media is submerged in the experience of the multimedia application. The idea of the integration taking place within a digital environment is crucial but does not of course imply that non-digital information cannot play an important role in multimedia, only that such information needs to be digitised and brought into the common environment. Hybrid systems using part-analogue, part-digital information will not survive in the long term. Pure analogue systems -such as traditional video discs, for example—are a technological dead end.

Why such uncompromising emphasis on the common environment being a digital one? Only if multimedia is digital can it be enriched by the unique features of digital information which are themselves what are driving the profound and comprehensive changes in the media industries which we have touched on earlier. Being able to apply these unique features to multimedia, of course, serves to define multimedia's ultimate power, impact and scope of application. Quite simply, multimedia, lying at the heart of electronic media development, can have no serious future unless it is also digital.

Maverick Compression Schemes

Despite improvements in the software-based schemes, they are principally a pragmatic solution to a commercial publishing problem rather than a realistic way of handling extreme video compression. However, there are some mavericks seemingly challenging the power and influence of MPEG. In the early 1990s, for example, the most important of these was a system called fractal compression, based on the then highly fashionable new mathematical development known as chaos theory. Fractals are fundamental redundancies in the natural world—the detailed layers of repetition in the structure of physical objects, for example — which enable quite complex formations to be described very simply. This same principle was applied by a US company called Iterated Systems to produce a software—based compression based on fractal mathematics. Although an immensely powerful means of compressing image data-used, for example, to good effect in the early editions of Microsoft's Encarta CD-ROM encyclopedia—its competitive advantage has declined in the face of other software schemes. The great weakness of the fractal scheme was not in the principle on which it was founded or on its ultimate performance. It was the fact that while it was easy to decompress fractal data it remained difficult, time consuming and expensive to compress the data in the first place.

This relationship between the ease of compressibility and decompressability is crucial to determining the commercial viability of compression schemes. MPEG, for example can now be compressed in real-time with fairly modest computers. This means that one hour of linear video will take an hour to compress. This makes MPEG nowadays a 'symmetrical' compression scheme. Asymmetric schemes like fractal compression are always less attractive because of the commercial need to get compression done quickly and cheaply.

But other new compression developments are emerging which could yet turn the world of data compression on its head. For example, in 1995, the Houston Advanced Research Centre (HARC) in the United States announced that it was on the point of commercialising a new form of compression based on a mathematical technique called wavelet analysis. The scheme—known by its originators as HARC-C essentially reduces descriptions of image data to terse mathematical formulations. These alone are then transferred to the delivery device either via a network or CD-ROM system and the original image information is reconstructed at the users' end by their computer. The key to HARC's promise lies not in the fact that it uses wavelet analysis-many research teams had been working on this for some years—but in the apparent ability of the new scheme to work with computers of modest performance. It therefore looks like a scheme that could be commercially exploitable. If it lives upto the promises of its inventors—and, at the time of writing, HARC-C still has to demonstrate its claimed potential in commercial applications—it could soon be challenging MPEG as the dominant form of video compression. It offers some starding prospects. For example it is claimed that it can deliver MPEG quality video over ordinary telephone lines with the software decompression algorithm included in the signal. This means that anyone receiving it could decompress the video because the can opener would be sent with the can. Ultimately, of course, MPEG is probably secure in the medium term because of its established position in the orthodoxy of world standards but—whatever happens to HARC-C in the bright light of the market-place—unexpected developments like it always need to be factored into any assessment of future compression developments and what they will be able to deliver in media terms. In other words, in this abstruse and highly mathematical sector of the industry, it is as well to expect the unexpected.

One thing is clear. Comfortable assumptions of the recent past about MPEG's universal dominance, and the fact that it would necessarily be hardware-based, are now being fiercely challenged. The medium-term reality looks more like a world in which no single scheme dominates but a rich variety have influence in different sectors of application. MPEG, for example, is likely to be the de facto standard in the field of digital broadcasting while proprietary software-based schemes such as advanced variants of QuickTime, HARC-C, Duck Technology's Truemotion and software implementations of MPEG hold sway in CD-ROM publishing and online multimedia.

This chapter sets in motion a massive but useful simplification which we will use to structure the rest of this book. We are going to pretend that the digital world is a simple place where there are essentially two forms of media. One kind is more familiar than the other. This is 'offline' media, packaged in a stand-alone physical form, palpable to the real world and dominated by developments in optical disc technology in general and compact disc technology in particular. The other realm is transmitted media -abstract and invisible, where information is delivered via different forms of networks ranging from Largely non-interactive broadcasting systems—radiating the same information from point to multipoint—to heavily switched systems which provide the uniquely one-to-one routeing of information which characterises interactive networks.

In practice, you cannot separate offline and transmitted media so easily. It is a convenient division but increasingly the realities of the market-place are creating a marriage of the two, combining their strengths in a powerful merger of technologies and publishing models which we will touch on at the close of this chapter.

Sometimes, however, it is helpful to pretend the world is simpler than it is—so long as you never forget that it isn't!

Using Video in CD Media

Although there seems little to stop rapid progress in the development of powerful video technologies for CD media, it is worth pausing to consider just how important high quality, full screen, full motion video is in the first place. As with most things in publishing and media distribution, the heart of the issue lies in the notion of fitness of purpose. In other words, the needs of the market are paramount and products must be designed with those needs firmly in mind. For example, it hardly requires saying that the best quality, full screen, full motion video is essential if the CD product is designed to deliver a filmgoing experience. If the product is a movie-or a music video, which is a special case of the same thing -nothing else will do. Indeed, as we have already argued, the real driver behind the nest generation of high density CD media is Hollywood and the search by studio moguls and others for an added value replacement medium for videotapes. The hugely increased storage capacity will eventually also be utilised for interactive products — especially video-rich ones-but the movie industry is first in line.

In edutainment, infotainment and games, however, the value of using full screen video of any kind is more arguable. The games industry right now is embracing CD video-at least, video decompressed in software so that it is played back in a smallish window-but it has special reasons for doing so. The cash cow of that industry-solid state cartridge games with the advantage of speed but the drawback of limited storage capacity-is in rapid decline. Most of the major console manufacturers are now moving their technologies increasingly towards CD-ROM based hardware. Nintendo is the major exception but even though it believes it has a super-magnetic disc technology up its sleeve, it is likely to fall into line with the rest of the industry in the long term. They are doing this both because CD-ROM is-for whatever reason-an attractive new product for games players and because they can use CD-ROM's capacity to deliver bigger games with more and better sound and graphics. The major problem which such manufacturers and their associated communities of software publishers have to address, however, is the slowness of the CD-ROM in delivering interactive experiences.

This relative slowness-especially compared to the lightning speed of cartridges-is due to the fact that CD-ROM drives have to physically move a stylus back and forth across the surface of a disc in order to locate and retrieve data. This mechanical process takes time and although careful design of where the data on the disc are placed and use of a modern PC's ability to hold large amounts of data in local buffers in its on-board memory, can disguise the limitation to a degree, games have to rely on much more than sheer speed of action to succeed. This has led games developers towards new genres of tides based more on cerebral values than the purely visceral appeal of fast action arcade games. The most obvious of these is the unfortunately named 'interactive movie'. This genre consists largely of traditional strategy games-with a leavening of arcade action -peppered with sequences of linear video in windows on the screen. When the video starts playing, however, the title stops being interactive. When the title stops being interactive, the experience of using it is fractured. In other words, instead of the video used this way becoming a cohesive and compelling feature within a CD-ROM title, it often fragments and ultimately undermines the experience of using it.

This highlights a key fact concerning digital video-currently it is a largely non-interactive ingredient in the interactive multimedia mix. Making it fully interactive, however, requires vastly more powerful technology than we can currently harness commercially. However, the immediate future looks promising not because linear video will be used any more wisely in interactive offerings but because a fully interactive alternative is in the wings. The next major move in uprating PC performance will come not via the wider use of MPEG video cards but through the emergence of accelerators that will allow ordinary PCs to handle 3D graphics and manipulate them in real time. This development-already partially visible among the most powerful games consoles-will turn PCs into virtual reality engines capable of delivering fully manipulable 3D experiences. In gameplay, this will mean that users will have complete control over their physical viewpoint and, more important, will have complete freedom to interact on a moment-by-moment basis with photorealistic 3D images. This, of course, is where the new role of video lies, Photorealism will partly come from the sophistication and resolution of the 3D images themselves but it will also increasingly spring from the ability to layer the images with video. This process-known as surface texturing-is already being used to add realism to 3D worlds. When we are able to texture with high quality video, the result will be breathtaking. It will also signal the end of the current generation of pseudo-interactive movies and the emergence of the real thing. Using video-textured, real-time 3D, users will be able to manipulate what appear to be normal video sequences. In reality, every element in each sequence will be computer generated with a video overlay texturing the graphics and, because of this, will be individually and independently manipulable by the user. The potential for immersing users in convincing 3D worlds will at last be available from ordinary desktop technology.

What about the role of video in information and education? Here the argument for full screen, full motion video is much weaker and the need for high levels of interactive 3D graphics is less obvious. Indeed, in even the best multimedia edutainment and infotainment products, the inclusion of full screen video segments would be a serious interruption to the flow of the title and add nothing worth having to the experience of using it. In other words, judiciously selected and well-implemented partial-screen video-even if it is of modest quality — is a good enough enrichment of underlying content. Why try to offer more? Indeed, the rule that emerges from these considerations suggests that where video is an enrichment rather than the central focus of a product, windowed video is not merely adequate but wholly appropriate. Where video is the central focus, full screen delivery is plainly important. However, the overriding issue is even more basic. Ultimately, the commercial success of the consumer CD-ROM market rests on how well the video is synthesised along with all the other elements of multimedia content to produce a product that satisfies its market.

Selling Content

First, sites can create revenue from attempting to sell content or, more likely, access to content. The distinction is a fine and important one. There is a deep-rooted fear among traditional content companies that once they post their copyright assets on the Web, they will quickly be plundered. Like much of the concern surrounding security on the Web, this particular fear is based more on a perception than a reality. It also represents a danger for such traditional players who have always created businesses out of a balance between both protecting and simultaneously exploiting copyrights. At any time it is a difficult balancing act But in the Web environment, there is a strong sense that protection is almost impossible and exploitation, at best, problematic. This analysis would, catastrophically, counsel content companies to steer clear of the Web altogether. Fortunately, it is becoming clear, even to newcomers to the field, that protection, is possible — at least to levels comparable to the real world — and that the best possible protection is not to make copyright materials accessible online in the first place. Instead, they can be showcased on the Web and sold via conventional channels. Showcasing itself can be a sophisticated process, including a sampling of the content products. Much here depends on the type of content involved. For television, video and film companies, showcasing and promotion is really the only option. Supplying product is still far beyond the capabilities of the Web. New forms of compression technologies, however, are beginning to make 'good enough' real-time video on a small window of the PC screen-probably adequate for sampling products-a near-term possibility.

For record companies, showcasing and sampling is already a possibility using existing, widely available software, although quality is still relatively poor, certainly inferior to normal CD quality sound. In other words, like the video companies, music companies (and the bands and artists themselves) are unlikely-with exceptions such as operations like the Internet Underground Music Archive in the United States and Cerberus in the UK-to attempt to deliver their products over the networks. Print publishers, of course, are the media players with most to lose and gain right now from posting their content directly on the Web because the environment is most immediately suited to text leavened with a few illustrations. There are, of course, resolution and convenience issues-resolution determined both by the way the content is stored in the server and by the limitations of the output printer and convenience by the fact that large volumes even of mere text can take time to download over ordinary dial-up connections. For publishers, therefore, the issue is most immediate but, even for them, the obvious solution is to consider promoting rather than selling their crown jewels. That way they can be stolen only in the real world, not in cyberspace. In any event, as we saw in the previous section, the notion of content of the Web needs careful definition. While the Web may become a place where some traditional content is traded, it more a place where trade will be based on very different notions of content than previously understood by the media industry. In fact, the old do not sit well in the new world. The type of content that flourishes Web is much more an experience than a fixed body of intellectual property in the traditional sense. This makes it much harder for Web content to be stolen. After all, how do you steal an experience? Only with great difficulty.

Even more difficult, right now, is actually generating revenue by selling to content-whether defined in traditional or new era terms. Content of course, drives the success of a site-by definition since there is site without content — but to get customers to part with money for to it is a real challenge. Those who have attempted to charge have the size of their constituencies plunge. On the face of it, this seems a strange difficulty. After all, most of the media industry is-on the surface, at least-based on the idea of selling access to content to those who want or need it. The direct exploitation of the content is the principal source of revenue generation. On the Web, by contrast, content is the honey that interest and helps build a constituency. Revenue generation seems to come later. In fact, closer analysis shows us that even in real world sectors, revenue generation is often more complex. Successful films produce substantial box office revenues but can often make more from video and merchandising exploitations. Magazines and newspapers rely on their content to sustain communities of regular readers which, in turn, are attractive to advertisers. Even book publishers-most obviously associated single revenue stream businesses-actually make substantial sums selling to third parties what they term 'subsidiary rights': the rights to serialise, adapt, anthologise original printed works or to turn books into different copyright forms such as films, plays, television programmes or even interactive products. So, in reality, the media world is less attached to just selling its content directly and is more multistream than one might pose.

Strategies for generating revenue from access to content resolve them-into four options. Selling access to an entire site by charging a subscription for entry is the most obvious approach. It also appears doomed to failure at present except for sites offering professional and corporate information with a strong 'need to know' character. The majority consumer sites would find it very difficult to persuade customers to pay in such a blunt fashion. Only slightly less blunt is the idea of charging for access to content on a 'pay as you go' basis. Instead of a fixed entry customers buy such content as they choose a la carte. More subtle and therefore more plausible is the widely favoured approach of providing site free and creating a high value, premium area within the site. Those wanting to get into the premium area have to buy a password which gives them access for a subscription period. Examples of early experiments with this approach include Penthouse, Hachette Fillipachi's 'Car and driver' site and the hugely successful Sportszone, run by US sports TV giant, ESPN. More subtle still-but possibly less plausible-is the move to blur the distinction between charging for content and charging for Internet access. A number of service providers — particularly news publishers-are now offering a subscription which includes an Internet access deal. The package is created by the content company sub-contracting the access provision to a third party company whose main business is providing such access. The content company hopes to negotiate preferential rates for its subscribers so the overall deal looks attractive. But the reality, of course, is that the charge for content and access combined always adds up to more than access alone and customers only have to do some simple mental arithmetic to appreciate the level of charging being made for the content to which they gain access. So the technique has some psychological value in fudging content charges but is not likely to fool many of the people for much of the time. That said, the deal could still look attractive if access was being provided at a heavily discounted rate. But to get a really good deal on access, the content company would have to guarantee some fairly high volume of trade.

The difficulty of selling content online is striking. In the real world there appears to be little difficulty so long as the content offering is compelling and the price is right. There is probably a slew of complex reasons but one is clear. In our current media culture, people value atoms more readily than they value bits. In other words, if a digital product is enshrined in a physical medium, immediately palpable to the senses, it is more easily regarded as an object of inherent value. By contrast, if a product is delivered online as a stream of bits, those accessing it seem less willing to appreciate its lasting value and are accordingly less inclined to pay for it. This phenomenon-which may decline as the generations roll by — is not helped by current Internet culture where information is widely seen-almost in terms of an ideology-as something that should be freely available. Even with the old altruistic culture fast being swept away by today's hardnosed commercial initiatives, the instinct that information delivered via the bitstream should be free lingers on and makes those initiatives that much harder to consummate.

REFERENCES

A. Hampapur, R. Jain, and T. Weymouth. Digital video segmentation. *Proc. of the Second Annual ACM Multimedia Conference and Exposition*, 1994.

A. Nagasaka and Y. Tanaka. Automatic video indexing and full-video search for object appearances. *Second Working Conference on Visual Database Systems*, pages 119-133, 1991.

A.A. Rodriguez. *Digital Video Compression On Personal Computers: Algorithms And Techniques (San Jose, Ca, February 7-8)*, volume 2187. SPIE, 1994.

A.M. Earnshaw and S.D. Blostein. An error analysis of camera translation direction estimation from optical flow using linear constraints. *IEEE International Conference on Image Processing*, 1995.

B. Shahraray. Scene change detection and content-based sampling of video. *SPIE*, 2419:2-13.

B.L. Yeo and B. Liu. Unified approach to temporal segmentation of motion jpeg and mpeg video. *International Conference on Multimedia Computing and Systems*, pages 2-13, 1995.

C. Bergeron and E. Dubois. Parametric block estimation of motion and application to temporal interpolation of video sequences. *ICPR-C*, 90:140-146.

C.C.J. Kuo and J. Storer. Guest eds., special issue on still and video image compression. *JVCIR*, 5(4):303-402, 1994.

C.T. Jones and K.D. Sauer. Bayesian approach to segmentation of temporal dynamics in video data. *SPIE*, 1605:522-533.

C-M. Fan and N.N. Namazi. Estimation of image motion parameters using the em algorithm. *IEEE International Conference on Image Processing*, 1995.

D. Le Gall. Mpeg: A video compression standard for multimedia applications. *Communications of the ACM*, 34(4), 1991.

D. Swanberg, C.F. Shu, and R. Jain. Knowledge guided parsing in video databases. *SPIE*, 1908, 1993.

E. Chalom and V.M. Bove. Segmentation of frames in a video sequence using motion and other attributes. *SPIE*, 2419:230-241.

E. Touradj, H.H. Chen, and B.G. Haskell. Joint motion estimation and segmentation for very low bit rate video coding. *SPIE*, 2501:787-798.

F. Arman, A. Hsu, and M.Y. Chiu. Image processing on compressed data for large video databases. *Proc. of the ACM Multimedia Conference*, pages 267-272, 1993.

F. Arman, A. Hsu, and M-Y. Chiu. Image processing on encoded video sequences. *ACM Multimedia Systems*, 1994.

F. Arman, R. Depommier, A. Hsu, and M-Y. Chiu. Content-based browsing of video sequences. *ACM International Conference on Multimedia*, 1994.

F. Dufaux, F. Moscheni, and A. Lippman. Spatio-temporal segmentation based on motion and static segmentation. *IEEE International Conference on Image Processing*, 1995.

F.C.M. Martins and J.M.F. Moura. 3-d video compositing: Towards a compact representation for video sequences. *IEEE International Conference on Image Processing*, 1995.

G.K. Wallace. The jpeg still image compression standard. *Communications of the ACM*, 34(4), 1991.

H. Sawhney, S. Ayer, and M. Gorkani. Dominant and multiple motion estimation for video representation. *IEEE International Conference on Image Processing*, 1995.

H.C. Liu and G.L. Zick. Scene decompostion of mpeg compressed video. *SPIE*, 2419:26-37.

H.J. Zhang, A. Kankanhalli, and S.W. Smoliar. Automatic partitioning of video. *Multimedia Systems*, 1(1):10-28, 1993.

H.J. Zhang, C.Y. Low, and S.W. Smoliar. Video parsing and browsing using compressed data. *Multimedia Tools and Applications*, 1(1):89-111, 1995.

H.J. Zhang, C.Y. Low, S.W. Smoliar, and J.H. Wu. Video parsing, retrieval and browsing: An integrated and content-based solution. *Proceedings ACM Multimedia*, 1995.

H.J. Zhang, C.Y. Yow, Y. Gong, and S.W. Smoliar. Video parsing using compressed data. *SPIE*, 2182:142-149, 1994.

I.K. Sethi and N. Patel. A statistical approach to scene change detection. *SPIE*, 2420:329-338.

J. Meng, Y. Juan, and S.F. Chang. Scene change detection in a mpeg compressed video sequence. *SPIE*, 2419:14-25.

J. Yeh, M. Vetterli, and M. Khansari. Motion compensation of motion vectors. *IEEE International Conference on Image Processing*, 1995.

J.Y. Wang and E.H. Adelson. Spatio-temporal segmentation of video data. *SPIE*, 2182:120-131.

K. Sauer and C. Jones. Bayesian block-wise segmentation of interframe differences in video sequences. *GMIP*, 55:129-139.

K. Shen and J. Delp. A fast algorithm for video parsing using mpeg compressed sequences. *IEEE International Conference on Image Processing*, 1995.

L-M. Po and W-C. Ma. A new center-biased search algorithm for block motion estimation. *IEEE International Conference on Image Processing*, 1995.

M. Cherfaoui and C. Bertin. Temporal segmentation of videos: a new approach. *SPIE*, 2419:38-47.

M. Kabuka, E. McVey, and P. Shironoshita. An adaptive approach to video tracking. *J-RA*, 4:228-236.

M. Khosravi and R.W. Schafer. Low complexity matching criteria for image/video applications. *ICIP-III*, 94:776-780.

M. Nagata and Y. Oonishi. Video image manipulation in multi-media pictorial database management. *CAPAIDM*, 86:340-347.

M. Rabbani and R.J. Safranek. *Image And Video Compression (San Jose, Ca, February 9-10)*, volume 2186. SPIE, 1994.

M. Rabbani, M.I. Sezan, and A.M. Tekalp. *Image And Video Processing (San Jose, Ca, February 3-4)*, volume 1903. SPIE, 1994.

M. Shibata. Temporal segmentation method for video sequence. *SPIE*, 1818:1194-1205.

N. Vasconcelos and A. Lippman. Spatiotemporal model-based optic flow estimation. *IEEE International Conference on Image Processing*, 1995.

P. Anandan, M. Irani, R. Kumar, and J. Bergen. Video as an image data source: Efficient representations and applications. *IEEE International Conference on Image Processing*, 1995.

P. Bouthemy and E. Francois. Motion segmentation and qualitative dynamic scene analysis from a moving camera. *IJCV*, 10:157-182.

R. Krishnamurthy, P. Moulin, and J. Woods. Optical flow techniques applied to video coding. *IEEE International Conference on Image Processing*, 1995.

R. Steinmetz. Data compression in multimedia computing-standards and systems. *Multimedia Systems*, 1(4):187-204, 1994.

R. Zabih, J. Miller, and K. Mai. Feature-based algorithm for detecting and classifying scene breaks. *ACM Multimedia*, 1995.

R.A. Samy and C.A. Bozzo. Dynamic scene analysis and video target tracking. *ICPR*, 84:993-995.

R.I. Taylor and P.H. Lewis. Colour image segmenation using boundary relaxation. *ICPR-C*, 92:721-724.

R.S. Jasinschi and J.M.F. Moura. Content-based video sequence representation. *IEEE International Conference on Image Processing*, 1995.

R.W. Picard. Light-years from lena: Video and image libraries of the future. *IEEE International Conference on Image Processing*, 1995.

S. Sullivan, L. Sandford, and J. Ponce. On using geometric distance fits to estimate 3d object shape: Form and deformation from range, ct, and video images. *CVPR*, 93:110-115.

S.A. Rajala and R.L. Stevenson. *Image And Video Processing II (San Jose, Ca, February 7-9)*, volume 2182. SPIE, 1994.

S.C. Brofferio. Integrated estimation of 2d motion field and image segmentation for videophone coding. *SPIE*, 2451:139-146.

S-F. Chang and D.G. Messerschmitt. A new approach to decoding and compositing motion-compensated dct-based images. *ICASSP*, 1993.

S-F. Chang and D.G. Messerschmitt. Manipulation and compositing of mc-dct compressed video. *IEEE JSAC Special Issue on Intelligent Signal Processing in Communications*, 13(1), 1995.

S-F. Chang, W-L. Chen, and D.G. Messerschmitt. Video compositing in the dct domain. *IEEE Workshop on Visual Signal Processing and Communications*, 1992.

S-F. Chang. Compressed-domain techniques for image/video indexing and manipulation. *IEEE International Conference on Image Processing*, 1995.

U-V. Koc and K.J. Ray Liu. Adaptive overlapping approach for dct-based motion estimation. *IEEE International Conference on Image Processing*, 1995.

V. Bhaskaran, W. Li, and M. Kunt. Segmentation-based scheme for very low bit rate video coding. *SPIE*, 2419:81-89.

W. Niblack and R.C. Jain. *Storage And Retrieval For Image And Video Databases II (San Jose, Ca, February 7-8)*, volume 2185. SPIE, 1994.

Y. Gong, H. Zen, Y. Ohsawa, and M. Sakauchi. A color video image quantization method with stable and efficient color selection capability. *ICPR-C*, 92:33-36.

Y. Huang and X. Zhuang. Motion-partitioned adaptive block matching for video compression. *IEEE International Conference on Image Processing*, 1995.

Y. Tonomura, A. Akutsu, Y. Taniguchi, and G. Suzuki. Structured video computing. *IEEE Multimedia*, 1(3):34-43, 1994.

Y. Wong. An efficient heuristic-based motion estimation algorithm. *IEEE International Conference on Image Processing*, 1995.

Y.F. Wang, N. Karandikar, and J.K. Aggarwal. Analysis of video image sequences using point and line correspondences. *PR*, 24:1065-1084.

Yeo B-L. and B. Liu. On the extraction of dc sequence from mpeg compressed video. *IEEE International Conference on Image Processing*, 1995.

Z. Kui, M. Bober, and J. Kittler. Variable block size video coding with motion prediction and motion segmentation. *SPIE*, 2419:62—70.

3

Computer Programming and Hardware Systems

Introduction to Computers Hardware

The hardware are the parts of computer itself including the Central Processing Unit (CPU) and related microchips and micro-circuitry, keyboards, monitors, case and drives (floppy, hard, CD, DVD, optical, tape, etc...). Other extra parts called peripheral components or devices include mouse, printers, modems, scanners, digital cameras and cards (sound, colour, video) etc... Together they are often referred to as a personal computers or PCs. Central Processing Unit (CPU)-Though the term relates to a specific chip or the processor a CPU's performance is determined by the rest of the computers circuitry and chips. Currently the Pentium chip or processor, made by Intel, is the most common CPU though there are many other companies that produce processors for personal computers. One example is the CPU made by Motorola which is used in Apple computers. With faster processors the clock speed becomes more important. Compared to some of the first computers which operated at below 30 megahertz (MHz) the Pentium chips began at 75 MHz in the late 1990's. As of mid 2003 speeds now exceed 3000+ MHz or 3 gigahertz (GHz) (check your local computer store for the latest speed). It depends on the circuit board that the chip is housed in, or the motherboard, as to whether you are able to upgrade to a faster chip. The motherboard contains the circuitry and connections that allow the various component to communicate with each other. Though there were many computers using many different processors previous to this I call the 80286 processor the advent of home computers as these were the processors that made computers available for the average person. Using a processor before the 286 involved learning a proprietary system and software. Most new software are being developed for the newest and fastest processors so it can be difficult to use an older computer system. Some of the keys have a special use. There are referred to as command keys. The 3 most common are the Control or CTRL, Alternate or Alt and the Shift keys though there can be more (the Windows key for example or the

Command key). Each key on a standard keyboard has one or two characters. Press the key to get the lower character and hold Shift to get the upper.

Disk Drives: All disks need a drive to get information off-or read-and put information on the disk-or write. Each drive is designed for a specific type of disk whether it is a CD, DVD, hard disk or floppy. Often the term 'disk' and 'drive' are used to describe the same thing but it helps to understand that the disk is the storage device which contains computer files-or software-and the drive is the mechanism that runs the disk.

Mouse: Most modern computers today are run using a mouse controlled pointer. Generally if the mouse has two buttons the left one is used to select objects and text and the right one is used to access menus. If the mouse has one button (Mac for instance) it controls all the activity and a mouse with a third buttons can be used by specific software programs.

One type of mouse has a round ball under the bottom of the mouse that rolls and turns two wheels which control the direction of the pointer on the screen. Another type of mouse uses an optical system to track the movement of the mouse. It is important to clean the mouse periodically, particularly if it becomes sluggish. A ball type mouse has a small circular panel that can be opened, allowing you to remove the ball. Lint can be removed carefully with a tooth pick or tweezers and the ball can be washed with mild detergent. A build up will accumulate on the small wheels in the mouse. Use a small instrument or finger nail to scrape it off taking care not to scratch the wheels. Track balls can be cleaned much like a mouse and touch-pad can be wiped with a clean, damp cloth. An optical mouse can accumulate material from the surface that it is in contact with which can be removed with a finger nail or small instrument.

Monitors: The monitor shows information on the screen when you type. This is called outputting information. When the computer needs more information it will display a message on the screen, usually through a dialog box. Monitors come in many types and sizes from the simple monochrome (one colour) screen to full colour screens. Most desktop computers use a monitor with a cathode tube and most notebooks use a liquid crystal display (LCD) monitor. To get the full benefit of today's software with full colour graphics and animation, computers need a color monitor with a display or graphics card.

Printers: The printer takes the information on your screen and transfers it to paper or a hard copy. There are many different types of printers with various levels of quality. The three basic types of printer are; dot matrix, inkjet, and laser.

- Dot matrix printers work like a typewriter transferring ink from a ribbon to paper with a series or 'matrix' of tiny pins.
- Ink jet printers work like dot matrix printers but fires a stream of ink from a cartridge directly onto the paper.

- Laser printers use the same technology as a photocopier using heat to transfer toner onto paper.

Modem: A modem is used to translate information transferred through telephone lines or cable.

The term stands for modulate and demodulate which changes the signal from digital, which computers use, to analog, which telephones use and then back again. A high speed connection also requires a modem but because the information is transferred digitally it isn't required to change the signal from digital to analog but is used to create the connection between your computer and the computer you are connecting with. Modems are measured by the speed that the information is transferred. The measuring tool is called the baud rate. Originally modems worked at speeds below 2400 baud but today analog speeds of 56,000 are common. Cable, wireless or digital subscriber lines (DSL) modems can transfer information much faster with rates of 300,000 baud and up. Modems also use Error Correction which corrects for transmission errors by constantly checking whether the information was received properly or not and Compression which allows for faster data transfer rates. Information is transferred in packets. Each packet is checked for errors and is re-sent if there is an error. Anyone who has used the Internet has noticed that at times the information travels at different speeds. Depending on the amount of information that is being transferred the information will arrive it's destination at different times. The amount of information that can travel through a line is limited. This limit is called bandwidth.

There are many more variables involved in communication technology using computers, much of which is covered in the section on the Internet.

Scanners: Scanners allow you to transfer pictures and photographs to your computer. A scanner 'scans' the image from the top to the bottom, one line at a time and transfers it to the computer as a series of bits or a bitmap. You can then take that image and use it in a paint program, send it out as a fax or print it. With optional Optical Character Recognition (OCR) software you can convert printed documents such as newspaper articles to text that can be used in your word processor. Most scanners use TWAIN software that makes the scanner accessable by other software applications.

Digital cameras allow you to take digital photographs. The images are stored on a memory chip or disk that can be transferred to your computer. Some cameras can also capture sound and video.

Case: The case houses the microchips and circuitry that run the computer. Desktop models usually sit under the monitor and tower models beside. They come in many sizes, including desktop, mini, midi, and full tower. There is usually room inside to expand or add components at a later time. By removing the cover off the case you will may find plate covered, empty slots that allow you to add cards. There are various types of slots including IDE, ASI, USB, PCI and Firewire slots.

Notebook computers may have room to expand depending on the type of computer. Most Notebooks also have connections or ports that allows expansion or connection to exterior, peripheral devices such as monitor, portable hard-drives or other devices.

Cards: Cards are components added to computers to increase their capability. When adding a peripheral device make sure that your computer has a slot of the type needed by the device.

Sound cards allow computers to produce sound like music and voice. The older sound cards were 8 bit then 16 bit then 32 bit. Though human ear can't distinguish the fine difference between sounds produced by the more powerful sound card they allow for more complex music and music production.

Colour cards allow computers to produce colour (with a colour monitor of course). The first colour cards were 2 bit which produced 4 colours [CGA]. It was amazing what could be done with those 4 colours. Next came 4 bit allowing for 16 [EGA and VGA] colours Then came 16 bit allowing for 1064 colours and then 24 bit which allows for almost 17 million colours and now 32 bit is standard allowing monitors to display almost a billion separate colours.

Video cards allow computers to display video and animation. Some video cards allow computers to display television as well as *capture* frames from video. A video card with a digital video camera allows computers users to produce live video. A high speed or network connection is needed for effective video transmission.

Network cards allow computers to connect together to communicate with each other. Network cards have connections for cable, thin wire or wireless networks. For more information see the section on Networks.

Cables: connect internal components to the Motherboard, which is a board with series of electronic path ways and connections allowing the CPU to communicate with the other components of the computer.

Memory: Memory can be very confusing but is usually one of the easiest pieces of hardware to add to your computer. It is common to confuse chip memory with disk storage. An example of the difference between memory and storage would be the difference between a table where the actual work is done (memory) and a filing cabinet where the finished product is stored (disk). To add a bit more confusion, the computer's hard disk can be used as temporary memory when the program needs more than the chips can provide.

Random Access Memory or RAM is the memory that the computer uses to temporarily store the information as it is being processed. The more information being processed the more RAM the computer needs.

One of the first home computers used 64 kilobytes of RAM memory (Commodore 64). Today's modern computers need a minimum of 64 MB (recommended 128 MB or more) to run Windows or OS 10 with modern software.

RAM memory chips come in many different sizes and speeds and can usually be expanded. Older computers came with 512 KB of memory which could be expanded to a maximum of 640 KB. In most modern computers the memory can be expand by adding or replacing the memory chips depending on the processor you have and the type of memory your computer uses. Memory chips range in size from 1 MB to 512 MB. As computer technology changes the type of memory changes as well making old memory chips obsolete. Check your computer manual to find out what kind of memory your computer uses before purchasing new memory chips.

Computer hardware is the physical part of a computer, including the digital circuitry, as distinguished from the computer software that executes within the hardware. The hardware of a computer is infrequently changed, in comparison with software and data, which are "soft" in the sense that they are readily created, modified or erased on the computer. Firmware is a special type of software that rarely, if ever, needs to be changed and so is stored on hardware devices such as read-only memory (ROM) where it is not readily changed (and is therefore "firm" rather than just "soft").

Most computer hardware is not seen by normal users. It is in embedded systems in automobiles, microwave ovens, electrocardiograph machines, compact disc players, and other devices. Personal computers, the computer hardware familiar to most people, form only a small minority of computers (about 0.2% of all new computers produced in 2003). See Market statistics.

Personal Computer Hardware

A typical pc consists of a case or chassis in desktop or tower shape and the following parts:

- Motherboard or system board with slots for expansion cards and holding parts ** Central processing unit (CPU)
  - — Computer fan-used to cool down the CPU
  - — Random Access Memory (RAM)-for program execution and short term data storage, so the computer does not have to take the time to access the hard drive to find the file(s) it requires. More RAM will normally contribute to a faster PC. RAM is almost always removable as it sits in slots in the motherboard, attached with small clips. The RAM slots are normally located next to the CPU socket.
  - — Basic Input-Output System (BIOS) or Extensible Firmware Interface (EFI) in some newer computers

- Buses
  - PCI
  - PCI-E
  - USB
  - Hyper Transport
  - CSI (expected in 2008)
  - AGP (being phased out)
  - VLB (outdated)
  - ISA (outdated)
  - EISA (outdated)

- Power supply-a case that holds a transformer, voltage control, and (usually) a cooling fan
- Storage controllers of IDE, SATA, SCSI or other type, that control hard disk, floppy disk, CD-ROM and other drives; the controllers sit directly on the motherboard (on-board) or on expansion cards
- Video display controller that produces the output for the computer display. This will either be built into the motherboard or attached in its own separate slot (PCI, PCI-E or AGP), requiring a Graphics Card.
- Computer bus controllers (parallel, serial, USB, FireWire) to connect the computer to external peripheral devices such as printers or scanners
- Some type of a removable media writer:
  - CD-the most common type of removable media, cheap but fragile.
    - CD-ROM Drive
    - CD Writer
  - DVD
    - DVD-ROM Drive
    - DVD Writer
    - DVD-RAM Drive
  - Floppy disk
  - Zip drive
  - USB flash drive AKA a Pen Drive
  - Tape drive-mainly for backup and long-term storage
- Internal storage-keeps data inside the computer for later use.

— Hard disk-for medium-term storage of data.

— Disk array controller

- Sound card-translates signals from the system board into analog voltage levels, and has terminals to plug in speakers.
- Networking-to connect the computer to the Internet and/or other computers

— Modem-for dial-up connections

— Network card-for DSL/Cable internet, and/or connecting to other computers.

- Other peripherals

In addition, hardware can include external components of a computer system. The following are either standard or very common.

Input or Input Devices

- Text input devices
- Keyboard
- Pointing devices
- Mouse
- Trackball
- Gaming devices
- Joystick
- Gamepad
- Game controller
- Image, Video input devices
- Image scanner
- Webcam
- Audio input devices
- Microphone

Output or Output Devices

- Image, Video output devices
- Printer Peripheral device that produces a hard copy. (Inkjet, Laser)
- Monitor Device that takes signals and displays them. (CRT, LCD)
- Audio output devices
- Speakers A device that converts analog audio signals into the equivalent air vibrations in order to make audible sound.

- Headset A device similar in functionality to that of a regular telephone handset but is worn on the head to keep the hands free.

PC Hardware

The newspaper ads scream out prices, MHz, ATA, DDR, PCI-e. Do you know what these buzzwords really mean? Does anyone? The PC may be the single most important tool for researchers and executives, but because it is purchased in a camera store or discount food warehouse it is often treated as a commodity item. It is not possible to buy a PC with poor quality core components. AMD and Intel don't make bad CPUs. Mainboards, disks, and video cards are uniformly decent quality. You can buy a cheap case (with sharp edges that cut your hands), but if you never open the covers you will never know. So in an era where game consoles cost $600, and you can spend real money on a flat panel TV set, you can still buy the least expensive Dell or HP system for $350 and get a pretty good computer. If that is all the advice you are looking for, read no farther. The rest of this article will be spent explaining how the technology works and what everything means. This information may have no immediate practical use, but it will increase your comfort level. If the PC is no longer a big investment in money, it is still an important tool in business or education. Knowing more about it should make concerned people more comfortable with their decisions. No technical background is assumed. Even very complex issues will be explained in terms that everyone can understand.

Who Made It?

IBM invented the modern PC design, but they recently sold that business to a Chinese company. This should not be a big surprise. Often the only American thing in a computer is the name on the cardboard box it came in. Apple assembles systems in Shanghai and ships them overnight to the US. If you buy a car from Ford, you expect the frame, engine, transmission, generator, and other parts to come from Ford or at least be built to Ford specifications. You do not expect to be able to put a Ford transmission in a GM car. In a PC, however, the CPU, memory, disk, CD, power supply, and case are all manufactured to industry standards. You can take a hard disk or memory out of a Dell computer and put it into a system made by HP. The brand names you know are the names of companies that assemble, distribute, and support the computers, not the companies that make the parts. This is an international business. The mainboard almost certainly comes from a Taiwan company (Asus, Abit, Shuttle, MSI, ...). Disks tend to come from Singapore or Indonesia (Seagate, Western Digital, Maxtor). Memory and LCD displays often come from Korea. The external case and the power supply probably come from China (though over time more and more parts will come from China). You can buy the components from CDW or NewEgg and assemble a computer yourself, but you won't save any money. The big computer makers buy parts in lots of a thousand, packaged in bulk to save packing and shipping. Nine screws attach the motherboard to the mounts on the case. Four screws attach the disk to the disk bay. Then the cables all plug into sockets. An unskilled worker can be quickly trained to assemble a computer every few minutes.

The advanced technology is in the manufacture of the chips, not the final assembly of the finished product. A CPU chip is constructed in a plant that costs billions of dollars. The building is on shock absorbers because the vibration generated by passing trucks would disturb the process. People wear spacesuits not to protect them from the environment, but to protect the chips from flakes of loose skin or the particles we exhale in every breath. Then the chip is packaged in plastic and shipped out. There is a socket on the mainboard. One corner of the chip has an arrow, and one corner of the socket has an arrow. Drop the chip into the socket while matching the two arrows, then drop a lever to hold it in place. It is harder to tie a shoelace than to install a CPU chip on a mainboard.

Trends

Lets assume you don't have the time to read everything about computers. What are the key concepts you need to know to be informed on the technology, even if you won't impress your teenage son?

The Intel blunder-Inside a computer there is an assembly line with stations (called the "pipeline"). There is a "clock" that signals periodically (like the bell in a highschool) when it is time for work to move on to the next station in the line. About 5 years ago Intel designed the Pentium 4 chip based on the assumption that clocks would get faster, so the time for any station to do work would get shorter. This meant building a longer pipeline with lots of stations, and simplifying the work done at each station. Its like creating an assembly line where each worker just turns one screw and then passes the work on to the next person. As you might imagine, there is some inefficiency passing work from station to station, but that would have been overcome as the clock speeded up. Unfortunately, problems in the materials used to construct chips made it impossible to significantly increase clock speeds for the entire five year period, and the inefficiency of the design was a drag on performance. Fortunately, Intel had an entirely different chip design for laptops, where efficiency improved battery life. So Intel reversed course and applied this more efficient laptop design to desktop computer chips, producing the current family of chips called Core Duo (or Core 2 Duo in a second generation).

The CPU and GPU-Inside every computer there are two processing units. The Central Processing Unit (CPU) from Intel or AMD runs the operating system (Windows, Mac, ...) and all the applications (Office, Web, Mail, ...). The Graphics Processing Unit is a specialized device that can perform certain operations 10 times faster than the CPU. It does not run ordinary programs. The operating system treats it as a device, feeds it data, and expects it to perform its specialized calculations. You can buy a system with two or four CPU "cores". Each core can run a different software program at the same time. If you are running a long program in the background, say compressing a TV show so it can display on a video iPod, then having a second core to run the rest of the programs can smooth out your performance. More than two cores can be very valuable on a corporate server, but is unlikely to help the home user. Similarly, you can plug two video adapter cards into the same computer and get 2 (or sometimes 4) GPU chips. Unlike a CPU core, they will not be used to run different programs. Rather, they will be tied together to do one bulk process even faster. Now compressing video for an iPod turns out to be something that the GPUs could do much, much faster than the CPUs if anyone wrote the software to use them. This has been promised for some time but never delivered. While Intel strategy seems to emphasize more CPU cores in the future, AMD has announced a strategy (called "Fusion") to produce chips with (probably) two CPU cores and then additional high speed specialized processing cores that look a lot more like a GPU. This will speed up games, multimedia processing, Photoshop, and the other specialized applications that can actually use more processing power.

Overclocking-The pipeline advances when the clock signals. To be sure that everything works properly, vendors like Intel test their chips with very fast clocks to make sure they work, but then ship them with slower clock speeds to protect against any possibility of error. If you are using your computer to run a business, you don't want to mess with the clock speed. You never, ever want the computer to crash. If you are playing games, however, then a setting that crashes the computer once a month (and you reboot) may be worth it if it makes the game run faster the rest of the time. Setting the clock to run faster is called "overclocking" and has become interesting because it is easy to do. It just isn't particularly useful.

Vista-Anybody who really knows computers spends a certain amount of time helping out friends who have loaded up their computers with trash, viruses, and spyware. So you spend a half hour cleaning things up, then turn the machine back over to someone who isn't smart enough to click the "No" button any time someone offers him free stuff. Windows was designed for TV's Mayberry, and then it got connected to the modern Internet. Microsoft spent 5 years creating a new tougher operating system that behaved the same as the old XP system. This is something like taking an armored Humvee that troops use in Baghdad and making it look and drive like a minivan that soccer moms use to pick up the kids after school. It is bigger and requires a more powerful computer, but is better suited for the dangerous real world we are in.

Standards

There are 8 basic parts to a computer:

1. Case

2. Power Supply
3. Mainboard
4. CPU (and cooling tower)
5. Memory
6. Video Card
7. Hard Disk
8. DVD Drive

Case

The case is the metal or plastic box that holds the computer. You can get small cases that look like stereo equipment, or large cases with room for a lot of disks and add on cards. Enthusiasts may buy a case that is transparent or one that looks sporty.

Things to look for in a case: A smaller case is more convenient. The large case is mostly empty, which may seem like a waste of space. However, a computer needs airflow to cool the CPU and video card. Bigger cases have more air and are easier to cool. Also, noise from a computer mostly comes from fans. A small case has a small fan that has to rotate very fast and is loud. A big case can have a 120 mm fan that can rotate more slowly and still move a lot of air. If you have the space on the floor, the bigger case has advantages. Other than this, look for a case with no sharp edges that cut your fingers if you open it up.

Mainboard

The mainboard must have a socket for at least one CPU chip, and sockets for typically 2 or 4 memory "sticks". The back panel will expose plugs for keyboard, mouse, USB, othernet, and maybe External SATA disks. Some mainboards have integrated video. It will then have slots and connectors for the things you add it: SATA connectors for disk and PCI and PCI-e slots for adapter cards. Things to look for in a mainboard: The CPU socket has to match the CPU chip. Mainboards come in large (ATX) and small (MATX) sizes with a few other (jumbo, tiny) sizes used only for specialty purposes. The small MATX board will only have two memory slots and room for four adapter cards, but it will fit in media center cases designed to look like stereo equipment. If you get a big case you can fit a full sized ATX board. Gigabit Ethernet is useful, particularly when you move large files from machine to machine in a home network. External SATA (eSATA) allows you to connect external disks to the computer at full speed. Integrated video is OK for running Office, but look for a DVI connector for modern flat panel screens. Otherwise, compare the adapter cards you want to install with the slots you have. Mainboards can have four PCI slots, but boards designed for running video games often have room for a second oversized video card and cut the PCI slots down to two.

Video

The video card will plug into the large PCI Express slot on the mainboard. Enthusiasts will spend more on the video card (or cards) than they do on the rest of the computer. Video cards can use more power than the rest of the system. This makes sense, however, because for the specialized type of computing they do, a video card can be 10 times faster than the CPU on the mainboard. Gamers want the most powerful card they can afford. Home "media center" users probably want a card that supports HDCP and can play High Definition TV recordings. Business users don't need any of this, and will be satisfied with the integrated video that comes on some inexpensive mainboards.

Things to look for in a Video card: Serious gamers already knew all this stuff and stopped reading long ago. You are therefore probably looking for integrated video or a single medium performance PCI Express video card. There are two main GPU chip makers: Nvidia and ATI. Since you are not looking to spend a few thousand dollars for the biggest and badest machine on the planet, the two vendors are approximately interchangeable. Minimally, you want video that supports DirectX 9 (Windows XP) and has some hardware support for decoding standard definition MPEG (DVD). If you read carefully, for the same money you can find integrated video or inexpensive adapters that will decode High Definition TV (broadcast and cable). In cards this means some type of ATI 1xxx (1600, 1900, 1950) GPU or an Nvidia 7xxx (7600, 7900) GPU. If you get 256 megabytes of memory, this card will be ideal for Vista. However, if you plan to add a Blu-Ray or HD-DVD drive to your system and view recorded high definition movies on a big screen display, then you need a display and adapter card that support "HDCP" and, to be safe, a GPU that can decode a format called "H.264" (generally the same ATI 1xxx or Nvidia 7xxx, but read the specs). To do everything except high performance gaming, expect the video card to cost $150 to $200. Vista supports DirectX 10, but at the start of 2007 the only cards that support this (Nvidia 88xx) start at $400. If you have only flat panel displays, the DVI connectors are much better than old analog connectors. A few cards support the smaller digital HDMI connector normally associated with flat panel TV sets.

Power Supply

The Power Supply is rated by the maximum amount of power it must provide to the rest of the computer. Most business systems will get along with 350 watts, but a system with four cores or high end video cards can require 500 watts or more. The Power Supply is the component most likely to fail sometime during the life of the computer. It may overheat or the cooling fan may fail. As it starts to fail the voltage levels go bad (the 12 volt wires may carry only 11 volts) and that can make the computer unstable and it will start to crash.

Things to look for in a Power Supply: I would say that you should read reviews and buy one from the company that has the best reputation for reliability, but even the best company produces the occasional bad unit. So look for a unit with two 12 volt "rails" instead of one, and one with a 120 mm fan will make less noise than one with 80 mm fans. Spend 10 minutes reading reviews at http://www.newegg.com/ and don't buy a real stinker that customers all hate. If you have a small case or one with a compartment for the Power Supply, watch out for units that are slightly larger than normal, especially if they have "modular cables" that plug into one end of the supply, because when you assemble everything the Power Supply may not fit. If you don't stock a spare Power Supply in your house, then know where to find a CompUSA or computer repair store where you can get one when you need it, or your computer may be down for a few days waiting for an internet vendor to ship one.

Disk

SATA is simpler and faster than the old parallel ATA. There is one high speed disk from WD called the "Raptor" that is at twice as fast as all other disks. Otherwise, you buy disks based on price, capacity, and reliability. Things to look for in Disk: First consider your case. A small case may have only room for one or at most two disks, so you may want to buy the biggest disk you can get. A large case can have room for 6 disks, and you can add buy rails that adapt the unused front 5.25" CD-sized slots to hold even more disks. Now if you look carefully at prices, you will see that two 250 gigabyte hard drives are often less expensive than one 500 gigabyte disk. A disk has movable "arms" that position somewhere on the surface to read or write data. Each disk has its own position. So if you are copying data from one disk to another the arms on each disk can remain positioned in one place, but if you process data from one file to another on the same disk, the arms move back and forth and the same processing can take 20 times longer than a two disk operation. So if you have room and are willing to think about optimizing your data layout, more small disks is better than fewer big disks.

All You Need is a Phillips Screwdriver

You can buy every part (except the CPU) from a dozen different vendors. There are only two CPU choices. Everything will fit together because there are standards. Lets build the system.

1. The Power Supply is a metal box with cables that dangle from it and connect to devices inside the case. You slide it into place and attach it to the back of the case with four Phillips screws (that come with the Power Supply).
2. The mainboard sits on screw holes on top of nine "standoffs" that keep the bottom of the board a quarter inch away from the metal of the case trey. Standoffs and the screws that attach the mainboard come with the case. In almost every case these are the same size screws as the ones that hold the Power Supply.

3. A modern power supply has a 24 pin connector that plugs into a slot on the mainboard. There is a second 4 pin connector. There is a latch on one side of each plug that attaches to a plastic notch on one side of the mainboard socket, but the plugs have shapes so they cannot be plugged in upside down.
4. The CPU drops into the socket and clamps in place. A cooling tower (heat sink and fan) clamps on top of the mounting assembly on the mainboard. Plug the fan into the little 3 pin power connector on the mainboard.
5. Plug memory into the memory slots. If they don't go in at first, you may be trying to plug them in backwards.
6. Plug the video card in the long PCI Express slot.
7. The hard disk and DVD drive connect to the case with four screws, typically two screws on each side. These screws also come with the case, but they are slightly smaller than the screws that hold the mainboard to the standoffs. There are only the two sizes of screws.
8. Now plug the long thin SATA cable to SATA socket number 1 on the mainboard and connect it to the back of the disk. There is an L shaped connector so it cannot go in wrong. Connect a power cable from the power supply to the back of the disk.
9. Now there is a block of pins on the mainboard and some little cables from the front panel of the machine. Typically you connect the power switch, power light, disk light, and speaker cables. There will be a diagram in the manual for the mainboard. The power and disk light connectors are the only things in the computer that you can plug in backwards. If either light does not go on, open the case later and flip the connector around.
10. Connect the monitor, keyboard, and mouse. Plug the power cable in the wall and turn the machine on. It is time to install an operating system.

The first time you do all this you may spend hours checking and rechecking everything. When you get used to it, the whole process can take as little as 20 minutes. On an assembly line, a worker probably builds a system in 3 minutes.

Carburetor or Cup Holders?

Back in the 1950's, before fuel economy and pollution controls, people judged a car by the power of its engine. Today, however, cars are sold to the mass market based on a quiet smooth ride, side air bags, a nice sound system, and Cup Holders.

There is a "hot rod" market for custom computers today. As with the automotive hot rod, the target audience for high performance computers are young males playing games. They have even borrowed a word from automotive customization, buying "modding" hardware for their systems. Cases have transparent panels and low heat internal lights to show off the electronics. The CPU is "overclocked" (run at a speed higher than that recommended by the manufacturer) and the extra heat is removed with exotic cooling systems. As with cars, this is a specialty market.

Maybe its the lower speed limits, or maybe the boomers are just getting older. Big engines are less important than they used to be. Some people even dream of zipping though town on a Segway. The same thing may happen with computers. The 55 to 65 miles per hour boundary for computers may correspond to 700 MHz to 1 GHz. That is fast enough to run Windows, browse the Web, read E-Mail, listen to MP3 files, and run all the Office programs. Faster speeds are only useful if you play computer games, convert video files, or run a server.

This is not a message that the computer makers want you to hear. It might suggest to people that they keep their old computer for another year rather than replacing it with a new model. However, technology continues to evolve across the board, and CPU may not be the most important thing. You didn't buy your last new car because the speed limit increased on the highway. Consider some other issues:

- *Power:* A few years ago a typical CPU used 100 to 120 watts of power. Today vendors build a version of their mainstream CPU chips that use only 65 watts (for two CPU cores!) and Intel makes specialty processors that can drop the power use as low as 10 watts. However, video cards can draw 200 watts each and high end gamers add a second power supply to their system just to power the video. If you can select your own components, and you do not happen to own your own electric company, then it will certainly be worth the $4 difference to buy a 65 watt processor than the 100 watt version of the same CPU. During the lifetime of the system you will save a lot more than $4 worth of electricity. If you buy a preassembled system from a vendor, they have no incentive to add $4 to the purchase cost of a system for a feature that most consumers are not smart enough to look for.
- *Noise:* The cheapest way to deal with the heat generated by the CPU, mainboard, and video card is to put a small fan on each device and run it at a high speed. This generates a lot of noise. For only a little more money one can carefully design the airflow, install larger metal radiators to spread the heat more widely, and run a few much larger fans at much lower speed. A quiet computer doesn't cost much more, and has a big effect on either your office or your living room.
- *Keyboard and Mouse:* The keyboard is the one part of the computer system that arguably has gotten worse over the years instead of better. When IBM first designed its personal computer, they used the same keyboard technology used in other IBM devices designed for full time professional use. Some people believe that the old "clicky key" IBM keyboards of the 1980's represented

the peak of technology. Today a "keyboard" is a no-cost item you can select on the Dell Web page, and replacement keyboards are sold in computer stores for $15. Compare this cost to the medical expenses of a repetitive stress injury. Fortunately, keyboards are interchangeable across systems, and a good one never breaks (although it doesn't improve if you spill pancake syrup into it). If you get a computer with a lousy keyboard, invest in a better one. Similarly, you can spend a few extra dollars getting a comfortable mouse and save your hand (although it is a lot easier to find mice shaped for right handed than left handed people).

- *Screens:* Size matters. Anybody reading this document wants some kind of LCD monitor. They come in two flavors. Devices sold as computer monitors have a limited brightness and tend to have high resolution on small screen sizes. Today the 19" monitor has become standard, but there are 20" and 24" monitors, some with wide screens. For a bit more you can buy an LCD TV. When sold as a TV, the screen is typically twice as bright as a computer monitor. TV panels (32" to 42") have resolutions of approximately 1280x768 or 1920x1080. A smaller 24" screen sold as a computer monitor will have resolutions of 1600x1200. Baby Boomers will discover that higher resolution isn't necessarily a good thing. While it makes photographs sharper, it also makes text too small to read comfortably.

High performance computers run games that appeal to the teenager. For the rest of us, a comfortable keyboard, easy to read screen, and quiet room may be more important.

The Q Bridge

In downtown New Haven, CT where I-91 meets I-95, the "Q Bridge" crosses the harbor area. It must be one of the hottest attractions in southern New England, because every morning and afternoon cars line up for miles to cross it. It defines the rush hour commute, and nothing that you do to the other roads or exits in West Haven or East Haven will materially speed things up.

Inside your computer there is an electronic version of the Q Bridge. Depending on the application, some component will become the choke point, and all the data bytes will line up waiting to get through. But while the real Q Bridge never changes, the PC choke point moves as you change use.

A Porche and a Yugo get caught in the backup at the same point in West Haven. Twenty minutes later they cross the bridge at the same time. It doesn't do any good to spend a lot of money on a fast car and a big engine if the limiting factor is traffic moving five miles an hour. Yet customers often select a server with a fast CPU, without first considering what the bottleneck will be.

If you play video games or edit video, then the speed of your computer depends on the speed of the CPU. If you record TV shows on your computer and then edit out undesirable material periodically inserted into the program, processing may be 10 times faster if you read from one disk and write to another than if you use a single disk. The performance of a database is typically determined by the amount of memory you have. Copying files from one machine to another depends on the network speed.

Summary and Links to Topics

Each main point will be summarized here. The summary is then linked to a secondary page where you can learn more about a particular topic. Readers are urged to follow each such link to get the full story, but you can make your own decision.

Circuit Size, Voltage, and Heat

All the electronic components of a computer follow some basic design principles. To make a computer circuit operate faster, you have to make it smaller. Smaller circuits can run at a higher speed, using less voltage, and producing less heat. By analogy, if the only question is 0 or 1, empty or full, then it is much faster and requires much less work to fill a shotglass with water than to fill a bathtub. These four factors (size, speed, voltage, and heat) are always in balance. You can increase speed on a given chip by increasing the voltage, but that produces more heat and requires more expensive cooling.

Clocks and Cycles

Components of a computer (the CPU, memory, adapter cards) are coordinated by a "clock" signal measured in Megahertz (millions of ticks per second) or Gigahertz (billions of ticks per second). Generally we say that speeding up the clock makes the computer run faster, but that is slightly misleading. The clock tells all the components when they should all be done with their previous operation and when they should begin the next step. Components all run at whatever speed their design permits. If all the components can complete their longest operation with lots of time to spare, then there is room to speed up the clock, shorten the periods, and get more work done in the same amount of time. Set the clock too fast ("overclock") and it ticks before one of the components is quite done with its last operation. Then the system crashes.

CPU, Instructions

A computer chip can do simple arithmetic, compare numbers, and move numbers around in memory. Everything else, from word processing to browsing the Web, is done by programs that use those basic instructions. CPUs get faster in three ways. First, better designs can do the simple operations faster. Second, better design can do as many as six simple operations at the same time in different areas of the CPU. Thirdly, since a lot of time is lost if the CPU has to wait for data from slower memory, techniques that reduce the memory wait time appear to speed up the CPU.

Hyperthreading and Multi-Core

The processing steps of a computer program can be decomposed into a set of independent "threads". To display a Web page, the Browser has to read in the page itself plus each individual file representing the pictures and ads displayed within the page. Then the text has to be arranged on the page and each picture has to be decompressed. Finally, the page has to be arranged and displayed on the screen. Each of these operations can be assigned to a thread. If a computer has (or appears to have) two CPUs, Windows will assign a separate thread to each processor and the computer will process two different streams of data at the same time. No matter how fast Intel makes its chip, a modern CPU spends 50% or more of its time waiting for data to arrive from main memory. This is only getting worse, because CPU speed increases much more quickly than memory speed. A larger cache provides some help. Another idea, however, is for the CPU to have some way to switch from the instruction and thread that is blocked waiting for data to another thread that is ready to execute. This is the idea behind "Hyperthreading". Each CPU pretends to be two processors. The OS assigns a thread to each pretend processor. When one thread is blocked waiting for data, the CPU can switch over to the other thread and get more work done.

Memory and "Burst" Speed

Technology has been applied to increase memory speed only when it can be done without reducing size or increasing cost. Current mass market designs favor Double Data Rate SDRAM. When a CPU instruction requires data from memory, it presents the address and then has to wait several cycles. Once the first block of data has been located by the memory hardware, the 32 bytes immediately surrounding the address can also be transferred in a "burst" of activity. DDR memory transfers the data at twice the ordinary speed of the memory bus by transferring bytes on both the tick and the tock of the clock.

The Mainboard (Motherboard)

The mainboard contains slots for the CPU, memory, and I/O devices. In current designs, one chip called the Northbridge sits between and connects the three high speed devices: CPU, memory, and AGP video port. It is then connected to a second chip called the Southbridge that provides logic for all the slow speed devices: the keyboard, mouse, modem port, printer port, IDE controller, PCI, USB, and any other devices.

Hard Disks and CD Drives

Apple adopted an industry standard technology called SCSI for its Macintosh computers. It was a standard that applied to desktops, servers, and even mainframe computers. PC makers, however, followed a path of tricks and gimmicks to design the lowest cost disk attachment. The simplest possible electronic interface was a chip that duplicated exactly the mainboard I/O bus available at the time. A simple 40 wire cable connected this chip to logic chips on the disk. The mainboard bus had been introduced on the IBM PC AT in 1985, so the disk connection became knows as AT Attachment or "ATA". It is also popularly known as "IDE" but some manufacturer claimed that as a trademark barring its use as an official name. Then a dozen years passed, and each year the chips got twice as smart as the year before. ATA evolved from an 8 MHz connection to a 133 MHz connection and became smart enough to handle other types of devices. However, the physical connectors and programming interface had to build on and remain compatible with an idea that some engineers developed to build the lowest cost possible interface based on the primitive electronics available at that moment in time. Today computers are transitioning to a new simpler and higher speed interface called Serial ATA.

Video and Monitors

The video adapter requires higher data transfer speeds than any other device. While the disks and network plug into the PCI bus or Southbridge mainboard chip, the video adapter is connected at high speed to the CPU and memory. For a decade, the video connector has been an AGP slot rated by speed (2x, 4x, or 8x). In the last few months, Intel has begun to offer a new slot design called PCI-Express that on paper can operate four times as fast as the fastest AGP slot. However, at the currently available technology, no video adapter card requires that much extra speed.

PCI and PCI Express

For a decade starting in 1985, PC adapter cards all plugged into the "ISA" bus. Then Intel came up with a better, faster PCI bus, which has dominated the last decade. The good news from such a long period of stability is that there are lots of fast, cheap, compatible adapter cards to upgrade your computer with an extra disk controller or a better audio system. The bad news is that ten years are up and it is time for a new I/O bus. The only part of PCI-Express that is similar to the old PCI bus is its name. It provides a much higher speed in a much smaller socket. However, although there are a few PCI-Express video cards available, there are no PCI-Express adapter cards. Systems will continue to need PCI slots for at least the next few years.

Ethernet

An Ethernet adapter card connects an office PC to the corporate network. At home it connects several computers to each other for file sharing, and it allows all the computers to share a single high speed Ethernet connection over a DSL or Cable modem.

USB and FireWire

To connect external devices (printers, scanners, disks, CD or DVD writers) to a computer there are two popular connection standards. USB 2.0 and FireWire provide full speed support for large numbers and a broad variety of external plug and play devices.

Introduction to Computer Programs & Programming

A computer program is a collection of instructions that describe a task, or set of tasks, to be carried out by a computer.

The term *computer program* may refer to source code, written in a programming language, or to the executable form of this code. Computer programs are also known as *software, applications programs, system software* or simply *programs*.

The source code of most computer programs consists of a list of instructions that explicitly implement an algorithm (known as an imperative programming style); in another form (known as declarative programming) the characteristics of the required information are specified and the method used to obtain the results, if any, is left to the platform.

Computer programs are often written by people known as computer programmers, but may also be generated by other programs.

Terminology

Commercial computer programs aimed at end-users are commonly referred to as application software by the computer industry, as these programs are focused on the functionality of what the computer is being used for (its application), as opposed to being focused on system-level functionality (for example, as the Windows operating system software is). In practice, colloquially, both application software and system software may correctly be referred to as *programs*, as may be the more esoteric firmware—software firmly built into an embedded system. Programs that execute on the hardware are *a set of instructions* in a format understandable by the instruction set of the computer's main processor, which cause specific other instructions to execute or perform a simple computation like addition. But computers process millions of such per second and that is the program, the sequence of instructions strung together such that when executed, they do something useful, and usually repeatable and reliable.

For differences in the usage of the spellings *program* and *programme*, see American and British English spelling differences.

Program Execution

A computer program is loaded into memory (usually by the operating system) and then executed ("run"), instruction by instruction, until termination, either with success or through software or hardware error.

Before a computer can execute any sort of program (including the operating system, itself a program) the computer hardware must be initialized. This initialization is done in modern PCs by a piece of software stored on programmable memory chips installed by the manufacturer, called the BIOS. The BIOS will attempt to initialize the boot sequence, making the computer ready for higher-level program execution.

Programs Vs. Data

The executable form of a program (that is, usually object code) is often treated as being different from the data the program operates on. In some cases this distinction is blurred with programs creating, or modifying, data, which is subsequently executed as part of the same program (this is a common occurrence for programs written in Lisp), see self-modifying code.

Programming

A program is likely to contain a variety of data structures and a variety of different algorithms to operate on them.

Creating a computer program is the iterative process of writing new source code or modifying existing source code, followed by testing, analyzing and refining this code. A person who practices this skill is referred to as a computer programmer or software developer. The sometimes lengthy process of computer programming is now referred to as "software development" or software engineering. The latter becoming more popular due to the increasing maturity of the discipline.

Two other forms of modern day approaches are team programming where each member of the group has equal say in the development process except for one person who guides the group through discrepancies. These groups tend to be around 10 people to keep the group manageable. The second form is referred to as "peer programming" or pair programming.

Trivia

The world's shortest useful program is usually agreed upon to be the utility cont/rerun used on the old operating system CP/M. It was 2 bytes long (JMP 100), jumping to the start position of the program that had previously been run and so restarting the program, in memory, without loading it from the much slower disks of the 1980's.

According to the International Obfuscated C Code Contest, the world's smallest "program" consisted of a file containing zero bytes, which when run output zero bytes to the screen (also making it the world's smallest self-replicating program). This "program" was qualified as such only due to a flaw in the language of the contest rules, which were soon after modified to require the program to be greater than zero bytes.

Ada Lovelace wrote a set of notes specifying in complete detail a method for calculating Bernoulli numbers with the Analytical Engine described by Charles Babbage. This is recognized as the world's first computer program and she is recognised as the world's first computer programmer by historians.

Components

At the heart of a digital computer is the central processing unit (CPU) which performs the logical and arithmetical operations on streams of numbers as controlled by a "program" which is itself a stream of numbers. The CPU has privileged access to the computer memory which can be thought of a large number of pigeonholes in which numbers can be stored and later retrieved. The CPU can also send and receive numbers from a set of input-output ports. These act as gateways from the CPU to other devices, such as keyboards, displays, printers, disks, analogue I/O devices, or network connections to other computers. Collectively these external devices are called peripherals. The CPU can select a peripheral and control its operation by sending appropriate number streams to the port to which it is connected.

Working with Numbers

The CPU can only manipulate numbers, so all pieces of information that we want the computer to manipulate must be stored as numbers. Such information includes: numerical values, keyboard or display characters, arithmetic operations, the addresses of memory locations, the addresses of ports, and even the possible set of operations that the CPU can perform. All these must be stored as numbers.

The philosophy of numbers for anything and everything is the basis of the power of the computer. When the CPU does a calculation and generates a numerical answer, that number need not be just the size of something, but it can be a character, a memory address or even the next operation of the CPU. It is like a calculator doing a calculation and coming up with a result that meant the calculator should next perform the square root calculation. i.e. producing a result that was an operation, not just a value. Computers have programs, called compilers, which produce numerical results which are nothing less than other programs.

Machine Code

The essential operations of a CPU are actually very limited. A CPU can

1. Load from memory. Given a memory address, retrieve the number stored at that address.
2. Store to memory. Given a memory address and a number, store the number at that address.
3. Load from port. Given a port address, get a number from the port.
4. Store to port. Given a port address and a number, send the number to the port.
5. Arithmetic. Given one or more numbers, perform some basic arithmetic, such as add, subtract, multiply, divide and other logical operations such as less-than, equals or greater than. Result is another number.

6. Test. Given a number, change the status of the CPU according to properties of the number, e.g. equal to zero, less than zero
7. Conditional jump. Depending on the status of the CPU jump to a different list of operations stored in the memory. For example, if the last test operation returned "equal to zero", then start executing the instructions at memory location 1000, otherwise start executing the instructions at memory location 2000.

Software Hierarchy

The lowest level description of a computer program is just the sequence of numbers which encode the basic CPU operations. This level is called machine code. Machine code is specific to a given CPU manufacturer and often specific to a given model type (for example the Pentium CPU has some codes not used by earlier 8086 CPUs). Machine code is very difficult for a human to read or write, so the lowest level of programming done by humans is in a language in which each basic operation is given a mnemonic code called assembly language. Humans can read and write using assembly language which can be converted into machine code using an assembler. Assembly language, like machine code is often specific to a particular CPU manufacturer or model.

The development of high-level languages meant that humans could program using a formalism that was closer to their conceptual models of the data being manipulated: characters, real numbers, lists, tables or database records. Such languages are easier for humans to learn and to use, and furthermore they tend to be available across different computers; with each manufacturer supplying a conversion program between the high-level language and the assembly language for their CPU. Examples of high-level languages are Fortran, Pascal, Basic, C, C++, Java and MATLAB.

Modern computer systems need to deal with complex tasks involving multiple programs interacting simultaneously, and the sharing of access to files on disks, to network resources and displays. To cope with these demands, manufacturers supply operating systems (e.g. Windows, Linux), which are themselves programs which help the user operate the computer and run other application programs. Often individual application programs need to work together to achieve an objective: for example a word processing application might call on a drawing package or on a spreadsheet program to do some specific processing within a document. This idea of combining programs is called scripting, where the specifications for which programs are to be executed and how they should interact is specified in a script.

Programming Language

A programming language is an artificial language that can be used to control the behavior of a machine, particularly a computer. Programming languages, like human languages, are defined through the use of syntactic and semantic rules, to determine structure and meaning respectively.

Programming languages are used to facilitate communication about the task of organizing and manipulating information, and to express algorithms precisely. Some authors restrict the term "programming language" to those languages that can express *all* possible algorithms; sometimes the term "computer language" is used for more limited artificial languages.

Thousands of different programming languages have been created, and new ones are created every year.

Definitions

Authors disagree on the precise definition, but traits often considered important requirements and objectives of the language to be characterized as a *programming language*:

- *Function:* A programming language is a language used to write computer programs, which instruct a computer to perform some kind of computation, and/or organize the flow of control between external devices (such as a printer, a robot, or any peripheral).
- *Target:* Programming languages differ from natural languages in that natural languages are only used for interaction between people, while programming languages also allow humans to communicate instructions to machines. In some cases, programming languages are used by one program or machine to program another; PostScript source code, for example, is frequently generated programmatically to control a computer printer or display.
- *Constructs:* Programming languages may contain constructs for defining and manipulating data structures or for controlling the flow of execution.
- *Expressive power:* The theory of computation classifies languages by the computations they can express (see Chomsky hierarchy). All Turing complete languages can implement the same set of algorithms. ANSI/ISO SQL and Charity are examples of languages that are not Turing complete yet often called programming languages.

Non-computational languages, such as markup languages like HTML or formal grammars like BNF, are usually not considered programming languages. It is a usual approach to embed a programming language into the non-computational (host) language, to express templates for the host language.

Purpose

A prominent purpose of programming languages is to provide instructions to a computer. As such, programming languages differ from most other forms of human expression in that they require a greater degree of precision and completeness. When using a natural language to communicate with other people, human authors and speakers can be ambiguous and make small errors, and still expect their intent to be understood. However, computers do exactly what they are told to do, and cannot understand the code the programmer "intended" to write. The combination of the language definition, the program, and the program's inputs must fully specify the external behavior that occurs when the program is executed.

Many languages have been designed from scratch, altered to meet new needs, combined with other languages, and eventually fallen into disuse. Although there have been attempts to design one "universal" computer language that serves all purposes, all of them have failed to be accepted in this role. The need for diverse computer languages arises from the diversity of contexts in which languages are used:

- Programs range from tiny scripts written by individual hobbyists to huge systems written by hundreds of programmers.
- Programmers range in expertise from novices who need simplicity above all else, to experts who may be comfortable with considerable complexity.
- Programs must balance speed, size, and simplicity on systems ranging from microcontrollers to supercomputers.
- Programs may be written once and not change for generations, or they may undergo nearly constant modification.
- Finally, programmers may simply differ in their tastes: they may be accustomed to discussing problems and expressing them in a particular language.

One common trend in the development of programming languages has been to add more ability to solve problems using a higher level of abstraction. The earliest programming languages were tied very closely to the underlying hardware of the computer. As new programming languages have developed, features have been added that let programmers express ideas that are more removed from simple translation into underlying hardware instructions. Because programmers are less tied to the needs of the computer, their programs can do more computing with less effort from the programmer. This lets them write more programs in the same amount of time.

Natural language processors have been proposed as a way to eliminate the need for a specialized language for programming. However, this goal remains distant and its benefits are open to debate. Edsger Dijkstra took the position that the use of a formal language is essential to prevent the introduction of meaningless constructs, and dismissed natural language programming as "foolish." Alan Perlis was similarly dismissive of the idea.

Elements

Syntax

A programming language's surface form is known as its syntax. Most programming languages are purely textual; they use sequences of text including words, numbers, and punctuation, much like written natural languages. On the other hand, there are some programming languages which are more graphical in nature, using spatial relationships between symbols to specify a program.

The syntax of a language describes the possible combinations of symbols that form a syntactically correct program. The meaning given to a combination of symbols is handled by semantics. Since most languages are textual, this article discusses textual syntax.

Programming language syntax is usually defined using a combination of regular expressions (for lexical structure) and Backus-Naur Form (for grammatical structure). Below is a simple grammar, based on Lisp:

```
expression ::= atom | list
atom ::= number | symbol
number ::= [+-]?['0'-'9']+
symbol ::= ['A'-'Z''a'-'z'].*
list ::= '(' expression* ')'
```

This grammar specifies the following:

- an *expression* is either an *atom* or a *list*;
- an *atom* is either a *number* or a *symbol*;
- a *number* is an unbroken sequence of one or more decimal digits, optionally preceded by a plus or minus sign;
- a *symbol* is a letter followed by zero or more of any characters (excluding whitespace); and
- a *list* is a matched pair of parentheses, with zero or more *expressions* inside it.

The following are examples of well-formed token sequences in this grammar: '12345', '()', '(a b c232 (1))'

Not all syntactically correct programs are semantically correct. Many syntactically correct programs are nonetheless ill-formed, per the language's rules; and may (depending on the language specification and the soundness of the implementation) result in an error on translation or execution. In some cases, such programs may exhibit undefined behavior. Even when a program is well-defined within a language, it may still have a meaning that is not intended by the person who wrote it.

Using natural language as an example, it may not be possible to assign a meaning to a grammatically correct sentence or the sentence may be false:

- "Colorless green ideas sleep furiously." is grammatically well-formed but has no generally accepted meaning.
- "John is a married bachelor." is grammatically well-formed but expresses a meaning that cannot be true.

The following C language fragment is syntactically correct, but performs an operation that is not semantically defined (because p is a null pointer, the operations p->real and p->im have no meaning):

```
complex *p = NULL;
complex abs_p = sqrt (p->real * p->real + p->im * p->im);
```

Type System

A type system defines how a programming language classifies values and expressions into *types*, how it can manipulate those types and how they interact. This generally includes a description of the data structures that can be constructed in the language. The design and study of type systems using formal mathematics is known as *type theory*.

Internally, all data in modern digital computers are stored simply as zeros or ones (binary). The data typically represent information in the real world such as names, bank accounts and measurements, so the low-level binary data are organized by programming languages into these high-level concepts as data types. There are also more abstract types whose purpose is just to warn the programmer about semantically meaningless statements or verify safety properties of programs.

Languages can be classified with respect to their type systems.

Typed Vs Untyped Languages

A language is *typed* if operations defined for one data type cannot be performed on values of another data type. For example, "this text between the quotes" is a string. In most programming languages, dividing a number by a string has no meaning. Most modern programming languages will therefore reject any program attempting to perform such an operation. In some languages, the meaningless operation will be detected when the program is compiled ("static" type checking), and rejected by the compiler, while in others, it will be detected when the program is run ("dynamic" type checking), resulting in a runtime exception.

By opposition, an *untyped language*, such as most assembly languages, allows any operation to be performed on any data type. High-level languages which are untyped include BCPL and some varieties of Forth.

In practice, while few languages are considered typed from the point of view of type theory (verifying or rejecting *all* operations), most modern languages offer a degree of typing. Many production languages provide means to bypass or subvert the type system.

Static Vs Dynamic Typing

In *static typing* all expressions have their types determined prior to the program being run (typically at compile-time). For example, 1 and (2+2) are integer expressions; they cannot be passed to a function that expects a string, or stored in a variable that is defined to hold dates.

Statically-typed languages can be *manifestly typed* or *type-inferred*. In the first case, the programmer must explicitly write types at certain textual positions (for example, at variable declarations). In the second case, the compiler *infers* the types of expressions and declarations based on context. Most mainstream statically-typed languages, such as C++ and Java, are manifestly typed. Complete type inference has traditionally been associated with less mainstream languages, such as Haskell and ML. However, many manifestly typed languages support partial type inference; for example, Java and C# both infer types in certain limited cases.

Dynamic typing, also called latent typing, determines the type-safety of operations at runtime; in other words, types are associated with runtime values rather than textual expressions. As with type-inferred languages, dynamically typed languages do not require the programmer to write explicit type annotations on expressions. Among other things, this may permit a single variable to refer to values of different types at different points in the program execution. However, type errors cannot be automatically detected until a piece of code is actually executed, making debugging more difficult. Lisp, JavaScript, and Python are dynamically typed.

Weak and Strong

Weak typing allows a value of one type to be treated as another, for example treating a string as a number. This can occasionally be useful, but it can also cause bugs; such languages are often termed *unsafe*. C, C++, and most assembly languages are often described as weakly typed.

Strong typing prevents the above. Attempting to mix types raises an error. Strongly-typed languages are often termed *type-safe* or *safe*, but they do not make bugs impossible. Ada, Python, and ML are strongly typed.

An alternative definition for "weakly typed" refers to languages, such as Perl, Javascript, and C++ which permit a large number of implicit type conversions; Perl in particular can be characterized as a dynamically typed programming language in which type checking can take place at runtime. This capability is often useful, but occasionally dangerous; as it would permit operations whose objects can change type on demand.

Strong and *static* are generally considered orthogonal concepts, but usage in the literature differs. Some use the term *strongly typed* to mean *strongly, statically typed*, or, even more confusingly, to mean simply *statically typed*. Thus C has been called both strongly typed and weakly, statically typed.

Execution Semantics

Once data has been specified, the machine must be instructed to perform operations on the data. The *execution semantics* of a language defines how and when the various constructs of a language should produce a program behavior.

For example, the semantics may define the strategy by which expressions are evaluated to values, or the manner in which control structures conditionally execute statements.

Core Library

Most programming languages have an associated core library (sometimes known as the 'Standard library', especially if it is included as part of the published language standard), which is conventionally made available by all implementations of the language. Core libraries typically include definitions for commonly used algorithms, data structures, and mechanisms for input and output. A language's core library is often treated as part of the language by its users, although the designers may have treated it as a separate entity. Many language specifications define a core that must be made available in all implementations, and in the case of standardized languages this core library may be required. The line between a language and its core library therefore differs from language to language. Indeed, some languages are designed so that the meanings of certain syntactic constructs cannot even be described without referring to the core library. For example, in Java, a string literal is defined as an instance of the java.lang.String class; similarly, in Smalltalk, an anonymous function expression (a "block") constructs an instance of the library's BlockContext class. Conversely, Scheme contains multiple coherent subsets that suffice to construct the rest of the language as library macros, and so the language designers do not even bother to say which portions of the language must be implemented as language constructs, and which must be implemented as parts of a library.

Practice

A language's designers and users must construct a number of artifacts that govern and enable the practice of programming. The most important of these artifacts are the language *specification* and *implementation*.

Specification

The specification of a programming language is intended to provide a definition that language users and implementors can use to interpret the behavior of programs when reading their source code.

A programming language specification can take several forms, including the following:

- An explicit definition of the syntax and semantics of the language. While syntax is commonly specified using a formal grammar, semantic definitions may be written in natural language (e.g., the C language), or a formal semantics (e.g., the Standard ML and Scheme specifications).
- A description of the behavior of a translator for the language (e.g., the C++ and Fortran). The syntax and semantics of the language has to be inferred from this description, which may be written in natural or a formal language.
- A *model* implementation, sometimes written in the language being specified (e.g., Prolog). The syntax and semantics of the language are explicit in the behavior of the model implementation.

Implementation

An implementation of a programming language provides a way to execute that program on one or more configurations of hardware and software. There are, broadly, two approaches to programming language implementation: *compilation* and *interpretation*. It is generally possible to implement a language using both techniques.

The output of a compiler may be executed by hardware or a program called an interpreter. In some implementations that make use of the interpreter approach there is no distinct boundary between compiling and interpreting. For instance, some implementations of the BASIC programming language compile and then execute the source a line at a time.

Programs that are executed directly on the hardware usually run several orders of magnitude faster than those that are interpreted in software.

One technique for improving the performance of interpreted programs is just-in-time compilation. Here the virtual machine monitors which sequences of bytecode are frequently executed and translates them to machine code for direct execution on the hardware.

History

Early Developments

The first programming languages predate the modern computer. The 19th century had "programmable" looms and player piano scrolls which implemented, what are today recognized as examples of, domain-specific programming languages. By the beginning of the twentieth century, punch cards encoded data and directed mechanical processing. In the 1930s and 1940s, the formalisms of Alonzo Church's lambda calculus and Alan Turing's Turing machines provided mathematical abstractions for expressing algorithms; the lambda calculus remains influential in language design.

In the 1940s, the first electrically powered digital computers were created. The computers of the early 1950s, notably the UNIVAC I and the IBM 701 used machine language programs. First generation machine language programming was quickly superseded by a second generation of programming languages known as Assembly languages. Later in the 1950s, assembly language programming, which had evolved to include the use of macro instructions, was followed by the development of three modern programming languages: FORTRAN, LISP, and COBOL. Updated versions of all of these are still in general use, and importantly, each has strongly influenced the development of later languages. At the end of the 1950s, the language formalized as Algol 60 was introduced, and most modern programming languages are, in many respects, descendants of Algol. The format and use of the early programming languages was heavily influenced by the constraints of the interface.

Refinement

The period from the 1960s to the late 1970s brought the development of the major language paradigms now in use, though many aspects were refinements of ideas in the very first Third-generation programming languages:

- APL introduced *array programming* and influenced functional programming.
- In the 1960s, Simula was the first language designed to support *object-oriented programming*; in the mid-1970s, Smalltalk followed with the first "purely" object-oriented language.
- C was developed between 1969 and 1973 as a *systems programming* language, and remains popular.
- Prolog, designed in 1972, was the first *logic programming* language.
- In 1978, ML built a polymorphic type system on top of Lisp, pioneering *statically typed functional programming* languages.

Each of these languages spawned an entire family of descendants, and most modern languages count at least one of them in their ancestry.

The 1960s and 1970s also saw considerable debate over the merits of *structured programming*, and whether programming languages should be designed to support it. Edsger Dijkstra, in a famous 1968 letter published in the Communications of the ACM, argued that GOTO statements should be eliminated from all "higher level" programming languages.

The 1960s and 1970s also saw expansion of techniques that reduced the footprint of a program as well as improved productivity of the programmer and user. The card deck for an early 4GL was a lot smaller for the same functionality expressed in a 3GL deck.

Consolidation and Growth

The 1980s were years of relative consolidation. C++ combined object-oriented and systems programming. The United States government standardized Ada, a systems programming language intended for use by defense contractors. In Japan and elsewhere, vast sums were spent investigating so-called "fifth generation" languages that incorporated logic programming constructs. The functional languages community moved to standardize ML and Lisp. Rather than inventing new paradigms, all of these movements elaborated upon the ideas invented in the previous decade.

One important trend in language design during the 1980s was an increased focus on programming for large-scale systems through the use of *modules*, or large-scale organizational units of code. Modula-2, Ada, and ML all developed notable module systems in the 1980s, although other languages, such as PL/I, already had extensive support for modular programming. Module systems were often wedded to generic programming constructs.

The rapid growth of the Internet in the mid-1990's created opportunities for new languages. Perl, originally a Unix scripting tool first released in 1987, became common in dynamic Web sites. Java came to be used for server-side programming. These developments were not fundamentally novel, rather they were refinements to existing languages and paradigms, and largely based on the C family of programming languages.

Programming language evolution continues, in both industry and research. Current directions include security and reliability verification, new kinds of modularity (mixins, delegates, aspects), and database integration.

The 4GLs are examples of languages which are domain-specific, such as SQL, which manipulates and returns sets of data rather than the scalar values which are canonical to most programming languages. Perl, for example, with its 'here document' can hold multiple 4GL programs, as well as multiple JavaScript programs, in part of its own perl code and use variable interpolation in the 'here document' to support multi-language programming.

Taxonomies

There is no overarching classification scheme for programming languages. A given programming language does not usually have a single ancestor language. Languages commonly arise by combining the elements of several predecessor languages with new ideas in circulation at the time [*citation needed*]. Ideas that originate in one language will diffuse throughout a family of related languages, and then leap suddenly across familial gaps to appear in an entirely different family.

The task is further complicated by the fact that languages can be classified along multiple axes. For example, Java is both an object-oriented language (because it encourages object-oriented organization) and a concurrent language (because it contains built-in constructs for running multiple threads in parallel). Python is an object-oriented scripting language.

In broad strokes, programming languages divide into *programming paradigms* and a classification by *intended domain of use*. Paradigms include procedural programming, object-oriented programming, functional programming, and logic programming; some languages are hybrids of paradigms or multi-paradigmatic. An assembly language is not so much a paradigm as a direct model of an underlying machine architecture. By purpose, programming languages might be considered general purpose, system programming languages, scripting languages, domain-specific languages, or concurrent/distributed languages (or a combination of these).[*citation needed*] Some general purpose languages were designed largely with educational goals.

A programming language can be classified by its position in the Chomsky hierarchy. For example, the Thue programming language can recognize or define Type-0 languages in the Chomsky hierarchy. Most programming languages are Type-2 languages and obey context-free grammars.

A programming language may also be classified by factors unrelated to programming paradigm. For instance, most programming languages use English language keywords, while a minority do not. Other languages may be classified as being esoteric or not.

Computer Systems: An Overview

The word *computer* refers to a system composed of many components. A computer system has both *hardware* and *software* components. This chapter discusses these components.

Hardware and Software

In thinking about *Monsters, Inc.*, you are thinking about something conceptual. It is intangible. You can't grab it and throw it against a wall, or break it in half, or weight it on a scale. It does not have a physical existence. You might record *Monsters,*

Inc. on a VCR tape. The tape is physical, but the movie is conceptual. When you speak of the movie, you usually mean the conceptual movie, not a particular tape that has a record of it. Sometimes the phrase "intellectual material" is used for movies, TV programs, novels, music, and computer programs. Sometimes the word "software" is used for the same purpose, although usually "software" refers to computer programs and data. The TV set you used to watch *Monsters, Inc.* is tangible. It has a physical existence. You can weigh it on a scale, you can throw it against a wall, you can break it in half, you can pound it to pieces with a hammer (and your grades will improve if you do). TV sets are useful because they combine the tangible (the TV set itself) and the intangible (TV programs). Computer systems are useful in the same way—they combine tangible components called *hardware* and conceptual components called *software*.

Components of a Computer System

Software is *stored* on hardware such as hard disks or tape. *Monsters, Inc.* can be recorded on a VCR tape. But the computer program (and the TV episode) is intangible. It is not the physical storage medium. The hardware components of a computer system are the electronic and mechanical parts.

The software components of a computer system are the intangible parts: the data and the computer programs.

The major hardware components of a computer system are:

- Processor
- Main memory
- Secondary memory
- Input devices
- Output devices

You probably have a computer in front of you. The processor, main memory, and secondary memory devices are inside the *systems unit*. This is the metal box that is sometimes called "the computer." The monitor (the TV-like screen) is an output device.

Hardware Components

The terms "input" and "output" say if data flow into or out of the systems unit. The picture shows the major hardware components of a computer system.

The bus is a group of wires on the main circuit board of the computer. It is a pathway for data flowing between components. Most devices are connected to the bus through a controller which coordinates the activities of the device and the bus.

The processor is an electronic device about a one inch square, covered in plastic. Inside the square is an even smaller square of silicon containing millions of tiny electrical parts. A processor may contain 100 million transistors. The processor is the "brain" of the computer system. It does the fundamental computing within the system, and directly or indirectly controls all the other components.

The processor is sometimes called the Central Processing Unit or CPU. A particular computer will have a particular type of processor, such as a Pentium or a SPARC chip. (processors are often called "chips.")

Memory

The processor is the brain of the computer. All fundamental computing takes place in the processor. Other components contribute to the computation (by doing such things as moving data in and out of the processor), but the processor is where the fundamental action takes place.

Unlike a human brain, which combines memory with processing power, a computer processor has very little memory. It must rely on other components to hold data and programs and to save results. The memory in a computer system is of two fundamental types:

- **Main memory:**

— very closely connected to the processor.

— the contents are quickly and easily changed.

— holds the programs and data that the processor is actively working with.

— interacts with the processor millions of times per second.

- **Secondary memory:**

— connected to main memory through the bus and a controller.

— the contents are easily changed, but this is very slow compared to main memory.

— used for long-term storage of programs and data.

— The processor only occasionally interacts with secondary memory.

Main memory is where programs and data are kept when the processor is actively using them. When programs and data become active, they are copied from secondary memory into main memory where the processor can interact with them. A copy remains in secondary memory. Main memory is intimately connected to the processor, so moving instructions from the program and data into and out of the processor is very fast. Main memory is sometimes called RAM. RAM stands for Random Access Memory. "Random" means that the memory cells can be accessed in any order.

When people say that a computer has "128 megabytes of RAM" they are talking about how big its main memory is. One megabyte of memory is enough to hold approximately one million characters of a word processing document. (There will be more about bytes and megabytes later on in these notes.) Nothing permanent is kept in main memory. Sometimes data are placed in main memory for just a few seconds; only as long as they are needed.

Secondary Memory

Secondary memory is where programs and data are kept on a long-term basis. Common secondary storage devices are the hard disk and floppy disks.

- The hard disk has enormous storage capacity compared to main memory.
- The hard disk is usually contained in the systems unit of a computer.
- The hard disk is used for long-term storage of programs and data.
- Data and programs on the hard disk are organized into files—named sections of the disk.

A hard disk might have a storage capacity of 40 gigabytes. This is about 300 times the amount of storage in main memory (assuming 128 megabytes of main memory.) However, a hard disk is very slow compared to main memory. The reason for having two types of storage is this contrast:

Primary memory	*Secondary memory*
1. Fast	1. Slow
2. Expensive	2. Cheap
3. Low capacity	3. Large capacity
4. Connects directly to the processor	4. Not connected directly to the processor

Floppy disks are mostly used for transferring software between computer systems and for casual backup of software. They have low capacity, and are very, very slow compared to other storage devices.

Input and Output Devices

Input and output devices allow the computer system to interact with the outside world by moving data *into* and *out of* the system. An *input device* is used to bring data into the system. Some input devices are:

- Keyboard
- Mouse
- Microphone

- Bar code reader
- Graphics tablet

An *output device* is used to send data out of the system. Some output devices are:

- Monitor
- Printer
- Speaker

Input/output devices are usually called I/O devices. They are directly connected to an electronic module inside the systems unit called a device controller. For example, the speakers of a multimedia computer system are directly connected to a device controller called an audio card (such as a Soundblaster), which in turn is connected to the rest of the system.

Sometimes secondary memory devices like the hard disk are called I/O devices (because they move data in and out of main memory.) What counts as an I/O device depends on context. To a user, an I/O device is something outside of the system box. To a programmer, everything outside of the processor and main memory looks like an I/O devices. To an engineer working on the design of a processor, everything outside of the processor is an I/O device.

Software

A computer that is dedicated to running a program that controls another device is an embedded system. An embedded system is usually embedded inside the device it controls. Usually they run just one program that is permanently kept in a special kind of main memory called ROM (for Read Only Memory). More processor chips are sold per year for embedded systems than for all other purposes. Software is the programs and data that a computer uses. Software is kept on some hardware device such as a hard disk or floppy disk, but it itself is intangible. Say that you have a floppy disk with a program saved on it. Now say that you erase the program from the disk. The atoms and molecules of the disk are the same ones as before, but now the program is "gone." The intangible software has been removed without removing anything tangible.

Software consists of both *programs* and *data*. Programs are lists of instructions for the processor. Data can be any information that a program needs: character data, numerical data, image data, audio data, and countless other types. The distinction between programs and data is not as clear-cut as you might think, however.

Fundamental Idea: Both programs and data are saved in computer memory in the same way. The electronics of computer memory (both main memory and secondary memory) make no distinction between programs and data.

The insight that both programs and data can be saved using the same electronic methods is one of the most important ideas in computer science. Computer systems can use their memory for whatever needs arise.

Types of Programs

There are two categories of programs. Application programs (usually called just "applications") are programs that people use to get their work done. Computers exist because people want to run these programs. Systems programs keep all the hardware and software running together smoothly. The difference between "application program" and "system program" is fuzzy. Often it is more a matter of marketing than of logic.

Application Programs	*Systems Programs*
• Word processors	• Operating system.
• Game programs	• Networking system.
• Spreadsheets	• Database system.
• Data base systems	• Programming language software.
• Graphics programs	• Web site server.
• Web browsers	• Data backup.

The most important systems program is the operating system. The operating system is always present when the computer is running. It coordinates the operation of all the hardware and software components of the computer system. The operating system is responsible for starting application programs running and finding the resources that they need. When an application program is running, the operating system manages the details of the hardware for it. For example, when you type characters on the keyboard, the operating system determines which application program they are intended for and does the work of getting them there.

Modern operating systems usually come with a user interface that enables users to easily interact with application programs (and with the operating system itself) by using windows, buttons, menus, icons, the mouse, and the keyboard. Examples of operating systems are Unix, Windows 98, Windows NT, Linux, Solaris, and System 7.

Operating Systems

The operating system is a complex collection of many programs concerned with keeping the hardware and software components of a computer system coordinated and functioning. It is like a shop keeper who keeps a shop in order by attending to customers, handling supplier deliveries, stocking the shelves, doing the bookkeeping, and so on.

The operating system is software; the same hardware can be used with many different operating systems (although only one at a time.) Sometimes the operating system on a computer becomes corrupted (perhaps because of a computer virus) and must be tediously re-installed. Until it is up and running again, other programs will not be available.

Starting a Program

When a computer is started up, the hardware will automatically load the operating system and start it running. This process is called booting. The reason for this odd term is that the operating system is itself involved in getting itself running—a process that is like someone "pulling themselves up by their bootstraps." Once the operating system is running, it is used to start up any other program.

Here is a (simplified) list of what happens when the user (you) starts up an application. Assume that the operating system (OS) is already running.

1. The user asks to run an application.
   - This could be done by clicking on an icon, making a menu choice, or other means.
2. The OS determines the name of the application.
3. The OS finds the section of the hard disk where the application program and its data are stored.
4. The OS finds an unused section of main memory that is large enough for the application.
5. The OS makes a copy of the application and its data in that section of main memory.
   - The software on the hard disk is unchanged; a *copy* of it has been made in main memory
6. The OS sets up resources for the application.
7. Finally, the OS starts the application running.

As the application runs, the OS is there in the background managing resources, doing input and output for the application, and keeping everything else running.

Networks

A computer network consists of two or more computers connected so that they can exchange data and programs. When a computer is a member of a network, the programs it runs and the data it uses can be on the hard disk of some other computer on the network. In business and industrial settings, most computers are on a network. The operating system that runs on a networked computer must manage its share of the network (along with managing all its other responsibilities.) The operating system is able to find programs and data that are stored on other network computers, and copy them into its own main memory.

In a local-area network only a few dozen computers are connected together, usually all located within the same building. Each computer has a network address that the other computers use to access it. Usually the computers share a printer. There may be an especially powerful computer called a server whose hard disk holds all the application programs and data that the other computers are expected to need.

Each computer in a network has a network interface card in its systems unit. This is an input/output device that sends and receives data over cables. The network interface cards of computers on a network are connected together with cables.

Wide-Area Networks

Large organizations need to connect many more computers than can be handled with a local area network. A wide-area network can connect thousands of computers together over great distances. The long distance connections are made by using fiber optic lines, telephone lines, microwave communications, and satellite communications. Each computer in the network has a network address (as with local-area networks) to uniquely identify it.

Wide-area networks use a variety of special hardware to manage the flow of data. When two computers share data, this hardware makes it appear that the two computers are connected together directly. In reality, there may be dozens of network devices between the two computers.

All these devices use the same method for dealing with data. Without a common method of dealing with data, a large network would become a hopeless muddle. An agreement about how to represent and transmit data over a network is called a protocol. Usually large networks use a protocol called TCP/IP (for transmission control protocol/internet protocol.)

The Internet consists of many wide-area networks that have been connected together to form one huge worldwide network. Even on this huge network, each computer must have a unique network address, much like each telephone in the world has a unique telephone number (if you include the country code and area code.)

World Wide Web

Remember that important idea (discussed several pages back):

> Fundamental Idea: Both programs and data are saved in computer memory in the same way. The electronics of computer memory (both main memory and secondary memory) make no distinction between programs and data.

Communications equipment makes no distinction between programs and data, either. It is all information as far as it is concerned, and all information is transmitted the same way. The Internet is like a worldwide package delivery service. It is concerned with moving packages from one address to another, without concern about what is in the packages.

The Internet provides the hardware and the information transmission protocols for the World-Wide Web. Data intended for the Web is transmitted over the Internet just like any data. What makes Web data special is that it is intended for Web browsers (such as the one you are probably looking at.) A browser is a program that can read Web pages and display them in a nicely formatted way.

A Web page is a package of data that contains information on how it is to be displayed on a monitor. This information is given using a language called Hypertext Markup Language (HTML). If you want to see an example of what this looks like, left-click on View in your browser, then left-click on Page Source. After you are done viewing, click on the close button in the upper right corner (the button marked with X).

Hyperlinks

One Web page is connected to another with a hyperlink. If you have been reading these notes over the Web, you have been linking between Web pages by using hyperlinks.

A web browser (such as Netscape Navigator) usually displays a hyperlink in a distinguishing color (usually blue.) When you click on it, the browser asks the operating system of the computer to get a particular Web page from another computer connected to the Internet. The Web page to get is specified with a uniform resource locator URL. A URL specifies both the computer (among all the Internet computers in the world) and the exact Web page on that computer.

Compression in Hardware and Software

Although MPEG is now a widely accepted standard and, in its original and evolved forms, is likely to shape the future of all kinds of multimedia delivery, it is only one basis for compression and remains a very demanding one, particularly at the level of playback. In other words, while it is relatively easy and cheap to create MPEG files from analogue video masters, it is still hard to find the computing power in personal computers to decompress them for end users to enjoy. What is needed in most computers is a special set of chips designed to do the grunt work on behalf of the host computer. Currently such cards cost a few hundred dollars to buy and are far from easy to install and use. In other words, they remain gadgets for enthusiasts rather than the mainstream of media and information users.

None of this matters if you are selling multimedia via a proprietary set-top box or stand-alone multimedia player. While these are computers of a kind, they are not general purpose devices. They are specifically created to decode and deliver digital satellite broadcasts, for example, or to play videos or video-rich interactive games from a compact disc. In other words, these devices are proprietary systems customised to a particular commercial purpose. The creators of these systems can ensure that they handle MPEG decompression by simply supplying them with the appropriate chips built into them. In the case of general purpose computers, by contrast, specialised chips sets add cost to the product to deliver a facility only a few at present may wish to use. In other words, a computer manufacturer is likely to include MPEG decompression as a routine feature of its products only when full screen digital video is a routine prerequisite of the desktop computing market.

From a multimedia publisher's point of view, MPEG can be utilised in products only if the means to decompress the MPEG files is readily and widely available. In the world of digital television, the commercial battleground is initially focused on the struggle to get appropriate MPEG-based set-top boxes into enough living rooms to create a market for digitally compressed television. In compact disc multimedia, proprietary systems such as CD-I (compact disc interactive) offer on-board MPEG decoding but need to establish a large enough installed base of users to make the video software market viable. Multimedia aimed at personal computers — usually delivered by another form of compact disc usually called PC CD-ROM (compact disc read only memory)—can address a very large potential audience but with very few machines equipped with the special chips needed to make sense of MPEG.

But MPEG is really important only where full screen, full motion performance is crucial. In applications where something less is tolerable, MPEG and its problems can be laid aside in favour of less demanding solutions. For partial screen, reduced frame rate video specialised software engines are now widely available which allow most PC users to decompress video files without having to modify their hardware in any way. The best known of these programs are Microsoft's Video for Windows, Apple's QuickTime and Intel's Indeo. They all offer the same prospect for a multimedia publisher—the opportunity to sell the razor with the razor blade. In other words, a publisher can include video files in its product compressed by one or other of the proprietary software schemes. To make the video accessible to customers, the publisher adds the decompression software to the multimedia product. When the customer installs the product for the first time, the decompression software automatically transfers itself to the host machine's hard disk and waits, ready to go to work as soon as any video files are accessed. From a commercial publishing point of view, the advantages of this kind of software-based scheme are obvious. You do not have to rely on users to have special chips inside their computers. You do not even require them to acquire the particular decompression software needed for your offerings because you give it to them as a part of your publication. And the whole process is transparent to your customers and therefore is friendly as well as efficient. But the disadvantages are obvious as soon as the video files are retrieved. While software schemes can sometimes deliver excellent results, to do so they must rely on a very powerful PC. These are, of course, increasingly becoming the norm, but publishers still have to direct their publishing towards some kind of common denominator and right now that usually means configuring the playback software to run on fairly modest machines. This in turn means that the resulting video tends to be of relatively poor quality, covering only a small window on the screen. Good enough—if the video is chosen carefully—to enrich a consumer title but far from adequate if video is to be the centrepiece of the product.

It is interesting to speculate on how this situation might change. Mainstream computers are getting increasingly powerful. Even home users are buying top end machines. In 1994, for example, in the United States more Pentium-based machines were sold for use in homes than in the large corporations for which they were originally expected to be destined. As this trend gathers pace, the common denominator of software-based video performance will be capable of working the software systems very hard indeed. Video windows will get larger, frame rates will rise to full motion and colour resolution will improve dramatically. At the level of PC multimedia, there is now a contest growing between hardware-based solutions to MPEG and the ability to decompress good quality video in software. Indeed, it seems likely that by 1988 or 1999, mainstream host machines those PCs in widespread and common use — will be powerful enough to decompress MPEG in software alone without any special chip set to support them. At the same time, MPEG will anyway become cheap and compact enough to include routinely on the motherboards of PCs or within the silicon of their central processors whether purchasers particularly want it or not. One way or another, therefore, MPEG is well on its way to becoming a widely used standard for handling digital video within PCs.

This means that whatever may happen in detail at a technical level, the direction is clear. We are moving towards a widely available facility to include full screen video on computer screens as naturally as we have come to expect it from television screens. Perhaps even more pressing a question now is how well such compression schemes will allow the easy transfer of video over computer networks relying on ubiquitous but inherently narrowband links such as telephone lines.

How Does a Compact Disc Work?

While we do not want to delve into underlying technology, it is worth giving at least a brief account of how a compact disc works. We have already touched on the basic principles when we examined the rise of the video disc and we cover similar ground again here but with the profound distinction that while video disc technology is an analogue media system, the compact disc is digital.

The old fashioned gramophone is a useful—and appropriate—metaphor for understanding compact disc technology. We are all familiar with the vinyl recordings of music that, in past years, were the underpinnings of a huge world wide leisure industry. The single, long spiral groove on a record carries in it mechanical wiggles that make a styles tracking through it vibrate. Gramophones work by spinning the plastic disc at a constant number of revolutions every minute while the styles passes along the entire length of the groove. The vibrations in the styles are converted into a tiny electrical signal which changes in intensity with the changes in the vibration. This rapidly varying signal is cleaned up, amplified and converted into audible sound via a speaker. In this way, the mechanical variations in the surface of the disc are preserved through a number of key stages. First, they are detected and converted into a sympathetically varying electrical current. Then the variations are amplified. Finally, they are turned back into mechanical variations in the form of oscilations in the air which we interpret as sound. Throughout, the information—whether a symphony by Beethoven or a gig by Blur—is being conveyed by a continuously varying quantity. In other words, the entire system is analogue.

In a compact disc, the information is coded in a similar way. A stylus runs through a spiral track and detects mechanical variations in it. But compact disc media need to carry a lot of information so we have to make two important modifications. First, we change the plane of the spiral track so that the mechanical fluctuation in it is vertical not horizontal. Second, we use a tiny laser as the stylus and use this to detect mechanical variations.

If you look at a compact disc you will be struck by the beautiful silvered appearance it shares with video disc. Like the video disc, its surface is covered by a highly reflective aluminium layer that allows a laser beam to bounce off its surface with practically no loss of intensity. What you cannot see easily with the naked eye is the single, tightly packed spiral track covering the surface. Typically, the spiral is packed to within 1.6 millionths of a metre of itself. If it was peeled off the disc and laid out in a straight line, it would measure nearly 3 miles in length.

If you looked at the track through a powerful microscope you would see the key to CD technology. Unlike a gramophone record, which has wiggles in the side of its track, here you would see variations in the floor. A series of minute pits are etched into the surface. In other words, if we imagine the track on a vinyl record as a meandering river whose banks wander from side to side, the compact disc's track is more like a steep and smooth-sided canyon with a bumpy floor along which the stylus hurtles.

A major advantage of using a stylus made of light is that it makes no physical contact with the surface of the disc. This means that neither the stylus nor the disc can ever wear out. Also, because a laser can be focused with pinpoint accuracy, it is possible to coat the surface of the disc with a tough, clear plastic. This protects the disc from dust and scratches while allowing the laser beam to penetrate and focus on the 'floor' of the information carrying track. As the beam sweeps along the floor it identifies the presence of the pits in the silvered substrate by the drop in reflectivity they cause. The fluctuations in the reflected laser beam are read at the head of the stylus as 'pit', 'no pit'. Two states: there or not there. On, off. Zero, one. In other words, binary code—the language of computers. So compact discs carry information in digital form, packed tightly in the single spiral track of a 12-centimetre diameter silver disc.

Unlike the video disc, what is being measured is not the length of the pits—the constantly varying value which gives video disc its analogue character—but merely whether or not a pit is there. This means the pits can be very small and a huge number can be carried in the 3 miles of track. In fact, translated into the measure of computer memory, a single compact disc can carry about 650 megabytes (65 million bytes) of information. Even today when magnetic hard disks are commonly offering hundreds of megabytes, this is a formidable amount of capacity. In 1985, when compact discs were first used to store computer data rather than digital music, a single megabyte of hard disk storage in a computer was substantial. So the 650 megabyte capacity of what became known as a compact disc 'read only memory' (CD-ROM) was nothing less than staggering. Even more striking than the sheer capacity was the low cost per byte of the medium. No other medium—either then or now — has even come close to the economy of optical storage. Depending on the numbers manufactured at one time, a compact disc can cost between about 50 pence and £1 sterling to produce. On this basis, each byte can cost as little as 0.00001 pence—orders of magnitude cheaper than solid state memory and vastly cheaper than any existing magnetic medium.

The Evolution of CD-ROM Markets

When CD-ROM appeared in 1985, it was a solo initiative by Philips and Sony, the creators of the compact disc, backed extensively by the computer hardware industry which scented a new line of product development to exploit Unlike its predecessor, the blockbuster entertainment medium, compact disc audio, CD-ROM was a medium firmly designed for computer users, requiring expensive new disk drives to be connected to desktop PCs to let users access the digital data stored on the discs. The step from CD-audio to CD-ROM had not been a simple one. Although in both cases, the information on the discs consists entirely of bits, in the case of CD-ROM the bits had to be stored in a specific and standard fashion so that all kinds of computers could get at the information. In other words, while CD-audio demanded a physical standardisation, CD-ROM required a deeper level of standardisation affecting the logical structure of the data on the discs. The process of agreeing the standardisation is an epic story in itself but it resolved itself when-in the late 1980s-the International Standards Organisation agreed a universal specification for all CD-ROM discs, designated as ISO 9660. From a publishing point of view, this was a crucial step because standardisation meant that all discs produced to ISO 9660 could be played of all CD-ROM drives manufactured to the same standard. Although, in the very early stages after the launch of CD-ROM, there were some maverick formats around, very quickly the industry settled into conformity and, to all intents, ISO 9660 became the defining specification for all forms of CD-ROM technology.

From the point of view of market development, however, the key factor was the rather arcane and isolated nature of early CD-ROM technology. It was overtly computeresque, demanding computer equipment for play-back and computer expertise from its users to make sense of the processes of loading and running the disc and manipulating the search and retrieval software either embodied on the CD-ROM or supplied separately. Viewed the present day, these characteristics of CD-ROM may not look particularly arcane or isolating. But in the mid-1980s, the personal computer was only just staggering to its feet as a pervasive and powerful new tool. Computers were expensive, unfriendly and largely unknown devices-except in those niches where access to electronic information was at least a partially established tradition. In other words, the original market for CD-ROM, and its commercial centre of gravity for many years afterwards, was those sectors in which computers were widely used and where electronic information was appreciated. This translates into professional information users-predominantly public and corporate librarians, academics and, slowly at first but gathering pace, managers in corporations with direct access to PCs.

This tight focus in terms of the users of CD-ROM did not mean there was any serious early volume in the market. David Worlock, now head of the London-based consultancy Electronic Publishing Services, recalls that he was one of the first British publishers to issue a CD-ROM title when in late 1985 he released a high priced CD-ROM database of legal information. He still reckons it was one of the boldest strokes in the history of publishing because, at the time, there were only about two CD-ROM drives in the UK-and one of those was on his desk! In other words, the early CD-ROM publishing industry suffered from a serious 'chicken and egg' problem. Publishers were reluctant to release tides because there were no CD-ROM drives in the hands of potential customers. Potential customers were reluctant to purchase drives because there were no titles to buy. It is not surprising, therefore, that one of the first CD-ROM directories, published as a thin, loose leaf folder by the London firm, TFPL, recorded only about 50 commercially available titles at the end of 1986. At that time, worldwide, the installed base of drives was about 6,500. At the end of 1994, by contrast, the same directory was a weighty tome with over 1,000 pages, printed on near bible paper to reduce bulk, containing details of around 8,000 titles. The worldwide base of drives, meanwhile, had grown to about 25 million.

As the 'chicken and egg' problem was gradually cracked by innovative, bold and both non-commercial and uncommercial publishers issuing CD-ROM titles in the teeth of a market of first a few hundred, then a few thousand drives, the initial commercial orientation remained fixed. The CD-ROM publishing industry addressed a market of desktop computer users. This meant professional, academic and-increasingly as the 1980s wore on-corporate users. The business model for this kind of publishing unsurprisingly followed the already well-established one familiar in online database markets. Very expensive products were sold to the few organisations who could afford to buy them. It was a high priced, low volume business with titles typically selling a few hundred copies at prices which varied from a few hundred to a few thousand pounds sterling. The products themselves were predominantly textual databases, often offcuts of some of the massive online databases that had been hosted for years on huge centralised computer systems and sold expensively via networks to small groups of academics and professionals with a strong 'need to have' motivation to pay the high cost of access.

Two basic pricing models emerged and are still commonplace for professional CD-ROM products. The simplest and most obvious is a straightforward one-off sale, usually-because of the market orientation-at very high price. More commonly, however, subscriptions are sold which give users access to a series of discs in the course of the year embodying monthly, quarterly or six-monthly updates of the underlying information. Clearly, the frequency of updates depends on how important the currency of the information is for users. Because of the technical and physical problems of creating updates on short timescales — except, of course, an extravagant premium prices-monthly updates are generally the most frequent. The idea of selling users 'access' in this pricing model is a key idea. Selling access means not selling the physical discs. In other words, all the customer purchases by paying a subscription is a licence which permits them-under certain stated conditions — to have access to the information stored on the discs. This is a vital point for publishers because it makes it easy for them to craft careful licence agreements to protect the valuable content of the discs from illicit use. A signature on such an agreement, and an unambiguous link between vendor and purchaser through such a licence contract, make it easier for publishers to enforce limitations on use and take sanctions against downright criminality. The most obvious dangers are resale of data, downloading and illegal copying, placing the CD-ROM on a network to enable large numbers of simultaneous users to benefit from the purchase of a single disc and-increasingly important as cheap, plug-and-play recordable CD-ROM systems become widely available-the illegal duplication of discs either for internal use by the purchaser's corporation or for straightforward commercial piracy. Subscription-based selling also ensures publishers get the outdated discs back from customers when a new version is issued. Early on, publishers found that if they did not do this a 'black market' trade rapidly emerged in 'old discs' resold by original purchasers at discounted prices to others who were less fussy about how up to date the products were

While these pricing models ensure potential profitability and-through subscriptions-reasonable control over high-value content, the marketing of tides has the attraction of requiring no radically new strategies, Traditional, print-on-paper specialists, for example, with experience of publishing for defined vertical markets can simply apply their established marketing approach. The key-as ever-lies in knowing the market and reaching it as cost effectively as possible with suitable product information and pricing deals. As with all electronic product, of course, CD-ROM databases cannot be subjected to the 'flick test', beloved by purchasers of books and periodicals. To gain a sense of the value of a major CD-ROM title, potential purchasers usually need to use or sample it. This has the fairly obvious message, that publishers of these kinds of products must either arrange a try-before-you-buy system or provide a money-back guarantee of some kind. So, in addition to conventional direct marketing strategies commonplace in vertical market sectors, publishers commonly dispense sample discs and run 'satisfaction guaranteed' schemes. The other minor divergence from traditional marketing practices — although based on established models-is the use of specialist distributors who offer a wide range of products from different publishers via catalogue mailings and- in the case of high added value reselling — also run road-show-style demonstrations of product. The main headline for this genre of product, however, is that-with some obvious, minor exceptions-it is business as usual for vertical market publishers. The products may be silver discs rather than print-on-paper books or journals but selling them is not a lot different. The more fundamental challenge is not marketing strategy but product design. Here, traditional publishers are at a serious disadvantage. There is a common assumption that publishers-especially specialist publishers -know their market-place. In a sense, of course, they do or they would not survive long. But publishing is not yet about understanding what people do with the information printed inside books. It is purely about trying to get as many people to buy the books in the first place. Now, to most outsiders, it would seem obvious that the two are connected. But the publishing industry has thrived on being good at packaging and marketing content while remaining ignorant of the detailed way in which their customers use-or may wish to use-the information and knowledge contained in the products. Publishers have a broad brush understanding that certain categories of people like books and periodicals on particular themes. But they are blissfully unaware of how much of what they publish is actually read, the detailed way in which information is utilised, shared or analysed by customers and what people do with the information when (and if) they access it. A book sale is a book sale. That is the only statistic a publisher cares about. If a book sells a lot of copies, it is successful and the publisher has shown flair. If it sells badly, the publisher has demonstrated bad judgement and an editor-probably-gets fired. The perfect example is Stephen Hawking's remarkable but largely impenetrable *A Brief History of Time*. It must be the only book to have sold in its millions because people wanted to possess the book rather than read it. The publishers, however, are far from concerned whether anyone was actually able to get beyond page 2 because — for whatever reason-the volume and rights sales were phenomenal. Understandably, this was the only arbiter of success that the publisher required. CD-ROM publishing for professional, corporate markets and academic markets is different— in spades.

Users of high priced CD-ROM tides do not want copies of discs to leave on coffee tables to impress guests. Neither do they buy them because they are fashionable or because they think that by physically owning the discs they possess the knowledge they contain. Instead, they buy discs because of specific, operational needs. And they are not merely seeking the raw information. The powerful appeal of CD-ROM in this market which makes it possible to sustain such high prices, is the power of the technology to offer rapid search and analysis features, added values that deliver high levels of benefit either because they save time or because they help users make more accurate decisions or both. This suggests two things. First, with such a high procedural element behind the customer's requirements, it is possible to draw up a clear, detailed blueprint for any particular product. In other words, publishers can literally define exactly what a customer needs and then design into the software on the CD-ROM an answer that addresses those needs. Second, while it is possible to blueprint products in principle, in practice it demands that publishers get to know their customers very well-something that they have been notably reluctant to do in the past. It is not surprising therefore that some of the most successful CD-ROM publishers for vertical markets have not come from the print-on-paper industry but from electronically based sectors such as online. There is a clear message here. For corporate, professional, academic markets-and in any form of electronic publishing aimed at such sectors-publishing success lies in defining the customers' needs and designing a functionality into the products that addresses them.

REFERENCES

Antoniazzi, S. and e. al. "A Methodology for Control-Dominated Systems Codesign", in Third International Workshop on Hardware/Software Codesign. 1994. Grenoble, France: IEEE Computer Society Press, 2-9.

Auguin, M. and e. al. "Towards a Multi-Formalism Framework for Architectural Synthesis: The ASAR Project", in Third International Workshop on Hardware/Software Codesign. 1994. Grenoble, France: IEEE Computer Society Press, 25-32.

Auguin, M., F. Boeri, and C. Carriere. "Automatic Exploration of VLIW Processor Architectures from a Designer's Experience Based Specification", in Third International Workshop on Hardware/Software Codesign. 1994. Grenoble, France: IEEE Computer Society Press, 108- 115.

Barros, E. and A. Sampaio. "Towards Provably Correct Hardware/Software Partitioning Using Occam", in Third International Workshop on Hardware/Software Codesign. 1994. Grenoble, France: IEEE Computer Society Press, 210-217.

Brage, J.P. and J. Madsen. "A Codesign Case Study in Computer Graphics", in Third International Workshop on Hardware/Software Codesign. 1994. Grenoble, France: IEEE Computer Society Press, 132- 139.

Buck, J.T. "A Dynamic Dataflow Model Suitable for Efficient Mixed Hardware and Software Implementations of DSP Applications", in Third International Workshop on Hardware/Software Codesign. 1994. Grenoble, France: IEEE Computer Society Press, 165-172.

Calvez, J.P. and D. Isidoro. "A Codesign Experience with the MCSE Methology", in Third International Workshop on Hardware/Software Codesign. 1994. Grenoble, France: IEEE Computer Society Press, 140- 147.

Caron, O. and e. all. "New architectures for smart cards: the OCEAN approach", in Third International Workshop on Hardware/Software Codesign. 1994. Grenoble, France: IEEE Computer Society Press, 148- 155.

Coelho, C.N. and e. all. "Redesigning Hardware-Software Systems", in Third International Workshop on Hardware/Software Codesign. 1994. Grenoble, France: IEEE Computer Society Press, 116-123.

D'Ambrosio, J.G. and X. Hu. "Configuration-Level Hardware/Software Partitioning for Real-Time Embedded Systems", in Third International Workshop on Hardware/Software Codesign. 1994. Grenoble, France: IEEE Computer Society Press, 34-41.

Deegener, M. and S.A. Huss. "Hardware/Software Co-Design in the MuSE Environment", in Third International Workshop on Hardware/Software Codesign. 1994. Grenoble, France: IEEE Computer Society Press, 195-202.

Eles, P., Z. Peng, and A. Doboli. "VHDL System-Level Specification und Partitioning in a Hardware/Software Co-Synthesis Environment", in Third International Workshop on Hardware/Software Codesign. 1994. Grenoble, France: IEEE Computer Society Press, 49-55.

Green, P., P. Rushton, and R. Beggs. "An Example of Applying the Codesgn Method MOOSE", in Third International Workshop on Hardware/Software Codesign. 1994. Grenoble, France: IEEE Computer Society Press, 65-72.

Gupta, R.K. and G.D. Micheli. "Constrained Software Generation for Hardware-Software Systems", in Third International Workshop on Hardware/Software Codesign. 1994. Grenoble, France: IEEE Computer Society Press, 56-63.

Herrmann, D., J. Henkel, and R. Ernst. "An Approach to the Adaptation of Estimated Cost Parameters in the COSYMA System", in Third International Workshop on Hardware/Software Codesign. 1994. Grenoble, France: IEEE Computer Society Press, 100-107.

Hoeg, F., N. Mellergaard, and J. Staunstrup. "The Priority Queue as an Example of Hardware/Software Codesign", in Third International Workshop on Hardware/Software Codesign. 1994. Grenoble, France: IEEE Computer Society Press, 81-88.

Ismail, T.B., M. Abid, and A. Jerraya. "COSMOS: A CoDesign Approach for Communicating Systems", in Third International Workshop on Hardware/Software Codesign. 1994. Grenoble, France: IEEE Computer Society Press, 17-24.

Kalavade, A. and E.A. Lee. "A Global Criticality/Local Phase Driven Algorithm for the Constrained Hardware/Software Partitioning Problem", in Third International Workshop on Hardware/Software Codesign. 1994. Grenoble, France: IEEE Computer Society Press, 42- 48.

Koch, G., U. Kebschull, and W. Rosenstiel. "A Prototyping Environment for Hardware/ Software Codesign in the COBRA Project", in Third International Workshop on Hardware/ Software Codesign. 1994. Grenoble, France: IEEE Computer Society Press, 10-16.

Lavagno, L. and e. all. "A Case Study in Computer-Aided Codesign of Embedded Controllers", in Third International Workshop on Hardware/Software Codesign. 1994. Grenoble, France: IEEE Computer Society Press, 220-224.

Luk, W. and T. Wu. "Towards a Declarative Framework for Hardware-Software Codesign", in Third International Workshop on Hardware/Software Codesign. 1994. Grenoble, France: IEEE Computer Society Press, 181-188.

Ravn, A.P. and J. Staunstrup. "Interface Models", in Third International Workshop on Hardware/Software Codesign. 1994. Grenoble, France: IEEE Computer Society Press, 157-164.

Sutarwala, S. and P. Paulin. "Flexible Modeling Environment for Embedded Systems Design", in Third International Workshop on Hardware/Software Codesign. 1994. Grenoble, France: IEEE Computer Society Press, 124-130.

Voss, M. and e. all. "Towards a Theory for Hardware/Software Codesign", in Third International Workshop on Hardware/Software Codesign. 1994. Grenoble, France: IEEE Computer Society Press, 173- 180.

Wilberg, J., P. Camposano, and W. Rosenstiel. "Design Flow for Hardware/Software Cosynthesis of a Video Compression System", in Third International Workshop on Hardware/ Software Codesign. 1994. Grenoble, France: IEEE Computer Society Press, 73-80.

Wilson, J. "Hardware/Software Selected Cycle Solution", in Third International Workshop on Hardware/Software Codesign. 1994. Grenoble, France: IEEE Computer Society Press, 190-194.

Wolf, W. and e. all. "TigerSwitch: A Case Study in Embedded Computing System Design", in Third International Workshop on Hardware/Software Codesign. 1994. Grenoble, France: IEEE Computer Society Press, 89-96.

4

Internet, E-mail, Network System and Computer Security

Internet: An Introductory Overview

The internet is made up of millions of computers linked together around the world in such a way that information can be sent from any computer to any other 24 hours a day. These computers can be in homes, schools, universities, government departments, or businesses small and large. They can be any type of computer and be single personal computers or workstations on a school or a company network. The internet is often described as 'a network of networks' because all the smaller networks of organisations are linked together into the one giant network called the internet. All computers are pretty much equal once connected to the internet, the only difference will be the speed of the connection which is dependent on your Internet Service Provider and your own modem. The internet has developed a very strong community base where information, software and expert advice are freely shared and for this reason users have developed a very strong protective stance on freedom of speech, freedom from commercial interests, netiquette and unsuitable material on the web. nThere are so many things you can do and participate in once connected to the internet. They include using a range of services to communicate and share information and things quickly and inexpensively with tens of millions of people, both young and old and from diverse cultures around the world. For example:

- You'll be able to keep in touch and send things to colleagues and friends using electronic mail, internet telephone, keyboard chat and video conferencing.
- You can also tap into thousands of databases, libraries and newsgroups around the world to gather information on any topics of interest for work or recreation. The information can be in the form of text, pictures or even video material.
- This means you can stay up to date with news, sports, weather and any

current affairs around the world with information updated daily, hourly or instantly.

- You can also locate and download computer software and other products that are available in cyberspace
- You can listen to sounds and music, and watch digital movies,
- There are also a growing number of interactive multimedia games and educational tools.

And as well as using the Internet for receiving things you will be able to publish information about your school or hobbies. Although it may seem like a new idea, the net has actually been around for over 40 years. It all began in the US during the Cold War, as a university experiment in military communications. By linking lots of computers together in a network, rather than serially (in a straight line), the Pentagon thought that in the event of a nuclear attack on the US it was unlikely that the entire network would be damaged, and therefore they would still be able to send and receive intelligence. At first each computer was physically linked by cable to the next computer, but this approach has obvious limitations, which led to the development of networks utilizing the telephone system. Predictably, people found that nuclear strike or not, they could talk to each other using this computer network, and some university students started using this network to do their homework together. It seems a natural human characteristic to want to communicate, and once people realized that they could talk to other people via this computer network they began to demand access, although initially the users were only from the university and government sectors. But more and more people could see the potential of computer networks, and various community groups developed networks separate from the official networks for the use of their local communities. The sum of all these various local, regional and national networks is the Internet as we experience it today, an ever expanding network of people, computers and information coming together in ways the Pentagon never dreamed of 40 years ago. So what began as an exercise in military paranoia has become a method of global communication. Cyberspace" is a term coined by William Gibson in his fantasy novel *Neuromancer* to describe the "world" of computers, and the society that gathers around them. Gibson's fantasy of a world of connected computers has moved into a present reality in the form of the Internet. In cyberspace people "exist" in the ether—you meet them electronically, in a disembodied, faceless form. Sometimes people use the words Internet and World Wide Web (WWW) synonymously but they are different. The WWW is a component of the Internet that presents information in a graphical interface. You can think of the WWW as the illustrated version of the Internet. It began in the late 1980's when physicist Dr. Berners-Lee wrote a small computer program for his own personal use. This program allowed pages, within his computer, to be linked together using keywords. It soon became possible to link documents in different computers, as long as they were connected to the Internet. The document formatting language used to link documents is called HTML (Hypertext Markup Language.) The Web remained primarily text based until 1992. Two events occurred that year that forever changed the way the Web looked. Marc Andreesen developed a new computer program called the NCSA Mosaic and gave it away! The NCSA Mosaic was the first Web browser. The browser made it easier to access the different Web sites that had started to appear. Soon Web sites contained more than just text, they also had sound and video files. The development of the WWW has been the catalyst for the popularity of the internet and is also the easiest part of the internet to use. We now have Internet Chat, Discussion Groups, Internet Phone capabilities, Video conferencing, News Groups, Interactive Multimedia, Games and so much more. TCP/IP is a communications protocol used to transfer digital data around the internet. TCP and IP were developed by a Department of Defense (DOD) research project to connect different networks designed by different vendors into a network of networks (the "Internet"). TCP/IP is often referred to as the 'internet protocol'. As with all communications protocols, TCP/IP is composed of layers:

IP - is responsible for moving packet of data from node to node. IP forwards each packet based on a four byte destination address (the IP number). The Internet authorities assign ranges of numbers to different organizations. The organizations assign groups of their numbers to departments. IP operates on gateway machines that move data from department to organization to region and then around the world.

TCP - is responsible for verifying the correct delivery of data from client to server. Data can be lost in the intermediate network. TCP adds support to detect errors or lost data and to trigger retransmission until the data is correctly and completely received.

Sockets - is a name given to the package of subroutines that provide access to TCP/IP on most systems.

Exploring the Web

In order to explore the web you will need a special piece of software known as a web browser. The two most commonly used web browsers are Netscape Navigator and Internet Explorer. They both operate in a similar manner using menus and buttons to help you navigate around the web. You can try these Webhints for some specific help with using your browser or see What To Expect for an explanation of the major functions of the browser. If you are using Netscape try this Tutorial Don't be overwhelmed by Cyberspace! Feeling lost is normal and should be anticipated. Much like journeying to a foreign country you know there are many things to see and do, but everything at first will seem so—well, foreign. When you first arrive, you'll have trouble reading the street signs. You'll get lost. And don't be timid! As you travel the Net, your computer may freeze, your screen may erupt into a mass of gibberish. The Net and your computer are hardier than you think, so relax. You can't break the Net!

If something goes wrong, try again. If nothing else, you can always restart your computer.

Finally, a warning—this territory is addictive and there is so much to see and do. It can become a fantastic time-sink. Hours can slip by, people can come and go, and you'll be locked into the Internet. Happy Surfing! On any web page you'll normally find text, images and hyperlinks. Hyperlinks allow you to move from page to page just by clicking on them with your mouse. Effectively a hyperlink can take you to pages on the same computer or other computers all around the world. Text hyperlinks will normally be differentiated from the rest of the document by a different color or underlined. Images can also be hyperlinked but are sometimes a little more difficult to tell immediately if they are hyperlinked, except that for any hyperlinks, whether it be from text or an image, when your mouse is over the hyperlink it will change from an arrow to a hand, letting you know if you click then, you will move to a new web page or a new part of the current web page, or even to audio and video files that you click on in the same way to hear or see them. When you have visited a link and return to the page you accessed it from, most times the link will change color allowing you to see which links you have already visited on that page which is helpful when you are looking through a long list of links. The operation of the web relies mainly on these hyperlinks as its means of linking resources from a range of locations. A web page can have many hyperlinks to other web pages sitting on web servers all around the world. When you select an item on a web page by clicking on it with your mouse, a copy of that item will be retrieved by your browser. You don't actually see this movement, only the document or image appearing on your screen. Sometimes images and programs can take some time to travel down the telephone to your computer. This is one of the greatest bug bears of the WWW. All we can do though in the interim is be patient, and wait for internet connections to be made faster. Now you can simply browse the web going from link to link but you may not find the information you want. The search button on your web browser will take you to a site that has a collection of search engines which compile databases of web pages. You select the search engine and then type in keywords, you can be very specific about the resources you're after.

Directories are another way to find what you want on the WWW. They are collections of resources organised into categories. They can focus on one subject area and some may collect and organise resources in a number of areas like the SOFWeb Resource Centre. Through your web browser you can also gain access to Electronic Mail and Newsgroups. If you like a page you have visited and would like to revisit it at a later date you can save it's location by clicking on the favorites button in Explorer or the bookmarks menu in Netscape. You select add to, then the next time you open the menu this page has been added to the list. You are also able to sort your favorite pages into directories.

You can use your back button on your browser for moving back through web pages you have previously viewed, this helps when you are viewing several links from one web page. You can also move forward through that same selection. You could also use Go on the Menu Bar which contains a history list of all the pages you have visited. You can select a particular page without having to move through all the pages in-between. If a web page is taking too long to load up you can use the stop button and try an alternate site. This sometimes happens if there are a lot of graphics on the page. The refresh or reload button gets you a new copy of the page from the WWW. You can use this for pages that update regularly. The home button will take you back to a page you have pre-selected to be your start up page. Don't confuse this with an actual home page which is the introductory page of a website that normally has a master menu of documents on that site. You can also send and receive email through your browser but it is not as sophisticated as the specialised electronic mail packages. As the range of materials on the web gets more complex and exciting it sometimes is necessary to add special add-on programs to the browser or your computer. There are two basic types, plugins and players. Plugins add new features to your browser and players to your computer or outside of your browser.

With the latest versions of Internet Explorer and Netscape Navigator you will have much of what you'll need to enjoy multimedia formats on the web like sound and video but occasionally you will across a file that won't work unless you get the appropriate plugin or player. Besides the obvious Sounds and Movies available for viewing on the web there are other types of interactive multimedia involving java, shockwave and cgi programs all written for the web for you to interact with. You can try this list of interactive shockwave games to see how shockwave works.

All of the documents that you will find on the Internet are differentiated by a unique address which is technically referred to as a URL which stands for Uniform Resource Locator. Think of it as a networked extension of the standard filename concept: not only can you point to a file in a directory, but that file and that directory can exist on any machine on the network, and can be served via a several different methods. They can look complicated but are easier to understand when you divide it into its component parts. Understanding how URL's are composed will enable you to locate and remember document locations with greater ease. A URL is always a single unbroken line with no spaces. For Example:

http://www.sofweb.vic.edu.au/internet/intro.htm

The first part http:// indicates that you wish to retrieve a document via the world wide web and stands for HypterText Transfer Protocol.

Most resources that you will access are located on World Wide Web servers and are thus named www at the beginning of the address. Each world wide web server will have a domain name. This is the domain name for SOFWeb - sofweb.vic.edu.au. Web pages can be organised into directories. This web page sits in a directory called internet. Lastly each web page has its own file name - this document is called intro.htm. All web pages end in.htm or html because they are documents prepared for viewing on the web through a web browser. To access a URL you only need to click on the Open Location button on your browser and type in the URL and press enter. All URL's or Web pages that you visit can be saved into your bookmarks file in your browser so that you don't have to remember them all. Sometimes you may come across a url that starts with ftp:// instead of http:// this means that the file is located on an FTP server instead of a WWW server. FTP servers are sometimes used for downloading files as they are a lot quicker than the standard WWW server. When you are accessing Newsgroups the urls will always start with news. eg. news:rec.gardening. These are the most common type of URL's you will come across. You can find more information on URLs here.

Downloading Files

The internet is full of sights to see and things to do like listen to sounds, view movies, play interactive educational games and transfer applications to your own computer like virus checkers, drawing programs, screen capturing programs and much more. In order to get and run these files you need to learn how to download and set them up on your own computer. Downloading refers to the actual transferring of the document from the internet to your own computer. Firstly you must make sure that you know what type of software is appropriate for your computer. That is you must know the specifications of your computer. Things like whether you are using a Personal Computer (PC) or a Mac (Macintosh) and if you are using a PC whether you are using Windows 3.1, Windows 95 or Windows NT as your operating system. You also need to know how much memory you have and whether the machine is a 486 or pentium if it is a PC. The type of computer, the operating system and specifications of your computer dictate what type of programs you can run on your computer. You may not have the capacity to run certain software or the software may not be available for the platform you are using and downloading it can be a complete waste of time. Setting up a separate download directory to store your downloaded files into is so they don't get mixed up with any other programs/files on your system, and so you always know where you can find them should you have to reinstall or find the files at a later date. Normally with software you receive on a disk the separate directory is the files on the disk and the file runs through it setup functions and creates a directory where the program will sit. By creating this download directory you are saving a lot of clean up time later. Most files you download will also be in a compressed format and when uncompressed will explode into many other files. By separating them you are able to clean up your file directories at a later stage with greater ease. If you are using Windows 95 you have the ability to create a new directory immediately to store the file in otherwise store them all in a download directory. You could create sub directories like that below.

Look at the file extension of the file you want to download Files like this one you are reading - download.htm have two parts separated by the (.). The name of the file refers to the first part, the file extension refers to the second part. The file extension is usually three letters and can be used to identify the type of file that it is. In this example download.htm means it is a hypertext markup language document (html). As you become more familiar with the internet and different file extensions you will be able to identify their file types and what you need to run them. A comprehensive list of file extensions and what they are can be found here. There are an amazing array of different file types around, you would probably be familiar with some more common ones such as word.doc and word.txt. Word.doc is a word document and word.txt is a plain text document. Compressed files are a way of storing many files into one, or making a big file smaller so by making it smaller it is quicker to download. For PC users the most common file extensions are zip files and exe files and for Macintosh users sea and hqx. Exe and Sea files are self extracting archives, that means you don't need other software to uncompress them and when you click on them in your file managing program they will automatically either run a setup program, explode into a larger file or explode into several files. All files can be compressed into these formats including all your sounds movies and programs to run them.

For Zip and Hqx files you will need other programs to decompress/unzip/expand them. For PC users winzip is the most popular and for Mac users stuffit expander.

Once you have this additional software you will be able to uncompress the files just by clicking on them in your file managing software. They will decompress onto your computer in the same manner as the exe and sea files. Further information on compressed file formats can be found here. Before you start downloading anything you should have virus protection. Computer viruses are just like the real thing they keep spreading until you get a cure and some are so bad they are deadly for your work and programs on your computer. You should try and get inoculated before you visit the virtual world. The Symantec AntiVirus Research Center is an excellent resource for information about viruses. Not only will you find a list of all currently know viruses, you can download software for both windows and Macintosh users that can protect you.

Viruses spread when you launch an infected application or start up your computer from a disk that has infected system files. Some viruses stay active in memory until you turn off your computer. Other viruses stay active only as long as the infected application is running. Turning off your computer or exiting the application removes the virus from memory, but does not remove the virus from the infected file or disk. Some viruses are programmed specifically to damage the data on your computer by corrupting programs, deleting files, or erasing your entire hard disk.

Trojan horses are not viruses; however, they are often thought of as viruses. A trojan horse is a program that appears to serve some useful purpose or provide entertainment, which encourages you to run it. But, like the Trojan horse of old, it also serves a covert purpose which may be to damage files or perhaps plant a virus on your computer. Remember if you want to have some fun on the internet - "Safe Downloading" means putting your anti-virus software on your computer before you start! Downloading technically means the transfer of one file on one computer to another computer. This can take several different forms when you are downloading using the internet. You can save individual web pages or images on a web page which are transferred in an instant or you can transfer whole programs and files by clicking on a link in a web page and the timing will depend on the size of the file. With simple files like this web page you are reading you can save just by clicking on File on the menu bar of your browser, then clicking on Save As. In the save as type menu you will have two options, either to save it as html file or a text file. If you want to save the html code that is used in it or only wish to ever read the file in a web browser save it as a html file. If you want to read the file in any text based programs like Microsoft Word save it as text. This will mean that you don't have to sift through the code that comes with all hypertext documents. If you are using Microsoft Word 97 with HTML options installed you will not have this problem.

All of the images on the web page will need to be saved individually if you wish to view the entire document, images included on your own computer. You will also need to store the images in the same directory that the images are stored in (or change the code). Getting confused? It's pretty simple. For this particular document I have stored all the images in a separate directory called images and when I have inserted them into the web page with html code I have told the browser that all of these images are in an images directory. You can view the source code by clicking on the view button on your button and clicking on source code or look at the sample below. Here you can see that the saveas.gif file is saved in an images directory. Now all you have to do is create a subdirectory for this page, call it images and save all the images individually into that directory. When you open this page up from your own computer all images will be intact and the file will be viewed as normal. With HTML files that are in frames, you will either need to click on the particular frame that you wish to save and save it or you will need to collect all the frames by clicking in each frame and then also saving the main frame which is the document if you would like the entire page. Sometimes this can get a little messy and confusing, it might be easier just to do a screen capture of the web page. The following instructions are based on downloading a file using the Netscape browser. Most web browsers operate in a similar manner so the basic concepts can be used for all browsers. When you click on the link for a file that you want to download a box similar to the one below will come

The browser is stating that the file that I am downloading is of a pdf format - see application/pdf. The browser doesn't recognise this file so it is asking for you to either pick an application to run it or whether we want to save it and work out what application we will use to run it later. As a beginner, always save the file unless you are very familiar with the file extension and know what program will run it.. There is nothing more annoying than picking the wrong application, waiting for it to download and then finding the wrong program has been chosen and having to download the file again. A box like that below will come up if you click on Save The File. This is where your separate directory comes in handy. If you are using windows 95 you have the ability to create a new directory immediately to store the file in. This all depends on the type of file that you have downloaded and its file extension. For example if you have downloaded a file to be used in another application like a movie or sound file, you may be able to use it immediately after downloading with your movie or sound player by opening up the application that you would use to play the file and then locating where you have downloaded the file to and playing it in the application. For instance if you downloaded a file called sing.wav you could tell that this is a wav sound file that can be played in any sound player. Sometimes though you will need to uncompress files before you can use them. As you become more familiar with the different file extensions it will become easier to know what you can and need to do for each file you download. Sometimes a file may be so big that it has been compressed so that it is quicker to download. If the file is a compressed file in the Exe, Zip, Sea or Hqx formats it will need to be uncompressed before you can use it. Remember to store it in a download directory so you can locate it easily. Exe files and Sea files can be uncompressed by clicking on them either in File Manager/Windows Explorer or on the Mac Desktop. Zip and Hqx files require other software to be installed firstly before they can be uncompressed. When you uncompress the file another file should pop out of it. For PC users remember to refresh your File Manager after decompressing if you can't see the file immediately. (This is the F5 function key). The file that pops out is the file that you will use when you open up your application like a sound player and locate the file to play it.

If the file that you have downloaded is a program/application file like a new web browser or a movie player, after clicking on it, it may decompress and commence a set up program which you would follow the instructions as you would normally installing any new software from a disk or cd. But it may initially uncompress with the installation file popping out of it (usually called setup.exe or install.exe) which you then just need to click on to start the installation process. If you are unsure of which file is the setup/ installation file there will also normally be a text file that explains how to install the program. This is the time where having separate download directories come in very handy. Imagine downloading some software called jelly.zip that you have saved into your download directory, sub directory jelly, you click on it in explorer, out pops setup.exe a few read me files and a couple of extra files the program needs to use to install. You then click on the setup.exe, the installation process commences, it creates a program in your programs files automatically. You can now return to your download directory and delete all the files in the jelly directory because they are only taking up space. The program files that are needed are all set up in a different directory and are safe. As the range of materials on the web gets more complex and exciting it sometimes is necessary to add special add-on programs to the software on your computer. There are two basic types, plugins and players/helper applications. A plugin is a piece of software or a program that operates within the web browser like the shockwave movie player and a player/helper application normally operates outside the browser like the Netoob movie player. Some plugins can also be helper applications like real audio, real video or adobe acrobat where you could play the file within your web browser or as a stand alone application without being connected to the internet. With the latest versions of Internet Explorer and Netscape Navigator you will have much of what you'll need to enjoy multimedia formats on the web like sound and video but occasionally you will across a file that won't work unless you get the appropriate plugin or player/helper application. If you don't have the appropriate plugin or helper application, when you click on the link you will get a message letting you know that you need to take a few minutes to download the tool or software before you can have any fun.

This isn't really difficult to do. On most occasions your browser will also direct you to the web page of the program you need to get, and you just follow the links until you get to a download option, click on download and save it to your computer. With Netscape you can view the plugins that you have installed by clicking on the Help button and then clicking on about plugins. To view helper applications with Netscape, click on Options, General Preferences and then Helpers. When you click on a hyperlink of a file your browser doesn't recognise it will give you the option to either save the file or pick an application to run the program with. Most times your browser will recognise the files that you have plugins or helper applications and run them automatically but sometimes it doesn't and you have to set them up manually. This will mean that whenever you come across that type of file the helper application will automatically load up.

The most important concept to understand when setting up helper applications is the concept of MIME (Multipurpose Internet Mail Extensions). MIME is a standardized method for organizing different file formats. The method organizes file formats according to the file's MIME type. When your browser retrieves a file from a server, the server provides the MIME type of the file. The browser uses the MIME type to establish whether the file format can be read by the software's built-in capabilities or, if not, whether a suitable helper application is available to read the file. For Netscape users you can view and configure the mapping of all MIME types to helper applications by clicking on Options, then General Preferences, then Helpers. The following screen should come up

From here you only need to click on the format, for example real audio and all files with the extension of ra rm and ram, click on launch the application and then associate the application by finding the executable file on your computer by using the browse button. For ra, rm and ram files it would be the Real Video Player application file in the Real Video Directory - rvplayer.exe.

For Macintosh Users, click here for a guide on setting up helper applications. Freeware are fully working models of products that you do not have to pay for but can not alter in anyway or sell or relabel, as the author of the program retains all rights to the program and just allowed you to copy and use it without paying. With Shareware the author again retains all rights to the product but this is more of a testing stage. You are usually allowed to use the product for a limited time, limited access or limited abilities of the product. They normally expire after 30 days if you do not register and pay the fee. Most software of this sort is around the $50.00 mark. This type of software is the most common. One other type of software is public domain software which allows you to relabel it, copy it, do virtually anything you like to it. Try SOFWeb's Software Resource Collection for some software sights to start downloading your own programs and files.

Internet Publishing

In order for people to access your Web site, your pages must be available 24 hours a day somewhere on the Web so before you start making your pages you should talk to your internet service provider to see if they can store your Web pages on their machines. This is normally a standard service of the Internet Service Provider but here are some questions you may like to ask.

- Is there are charge for this service?
- How much space is available?
- Is there direct FTP access? FTP is the quickest method of transferring files from your computer to your Internet Providers. Pages will be updated almost instantly.
- If not, how long will it take the provider to implement changes?

If you are really keen you can also inquire about registering your own domain name, which is a unique name for the location of your site. (This might cost, depending on your service provider). With a domain name you can type in an address like:

http://www.*myschool*.edu.au where *myschool* is the name of your school. Otherwise your Web site address will probably look like:

http://www.*your service provider*.net.au/~*myschool* where

your service provider *is the name of your service provider and* myschool *is the name of your dial-up account.*

It doesn't matter whether you register a domain name or not, but it is usually easier for people to remember a domain name address. If your Internet Service Provider is unable to store your web pages, never fear there are a couple of alternatives. There are WWW sites that allow you to store your web pages with them, some are quite limited with space and restrictions and may require you to present their logo on your pages. There are several factors you should considering free web pages.

- Is it enough for your requirements right now?
- Can you see yourself needing more in the future?
- If you need a commercial home page, is that allowed?
- Conversely, if you need a personal home page, is that allowed?
- Do you require or want graphics on your site?
- Can graphics be used?
- Are there any graphics provided for you to choose from? Are you limited to them?
- Can you upload your own graphics?
- Is the page intended only for a specific audience (e.g. musicians, artists, etc.)?
- Will it be available to all, not just the members of the service?
- Is it a requirement to credit the service on your page? Do you mind?
- Does your page meet all the guidelines?
- Do you have any questions about the service? If so, e-mail them.
- Will your page ever be removed without your knowledge?
- Will the service ever begin charging for the placement of your page?
- Make sure you ask about any additional charges that may come up also.

You can try these websites for free web pages. Remember, if all else fails contact SOFWeb to see if alternative arrangements can be made. Start collecting ideas for your home page (a home page is the very first page someone will see when they visit your site). Talk with your fellow teachers, students and the principal for ideas about what should be on your home page. You will need to liase with these people as you are developing your ideas. The best home pages are creative, original and fun! Try not to put too much text on the home page, save that for other files which you link from the home page. You will probably need at least a few links from the home page to other files on your Web site. Once you have a good looking home page, work on the other pages; these have a lot more 'content' than the home page, so feel free to put more information in them. Map your pages out. If you do not have a well-defined structure for the way a user will move through the webpages, both they and you will become lost.

- Make sure it flows
- Make it logical, easy to navigate
- Split large pages into groups of smaller ones when appropriate
- Leave room in your webspace structure for expansion later on
- If you must have links to pages which are "under construction" [i.e. to help conceptualise the completed webspace or indicate what is coming], turn off those links until there is actually something where they are pointing, something, that is, other than a boring "under construction" notice!
- Decide on filenames that are not too inflexible, as *ALL* the links to a page in the *ENTIRE* webspace will need to be changed if you need to rename it, say from KIDS97.HTM to KIDS98.HTM
- Include links back to such places as the Home Page or the start of a section on each page

Publishing on the World Wide Web means that you need to balance the content of your page, with the design elements. There is little point in creating a beautiful graphic for your Home Page that is so large no one waits for it to download. On the other hand, a page of all text and little white space may have lots of information, but is not inviting enough to encourage people to read it. Although the web is a fairly new publishing medium, there are already some stylistic guide lines which may help you as you begin to design your page.

Keep in mind that unlike normal school publications which will probably have a fairly limited circulation in the classroom, school, or local community, when you are publishing on the World Wide Web, your audience is potentially the whole world. Obviously you will want to do your best to ensure that your web page is an accurate reflection of your school's standards. Spelling mistakes in particular, can attract adverse comment from the Web community, and errors of usage or fact can spoil the amount of work your school puts into its publishing effort. For more information about making sure that your web page is a good advertisement for your school see some of the examples from Why Schools Publish Web Pages. You also need to remember that not everyone will have the same type of computer, browser or internet connection as you do, so you need to keep this in mind when designing your pages. For some tips on making your web page user-friendly, which is good "netiquette" read the World Wide Web guide from Arlene H. Rinaldi's excellent on-line guide to netiquette. A fairly technical but very informative guide is the Web Style Manual from the Yale Center for Advanced Instructional Media. For schools publishing on the web, as in other media, student and staff safety must be of paramount importance. This includes such obvious things as not publishing personal addresses and telephone numbers, and not publishing details which might enable the identification of individual staff and students. Where your school's home page provides an e-mail link to the school, the mailbox should be checked first by teachers. Schools who wish to publish student photographs or student work on the Web need to make sure that they get signed permission from parents using a release form.

SOFWeb recommends some simple steps to protect students when publishing student images or work on the web.

- Do not publish student's last names or other information which might make students individually identifiable.
- Do not publish student's personal contact details, i.e. home phone numbers, addresses or personal email addresses. Where contact details are to be included use class email addresses or the school's telephone number.
- Where possible publish group photographs rather than individual images of students. Schools might publish the image of a class or other group activity, and identify students generically by class or activity, i.e. "Grade 4A", or the "Year 7 hockey team".

For further resources about student safety on the Internet, please see SOFWeb's Taking Care on the Internet, which provides detailed advice for schools, as well as links to a range of useful resources.. There are an estimated 30 million web users, so your first answer might be, "the world"! Realistically though the whole world won't visit your Home Page, so you need to think about who you are writing for. Your audience might include:

- your own school
- the wider school community
- the local area, i.e. your geographic region.
- other students both local, national and international
- colleagues and others who might be interested in your school's work

There are a great many web pages in the world, in order to bring people to your page and to keep them returning to it, you need to think carefully about what you are going to offer the Internet community. Some of the elements you might include are:

- a site which changes frequently
- publishing student projects or writing

If you hope to influence viewers to actually read your webpages, you will need to arrest their attention within a very short time - remember that we now have several generations limited to a thirty second attention span *as maximum*. If you don't have their interest in the first five seconds, they are gone!

- The page should get attention immediately, either through 'eye candy' [graphics] or compelling content
- The page should offer the specific audience something appealing, ideally something which will make them want to come back to the page again
- The first screen [what appears in the browser window when the page first loads] should have enough in it to identify the interesting aspects of the page
- Too many graphics can actually lose your audience, as the Internet can be slow and graphics slow it down more. People [especially children] lose patience and move on
- Cut down on any unnecessary introductory pages where possible - get straight to the point

HTML, or Hyper Text Markup Language, is the language of the World Wide Web. You use it to format text and graphics into files ready for the Web. HTML consists of additional formatting in a text file, called TAGS. If you select Document Source from the View menu in Netscape (or the equivalent command in your browser) you will see the contents of the HTML file you are browsing. All of the text inside less than (<) and greater than (>) characters are called TAGS. Once you learn what these tags mean, you can add them to a text file to create a HTML file ready for the Web. Although HTML Editors are available it is worthwhile becoming familiar with the actual tags. HTML Programs can't do everything you want them to and if you have an understanding of HTML code you are able to both fix up errors and make quick edits in a text package like simple text on the Mac, or NotePad or WordPad on the PC. Also some of the html editors available have a tendency to load in extra code making files twice the time, sometimes three times the file size they would have been had you hand coded them. This means that your files will take twice to three times longer to download. Once you are ready to start coding you can use SOFWeb's Beginners HTML Guide for an informative guide on creating your web pages which includes all basic necessary tags for your web pages.

Some other guides include Teach Yourself Hypertext from Macquarie University. This tutorial will take you from beginning HTML to Frames and beyond to Shockwave and Java. A Beginner's Guide to HTML is a plain vanilla HTML tutorial, but for all it's lack of gloss it is very thorough and worth a look. Introduction to HTML offers a good introduction to HTML and then, when you are comfortable with the basics you can go on to Intermediate HTML to refine your skills. If you are interested in the technical aspects of HTML, including official code and developments, then you need to look at HTML, hyper-text markup language An HTML Editor is a software program which has been especially designed to make writing HTML easier. There are many of these editors available as shareware, for both PCs and Macintosh computers. Shareware means that after you are able to download the program for a trial run but are expected to pay for it after you have trialled it. The evaluation period is normally 30 days. PC users can download a copy of Hotdog. This is no longer free to schools but has the standard 30 day evaluation period. Macintosh users can download PageSpinner. If you would like to try some other HTML editors check out the TUCOWs software archives.

With a HTML Editor you can learn what the HTML tags are, and how to use them. These programs allow you to enter text and the appropriate HTML TAGS to create a HTML file. You do not have to rely on them to produce the code but use them as an extra in your learning. If you are using Netscape version 1.1 or above, you can use color codes to control the color of your page background, text colour, link colour and visited link colour. And, although it is not official HTML coding, later versions of Netscape will also allow you to specify the color of your text. You can do this by specifying the color by name or by RGB code. For example, if you wish to create color text, such as the heading above you can use the HTML code, <FONT COLOR=BLUE>. As usual you will need to turn the color off by using the </FONT> command. Note that you need to use the spelling “color” rather than “colour” otherwise Netscape won’t recognise the command. There are some colours you can use by name. With the World Wide Web you don’t need to be restricted to simply using text and pictures. You can use other media, for example you can add sound and movies to your web pages.

Try these links for some more information.

- Making Shockwave Movies
- Adding Quicktime, Avi, MPEG Movies To Your Web Pages
- Embedding Sounds Into Your Web Pages
- Using Real Video or Real Audio On Your Web Pages

Here are some other collections of on-line resources to help you publish on the World Wide Web.

webreference.com has a wealth of information about the Internet, from learning how to use it, to advanced web design.

How do they do that with HTML? is a collection of tips, from the simple to the bizarre, for HTML. To learn about frames, have a look at Netscape’s Frames: an introduction or So you want some frames, huh? is an entertaining and useful introduction to putting frames around your web pages. An Introduction to Java Script. Plug-ins are software programs that extend the capability of Netscape, for example, allowing you to play sound or movies, view 3D or animation. The number of available plug-ins are increasing every week. Check the official Netscape Navigator Components Page to find out about, and download the latest plug-ins.

Now that you have finished your site, you're probably excited and want to publish it straight away. Hang on a minute. Your World Wide Web page has a potential audience of millions of people! It is therefore important that you make every effort to ensure that your page is not only well designed, but that it is correctly spelled, that factual information is accurate, that you have tested your page by clicking on every link and made sure all the graphics work. Remember that your are presenting this information to the whole world, so you want it to work well with no errors in it. One important aspect of quality control is ensuring that you have appropriate guidelines for publishing and an acceptable procedure for signing the pages off before publication. This might mean that you form a publication committee which is finally responsible for signing off all electronic publishing. This committee could consist of students, teachers, parents and members of the wider school community. One of the responsibilities of such a committee would be developing guidelines for electronic publication. It is important that all information published by a school should be signed off by the principal or appropriate publishing committee. Before signing off any publishing ensure that all copyright is respected. In the case of student work this means that an appropriate model release form is signed. For other materials you need to ensure that you are not abusing their copyright. You need to ensure if the images, text or other material you publish is not copyright free you have permission to use it. If you are not sure you need to check SOFWeb's Copyright Statement. Be aware that many large corporations are aggressive about any contravention of their copyright, especially the use of well known corporate symbols and logos.

Sometimes it is appropriate to use copyrighted material if you provide appropriate acknowledgement of your sources. This is called referencing, and there are ways of referencing both text-based and electronic material. Remember that using material which is not your own without appropriate acknowledgement or permission is called plagiarism and is illegal and unethical. See SOFWeb's guide to Plagiarism and Referencing for more information. Now its time to transfer all your files to your web site, probably using an FTP program. Use an FTP program (FTP stands for File Transfer Protocol) to log on to your website, then transfer all the necessary files and directories onto your service providers machine. If you can't figure out what to do, call your service provider for further instructions. When you are sure that your pages are ready for publication, register them with SOFWeb, so that you can share all your hard work with other schools in Victoria and around Australia and publicise your site. When you register your page with SOFWeb, all you need to do is fill out the registration form on-line and submit it to us. You will then be asked to print out our automatic response, which needs to be signed by your Principal and faxed back to us. This is a good way to ensure that the information on your school's Home Page is accurate and approved for publication. Once we have received the signed form, we will add your school's Home Page to our list. The maintenance of the site can often take up more time than the original design. You have to ensure that information you have included is still up to date and that web sites you have linked to are still there. You should enter a date on your pages whenever you revise them so that people can tell how old the material is. When you put pages up on the web you have to be committed to their upkeep otherwise they might be beautiful on day one but if not maintained they can become worthless pieces of cyberjunk. Try to include links to sites home pages where you can, rather than actual pages on their site, this gives them more chance of not being altered in a hurry. Also you can ask website managers to advise you of any alterations to their site.

Video Conferencing

Video conferencing involves the visual communication of parties around the world. You can use Video conferencing to link up with specific parties or you can join Video conferencing communities that operate in the same way Internet Chat does. There are 38 Victorian Government schools using Video conferencing technology which allows teachers and students to communicate verbally, electronically and visually as if they were in the classroom. On-line discussion groups and electronic mail enable teachers and students to interact between lessons. Clusters of rural schools also purchase mobile technology resources jointly. These shared resources, ShareTeks, are rotated around the schools in the clusters for use by students and teachers. For more information on this Learning Technologies Project. The Education Department's SOFNet studio offers facilities for anyone to book their Video conferencing suite at 23 St Andrews Place - Melbourne. You can book these facilities by contacting Carmel Mauro. To book facilities held in schools contact the schools directly.

If you would like to set up your own Video conferencing facilities from your computer read on. If you would like to be a receiver - that is only 'see and hear the conversation', you will be able to do this with any standard Mac and if you have a Sound card and Video card on any standard PC. If you would also like to also be a sender that is - 'transmit your voice and video' you will also need a digital camera and PC users will need a microphone. These cameras can be purchase for about $100 for both MAC's and PC's and microphones for around $20.

And you will also need the software program!

The most popular program is CU-SeeME. It is a free Video conferencing program (under copyright of Cornell University and its collaborators) available to anyone with a Macintosh or Windows and a connection to the Internet. With CU-SeeMe, you can video conference with another site located anywhere in the world. If you want to conference with more than one other person/computer you need to connect to a reflector. By using a reflector, multiple parties at different locations can participate in a CU-SeeMe conference, each from his or her own desktop computer. With CU-SeeMe each participant can decide to be a sender, a receiver, or both. Receiving requires only a standard Mac and a connection to the Internet. Sending requires the same plus a camera and digitizer which can cost as little as $100 to add on. For PC User to send and receive video you will need a video card supports Microsoft Video For Windows and a video camera to plug into the video card. To send & receive audio you'll also need a Sound Card that conforms to the Windows MultiMedia Specification (Sound Blaster or better). Full Duplex audio is very desirable and Speakers (or headphones) and a microphone. Web cameras are available on the internet all around the world for you to take a peek at different parts of the world. Try some of these links.

- New Zealand - Ruapehu Volcano
- View the earth from many different satellites orbiting the earth
- Earth & Moon Viewer

Chat

Imagine a room full of people from all around the world talking to each other with everybody in the room being able to hear everyone elses conversation and join in any one of them at any time. Then imagine this room always having people in it any time of day or night for you to drop in and have a conversation with. That's basically what chat is.

Chatting is one of the most popular activities on the Internet and involves people from all walks off life and just about all ages to coming together in areas where they can join in on in a variety of topics that they are interested in with people all around the world. Traditionally chat is text based but can also involve audio and video. In public chat areas people use "user names" or "nicknames" or sometimes represent themselves as graphical icons or "avatars" as they are known in the chat world.

Chatting can be great fun, but because it is basically an anonymous encounter the risk of being deceived is high if you are entering public chat areas where the other users aren't known to you. There are public chat areas just for children, but because it is impossible to know anything about people on the Internet except what they choose to tell you, there is no guarantee that the users of children's chat areas are in fact, children, While real time communication can be engaging and educationally useful, we strongly suggest it be used with students in a controlled environment using programs that enable direct links with specific parties rather than joining these public areas. In all cases where students are going to communicate on-line they should be aware of Netiquette and My Rules For Online Safety. There are two main types of internet chats. One is the web based chat room. These are graphical where people can choose images to represent themselves and offer elaborate virtual environments. They are not real time, messages will come up on your screen if you press the refresh or reload button. Some of the latest web based chats use server push technology or java, so that you don't have to press the refresh button but it still isn't as quick as the second type of chat called internet relay chat or IRC. This is not on the world wide web, but found directly on servers. It is a text-based chat (no pictures) and real time (all messages immediately come on screen when entered).

IRC is a multi-user chat system, where people meet on Channels (rooms, virtual places, usually with a certain topic of conversation) to talk in groups, or privately. There is no restriction to the number of people that can participate in a given discussion, or the number of channels that can be formed on IRC. IRC uses a streaming technology so basically how fast you type is how fast your messages are up. With traditional IRC software like Mirc you would download the software, select a nickname, choose and connect to an IRC server using that software and then choose one of the thousands of channels (virtual rooms) you see on the list. The content of many IRC chat areas can be rough and uncensored, and because they are publicly accessible they attract a very diverse range of people. There are other programs available that connect to a specific IRC server and run theme based colorful chats, in order to participate in these chats, you need to have particular chat software, not generic software such as mIRC. The Palace is a popular shareware program in which you can use your own images as your avatar or use the standard images provided until you pay and register. There are many rooms to visit like the Haunted Palace, a cyberspace amusement park, the original Time Warner Palace with over 30 rooms, and a host of others. When you speak a balloon image comes up with the text inside and you can use sounds and animations provided to provide some emotion to your conversation.

Worlds Chat is a 3d chat program in which each visitor is represented by a 3d image, or avatar, of their choice which you can then use to move around the 3d Worlds. The visuals in this one are fantastic. You can even build your own 3d house in this program. Only available for PC users though. To find other 3d Worlds chat software try Yahoos selection. Virtual Places allows you to use a selection of images or your own as your avatar. Your messages come up in a bubble over your image. You can also play sounds and animations provided. There is a wide selection of theme based rooms, virtual streets and virtual cafes to chat in.

This uses a comic strip as the theme for the chat where you are a character and all messages are shown as a cartoon strip. Visually this is really great to see. There are programs available that can be used to dial up specific parties only. In a classroom environment this type of program can be used to set up discussions between students or teachers working on collaborative projects with other schools around the world. Sometimes they can get a little slow. Some of them will use java, server push technology and some will require you to press the refresh/reload button for you to see any new messages.

Several programs have become available that will let you, equipped with the right computer hardware, an Internet connection, and special software, to speak (voice) in real-time over the Internet - in effect using the network like a telephone.

These audio conferencing programs work by digitizing your speech as you talk and sending the digital data over the Internet. If you have a good Internet connection then the sound quality is comparable to a regular phone call. However the sound quality varies dramatically between applications and depends largely on the local capacity at each end. In nearly all cases, the limiting factor will not be the speed and capacity of the Internet, but will depend on the local network at each end. The newer software operates in full duplex - that is In a full duplex conversation, you can speak and hear the other person at the same time. In half duplex, only one person can speak at the same time, and if you speak while the other person speaks, then you will not be able to hear each other. Your sound card will either be full duplex or half duplex, which will control which mode you can operate in. Most new Macs come equipped with full duplex sound cards, but most PC's do not. When you load the application, if it does not let you choose full-duplex mode, then you probably have a half duplex card. Speak Freely is free and one of the best applications available. It offers many features more advanced than commercial software such as voice mail, compression, multicasting, encryption, and usually offers excellent sound quality. Operates in Full & Half Duplex mode. Windows based program.

VocalTec's Internet Phone has quickly become the most popular Internet telephony software. The latest version offers an incredible user interface, and many advance features including an excellent user directory, full/half duplex, low bandwidth demands. It runs on top of Internet Relay Chat, providing you with a list of on-line users and topics of conversation, making it easy to find new people to chat with. The demo version only gives you one minute online time. You can purchase it for $US99. For MAC's & PC's.

With Internet phone you are able to use it to call someone who has a regular telephone by connecting to what is called a "phone gateway." There is a volunteer project known as Free World Dialup which allows people using Internet Phone to make calls to regular phone networks using a phone gateway. Netmeeting includes many advanced features such as text chat, whiteboard, file transfer and is set up to make large conferences easy to use. One of the most useful features is that it allows application sharing where one user can take control of the other user's computer and see their applications. Platform: Windows. For more information about NetMeeting, see A Beginner's Guide to NetMeeting written by Lindsay Clapperton, Principal of Porepunkah PS. A MUD (Multiple User Dimension, Multiple User Dungeon, or Multiple User Dialogue) is a program where you choose a character or avatar to represent yourself and then you walk around, chat with other characters, explore dangerous monster-infested areas, solve puzzles, combat evil tyrants, and build on the existing

MUD world. Most MUDs you will find are social games but they are also used for education and research. There are different types of MUDs such as MOOs, UnterMuds, MUSHes, etc., each of them have their own style.

After you have decided on the chat you want to enter you will need to choose a 'nickname' or 'handle'. You want to use something very original and imaginative. Most standard names will usually already be taken and your name is going to be what initially catches peoples eye. Some web based chats, Virtual Places and The Palace allow you to put your own images up next to your 'nickname'. You want to select a picture that is small that represent you or the name you have chosen. You can include your own photo here if you want people to know what you look like but mostly people use comical images of something that represents them. For example choosing Batgirl as a name along with a batgirl picture or a picture of a bat. To post it to the website will normally involve set instructions or you would use basic html code to do this.

Public Chatrooms and IRC Channels may seem a little intimidating at first. People are either ignoring you or saying hello left, right and center. It may look like they are speaking a foreign language which they are - Chatters Jargon". Sometimes it is difficult to keep up with a number of conversations if you don't read and type fast! When you first enter a chat room or an IRC Channel you should perhaps just listen for a while (or "read" as the case may be") before speaking (or "typing"). When you feel game enough to speak saying a nice greeting to everyone is the best way to catch someone's attention. If that doesn't work usually it's best to address someone with a question. If you want to talk to someone specific you have to type their 'username' before your message so they know you are talking to them. Try not to get peoples attention by typing in capitals or editing your font size it's considered yelling and bad netiquette. You can change the color to make your messages more unique and personalized. The IRC chat programs and some web based programs will not allow you to edit the font. To cut down time on typing, many people have started using abbreviations for various actions like ROFL means Rolling On The Floor Laughing. And to give some emoticon to the text people have started using actions or Emoticons like :-) means "Smile, I'm joking". Many of the Emoticons and Acronyms used in chats have pretty much become universal and used in Newsgroups and Email Message. They are a lot of fun. You can try this SOFWeb's list of Emoticons & Acronyms. For a more extensive list try the WBS Chat Book. In a lot of web based chat programs you are also able to post links or email addresses. This can usually done just by using your basic html code. There are a few common courtesies to follow when in chats.

- Respect others privacy. Don't spy on others in different chat rooms. It's just like in real life when someone needs to talk to someone in private.
- Be kind to chat room newcomers. You will know what it was like, bit unsure of what to do or say. Be friendly and welcome them into the chat room.

- Don't write really long or big messages. A lot of chatters do not like scrolling down a lot just to see a few messages after yours. If you do have to type a long message to another person either send it private or send them an email.

Check our Netiquette Guide for more information. Just as you meet people in the real world, you can make friends in the virtual world. Some people have even met their future husbands and wives through chat, but there are a few things you should be aware of. People can, and do, pretend to me anything they want on the Internet, so you have no real guarantees that your cyberfriend is who they say they are. If you decide you would like to meet in real life someone you have met on the Internet, you need to be cautious. If you are a student you should talk this over with your parents and/or teachers to decide whether this is a good idea. Under no circumstances should you give anyone your personal details (home address, telephone number, school) over the Internet without permission from your parents or teacher. People tend to be a lot braver online than in person and a lot braver can mean being more aggressive or just stupid. If you have a disagreement with someone or someone has just picked you out of the crowd (flamed you) usually the best thing to do is just ignore them, they'll get bored if you don't bite. Some chats even have an ignore option so you can just turn this person off. If the person is persistent report them to the webmaster of the chat. A lot of chats have monitors in the rooms that will either warn them or kick them out.

Electronic Mail (E-mail)

Electronic mail, or Email, is the term used to describe the tool which allows one computer user to send a message to one or more other computer users over a computer network in a digital form. Email can be sent internally to members of an organisation through their internal computer network or they can be sent externally to anyone in the world by using the network of computer networks that make up the internet.

It's very similar to our traditional mail system with post boxes, post offices, envelopes and addresses. The difference is that instead of Australia Post delivering your messages around the globe for you, messages are sent electronically to other computer users via the computer network (the internet) taking a fraction of the time to get there AND, you don't have to walk to the letter box! Just as you can send attachments with your letters in the normal post (snail mail) you can also send computer documents, graphics, software or anything else that can be turned into a digital form attached to an email message.

In order for messages to be sent from one computer to another, your message needs to be converted into a digital form and forwarded to a computer that acts as a mail server or post office. This mail server sorts and directs your mail for you. The only way this mail server can direct mail though, to all users is by being connected to a network that all the users are also connected to. This network can be internal (a stand-alone network) which means you can only send email to other users on that network. If your mail server is connected to the Internet you can also send your email messages to any other computer user that is connected to the internet anywhere in the world because the internet is a network of all the little networks of organisations around the world.

This mail server can be within your organisation or with an Internet Service Provider, so you would connect to it by logging into your email account. When you send your email message, the mail server decides whether the message is to be passed on to a user on its immediate network or it will pass it onto another mail server on another network closest to it through these combination of networks and each mail server keeps passing it on until it reaches its intended destination. This is known as the 'store' and 'forward' system, storing your message at various points on the path to its receiver waiting for the link to be free for it to forward your message on the next part of its journey.

The digital data can be broken up and follow different paths (go through different mail servers) to gets to its destination but always meets up when it gets to the post office or mail server of the recipient. The mail will stay at the post office until the recipient decide to collect it which is done by logging into their email account.

In order to read or send any electronic mail you will need special software. Eudora is one of the most commonly used software packages and comes in two versions. Eudora Lite can be downloaded from the Eudora website and used without charge. Eudora Pro - a more advanced version of the software can be purchased for approximately $89 from most leading software suppliers. The Eudora website can help you locate a supplier closest to you. Eudora can be used on both IBM compatible and Macintosh computers. Web browsers like Netscape and Explorer now have an email function also but they are not as sophisticated and reliable as Eudora. One benefit of this type of email package is that where addresses of World Wide Web pages are given in the body of the message you can click on the address and the browser will automatically display the page. Eudora also has this ability.

If your school is connected to the statewide VicOne network you can to the Edumail site to obtain information relating to email software available to Victorian schools. You will need your school username and password to access this site.

To become an email user you need to have an email account set up for you by an Internet Service Provider or your organisation. This would normally occur automatically when you get your internet connection if you're setting up your account privately. With a school or business you would normally gain access to email by talking to your technical advisor where a user account will be set up for you. When you get your account you will be given an email address, a Username and a password which you would use to access your email. You can obtain free email accounts through certain web sites on the internet. You check your mail through your web browser by looking at a web page, typing in your name and password. These types of services are nowhere near as secure as having your own email software on your own computer and can be slow with delays. They are free though and provide additional services such as receiving regular news from various sites of your choosing. One such site is the Hotmail Site. Each email user is given an email address which distinguishes them from each other like your name and street address distinguish your house from your neighbors. Your email address is usually your Username or User ID, plus the domain name of the computer through which you normally gain access to the internet with an @ symbol in-between.. - (sofweb@edumail.vic.gov.au). As you can see here my Username is 'sofweb' and the domain name for the Department of Education, Employment and Training (where I work) is edumail.vic.gov.au. Your Username doesn't necessarily have to be your real name it can be a variation or any name of your choosing - eg. (wizard@edumail.vic.gov.au)

After Downloading your Email Software and setting up your email account with your Internet Service Provider, you need to set the software up with details like your Username, password, email address and mail server. The Internet Service Provider will normally give you all of this information which you will need to include in the set up. With Mac or Windows 95 you follow the prompts and include the details the provider has given you. If you are not setting your account up privately your technician should do all of this for you. With free email accounts like Hotmail you do not need to download any software and the instructions are usually simple to follow, and provided on the website.

A domain name is the Internet address of a computer. All computers connected to the internet have a domain name. Your computer itself may not have a domain name but the computer that you connect to firstly to enable you to gain access to the internet will have a domain name. For example you may connect to the internet through a computer which is called a server belonging to your organisation or through your Internet Service Providers server. By having a domain name all computers on the internet are able to locate each other and forward messages and requests. When you specify an email address or IP address of a website it accesses the server/computer by the domain name that you specify by accessing a database known as a DNS Name Server. You may have seen the error messages "No DNS Entry" before when typing in a web site address. This means it is unable to locate the domain address of the computer where the web page is that you specified. A domain name is separated by periods (.) and will normally include the name of the organisation (or an acronym of it), for example the domain name for SOFWeb is www.sofweb.vic.edu.au, this includes our name (SOFWeb), which is in Victoria (VIC) which is part of the Department of Education, Employment and Training (EDU). Two-letter country codes are used, such as AU for Australia.

The email system at the Department of Education uses names such as sofweb followed by @edumail.vic.gov.au which is the domain name of the server/computer that forwards electronic mail to each user on the network. Standard naming rules are used for domain names which show the type of organisations and country the people have internet accounts with, and because of this you can remember email addresses as well as web site addresses with greater ease. You can also work out where a person comes from by looking at the email address.

For example, if you received an email message from J.Smith@zoo.org.au you could tell from the domain name that this message came from Australia (AU) from a non-profit organisation (ORG) which is the Zoo which is an acronym for Melbourne Zoo.

Here is a sample of some of the standard naming rules used.

Name	*Description*	*Name*	*Description*
com	Commercial Organisations	au	Australia
edu	Educational Institutions	uk	United Kingdom
org	Non-profit organisations	fr	France
net	Networks		
gov	Non-military government organisations		
mil	Military government organisations		
int	International organisations		

In some cases email addresses do not include a country code. This is often the case with email addresses of users from the United States but this is also becoming more common in other countries.

Email messages are often less formal than letters and can sometimes be as short as one single word. Because it is treated more casually than a formal letter sometimes people aren't as careful with what they say in an email message. You should refer to our Netiquette guide and Email Style Guide for some tips on writing your email messages. You can't send email without having the other person's full email address. Without it its like mailing an envelope without any address on it. Just as you would put the person's name and address on the envelope, you would put their email address, comprised of their Username and domain name, on the email message. You can include their real name in the message also.

You may be able to find an Australian users email address at the SOFCOM site. Most email packages allow you to set up an email address book so that you only need to click on the person you would like to send the message to once you have put them in your book. All you need to do is use the automatic addressing feature to transfer the address to your new message. As you would normally put your return name and address on the back of an envelope so the message can be returned to you if there is a problem - you can include this on your email software when you set it up so it does the same with the email messages you send. If you type in the subject, this subject header will show up on their email program so that they get an idea of what your message is about - you can type in Urgent! to let the recipient know to open it right away.

The email program automatically puts in the time, the date. This is where you type the main body of your message. Check out Style Guide for some tips on writing your messages. Documents can also be attached to email messages. To attach a document or other type of digital file to an outgoing message, select *Attach* File from the *Message* menu.. A standard dialogue box will be displayed. Select the document you want to send and click OK. The location of the file will appear after the Attachments: field of the header. When the message is sent the attachment will be located and sent also.

Receiving Attachments - Select the directory or folder you want the attachments to be saved to. You can do this by going to Settings menu, then clicking of Attachments, followed by the box under Attachment Directory. Select a directory/folder for your attachments to be saved into. If you do not select a specific directory, incoming attachments will be saved into the Eudora directory.

Beware!! When you are sending attachments please ensure that the person you are sending to will be able to "read" (open) the file. Check to find out if they have the correct software and the correct version of that software. If in doubt save word processor documents as .rtf - most word processors can read this type of file, although you may lose some formatting in the process. You can forward a copy of your message to the user you include here. All you need to do is include their email address in this section. This field allows you to send to send a copy of a message to someone else without the original recipient knowing. To check if there is any new mail you have to log in to your email software with your account. To do that you open the software, your Username will automatically come up and your password will be requested. After you type in your password your email program will connect to your mailbox at your post office to see if there is any mail waiting for you. If there is it will download the messages to your computer and tell you, you have new mail. You click on OK, and then just click on the new messages that you have to open them. You can tell they are new by the unopened markers next to them.

If you want to make the best use of email make sure to check regularly for incoming mail and reply as soon as possible. The benefit of email is its ease of use in sending, receiving AND replying promptly. You don't have to use the same computer to access your email, you can access it remotely from other computers as long as the computer has email software and you know the domain name of your mail server and your user details. The email program has an automatic reply command, which will instruct it to prepare an email reply to go to the sender of the email. The program automatically insert the senders email address, and by default the same subject header. You have the option of including the original text in the message when you reply so that you can refer to points in it. Occasionally you will get email returned to you that has "bounced", this happens if you type the address incorrectly or the user has cancelled their account. It will be returned to you with an error message telling you why it couldn't be delivered like - "this message could not be delivered as there was no email account or mail box for this person". It is very important to get the address exactly right including all underscores and full stops. Electronic Mail in the classroom is an exciting adventure for both students and teachers. Some of the benefits of using electronic mail include:

- Students are writing messages for a purpose and a real audience
- Increased focus on literacy
- Increased motivation
- Co-operative team work
- Less emphasis on teacher-directed learning
- Improved research skills
- Increased communications
- Provides stimulus for students to learn about other cultures
- Increased comprehension, hand-eye coordination and typing skills

There are many fun and educational projects can be joined through the Global Classroom Project site. An electronic mail list is simply a discussion group which operates via electronic mail. In its simplest form an e-mail list can be a small number of people who send mail backwards and forwards to each other, possibly a professional group, or people with a particular interest in common. Imagine that at one stage this group of people decided to formalise things a bit, and appointed one person to operate as the maintainer of the discussion. One way of doing this would be for that person to maintain the list of e-mail addresses of the other members. Then each member of the list who wanted to join in the discussion would forward their message to that one person, who would then distribute it to everyone else. This would work quite well if there were only a small number of participants, but what if the discussion was so interesting that lots of people wanted to join in? It would become a lot of work for the person who was running the list. In order to make life simpler for the person who runs the list (the list owner), there are several kinds of software which automate the running of an e-mail list, including enrolling new members (subscribing), removing members (un-subscribing), changing mail preferences and distributing the messages.

There are several different kinds of software which do this, one of the most common is known as Listserv software, so you will often see e-mail discussion lists called Listservs, after this software. However there are other kinds, including Majordomo. All of this list software operates in a similar fashion, so once you have learned how one kind works, it is easy to learn the others if you need to. Schools who choose to connect to the Internet through EduNet, will be able to use the SINA Administrator tools to create and administer their own email lists. Simply, once you have subscribed to the list (see below), all you need to do is send your mail message to the list's address and your message will be automatically distributed to every other member of the list.

Electronic mail lists are an excellent way of participating in discussions with people who share an interest in your particular subject area. They are a good way of keeping up with the latest developments in your field by belonging to a network of people all over the world who are working in your area. You can share ideas or concerns, ask questions, find out about research, conferences or professional development activities and discover what is going on in other regions, states or countries Electronic mail is a relatively low cost form of communication and e-mail lists are free. It costs you nothing except your dial-up time to subscribe and participate. The only cost you might find is in time, if you join a high volume mail list, or find yourself participating in a lot of discussions!

For people who may be isolated from other professional networks because of distance, or for any other reason, electronic mail lists are an excellent way of remaining in touch with your colleagues, researchers in your field and other interested people. There are tens of thousands of e-mail lists in the world covering a huge variety of subjects. If you are looking for a list in a particular subject area here are some places to look. PAML, (Publicly Accessible Mail Lists) at: http://www.neosoft.com/internet/paml/ has possibly one of the most comprehensive lists of electronic discussion lists on the web. Another place to look is LIZST at: http://www.liszt.com/ where you can search more than 66, 000 lists for one that interests you.

Once you have found a list you need to let the list know that you want to join in the discussion by subscribing to the list. You do this by sending a subscription message (request to join the list) to the list address. The subscription message will vary depending on which list administration software is being used. Here is a table of the subscription messages for the major list administration software.

Package	*Command*
LISTSERV	subscribe listname yourfirstname yourlastname
LISTPROC	subscribe listname yourfirstname yourlastname
MAILBASE	join listname yourfirstname yourlastname
MAJORDOMO	subscribe listname

Depending on the list you will get a message back, either letting you know that you are subscribed to the list, or that your subscription to the list has gone to the list owner for approval. Some lists are moderated or closed lists, which means that the list is open only to a particular group of people, or that all messages sent to the list need to be approved by the list owner before they circulate to other members. Note that most lists are publicly accessible, so that all you need to do is send your subscription message in order to be allowed to join.

All e-mail lists have two addresses. One address is that of the automatic list software (for example listserv or majordomo), the other is the address to which you send your messages when you want to participate in the discussion. The first address will have the name of the e-mail software as the first element, (the bit before the @). The second address has the same element after the @ as the first address, but the bit before the @ is the name of the list. So if we invent a listserv called list-l, which is held at an address called address.edu.au, the two addresses would be:

listserv@address.edu.au and list-l@address.edu.au.

The first address is where you send your subscription detail, the second address is where you can send your messages to join in the discussion. An easy way to sort this out is to think of the e-mail list as a club you want to join. Most clubs will have a secretary who is responsible for such things as requests to join, membership subscriptions, changes of address and other administrative details. This is the equivalent of the first address (majordomo@edx1.educ.monash.edu.au). However, if you wanted to submit an article to the club's newsletter you wouldn't send it to the secretary, you'd send it to the person responsible for that particular activity, possibly the newsletter editor. This is the equivalent of the second address (called the list address), the one where you send your thoughts, comments, information and questions.

It is important that you are sure of the difference between the two addresses because if you try and send a question to the majordomo address you will simply get an error message back, while if you send a query about your subscription to the list address you won't get any action. One important thing to remember about subscribing to a list is that in order to use the list, you need to send any messages, to either address, from the original e-mail address you subscribed from. It is the equivalent of having the club's newsletter sent to your home address, if you move and don't let the secretary know you have changed addresses, you will no longer get your mail. So if you change e-mail addresses you will have to unsubscribe from the list using your old address and resubscribe using your new address. If you send a message to the list and get a reply saying that you are no longer subscribed to the list, check to make sure that you are sending your message from the e-mail address you used to subscribe.

There are other commands you can send to the majordomo which can be very useful to know. One of the most useful, and the easiest to remember is the word HELP.

If you send a message to you majordomo address with just this in the body of your message you will receive a list of the commands that majordomo recognises, including instructions for subscribing and unsubscribing. But remember that their is more to e-mail than just joining a list, you need to remember that there are real people on the other end of the list. This is where Netiquette is important.

Because e-mail is fast and easy to use, there is a tendency to write before you think. In order to make and keep friends using e-mail it is a good idea to learn about Netiquette, but it is also important to learn a few e-mail style guidelines which will make your messages welcome in the mail boxes of your correspondents.

- Most e-mail programs are strictly text only, and use only the letters, numbers and keyboard punctuation marks, without any of the formatting you are used to being able to use in word-processing.
- Keep it short. Unformatted text is not particularly easy to read on screen, so your chances of someone reading your whole message are better if you keep it as concise as possible. The length of a message might not seem important if you don't get much mail, but for people who receive a lot of e-mail there may not be time to read long messages.
- If you need to write a longer message, flag it in the subject line of the message, i.e. "Why the Cat in the Hat Came Back (long)". This way people know that it's a long message and can decide whether they have time to read it immediately.
- Always use a subject line and try and make it as relevant as possible to your message. This is the first part of the message anyone sees when they open their e-mail program and many people choose whether or not to read the message on the basis of the subject line.
- A whole screen of text is not easy to read either, so try and break your message up into short paragraphs with breaks in between. White space makes text easier to read.
- For much the same reasons don't use all capitals in a message. In the culture of cyberspace, messages written in all capitals are seen as shouting. This is because a message composed entirely of capital letters is uncomfortable to read. It's okay though to use all capitals IF YOU WANT TO EMPHASIZE SOMETHING, as long as it's not a whole message.
- There are other ways of creating emphasis. You can use *.* to indicate italics. This can be *very useful*.
- If you want to underline you can use underscores _. For example if you wanted to underline the title of a book, _The Cat in the Hat_.

- Keep your line length shorter than 80 characters and preferably no longer than 60 characters. Otherwise when your message is received it might break in strange places which is very irritating to read.
- If you are sending a message to a mailing list, don't start your message with a space. Some mailing lists gather a group of messages together and send them to subscribers all at once (this is called a digest). A message with a space at the beginning can cause the digest to truncate at your message.
- Always include your name and e-mail address at the bottom of your message. Some mail programs don't receive the message header which generally includes your name and e-mail address, so if they wanted to answer you they might not be able to.
- Some people have created remarkable signatures from simple ASCII text, but they tend to be quite large. Try and keep your signature file to no more than four lines. Some people have to pay for their e-mail by the amount they download, so it is considerate to save message size by keeping your signature short.
- If you receive a message with what looks like a signature file but you can't make any sense of it, try and change the font on your browser to a proportional font such as Courier, (a proportional font is one in which each character takes up the same amount of space in a line).
- There are other ways of adding personality and meaning to your e-mail message, these are known as emoticons and acronyms.
- If you are responding to a previous message, quote the relevant bit of the post you are replying to in your own message and if possible quote the name of the sender. Don't go overboard and re-post the entire thing, but give enough information so that it is clear what you are talking about.

For example:

Last week Jane Austen wrote:

>If you are responding to a previous message,
>quote the relevant bit of the post your are replying too
>in your own message.

There are many ways of adding personality and meaning to your e-mail message, these are known as emoticons and acronyms. There are lots of them, but the most common are the ones to indicate humour. There is the smiley face :-) (try looking at it sideways), the grin, and the very big grin. Try some of these in your messages.

Acronyms			
FOFL	Fall on the floor laughing	IRL	In real life
LOL	Laugh out loud	YMMV	Your mileage may vary
ROTFL	Roll on the floor laughing	ITRW	In the real world
TTFN	Ta ta for now	BTW	By the way
Grin	Grin, joking	BG	Big grin
VBG	Very big grin	RTFM	Read the flaming manual
TIA	Thanks in advance	IMHO	In my humble opinion
IMNSHO	In my not so humble opinion	IOW	In other words

Emoticons			
:-)	Smile, "I'm joking"	:-(	Frown, "I'm not happy"
:)	Smiley for lazy typists	:(	Frown for lazy typists
;-)	Wink, a sly grin	:-O	Shocked
*	Kiss	{ } [ ]	Hugs
{{{***}}}	Hugs and kisses	:-P	Sticking out your tongue
:,-(	Crying	:-|	Can't decide how to feel

Overcoming Email Overload with Eudora 5 : A Case Study

Do you ever feel overwhelmed by email? Do you ever have to struggle to get through all of your messages between meetings? Does getting one more frivolous message ever make you angry?

It probably wasn't always this way. When you started using email, you probably only got a trickle of email messages each day. After a few months, perhaps ten messages arrived in your inbox daily. A few months after that, you changed to a different department at work and started getting thirty messages per day. And yesterday you came to work and found ten messages about the facilities shutdown, five announcements that people have changed jobs, three jokes, seven messages complaining about the new lobby furniture, four announcements of new projects, eight direct questions about some aspect of your job, two notices that a red minivan's lights are on, confirmation that the book you bought on-line has shipped, and fifty other similarly random messages.

Little by little, your trickle turned into a flood, and now you are gasping for air.

Does this sound like you? If so, cheer up—you've come to the right place. This book will save your time and perhaps your sanity. Some techniques might require a little bit of work at first, but they will be worth it over time.

If you don't get this much email, count yourself lucky—for now. This book will show you how to keep from getting overwhelmed in the future. This book is for anybody using Eudora 5 who gets too much email. While you need to know a few very basic things, you do not need to be an expert on Eudora 5. This book explains all the advanced features that you need to know—and doesn't waste your time explaining every single possible thing you can do with Eudora 5. Even if you are a Eudora power user, this book will still be useful. Three-quarters of the book is on email strategies, not which button to push or which menu to pull down. If this were a book on writing, it would be something like Effective Business Communication, not Mastering WordPerfect 7.3.2 in Ten Easy Steps Unleashed. When there is more than one page of "buttons and menus" instruction, I give the page number of the next strategy section. This lets you easily skip over material you already know. I do assume that you are familiar with the basic operations of Eudora and:

- can send and receive email messages
- can add nicknames to your address book
- can use the Find and Search tools
- can open a message in its own window
- know what mailing lists (also called listservs, list servers, listbots, or distribution lists) are

There were a few topics that clearly some people know and others do not. To give the information some people need without boring the ones who know it already, I put a very brief discussions of mailboxes and labels in Mailboxes and Labels.

If you need a comprehensive reference manual for Eudora, you should find another book. Eudora for Windows and Macintosh: Visual Quickstart Guide by Adam Engst (Peachpit Press, 1999) should tell you what you need.

If you are a teacher, you will find this book suitable for classroom instruction at many levels. The language in the book is easily accessible, even for teenagers. On the other hand, its deconstructions of the medium can be jumping-off points for collegiate classroom discussions. Homework exercises are available at

http://www.OvercomeEmailOverload.com/exercises/

While there is material that applies to anybody, I wrote this book for people who get too much email at work. Very few people are overwhelmed by messages from their closest personal friends.

Here's a preview of what you will learn in each chapter.

This book starts by explaining filters —instructions that you can give to your email program to organize and prioritize your messages automatically. Organize and Prioritize Your Messages and Useful Filter Recipes are by far the most technical of the chapters, but also the ones that I believe are the most useful. When I started using filters, I was able to get through my email messages in half the time it took before.

- Organize and Prioritize Your Messages, gives strategies for grouping messages, shows how to create filters, and gives strategies for showing a message's importance.
- Useful Filter Recipes, is a "cookbook" with examples of useful filters.

Finding and selecting a message in Eudora doesn't take much time, but it's something you do over and over. A little bit of time saved on each operation can add up quickly.

- Move Around Your Messages Quickly, shows keyboard and mouse shortcuts for navigating through your messages more efficiently.

Reading messages more efficiently helps enormously, but if you still have to read and respond to a hundreds of messages per day, it might not be enough.

- Reduce the Number of Incoming Messages, gives strategies for reducing the number of messages you get.
- Spend Less Time on Responses, shows how to cut down on the amount of time you spend composing replies, while still being responsive to the messages that matter.

Another way to save time is to write better messages. A miscommunication means more work for you—which usually means more email. Reducing your load by writing well is such an important topic that it's split into four chapters.

- Reduce Ambiguity, shows how to make the content of your messages more clear. If you write clear messages, people won't have to send you further messages asking for an explanation.
- Convey Emotional Tone, gives strategies the emotional tone more clear. You won't have to spend as much time explaining your intentions.
- Make Messages Legible, shows how to send messages that your correspondents can read easily. This reduces the number of times you'll have to send a message.
- Get and Keep Attention, shows how to improve the chances that your correspondents will notice, understand, and reply to your messages. This means less time you'll spend on getting a response or action from your correspondents.

At some point, regardless of how well you manage your own email, you'll be limited by your coworkers' email habits.

- Improve Your Company's Email Effectiveness, discusses techniques for improving email efficiency for your whole organization.

Each chapter ends with a set of summarizing bullet points.

Appendix A has an extensive glossary. I do define almost all technical terms, abbreviations, and jargon the first time I use them, but I realize that you might not read the whole book straight through. I also don't define some of the more elementary terms. Finally, the Glossary defines some email terms that this book doesn't use, but that you might see in other places.

As mentioned earlier, Mailboxes and Labels discusses mailboxes and labels.

There are many different versions of Eudora. There are Windows and Mac OS versions of all three Eudora 5 modes: Paid, Sponsored, and Light. As far as the material in this book is concerned, the three versions have very few differences. I will point differences out as they come up.

(If you are using Eudora 5 at work, you probably have Paid mode. Paid mode costs money and has all the features. Sponsored mode has all the features and is free, but you have to look at advertising. Light mode is free but doesn't have as many features as Sponsored and Paid mode.)

There are many older versions of Eudora, but fortunately Qualcomm is very good at maintaining compatibility between versions. If you use an older version, the pictures might look different, but most of the features discussed in this book are essentially the same. You can learn more about how your version's lack of features affects material discussed in this book at:

http://www.OvercomeEmailOverload.com/eudora/versions.html

While I only have a limited amount of space in this book to cover material, the Web is not limited. There is additional material at this book's Web site:

http://www.OvercomeEmailOverload.com/eudora

The site has:

- exercises for students
- visual aids (overheads) suitable for lectures
- a list of errors that were found after the book went to the printers
- template files that you can download and use
- links to sites with further information

Please take a moment to read about the notation and terminology. Understanding the notation will help you spot examples more easily and recognize how I've simplified things. Understanding the terminology will make the explanations easier to follow. Sections that mainly cover which buttons to push and which menus to pull down have section headers that start with "How to..."

I use a fixed-width font for anything that the computer would print or that you would type.

If you need to select something from a menu, I use arrows (->) to show the order of the menu selection. For example, if I tell you to select Message -> New Message, that means that you should first select the Message menu, then select New Message from the choices that appear.

I sometimes combine Mac OS and Windows commands with a slash. For example, almost all keyboard shortcuts are identical between Mac OS and Windows except for the modifier keys. I sometimes write instructions like "press Command / Control-w to close the window." That means that if you are using Mac OS, then you should press Command-w; if you are using Windows, you should press Control-w.

All filter recipes (covered in Organize and Prioritize Your Messages and Useful Filter Recipes) are boxed like this:

when a message arrives
if To: *contains roses-talk@rosegardens.org*
then Transfer To mailbox RoseGardening

Figures showing Eudora windows don't reproduce particularly well and have a lot of unimportant details. I therefore usually show email messages as text instead of as screen shots. Email messages have a light grey background like this:

Subject: This is in the header of an example message.
Date: Mon, 1 Jan 2000 20:09:59 -0800
From: sender@catfloss.org
To: receiver@catfloss.org

This is the body of an example message.

I need to explain some of the email terms as well. Unfortunately, the terminology of email is a bit odd.

- Body: The body is the actual text of the conversation. In the example above, the body is This is the body of an example message.
- The header: The information about a message is called the header. That's what's above the line in the example above. The header includes things like

who the message is to, who it is from, when it was sent, what the subject is, and so on.

- Headers: Each line in the header is called a header. For example, the Subject: line is a header. So is the Date: line; so is the From: line. They are all headers. (I didn't come up with this terminology, I'm just reporting it.)

I don't show all possible headers. Email messages usually have ten to twenty headers, most of which are only interesting to email programs or the programmers who write them. These headers are so dull, in fact, that Eudora usually hides most of the headers from you.

Unless a header is important to an example, I leave it out. For example, if I am not discussing dates or times, I leave out the Date: header. I even leave out the From: and To: headers frequently.

When I show the header in an example, a thin black line separates the header and body. The header is above the line and the body is below the line.

I usually leave out email signatures in examples. Signatures are useful, but they take up space that I'd rather use for explanations.

I put short pieces of advice that don't fit in the flow of the text into TIP boxes, like this:

Eudora usually shows quotes in email messages with black vertical lines that it calls excerpt bars. However, people using different email programs usually see ">" at the beginning of your quoted lines, even if you see excerpt bars when you create the message. Because of that—and because it is difficult for me to simulate excerpt bars in my text layout program—I almost always show quotes with ">".

E-mail for Users and Programmers: Introduction

This chapter starts with an introduction to electronic mail: we'll take a quick look at how email is sent and how UNIX handles it. There's a brief comparison of MH, *xmh*, and other UNIX mail agents. Whether you've used other mail agents or not, this chapter should help you understand why (and how) MH is special. Next are some guidelines for addressing email. Following that is an overview of the important file called the MH profile. The chapter ends with information about the latest versions.

MH and nmh: Email for Users and Programmers

Electronic mail, often called "email," is a way to communicate with people as close as your office or as far away as the other side of the world. You type a message and put addresses on it; email programs use your computer and a network such as the Internet to deliver the message. Email programs run everywhere from microcomputers to supercomputers (of course, this book covers MH and related email programs, which run under UNIX). The people who read your messages don't have to use the same mail system as you do; their computers don't need to run UNIX.

Messages usually arrive anywhere from a few seconds to a few hours after they're sent. (They're held at computers along the way if a connection can't be made; also, some computers send mail in batches periodically.) The recipient can read your message, print it, send a reply to you and other people who were copied, file it, remove it... right away or whenever it's convenient.

Email is getting to be a part of life. It connects people on all kinds of computers, handles an uncountable number of messages every day, and lets you stay in contact when you're not in your office. Email provides a handy way to get information to and from busy people without playing telephone tag or interrupting them with a phone call. You can use email to announce or arrange meetings, discuss problems, share opinions among members of a group, and much more. Of course, email isn't the answer for everything. Sometimes a phone call or a FAX is easier and quicker.

UNIX Email System

In general, each UNIX computer has two kinds of programs that handle mail:

- A *user agent* is a mail program that humans use. It collects the mail messages you send and shows messages you receive. The user agent is an interface to the second kind of program: the transfer agent.
- A *transfer agent* is a "system" program that you usually don't run directly. It accepts messages from the user agent and routes them to their destinations. A transfer agent usually also delivers mail into each user's *system mailbox*, a file where the user agent can get the new messages that other people send you. But a *mail hook* program can intercept and process the message before your mailbox — see the Chapter on Processing New Mail Automatically.

There are lots of user agent programs and there are several common transfer agents. How a mail message gets from A to B is a diagram that shows what happens when you send a message. Your user agent collects the message and gives it to your computer's transfer agent. Your transfer agent either delivers the message if you're sending it to someone on your computer or sends the message across a network to another computer's transfer agent. Then the person you sent the message to runs a user agent to bring in the message from the system mailbox, read it (view graphics, hear sounds, and so on) — and maybe also print the message, reply to it, delete it, etc.

Email Transfer Agents

Mail transfer agents (MTAs) are complicated programs. They have to understand all kinds of nasty details about message addressing, networks, error handling, and other functions. Some typical MTAs are *sendmail* and MMDF. This book doesn't cover transfer agents.

Email User Agents

If you send and receive only a few email messages, you probably don't need to learn much. Almost any user agent will do (and there are a lot of them). MH and *xmh* are fine for beginners: there are just a few basic concepts and commands to learn.

But when you start to do more with email, you'll want a user agent that saves you time, lets you organize messages the way you want to, and helps you find messages you've stored. You'll probably want to automate routine work. You might even customize your email setup so it works exactly the way you'd like it to. This is where advanced, flexible systems like MH stand out. Here's a quick comparison of user agents.

Monolithic Mail Agents

Most user mail agents are monolithic: you're in the mail program until you quit out of it. To start the program, you type its name, like *mail*, at a shell prompt. (The shell prompt is shown as a percent sign (%) here; your prompt may be a dollar sign ($) or something else.) Then that program takes over — it reads and executes all the commands you type until you use its *quit* command. For example, here's how you would read, print, and delete two mail messages with the standard UNIX program named *mail*:

```
% mail
Date: Mon, 09 Jan 1995 07:53:55 EST
From: nancyo (Nancy O'Leary)
To: jdpeek
Subject: meeting

I'm free at 3 today. Is that okay?

? s toprint
Date: Mon, 09 Jan 1995 08:54:22 EST
From: biffj (Biff Jameson)
To: jdpeek
Subject: the meeting

I can be there at 11 or 3 today.

? s toprint
% lpr toprint
% rm toprint
```

You show the first message on the screen. At the first prompt (which is a question mark (?) in this program), you give the command to save the message in a file named *toprint*, which also automatically deletes the message. (You're saving to a file because you can't print directly from this particular *mail* program.) You read and save the next message in the same file *toprint*. The mail agent automatically quits because it's given you all the messages. Then you print the messages you saved and delete the *toprint* file. Most mail agents have more commands built in. For instance, many have a command for printing a message directly. A lot can send a reply to or a copy of a message. Some let you organize messages into groups. Most also let you type a single UNIX command without leaving the mail agent: that's called a *shell escape*.

Monolithic mail agents keep all of the messages in your system mailbox or a file in your account named something like *mbox*. These are single files which hold all mail messages together. The messages are separated in one of several ways. The mail agent knows how to parse (split) them into separate messages, but this format makes it harder to do complex things like rearranging the order of the messages.

MH

Here's the same example using MH. (nmh, the new MH, works the same way.) Because MH commands aren't part of a monolithic mail agent, you type all the commands at the shell prompt:

```
% inc
Incorporating new mail into inbox...
1+ 01/09 Nancy O'Leary       Meeting<<I'm free at 3 today. Is that
2 01/09 Biff Jameson the     meeting<<I can be there at 11 or 3
% show
(Message inbox:1)
Date: Mon, 09 Jan 1995 07:53:55 EST
From: nancyo (Nancy O'Leary)
To: jdpeek
Subject: meeting

I'm free at 3 today. Is that okay?
% next
(Message inbox:2)
Date: Mon, 09 Jan 1995 08:54:22 EST
From: biffj (Biff Jameson)
To: jdpeek
Subject: the meeting
```

I can be there at 11 or 3 today.

% show 1 2 | lpr

% rmm 1 2

Because MH commands aren't part of a monolithic mail system, you can use them at any time; you don't have to start or quit the mail agent. It's fine to mix other UNIX commands between your MH commands, to leave your mail for a while and do something else, and to work at several terminals at the same time. Because you use MH commands from a shell prompt, you can use all the power of the shell. For instance, I used a pipe to send the output of the *show* command to the printer directly. I removed the two messages after sending them to the printer. If your shell has time-saving aliases or functions (and most do), you'll be able to use them with MH. And because MH isn't a monolithic mail agent, you can use MH commands in UNIX shell scripts or call them from programs in languages like C or *perl*. Unlike most mail agents, MH keeps each message in a separate file. The filename is the message number. To rearrange the messages, MH just changes the filenames. MH can use standard UNIX filesystem operations such as removing, copying, and linking on its messages. The message files are grouped into one or more *folders*, which are actually UNIX directories.

The MH setup has a lot of advantages. A significant disadvantage is that it takes more filesystem space to store the messages. See the Chapter Key Parts of the UNIX Filesystem for an overview.

nmh, The New MH

After almost twenty years, development of MH seems to have stopped. Most activity is with nmh, the "new MH". Although nmh is mostly backward-compatible with MH, its user interface is evolving. And the nmh internals are becoming a lot different than MH: old limitations are being removed, security is improved, and installation is much easier. This book explains differences between MH and nmh at the place that seems the most logical to me—usually in the general introduction to a command or feature. For a concise list of user interface changes, read the file *DIFFERENCES* in the top-level directory of the nmh source tree. (You can also compare the MH and nmh manual pages for a particular command. But the nmh manpages tend to be more complete—and to document MH features that weren't well-documented before.) The *ChangeLog* file in the top-level directory of the nmh source tree has a fairly detailed list of changes, version by version, as nmh evolved.

Front Ends to MH

The *xmh*, MH-E and *exmh* programs are something like a monolithic mail agent; they each have an interface with a limited set of commands. But they actually run MH commands for you; if you need to do something that you can't do with the interface, you can always use the MH command instead. MH-E, *exmh*, and *xmh* are examples of what I call a *front end*. A front end is a program or set of programs that is an interface to MH commands. They let you do some of the most common things you need from MH, usually by pressing a single key, clicking a button, or using a menu. In fact, if you know how to write a program in some UNIX programming language — such as the Bourne shell, Perl, or Tcl — you can write a front end to MH. One Chapter of this book has tips for programming with MH. The typical sessions with MH, *xmh*, MH-E, and *exmh*. If you decide that a front end to MH (like *xmh*) is right for you, it's still a good idea to get familiar with the rest of the MH commands and features. That's because there's a lot in MH that you might need — to make your email use easier or more efficient — that your front end may not let you do easily, if at all.

xmh comes with the X Window System from the X Consortium. It's built with standard parts of X. If you're familiar with X and know how to customize the X Toolkit, you'll feel right at home with *xmh*. Even if you don't want to customize *xmh*, the "out of the box" design makes it easy to use MH commands without using the UNIX command line. If you use the GNU Emacs editor, or you use a terminal that doesn't "do windows," MH-E can be a great choice for an MH front end. It gives you all the power of GNU Emacs — including the ability to divide a standard non-windowing terminal into multiple windows. Many of the commands take only a single character.

The *exmh* interface looks something like *xmh*. It also runs under the X Window System. But instead of the X Toolkit, *exmh* is built with Tcl/Tk. By default, *exmh* is far more powerful than *xmh*. One major difference is that *exmh* can read and send MIME multimedia mail. But, while *xmh* is stable and hasn't changed much in the last two major releases of X, *exmh* is evolving quickly. If you aren't interested in being on the "bleeding edge" of email technology and updating your software fairly often (as bug fixes and new versions are announced), *exmh* may be worth watching from a short distance away. There are many other interfaces to MH as well — too many to mention here. You can read brief summaries about them in the FAQ, the Frequently Asked Questions document that is posted regularly to the Usenet newsgroup *comp.mail.mh*. In fact, the FAQ contains so much good information that it could be a part of this book. But, because the FAQ changes so often, we thought it would be better just to tell you how to get it.

MIME

Until recently, email could transmit only plain English text. Words in other languages, with characters that don't belong to the character set used in English, couldn't be sent. For instance, Spanish-speaking email users had to use kludges like montana to stand for the word *montaña*. If you wanted to send data, pictures, word-processor documents, sound, video, and other non-text messages, you had to use workarounds that many recipients couldn't handle.

In 1992, the Multipurpose Internet Mail Extensions, MIME, started to change that. The MIME standard lets users around the world send text and documents in a way that everyone can receive. If a recipient's email user agent can't display MIME messages, the messages will still be in a format that makes most of the text readable. Instead of trying to change everyones' mail transport systems, MIME was designed to work around limitations — to work with existing systems.

More and more email user agents support MIME. MH support started with a set of patches to MH version 6.7.2. Both *exmh* and MH-E can send and receive MIME mail. If you use *xmh*, there are patches in the Metamail package for MIME support.

Addressing Email

Email addressing varies. How you do it on your computer and your network might be different than what I show here. Basically, though, there are two kinds of email addresses:

- If you're sending a message to someone who has an account on your computer, address it to that person's username (login name). For instance, if Marty Waters logs on to his account with the username *mwaters*, you can address his mail to mwaters.
- If you're sending a message to someone who reads mail on another computer, you'll usually need to include that computer's name in your address. Two forms of addresses are pretty common:
  1. Internet addresses have a username, followed by an at sign (@) and the other computer's hostname. For example, if Edie Nisbaum's username is *edie* and her computer is named *giraffe.zoo.utx.edu* you'd address Internet mail to her as *edie@giraffe.zoo.utx.edu*.
  2. UUCP addresses have the other computer's name, followed by an exclamation point (!) and then the username. If Sandi Shore is *sandis* and her computer is named *beach*, you might address her mail as *beach!sandis*.

MH Profile

MH - and front-ends, like *xmh*, through the MH commands they run — use a file called the *MH profile*. By default, it's stored in your home directory and named. *mh_profile* (its name starts with a period, which makes it a hidden file that you won't see in an *ls* listing unless you use the *-A* or *-a* option). The MH profile defines your personal configuration for MH.

When you first use an MH command like *inc*, if your account doesn't already have an. *mh_profile*, the command will make one for you. The most basic MH profile has just one line: the Path: entry. (The MH manual pages use several different terms for these elements of the MH profile and similar files: *component*, *entry*, and *line*. In this book, I use the term *entry*.) You can add to or edit the file any time — in fact, as you learn more about MH, you'll probably want to make a few changes.

The Example below is a fairly short MH profile.

Example: Short MH Profile

Path: Mail
Folder-protect: 750
Msg-protect: 640
Signature: Emma H. User
repl: -annotate
scan: -form scan.time

That MH profile says that your MH directory is named *Mail* and stored in your home directory. It sets the default file access modes, with the numbers used by *chmod*(1), for folders and messages. The fourth entry tells MH how your name should look in the From: header field of messages you send. (The MH manual pages call these *header components*. Many email users call them *headers*. The term used in Internet standards documents like RFC 822 and RFC 1521 is *header fields*. I use that term in this book.) The last two entries make *-annotate* a default switch for the *repl* command and change the display format of the *scan* command. Your MH profile can't have blank lines in it. Another Section has detailed information and a longer example. Also see the *mh-profile*(5) manual page (for help finding online manual pages, see the Section Online Manual Pages).

Computers Supporting MH?

If you have a computer running UNIX, you can probably run MH — and you can almost certainly run nmh. Ports to non-UNIX operating systems aren't too likely, I think, because MH and nmh take advantage of UNIX filesystem features like hard links that aren't available on other OSes. (If you know of ports, please click the link at the bottom of this page and tell me!)

You can get MH on the Internet or on tape. Someone who has a fair amount of experience installing UNIX software can probably get MH running on your system. The latest version (which this book covers) is numbered 6.8.4. MH 6.8.4 runs under Berkeley UNIX, System V, SunOS, Solaris, and other versions of UNIX. Some UNIX versions need patches — so, if you have trouble building MH, check archives of the *comp.mail.mh* Usenet newsgroup or the mailing lists. Unless you have a reason to get MH, though, I'd recommend the new version called nmh. nmh has much improved security and many bugs fixed, has more complete documentation and is much easier to install. It's evolving rapidly but is fairly stable; the latest version (as of this writing) is 1.0. It's available on the Internet. What about the front-end interfaces to MH and nmh? The *xmh* program is part of the standard X distribution. The latest version runs under X Version 11 Release 6. You can also get MH-E and *exmh* from the Internet; the current versions are newer than the versions this book covers. MH and nmh can get mail from another machine with POP, the Post Office Protocol. As of this writing, I don't know of any support for IMAP. IMAP archives are nowhere near as rich and flexible as the UNIX filesystem model that MH uses, and IMAP doesn't support all of the features that MH provides. So my guess is that full IMAP support won't happen soon. For the latest, check the newsgroup and mailing lists.

Obtaining MH, nmh, xmh, exmh, and MH-E

All the programs described in this book are available without charge. *xmh* is a standard client in the X Window System distribution. See Appendix MH and nmh Source Code for instructions on getting MH, Appendix Getting exmh for instructions on getting *exmh*, and Section Getting MH-E in *The MH-E Manual* for instructions on getting MH-E.

Organizing and Prioritizing Messages

If you are like most people, you go through your messages in the order that they arrive. This can be very inefficient: you can spend so much time on low- or medium-priority messages that you don't get to a time-critical message until it's too late. Perhaps you skim the subjects and guess what is important and what isn't. Unfortunately, relying on your eyes and memory can be dangerous. You might see an urgent message that distracts you enough that you forget to go back and deal with an important but less-urgent message. You might even overlook an important message completely. Think about how you handle your paper mail. You undoubtedly sort your paper mail quickly before you read it. Having messages categorized helps you figure out what to look at first, what to read later, and what to ignore. Prioritizing your email messages can help as much as prioritizing paper mail. If your messages are sorted into groups of related messages, then you can:

- Match your response speed to message priority. You can look at high-priority groups of messages often and ignore low-priority groups until you have a free moment. For example, you might want to examine messages from your closest coworkers the moment the messages arrive but wait until the end of the day to read through a company-wide announcements list.
- Remember discussions. If you read all the messages on a topic one after another, you are likely to remember what was in earlier messages on that topic. If a lot of unrelated messages separate two related messages, you might not understand the later message without re-reading the earlier one.
- Judge the amount of traffic on a topic. Grouping related messages together makes it easy to see how many new messages on a particular topic have

arrived. The number of related messages can give you a clue about what action you should take. Suppose, for example, that someone sends a message that asks a question. If you see a lot of responses to that message, someone else has probably already answered the question. You will then know to read all the responses before replying, instead of composing a response right away.

Fortunately, Eudora has tools that can organize and prioritize messages for you. These tools—called filters —can move messages into different mailboxes based on rules that you set up. For example, you might set up your filters to file all messages from a mailing list into its own mailbox. Setting up filters is probably the single most important step to take to regain control of your email. It does take some effort to set up filters, but it is well worth it. This chapter gives strategies for prioritizing messages, discussing how to:

- group related messages together
- configure filters in Eudora
- keep track of messages you aren't done with
- test your filters
- keep messages and their responses together
- organize with multiple accounts

This chapter is by far the most technical chapter of the whole book. But while filters might look intimidating, they aren't actually very difficult. If you can follow written directions to bake a cake or change a sparkplug, then you can set up filters.

Group by Category

You may be tempted to use filters to move messages to different mailboxes. However, when messages are spread across many mailboxes, most people have a hard time keeping track of messages that they haven't finished with yet. In most cases it's better to prioritize by categorizing messages with labels. With labels, you can assign a category and a color to a message. To assign categories and colors to labels, select Special -> Settings... -> Labels (Mac OS) or Tools -> Options... -> Labels (Windows). (For more about labels, see Labels.) Assign labels to all your incoming messages, sort your inbox by label, and remove messages from your inbox when you have finished with them. This lets you see all of your "to-do" messages quickly and in priority order. The label's name is usually visible in a column towards the left side. Messages with labels Charlie, Payroll, CoWorkers, and Announce are visible. If your Label column is not visible, select Special -> Settings... -> Mailbox Display (Mac OS) or Tools -> Options... -> Mailboxes (Windows), and put a check in the box marked Label.

Note that when you sort a mailbox by label, it's sorted by the order of the labels in the Special -> Settings... -> Labels (Mac OS) or Tools -> Options... -> Labels (Windows) windows, not alphabetically by the name you give to the label. For example, messages with the label Payroll sorted before messages with the label Announce. You should assign your labels in order of priority.

When you sort a mailbox by label, Eudora shows messages with no labels before messages with labels. If you are using Eudora for Mac OS, messages with system labels will appear before messages with Eudora labels.

Organize Your Categories

If you are used to filing paper documents, you might want to have lots and lots of categories. However, categorizing electronic mail messages is very different from filing paper documents. Finding an old paper memo can take so long that retrieval time is much, much more significant than filing time. It makes sense to have lots of categories for paper. Eudora's excellent sorting and searching tools make finding old messages much faster, so filing speed is much more significant than retrieval speed. This means you don't need as many categories for your email as for your paper documents. Giving each of your projects its own label is usually not a good idea. In addition to requiring many labels, this strategy guarantees that some email messages will be difficult to categorize. Email messages that mention two different projects could go in either project's category. Furthermore, categorizing based on project is very difficult to do automatically. Computers are still a lot dumber than humans: they don't do a good job at figuring out what a message means.

It is much easier to categorize based on what group the sender belongs to. There is always one and only one sender of a message, and people usually fit into relatively well-defined groups in your life. Your groups might include:

- coworkers in your immediate group
- other people in your company
- relatives
- friends
- fellow members of volunteer organizations
- various mailing lists that you've subscribed to (both work and personal)
- retailers that you have a relationship with
- retailers who are trying to get your business (junk email)
- automated response programs (such as order confirmations or account information)

While mailing list messages can be from many different people, I think of the messages as being "from" the mailing list. They are usually to the same address and so are easy to group together. Grouping keeps the conversations intact. I make an exception for jokes and do not categorize by sender. Usually the sender didn't write the joke, and a joke almost never has anything to do with your relationship to the sender. Furthermore, jokes almost never need a response. If your filters can tell that a message is a joke, they should put it in a jokes-only category, regardless of who sent it.

If You Have More Categories Than Labels

Unfortunately, you probably will have more categories than labels. Eudora for Mac OS has fifteen labels, which might be enough if you don't subscribe to many mailing lists. However, Eudora for Windows only gives you seven labels to work with. If you don't have enough labels for all of your categories, you might think of using the same label for several categories. For example, you could use one label for all of your mailing list messages. Unfortunately, that would mean that all of your mailing list messages would be mixed together. A better strategy is to use treat categories slightly differently depending upon their priority. You will probably find that you have three types of categories:

- high-priority: with messages that might turn into "to-do" items,
- medium-priority: with informational messages that are not likely to turn into "to-do" items, and
- low-priority: with messages that you don't want to read.

Assign your labels to high-priority messages. If you don't have enough labels for your medium- and low-priority categories, group their messages together in their own mailboxes. Because the medium- and low-priority messages are not likely to turn into "to-do" items, your inbox should still have all of your important messages. Here's an example of how someone might set up her labels and mailboxes. Assume that Mabel Garcia is a recreational skydiver, the payroll manager at Floss Recycling Incorporated, and likes to grow roses. Mabel should use labels for these high-priority categories:

- Husband—messages from her husband
- Family—family correspondence
- Payroll—messages from colleagues in the payroll department
- Coworkers—messages from people at Floss Recycling, Inc. who are not in the payroll department
- Announce—company-wide announcements (that sometimes turn into to-do items)
- Friends—messages from friends
- Unknown —messages that her filters can't categorize

If Mabel uses Eudora for Mac OS, she will have enough labels for her medium-priority messages:

- ParachuteJumps—parachute jump announcement mailing list
- RoseGardening—rose gardening mailing list
- Parachuting—general skydiving mailing list
- ConfirmationsUpdates—merchandise order confirmations

Eudora for Mac OS even has enough labels for her low-priority messages:

- Humor—jokes
- ProbableJunkEmail—junk email

However, if Mabel uses Eudora for Windows, she won't have enough labels for her medium- and low-priority messages. She must group those messages in mailboxes. You should move messages out of your inbox when you've finished with them, so you can see your "to-do" items more easily. If you transfer them to mailboxes with the same names as their labels, they will be easier to find. ((Don't) Mark Messages Done by Deleting will talk more about saving old messages.) So even if you have enough labels for all of your categories, you still need to create some mailboxes.

(If you don't know how to create and delete mailboxes, please read Mailboxes, then come back to this page.)

Order Your Mailboxes

You might want to give mailboxes the exact same name as your labels. However, Eudora lists mailboxes in alphabetical order—which usually isn't the same as your priority order or the order of your labels. To make it easier to find a mailbox quickly, you might want to change the order of the mailboxes to match your priority order. To change your mailboxes' order, put a letter in front of the mailbox name:

Without Letter	*With Letter*
Announce	a-Husband
ConfirmationsUpdates	b-Family
Coworkers	h-Payroll
Family	i-Coworkers
Friends	j-Announce
Humor	m-Friends
Husband	p-ParachuteJumps
ParachuteJumps	q-Roses
Parachuting	r-Parachuting

Payroll	w-ConfirmationsUpdates
ProbableJunkEmail	y-Humor
RoseGardening	z-ProbableJunkEmail

Why aren't the letters consecutive? (For example, why doesn't Payroll start with c- instead of h- ?) Because at some point, Mabel might want to add a new mailbox in between two old mailboxes. If she leaves a few letters unassigned, she can use an unassigned letter for the new mailbox instead of having to reassign all of the letters.

Eudora Filters

Once you have made labels and mailboxes for the different categories of your messages, you can start grouping your messages. Filters, like mail-sorting clerks, help enormously. (If you are already very familiar with filters in Eudora, you can skip to Use Multiple Accounts to Group Messages.) When you become so rich and famous that you get a flood of paper mail, you will probably hire somebody to sort your mail. You'll ask him or her to put all your greeting cards in one box, all the bills in another box, all junk mail in the trash, and so on.

Filters can do similar sorting actions. Mail room clerks, however, are much smarter than computers, so you have to be much more precise with a filter. You could tell a mail clerk simply, "Put all junk mail in that box." With a filter, you'd have to say something like "When the envelope's finish is glossy, put that piece of mail into the box marked `Junk'." In addition, a single filter can't handle too much at once. It's as if you needed one clerk to pick out junk mail and a second clerk to pick out bills.

"Real-World" Filters

To help introduce filters, let's first spend a page writing instructions for mail room clerks. For each instruction, you need to tell your clerks what action to take and under what conditions to take it. In the previous example, you want the clerk that when a letter arrives, if

the envelope's finish is glossy

then he or she should

put the piece of mail in the box labeled Junk

Or, combining the condition and the action:

when a letter arrives
if the envelope's finish is glossy
then put the piece of mail in the box labeled Junk

Email filters are very similar to these mail room clerks. You just have to tell them (carefully) what you want them to do.

How to Organize Messages with Eudora Filters

When you create filters for email, you can't use the same type of rules as you'd give a mail clerk. Email messages don't have envelopes or handwriting to give clues about the message's nature. However, filters can look for specific words or phrases in the message. This is a very powerful capability.

For example, if Mabel wants assign the label Payroll to all messages from Andy Jain (andy@flossrecycling.com), she can set up a filter to change the label if the From: header matches his email address:

when a message arrives
if From: is andy@flossrecycling.com
then Make Label -> Payroll

To create this filter, Mabel needs to first select the menu option Window ->> Filters (Mac OS) or Tools -> Filters (Windows).

The Filters Window has several parts. On the left is a list of all the filters, with buttons at the bottom for creating new ones and deleting existing ones. Because Mabel doesn't have any filters yet, there aren't any filters in the lists. On the right-hand side is where Mabel sets up the filter conditions and actions. At the top of the right-hand side are three checkboxes labelled Incoming, Outgoing, and Manual. These boxes tell Eudora when to run the filters: on all incoming messages, on all outgoing messages, or on messages that Mabel selects. If you put a check mark in the box labelled Manual at the top center of the Filters Window, then you can run that filter on messages at any time—not just when it arrives. Outgoing filters are useful for keeping both sides of a conversation together. How to Keep Conversations Together discusses outgoing filters further. For now, Incoming is the only box Mabel needs. Fortunately, when she starts to create a new filter, Eudora puts a check mark in the Incoming box automatically.

Below the checkboxes are the filter's conditions, as indicated by the arrow marked Conditions. Mabel can look for any word or phrase in any of several places in the message.

To make the filter to assign the label Payroll to any message from Andy Jain (andy@flossrecycling.com) Mabel needs to first click on the New button. The name Untitled will appear in the list of filters in the left-hand side. Changing the box next to Header: changes where the filter looks for the specified word or phrase. Mabel needs to change that box to From:. Directly below the header selection box is where Mabel enters the word or phrase that the filter looks for. In this case, Mabel should enter andy@flossrecycling.com. Below the conditions section is the actions section. Filters can do up to five actions. The most important ones are Make Label (to assign a label to a message) and Transfer To (to move a message to another mailbox). How to Prioritize with Advanced Filter Actions will cover other actions in more detail. The only action

Mabel's filter needs right now is an action that assigns the label Payroll to the message, as shown by the arrow in the lower right.

Finally, Mabel needs to save the filter by pressing Command-s (Mac OS) or Control-s (Windows). (She could also simply close the window; Eudora will ask if she wants to save her changes.)

How to Use Nicknames in Conditions to Reduce the Number of Filters

Suppose Mabel wants to assign the Payroll label to any messages from someone in the Payroll department, not just to Andy's messages. Mabel could make a different filter for each person in the Payroll department, but that would be a lot of work. Fortunately, Eudora filter conditions can find messages from a group of people by using nicknames.

If Mabel creates a nickname payroll in her Address book and puts all of the payroll department employees into that nickname, then she can automatically file all messages from her payroll department colleagues with a filter like this:

when a message arrives
if the sender is in the nickname payroll
then Make Label -> Payroll

To make this filter, Mabel needs to change andy@flossrecycling.com to payroll and contains to intersects nickname.

(Why "intersects nickname"? Because that's what Eudora's author decided to call it. Don't worry about the wording, just know that's how a filter checks to see if an address is in a nickname.)

How to Use Phrases to Find Coworkers

You can look for any words and phrases, not just email addresses. For example, suppose that messages from people inside Floss Recycling, Incorporated always have @flossrecycling.com in the return address. Mabel can then find all messages inside the company with this filter:

when a message arrives
if From: contains @flossrecycling.com
then Make Label -> CoWorkers

This filter is very similar to the "Andy" filter in except for the text in the second box and the label.

Importance of Filter Order

Messages go through filters in the order that the filters are listed on the left of the

Filters Window. So with the two filters that Mabel has now, all incoming messages first go through the Payroll filter and then through the CoWorkers filter. For example, suppose Andy sends a message to Mabel. The first filter assigns the label Payroll to Andy's message. But then the second message assigns the label CoWorkers to Andy's message—not what Mabel wants!

When a filter has a Skip Rest action, Eudora will put a mark in the list of filters. Eudora for Windows will display a small "stop sign" icon, as shown by the upper arrow.

How to Use << Any Recipient>> to Find Mailing List Messages

There are many places besides the From: header where filters can look for a word or phrase.

Your filters should almost always look for words and phrases in the «Any Recipient header instead of the To: header. People sometimes put addresses in the Cc: header instead of the To: header, but «Any Recipient will find words or phrases (or email addresses) in either.

Note that with the filter order, a message from Andy to the Announce mailing list will end up with the label Payroll. If the message is to the Announce mailing list, it probably isn't about payroll business. Mabel should drag the Announce filter to the top of the filter list so that the Payroll and CoWorkers filters don't keep Announce messages from getting filtered properly.

Make Filters More Precise By Combining Conditions

You've probably noticed that there is room for two conditions in the Filters Window. Combining conditions is not something that you will do frequently, but it is very handy sometimes.

For example, Mabel might not want to see messages that a car's lights are on unless it is her car. She could get rid of messages about other people's lights with a filter that transfers messages with the word headlights in the Subject: header to another mailbox—unless it has a description of her car in the Subject: header as well. To combine conditions for this filter, Mabel must change the bar that says ignore to say unless, as shown by the diagonal arrow. (You have the option of and, or, and unless.) Than mabel must enter in the next condition:

Note that there are now two little circles and an arrow next to the headlights filter in the list of filters, as shown by the vertical arrow. With Eudora for Mac OS, filters that transfer a message to another mailbox do a Skip Rest automatically. Thus one of the little circles, from the Transfer To action and one is from the Skip Rest. (The small arrow shows that the headlights filter has a Transfer To action.)

With Eudora for Windows, a Transfer To action will not stop later filters from acting on that message. To remind the Windows users how important Skip Rest is, I will show it even in Mac OS screen shots. (Even though Skip Rest isn't necessary in Mac OS filters that have a Transfer To action, it won't cause any problems if it is there.)

Separate "To-Do" Messages from "Done" Messages

People use email for more than just communicating. Almost everyone uses email to remind them of things they need to do. Many people even send themselves email to remind themselves to do something. It is therefore critically important that you keep your "to-do" messages separate from the messages you are done with. For your high-priority messages (the ones in your inbox), the easiest way to mark them "done" is to move them to a different mailbox. Any messages that remain in the inbox are then either "to-do" items or Unread messages. The easiest way to move messages out of the inbox is with manual filters. For example, Mabel could set up a manual filter to transfer messages from people in her payroll nickname into the h-Payroll mailbox. Then, when Mabel finishes with a Payroll message, she can transfer that message out of the inbox by manually filtering. There are three ways to run all your manual filters on selected messages:

- press Command-j (Mac OS) or Control-j (Windows),
- select the menu command Special -> Filter Messages, or
- put a button in the toolbar to filter messages and click on that button. (See How to Put Buttons in the Toolbar.)

To use this technique, Mabel needs a second filter for each of her high-priority categories. The filter that assigns the label must run only on incoming messages, while the filter that moves it to a mailbox must be manual only. For example, to file Payroll messages when she's done with them, Mabel needs a filter with a check mark in the Manual box. Medium-priority messages (which you transfer into mailboxes as soon as they arrive) by definition are not supposed to turn into "to-do" items very often. However, if you do have to respond to or act upon a message that isn't in the inbox, you can move it to the inbox to show that it is a "to-do" item. When you are done with it, transfer it back to its normal mailbox.

Because the incoming filter for that message transfers it to a mailbox, you don't need a separate manual filter. Instead, put a check mark in the Manual box of the existing filter.

I think that filtering manually when you are done with them is the simplest way to go through your messages. However, if you don't like this technique, you will learn more techniques in Quickly Mark Messages "Done" or "To-Do".

How to Prioritize with Advanced Filter Actions

By this point, you have learned the basics of organizing your messages with filters. You've seen how to use Make Label, Transfer to and Skip Rest to make categories' importance obvious. However, there are several additional filter actions that can help make messages' importance even more obvious:

- Open to open a message or its mailbox in its own window
- Make Priority to raise or lower the priority of a message
- Play Sound to let you hear what type of message arrives

This section's advice, while useful, isn't as critical as the sections you've already read. If you are in a hurry, you can skip to How to Keep Conversations Together for now.

How to Show Importance by (Not) Opening Messages and Mailboxes

Eudora normally opens all mailboxes that have new messages. If you don't want to be bothered by low-priority messages, you might want to turn that feature off and use filters to open your medium-priority mailboxes. (You will probably leave your inbox open all the time, so you should not need to open it with filters.)

Select Special -> Settings... -> Get Attention (Mac OS) or Tools -> Options... -> Get Attention (Windows). Uncheck the box next to Open mailbox. Then, to make your filters open your medium-priority mailboxes, select the filter action Open and put a checkmark in the box next to Mailbox

If a message is really important, you might want to open it in its own window. Select the filter action Open and put a checkmark in the box next to Message. Mabel might want her filters to open messages from her husband in their own window, not open z-ProbableJunkEmail or y-Humor at all, and open the mailbox for all other incoming messages.

How to Make Importance More Obvious with the "Make Priority" Action

Eudora can attach a priority level to a message. These priorities usually reflect the priority that the sender thinks a message should have. The priority is shown as arrows up or down in a mailbox' second column (just to the right of the blue Unread balls).

Your filters can override the priority level of messages with the Make Priority action. The advantage of overriding the priority level is that the new priority level is more likely to reflect your opinion of the message's true priority. The disadvantage is that you can't tell what the sender thought the priority level was. Frequently, however, the sender's opinion of the priority level is very different from your opinion, so you might not mind. If you aren't comfortable throwing away the sender's priority, you can set the priority relative to the old priority. You can Raise or Lower the priority. This takes into account both your priority and the sender's priority. For example, Mabel might want to use Make Priority to lower the priority of anything marked FYI (For Your Information).

How to Hear Importance with the "Play Sound" Action

If your filters play sounds, you can tell when important messages come in, even if you're not focusing on your computer. For example, if a message from Mabel's rose gardening mailing list arrives, she probably won't put aside what she's doing to read it. If a message from someone in the Payroll department announces itself, she probably will.

If a sound has some connection to its category, it's easier to remember what the sound means. For example, you might associate the following sounds and message types:

- old-fashioned cash register ring or credit card slider sound for sale confirmations
- laughter for jokes
- rude noises for junk mail
- wedding bells for messages from your spouse.

If you have your filters play sounds, make sure that the sounds are very short—shorter than the time it takes to say the phrase "filter action." Your sounds will play over and over, and you will get tired of waiting for long sounds to finish. By default, Eudora plays a sound when a new message arrives. You can disable this by changing the Get Attention page in the settings. Select Special -> Settings... -> Get Attention (Mac OS) or Tools -> Options... -> Get Attention (Windows) and uncheck the box next to Play a sound.

How to Keep Conversations Together

The filters you've learned so far are good for organizing messages that you receive. It is also helpful to put outgoing messages in the same mailbox as related incoming messages. There are two ways to do this: by making outgoing filters for all of your high- and medium-priority categories and by using Eudora's Fcc (Folder Carbon Copy) option. Moving messages out of your Out box also might improve Eudora's performance. Eudora keeps all of the messages in your In, Out, and Trash mailboxes in memory. If any of those mailboxes get large, the memory demands can reduce Eudora's performance.

How to Keep Conversations Together with Filters

You can set up any filter to operate on outgoing messages by checking the Outgoing checkbox in the Filters Window. For example, Mabel could make a filter that moves all outgoing messages to anyone in the Payroll department into the h-Payroll mailbox.

How to Keep Incoming and Outgoing Messages Together with FCC

With the Fcc (File Carbon Copy) option, Eudora files any reply of yours in the same mailbox as the message you replied to—except if the original message is in the inbox. To use the Fcc option, select Special ->> Settings... -> Sending Mail (Mac OS) or Tools -> Options... -> Replying (Windows) and put a check mark in the box labelled Automatically Fcc to original mailbox. Telling Eudora to automatically Fcc messages to will only do part of the job: messages that are not replies will still end up in your Out mailbox. Still, it is much easier to put one check mark into one box than to create a lot of outgoing mail filters.

How to Test Your Filters

It is a good idea to test your filters when you set them up. If you make a mistake, your filters could put an important message into a mailbox that you never look at.

Manual filters are extremely useful for testing your filters. You should probably put a check in the Manual checkbox in all the filters except for your high-priority filters—the ones that change the label and leave the message in the inbox. (If you put a check in the Manual checkbox for messages that stay in the inbox, you won't be able to use manual filtering to move those messages out of the inbox as described in Separate "To-Do" Messages from "Done" Messages.)

If you need to test your high-priority filters, you can put a check mark temporarily in the Manual checkbox. Be sure to uncheck the Manual box when you are done testing. If you are using Eudora for Mac OS and your filters don't do what you expect, you can find out which filters a message activates. Select a message, hold down the Shift key, and then open the Filters window. Eudora will highlight all the filters whose conditions match the selected message. If a filter's condition appears to be correct, but the filter didn't do the appropriate action when you ran it manually, make sure that the Manual box is checked. It is very easy to forget to check the Manual box—even I do so with astonishing regularity.

Use Multiple Accounts to Group Messages

If setting up filters looks like too much work for you to do right now, you can use multiple email accounts to group your messages. You can frequently check the accounts that you use for higher-priority topics and only occasionally check your low-priority accounts.

In the past, having multiple email accounts was very expensive, but there are now numerous free Web-based email services. Furthermore, some of the Web-based services block junk email.

However, there are significant disadvantages to using free Web-based accounts:

- You have to check each account.
- Free services usually make you look at advertising.
- A free service might limit how many messages you can keep or how much disk space you can use.

Eudora will let you check messages from multiple accounts by using different personalities. (Select Help -> Using Personalities (Mac OS) or Help -> Topics -> Index -> personalities (Windows) to learn more about personalities.) Using Eudora to check the messages in all your accounts might make it easier to check your messages, but you would need to routinely switch between your different personalities. The more personalities you have, the harder it is to remember which personality you are using at any given moment.

You should have very few accounts—probably less than five. I recommend using three accounts: your work account, a personal account, and an account for junk mail.

Personal Accounts

Separating your work and personal email is one of the best things you can do. Besides making it easier to concentrate on work issues while you are at work, it has these benefits:

- If you suddenly lose your job, you won't also lose all the addresses in your email address book.
- Your personal email is more private. In some places, employers have the legal right to read email on your work computer at any time without your permission or knowledge. If your employer gets sued, lawyers from both sides might end up reading all your company email—regardless of whether it is related to the suit or even your work.
- You are less likely to get in trouble for using company time and equipment for personal use.

If you get a personal account, always checking it from your work copy of Eudora (by using different personalities) eliminates many of these benefits. It's better to use a web-based email system for your personal email or to only download personal messages to your home computer.

Junk Mail Accounts

Junk mailers have programs that scan the Web for email addresses. If your email address gets onto a Web page in any way—if you put it on a home page or if you post a message to a discussion group that is archived on the Web—junk mailers will find you.

Similarly, if you give a retailer your email address, they might send you advertisements in the future. They might also sell your address to other retailers. Even if they have a privacy policy that says that they won't give your address to anyone else, the privacy policy isn't guaranteed to continue if the company goes bankrupt. When a company files for bankruptcy, knowledge of your email address is considered part of the company's assets and might be sold to pay off creditors.

Therefore, you should have at least one account to give to Web sites and other retailers.

Improving Company's Email Effectiveness

Changing your own behavior—filtering, using pre-written responses, writing good subject lines, providing adequate context, and so forth—will make getting through your email much easier. However, at some point, you will be limited by how well your company deals with email.

Your company's email behaviors might have been the result of conscious decisions, but it's more likely that its culture evolved spontaneously. Your company can probably improve its email effectiveness.

There are three basic ways to change behavior in an company: improve resources, provide training, and set policy. This chapter will discuss each method and suggest specific examples of each that can help improve email efficiency.

Improve Resources

Providing good resources can make desirable behaviors easier and undesirable behaviors harder or impossible. Technology is one powerful resource for changing behavior. Unfortunately, technological changes almost always cost money—to buy (or develop), configure, and maintain the software.

If you are technically proficient, you might be able to influence your company's email usage by developing one or more of the following resources.

Web-Based Mailing List Interface

If your company sets up mailing lists for different functional groups, your company will be more productive. Not only do mailing lists make it easy to send messages to the right people, they make filtering extremely easily. This improves people's ability to organize and prioritize. Making it easy for people to set up mailing lists is thus good for the company. Something that works well is to have a web-based interface to mailing lists with information on

- what lists are available
- what their policies are

- who the "owner" of the list is
- who has subscribed
- how to subscribe
- how to unsubscribe

A searchable Web-based archive with all the messages from a list is also very useful.

- An archive helps people who delete a message and then decide later that they wanted to see it.
- It is easier to catch up after an absence if the mailing list messages are in an archive.
- An archive is a useful resource for training new employees.
- An archive creates a record of what decisions were made and why.
- People are sometimes a bit more polite and careful if they know that their comments are stored.

External Subscribers

Letting people from outside the company subscribe to mailing lists has benefits and disadvantages. If your company allows people from outside the company to be on a mailing list, employees can send confidential information outside the company accidentally. (Because senders don't see who is on a list when they mail to it, it is easy to make that mistake.) On the other hand, if your company does not allow external subscribers, then nobody can set up lists of customers and vendors that you might want to correspond with in bulk. One compromise solution is to have a privileged set of people who can create and maintain mailing lists with both internal and external subscribers.

Your company might also want to have a different naming convention for internal-only and internal/external lists. That way, people can see quickly how confidential messages to the list are.

Geographical Mailing Lists

There should be a mailing list for every geographical area so that messages that apply only to one location don't also go to other locations. The classic example of what happens if you don't have this is everyone worldwide getting messages like this:

Subject: blue Ford 2RSM183 - headlights on

Facilities closures, maintenance, and party announcements are frequently mis-addressed as well. Once your company has geographic mailing lists, training can impress upon people that they shouldn't waste people's time by sending to the wrong list. Peer pressure can keep people from making that mistake twice.

Reply-to-All vs. Reply-to-Sender

Mailing list servers should be configured so that the From: header has the author of the message, not the listname address. This will ensure that simple replies (including out-of-office messages) go to just the original author, not the whole list. (It would be nice if people wouldn't send automatic responses to mailing lists, but the more people you have on a list, the more likely that someone will make that mistake.)

Security

Email attachments can contain viruses. Hopefully, everyone will have the latest virus-checking software on their desktop computer. However, people are lazy. Unfortunately, if one person fails to install the latest virus-checker, that can affect the entire company. It is slower but safer to check all attachments automatically before the receivers have a chance to see them. Certain types of attachments are more prone to viruses than others. In particular, executable files (with extension.exe) can be deadly, and are rarely useful. Your company might wish to delete all .exe attachments that come from outside the company.

Eliminate Duplicates

If your company's mailing list software can remove redundant copies of messages, that can save people a lot of aggravation. There are times when a message is appropriate for several different mailing lists. If people subscribe to multiple lists, however, that means they could get multiple copies of the same message—which gets dull quickly. Sending each person only one copy of a message will help people get through their email faster.

Develop a Good Web Site

A good Web site for your company or department means that people can refer their correspondents to information on a Web page instead of creating it all themselves. For example, if your company has a Web page with a map and directions to its location, people won't have to spend time writing directions. They can instead send the URL of the map. Any sort of information that people ask about regularly is helpful to put on a Web site. These include things like benefit details, lists of medical providers, technical specifications, company charts, and even floorplans.

Develop Corporate- or Department-Wide Responses

It might save time for someone in the company to carefully develop stationery for common questions, then make them available to the whole company. For example, a non-profit might make a mission statement available. A corporation might want to have a blurb directing people to the public relations department:

> I'm sorry, I really am not the appropriate person to discuss this with. You need to talk to Sal Mgabi in our Public Relations department. His phone number is +1-217-555-7777x77.

A Customer Support department might have a large number of canned responses that would be useful to have easily available, like:

> The problem of the Harik Quicksilver Electric Bagpipes overheating has been fixed in release 3.1.4.1.5.9. To download the patch, go to
>
> <http://www.electricbagpipes.com/harik/rel314159.zip>
>
> The overheating is only a problem if all the drones are blocked. Keeping the drones clear will prevent this problem.
>
> Should you have any further questions, please do not hesitate to ask.

Good Email Software

Eudora is an excellent general-purpose email program. However, for people doing customer support, Customer Relationship Management software might be better. Customer Relationship Management (abbreviated CRM or eCRM) software makes it easier to keep track of and use a company's pre-written responses. While these are most useful for customer support personnel, they can also be useful for anybody who gets many routine questions. I have found that an "auto-suggest" filter action is extremely useful. I was able to get through messages about ten times faster when I had a system that let me select (with one click) from several suggested responses. I could then, if I chose, edit the response(s) before sending them. This isn't as fast as responding completely automatically, but allowing a human being to make the choices cuts down on the number of inappropriate responses. Humans are still a lot smarter than computers. Most CRM software will also allow you to track all communication that you have had with the sender of the incoming message. Again, this is most useful for support personnel, but anybody who manages a lot of communications—like people in sales or fund raising—could find it useful.

Provide Alternatives to Distracting Messages

People, left to their own devices, will generate all kinds of messages that are not directly related to work. Some of the most common non-work messages are about

- goods to buy, sell or give away (for example, "spare ticket to Monday's football game")
- requests for recommendations of products or services
- jokes
- notification that food is available (for example, "leftover bread and cheese in conference room C4")

- notification that automobile headlights are on

Eliminating these messages might be difficult and create bad will. What your company can do, however, is create better channels for sending non-essential messages, as I describe below.

Mailing Lists

If you set up specific mailing lists for the distracting messages, then people can filter them into low-priority mailboxes. For example, a mailing list for leftover food would be easy to filter.

Web-based Services

Another, more sophisticated, option is to set up web-based services. For example, your company could set up a simple Web-based application that would send mail only to the owner of the car whose lights are on. (People would have to enter their license plate numbers, but their reward for doing so is high.) Your company might also provide Web-based applications that tell where to find leftover food, a marketplace, and a place to review products and services.

Where Are Your Colleagues?

Another useful Web-based application is one that lets employees check in and check out of the office. Then people can use the Web application to find out where someone is. This is better than having coworkers send email to everybody whenever they leave the office: those who don't care that someone is gone won't have to read a message about it.

Out-of-Office Messages

Sometimes, casual users can set up their email system to automatically respond to incoming messages with a "out-of-office" message:

> *Subject: out of the office until 29 Feb*
>
> I am at the Floss Expo in Fargo, ND and will not be returning until 29 Feb. I will be checking my voicemail on a daily basis. If you need immediate assistance, please contact Chantelle Williams at x2202.

However, casual users usually set up their out-of-office messages to respond to ALL incoming messages. This means that anybody who sends a message to a mailing list frequently gets back several out-of-office messages. If both the sender and receiver have out-of-office messages, their email programs can get into a loop where they keep telling each other that they are out of the office. Additionally, people sometimes forget to turn their out-of-office messages off. Given all that, it is a good idea to set up a Web-based application that configures out-of-office messages so that

- only one message per absence (or per week) goes to any individual account

- out-of-office messages don't go to mailing lists (or perhaps to any external accounts)
- bounce messages don't generate a out-of-office message
- messages that contain the phrases "vacation" or "out of the office" don't generate a out-of-office message.
- out-of-office messages stop automatically at the scheduled end of the absence

Filters

It is very valuable for the company to set up filters that remove unsolicited commercial email before it gets anywhere close to the end user. Junk email can take up an enormous amount of time and energy. While the filters in Useful Filter Recipes are good starting points for filters, having a set of pre-made filters might help your company's productivity. Your company could then customize the filters for its specific situation. Employees could use the pre-made filters as guides in developing their own.

Confidential Material

Email makes it very easy to transmit confidential material, but email has very poor security. Anything highly confidential should be sent via a trusted courier. One way to make it more difficult to disclose confidential information is to have a computer program examine all outgoing messages for a set of words marking confidentiality. For example, Mabel's company could prevent people from emailing documents containing the phrase Floss Recycling Inc. Confidential.

Messages from the Company

From time to time, someone will need to send a message to the entire company about policy changes, facilities closures, and so on. For large companies, it can be dangerous to send that message from a personal account. The sender might get hundreds of messages from employees. (If nothing else, there could be a lot of out-of-office messages.) On the other hand, if updates come from an email address that is not attached to a person, it can seem very cold and impersonal. One way around this is to make the message from an impersonal address, but to give the name of the person who sent the message. Then ask that follow-up comments go to a web-based discussion forum. Ask that people not post messages unless they have something new to add, but add a way to count "I like this" or "I don't like this" votes.

Provide Training

Many of the tools above enforce good practice, but good training can encourage good practices. If your company does not have the technical resources to develop tools like the above, adding training on email effectiveness can be valuable. Even if your company has the time, money, and skill to develop resources, training might be useful. Good resources won't help everything; in particular, technical aids do a poor job of helping people write more understandable messages. Training is particularly productive if the unwanted behavior is the result of uninformed or unconscious decisions. Showing the benefits of doing things a different way might be all that it takes to change the behavior. If your company can come to agreement on what behaviors are acceptable, peer pressure can enforce those behaviors. If five hundred people all reply, "that wasn't appropriate" to an unacceptable message, the sender isn't likely to make that mistake again. To make this work, however, the culture must accept or encourage this type of vigilante justice.

The disadvantage of training everybody is that it takes time and energy—which usually means money.

Signal Words and Abbreviations in the Subject

Even if your company doesn't have the resources to make more appropriate homes for distracting messages, it can get similar results if everybody uses the same signal words in Subject: headers. If people use the signal words consistently, those who are not interested in a certain type of message can filter them into low-priority mailboxes or delete them outright. Examples of useful signal words are:

- OT: for messages that are Off-Topic—not directly related to a mailing list's topic
- REQ: for REQuest—meaning the sender wants the receiver to do something
- LIGHTS: for messages about cars whose headlights are on
- FOOD: for messages that there is leftover food available for the taking
- WHERE: to notify people of a temporary absence
- OOO: for automatic responses that the sender is out of the office
- FS: for messages advertising something For Sale
- WTB: for messages expressing a desire to purchase something (Wanted To Buy)
- EOM to show that the subject line contains the entire message
- TC: for Time Critical

It doesn't really matter what words people use, as long as everybody uses them consistently. Your company will be just fine if everybody uses AR: (for Action Request) instead of REQ:. But if some people use AR:, some use REQ:, some use AI:, and some use DIRECTIVE:, it will be harder for people to set up filters. Training can also reduce confusion about common abbreviations. While FYI (For Your Information) and BTW (By The Way) are relatively common outside of email, there are a number of abbreviations that aren't seen often except in email:

- IMHO - In My Humble Opinion
- RTFM - Read The Manual
- LOL - [I] Laughed Out Loud
- ROTFL - [I am] Rolling On The Floor Laughing
- RSN - Real Soon Now
- TIA - Thanks In Advance
- YMMV - Your Mileage May Vary (meaning "your experiences might be different")
- <g> - grin

In addition, every company has its own acronyms and code names. For example, Intel Corporation uses NCG to mean "New College Graduate." NASA has so many acronyms that its employees joke that it stands for "National Acronym-Slinging Agency."

Alas, frequently someone will send a message to a huge mailing list asking questions like, "What does IMHO mean?" If there are 500 people on the mailing list, the message will probably annoy 450 of them.

To let everyone know what these words and abbreviations mean, your company might want to have a Web page with a list of the signal words, abbreviations, and code words that your company uses. Even if someone explains the signal words and abbreviations once to every employee, there can still be trouble in the future. People will forget, new situations will call for new signal words, and new people will join the company.

The new hire orientation should impress upon people that if they don't understand a phrase, they should not ask everybody on a mailing list. Tell them to ask either the sender of the message or the person responsible for the acronyms Web page.

Signatures

Different companies have different attitudes towards signatures. It can be worthwhile to discuss signatures at new-hire orientation. Even if there isn't a company policy, it would be good for people to understand the issues surrounding signatures. Some people like to see signatures with the name, phone number, and/or position in the company for internal mail. Others prefer to receive uncluttered messages. They figure that if they want a colleague's contact information, they can look it up in the company directory. Some corporate cultures allow humorous sayings in the signature. This can be fun. It can also look unprofessional. For external mail, your company might want to ask people to include lots of information in a text signature. People outside the company probably can't see your company directory.

Priority Levels

Priority levels can be very useful—if everyone knows what the priority means. Unfortunately, left to their own devices, people will use radically different priorities for the same circumstances. Some will never set a priority and others will make everything top priority. Some will set priority according to how important it is to the sender while others will set priority according to how important it is to the receiver. Thus, many readers ignore priority levels completely. (Some even use filters to change the priority level.) Another problem is that priority is a combination of urgency and importance, but there is a big difference between the two. For example, "Do you want to go to lunch with me in an hour" is high urgency but low importance. On the other hand, "I will need a bone marrow transplant in a year. Please register to be a bone marrow donor" is high importance but low urgency.

Coming up with and training people on some company-wide guidelines for priority levels will make them more useful for everybody.

Voice Instead of Email

There are times when phone or face-to-face conversations are better than email. If the topic is emotionally charged or if there are many intertwined issues to resolve, voice is frequently better. Education is the key to getting people to use the right medium for the message.

Response Speed

Differences in response speed can cause problems. If someone who thinks that people should respond to email immediately sends email to someone who replies a week later, there could be trouble. It is difficult to set firm policy on response time because of unintended consequences. If the boss orders that everyone must respond within a certain amount of time, people will probably set up their filters to respond to all messages with "I got your message and am looking into your issue." This is not helpful. If your company makes a policy insisting that employees must answer messages in a certain amount of time or not at all, then people might choose to never respond. This is also not helpful. Your company might want to suggest to its employees that if they can tell it will take more than a day to find the answer to a question, that they should send a courtesy response. This response should say why they can't respond and when they expect to know enough to be able to respond. It could be that some people have slow response time simply because they are buried in email. In that case, some training on how to manage email might be appropriate. Give them a copy of this book or get them to email management training. If they still can't cope with the flood of messages, perhaps they need email management software (as described in Good Email Software) or an assistant to help them deal with all the messages.

Write Email Well

Writing clear messages can reduce the number of responses that people send. If quotes are not an appropriate length, if lines aren't wrapped well, if messages are too long, or if they cover too many topics, it will take longer to finish the conversation. It is difficult to order people to write messages well because people almost never try to write poorly. Training, however, can be useful. Give everybody a copy of this book, send them to a class, or develop a Web page with hints, tips, and links to resources for writing well.

Emoticons

Some people really hate emoticons, despite how helpful they can be in conveying emotional tone properly. Some language purists find emoticons to be an assault on proper usage. Some people think emoticons are unprofessional. Other people use text-to-speech processors, which render emoticons unintelligible or invisible. Your company might want to make sure that everyone understands the reasons for emoticons as well as their limitations.

Set Policy

One way to change behavior is to put it into the company policy. The benefits of doing things by decree are that it can be efficient and costs very little directly. The bad news is that the indirect costs can be high if people don't like the policy: grumbling and unhappiness can hurt productivity. Furthermore, there are always gray areas: behaviors that decrees can't cover or that can't be enforced. For example, "write better messages" is not a meaningful order. People don't usually write poorly on purpose. Email is a new enough medium for most companies that sometimes it isn't clear who is responsible for making high-level decisions about email. Even if you aren't part of the management chain, you might be able to affect your company's email culture by asking the senior management, "Who is responsible for email policy decisions?" Getting an answer to that question means that somebody now has ownership of the problem. This, by itself, might be a big enough step to lead to changes. Each company's management will have differing abilities to dictate policy, depending upon the company's overall culture. The military can tell people what to do much more easily than a charity staffed by volunteers. That said, there are times when management needs to set policies about email usage. Management should make policies clear for any issues with legal implications, as in the following examples.

Personal Use

If your company does not have a policy against it, people will use email for their personal use. This can be good. People might not need to leave work if they can take care of errands by email. Email is also quieter than talking on the telephone—which people who work in high-density offices will appreciate. Personal use can also hurt productivity. People can end up spending a lot of time on personal email. Jokes, hoaxes, and chain letters can be a particularly wasteful. However, limiting employees' email access can make them resentful, especially if other companies in your area allow it. Limiting email access might limit your ability to attract and retain employees.

Your company probably needs to have a policy on acceptable behavior, which could include a recommendation that employees use a separate account for personal messages.

Illegal Uses

Many things are just as illegal on-line as they are off-line. Depending upon your jurisdiction, the following can be illegal: harassment, stalking, libel, fraud, gambling, and pyramid schemes. Your company should have a clear policy stating that your company will not tolerate illegal uses of email. Be sure to give clear examples of unacceptable behavior.

Privacy

Depending upon your jurisdiction, your company might have the legal right to examine employees' email. There are some situations where clearly it makes sense for a company to exercise that right. For example, system administrators sometimes need to glance at someone's email to make sure that they fixed a problem with the email system properly. However, employees will probably get upset if someone reads their messages for no obvious reason. Your company might want to say who can read email under what circumstances. For example, the policy could say that reading someone else's email is cause for disciplinary action except when:

- fixing a problem in the email system
- developing a defense for a legal case
- providing subpoenaed material
- investigating illegal activities (including theft of intellectual property)
- authorized by a vice president

The company's email privacy policy should be stated clearly, perhaps at orientation or in the personnel policy.

Addresses

One thing that is definitely a policy issue is assignment of email addresses. Does your company allow people to choose any address that they like? Or does it insist on a formulaic address, like "first initial-last name"? People might want to choose their own email addresses, but others might have a better chance of finding addresses if your company uses a set formula. On the other hand, a formula might cause people to send email to the wrong place. For example, if a second lee shows up, the first lee might frequently get the second lee 's email. If everyone has an unusual email address, people have an incentive to look it up. Another issue is public visibility of email addresses. If everyone has a formulaic address, then it's easy for outsiders to guess email addresses. This can be good (customers who lose an employee's business card can still find him or her) and bad (recruiters from other companies can send email to your employees). Your company might choose to assign you two different email addresses: the formulaic one to give to outside people and a user-selected address to give to inside people. Which address someone uses will show where the email came from and make it easier to filter.

Your company might formally recommend that employees use a different email address for any public correspondence (like Usenet newsgroups).

Attachments

What formats are okay to send as attachments? If a minority isn't able to view attachments in a certain format, what is the policy? Is the minority obliged to find software that can read it or is the majority obliged to find a format that everybody can read? One way to address this issue is to have a list of approved formats and to issue a policy directive that everyone must have the appropriate software loaded on their computer. Another approach is to say that the person requesting the favor bears the burden of translating the document into a usable format. It is also helpful to set limits on the size of attachments people can send. Attachments can be very large, and if the attachment goes to 500 people, that's 500 disk drives that the attachment takes space on. Instead, your company might want people to put large documents on a file server or Web server.

People Who Circumvent Technology Channels

If your company has technically-savvy employees, they might be able to set up their own email servers and/or Internet connections. Sometimes there might be good reasons for doing this. For example, if someone is developing new email list software, they will have to set up their own list servers. However, these unofficial servers can sometimes bypass important security features. Your company might want to state that setting up an email server without the prior written permission of the Information Technology department is grounds for disciplinary action.

Email vs. Telephone

Some people don't like email. I know people who don't read their email because "if it's important, they'll telephone." This eliminates many of the benefits of email. Frequently this culture clash forms along age, gender, and job position. While many older workers are quite comfortable with email, the minority of people who are not comfortable with email tend to be older. Older men, particularly, don't always type well because typing used to be "woman's work" and low-status. The human-contact people—sales, marketing, human resources, and so on—also tend to like the telephone more than engineers do. Engineers tend to be more comfortable with email than non-technical people are. Given that senior management tends to be older men with non-technical backgrounds, there can be more email resistance as you move up the management chain. This can make it difficult to change policy. The senior executives might find it a loss of face to admit difficulty with email, so they might not be receptive to training or persuasion, either. The best way to get people to read their email is to make it part of everyone's performance evaluation: does the employee respond promptly to requests from others? If email messages are a significant part of your corporate communication, your company might also want to ask all job applicants how comfortable they are with email.

Summary

Developing resources, providing training, and setting policy are all ways of improving an company's email productivity. Useful resources include:

- Web-based applications to archive mailing lists, communicate with list servers, indicate where someone has gone configure out-of-office auto-responses, and discuss corporate announcements
- Web-based applications Web-based applications for
- software to monitor outgoing messages for confidential information
- software to eliminate duplicate messages
- software to remove viruses
- for messages about food, car lights left on, items for sale, and recommendations
- a good Web site
- pre-written responses
- pre-written filters

Training can improve understanding of:

- abbreviations and signal words
- signatures
- when to use voice instead of email transactions
- appropriate response times
- when to use Bcc:
- how to write clearer email messages
- when to use emoticons

Management should clarify what is expected regarding:

- personal use of email
- illegal uses
- privacy
- email addresses
- attachments
- setting up alternate email servers
- reading email

Computer Network System and Security

A computer network is two or more computers connected together using a telecommunication system for the purpose of communicating and sharing resources.

Experts in the field of networking debate whether *two* computers that are connected together using some form of communications medium constitute a network. Therefore, some sources will state that a network requires *three* connected computers. A computer connected to a non-computing device (e.g., networked to a printer via an Ethernet link) may also represent a computer network, although this article does not currently address this configuration. For example, states that "the term network describes two or more connected computers" while states that a computer network is "A network of data processing nodes that are interconnected for the purpose of data communication", the term "network" being defined in the same document as An interconnection of three or more communicating entities" (author's emphasis).

This article uses the definition which requires two or more computers to be connected together to form a network. The same basic functions are generally present in this case as with larger numbers of connected computers.

Basic Computer Network Building Blocks

Computers

Many of the components of an average network are individual computers, which are generally either workstations (including personal computers) or servers.

Types of Workstations

There are many types of workstations that may be incorporated into a particular network, some of which have high-end displays, multiple CPUs, large amounts of RAM, large amounts of hard drive storage space, or other enhancements required for special data processing tasks, graphics, or other resource intensive applications. (See also network computer).

Types of Servers

The following lists some common types of servers and their purpose.

File Server

Stores various types of files and distributes them to other clients on the network.

Print Server

Controls and manages one or more printers and accepts print jobs from other network clients, spooling the print jobs, and performing most or all of the other functions that a workstation would perform to accomplish a printing task if the printer were connected directly to the workstation's printer port.

Mail Server

Stores, sends, receives, routes, and performs other email related operations for other clients on the network.

Fax Server

Stores, sends, receives, routes, and performs other functions necessary for the proper transmission, reception, and distribution of faxes.

Telephony Server

Performs telephony related functions such as answering calls automatically, performing the functions of an interactive voice response system, storing and serving voice mail, routing calls between the Public Switched Telephone Network (PSTN) and the network or the Internet (e.g., voice over IP (VoIP) gateway), etc.

Proxy Server

Performs some type of function on behalf of other clients on the network to increase the performance of certain operations (e.g., prefetching and caching documents or other data that is requested very frequently) or as a security precaution to isolate network clients from external threats.

Remote Access Server (RAS)

Monitors modem lines or other network communications channels for requests to connect to the network from a remote location, answers the incoming telephone call or acknowledges the network request, and performs the necessary security checks and other procedures necessary to log a user onto the network.

Application Server

Performs the data processing or business logic portion of a client application, accepting instructions for operations to perform from a workstation and serving the results back to the workstation, while the workstation performs the user interface or GUI portion of the processing (i.e., the presentation logic) that is required for the application to work properly.

Web Server

Stores HTML documents, images, text files, scripts, and other Web related data (collectively known as *content*), and distributes this content to other clients on the network on request.

Backup Server

Has network backup software installed and has large amounts of hard drive storage or other forms of storage (tape, etc.) available to it to be used for the purpose of ensuring that data loss does not occur in the network.

Printers

Many printers are capable of acting as part of a computer network without any other device, such as a print server, to act as an intermediary between the printer and the device that is requesting a print job to be completed.

Dumb Terminals

Many networks use dumb terminals instead of workstations either for data entry and display purposes or in some cases where the application runs entirely on the server.

Other Devices

There are many other types of devices that may be used to build a network, many of which require an understanding of more advanced computer networking concepts before they are able to be easily understood (e.g., hubs, routers, bridges, switches, hardware firewalls, etc.). On home and mobile networks, connecting consumer electronics devices such as video game consoles is becoming increasingly common.

Building a Computer Network

A Simple Network

A simple computer network may be constructed from two computers by adding a network adapter (Network Interface Controller (NIC)) to each computer and then connecting them together with a special cable called a crossover cable. This type of network is useful for transferring information between two computers that are not normally connected to each other by a permanent network connection or for basic home networking applications.

Practical Networks

Practical networks generally consist of more than two interconnected computers and generally require special devices in addition to the Network Interface Controller that each computer needs to be equipped with. Examples of some of these special devices are listed above under Basic Computer Network Building Blocks / Other devices.

Types of Networks

Below is a list of the most common types of computer networks.

Local Area Network (LAN)

A network that is limited to a relatively small spatial area such as a room, a single building, a ship, or an aircraft. Local area networks are sometimes called a single location network.

Note: For administrative purposes, large LANs are generally divided into smaller logical segments called *workgroups*. A workgroup is a group of computers that share a common set of resources within a LAN.

Campus Area Network (CAN)

A network that connects two or more LANs but that is limited to a specific (possibly private) geographical area such as a college campus, industrial complex, or a military base.

Note: A CAN is generally limited to an area that is smaller than a Metropolitan Area Network (MANthe brnet work ois main one in ewibsdvfugrgvhfdxgjbfdvghgfdbghfdgbjfdvhfdg

Metropolitan Area Network (MAN)

A network that connects two or more LANs or CANs together but does not extend beyond the boundaries of the immediate town, city, or metropolitan area. Multiple routers, switches & hubs are connected to create a MAN.

Wide Area Network (WAN)

A network that covers a broad geographical area (i.e., any network whose communications links cross metropolitan, regional, or national boundaries) or, less formally, a network that uses routers and public communications links.

Types of WANs

Centralized: A centralized WAN consists of a central computer that is connected to dumb terminals and / or other types of terminal devices.

Distributed: A distributed WAN consists of two or more computers in different locations and may also include connections to dumb terminals and other types of terminal devices.

Internetwork

Two or more networks or network segments connected using devices that operate at layer 3 (the 'network' layer) of the OSI Basic Reference Model, such as a router. Any interconnection among or between public, private, commercial, industrial, or governmental networks may also be defined as an internetwork.

Internet: A specific internetwork, consisting of a worldwide interconnection of governmental, academic, public, and private networks based upon the Advanced Research Projects Agency Network (ARPANET) developed by ARPA of the U.S. Department of Defense – also home to the World Wide Web (WWW) and referred to as the 'Internet' with a capital 'I' to distinguish it from other generic internetworks. Synonyms for the 'Internet' also include the 'Web' or, in a more comical sense, the 'Interweb'.

Intranet

A network or internetwork that is limited in scope to a single organization or entity or, also, a network or internetwork that is limited in scope to a single organization or entity and which uses the TCP/IP protocol suite, HTTP, FTP, and other network protocols and software commonly used on the Internet. Intranets may also be categorized as a LAN, CAN, MAN, WAN, or other type of network.

Extranet

A network or internetwork that is limited in scope to a single organization or entity but which also has limited connections to the networks of one or more other usually, but not necessarily, trusted organizations or entities (e.g., a company's customers may be provided access to some part of its intranet thusly creating an extranet while at the same time the customers may not be considered 'trusted' from a security standpoint). Technically, an extranet may also be categorized as a CAN, MAN, WAN, or other type of network, although, by definition, an extranet cannot consist of a single LAN, because an extranet must have at least one connection with an outside network. Intranets and extranets may or may not have connections to the Internet. If connected to the Internet, the intranet or extranet is normally protected from being accessed from the Internet without proper authorization. The Internet itself is not considered to be a part of the intranet or extranet, although the Internet may serve as a portal for access to portions of an extranet.

Classification of Computer Networks

This article or section does not cite its references or sources.

Please help improve this article by introducing appropriate citations. (help, get involved!) This article has been tagged since December 2006.

By Network Layer

Computer networks may be classified according to the network layer at which they operate according to some basic reference models that are considered to be standards in the industry such as the seven layer OSI reference model and the five layer TCP/IP model.

By Scale

Computer networks may be classified according to the scale or extent of reach of the network, for example as a Personal area network (PAN), Local area network (LAN), Wireless local area network (WLAN), Campus area network (CAN), Metropolitan area network (MAN), or Wide area network (WAN).

By connection Method

Computer networks may be classified according to the technology that is used to connect the individual devices in the network such as HomePNA, Power line communication, Ethernet, or WiFi.

By Functional Relationship

Computer networks may be classified according to the functional relationships which exist between the elements of the network, for example Active Networking, Client-server and Peer-to-peer (workgroup) architectures.

By Network Topology

Computer networks may be classified according to the network topology upon which the network is based, such as Bus network, Star network, Ring network, Mesh network, Star-bus network, Tree or Hierarchical topology network, etc.

Topology can be arranged in a *Geometric Arragement*

By Services Provided

Computer networks may be classified according to the services which they provide, such as Storage area networks, Server farms, Process control networks, Value-added network, SOHO network, Wireless community network, XML appliance, Jungle Networks, khadar network, etc.

By Protocol

Computer networks may be classified according to the communications protocol that is being used on the network. See the articles on List of network protocol stacks and List of network protocols for more information.

Information Security Policy

This file is a DRAFT chapter intended to be part of the NIST Computer Security Handbook. The chapters were prepared by different parties and, in some cases, have not been reviewed by NIST. The next iteration of a chapter could be SUBSTANTIALLY different than the current version. If you wish to provide comments on the chapters, please email them to roback@ecf.ncsl.gov or mail them to Ed Roback/Room B154, Bldg 225/NIST/Gaithersburg, MD 20899.

Introduction to Computer Security Policy

Organizations rely on IT resources today to handle vast amounts of information. Because the data can vary widely in type and in degree of sensitivity, employees need to be able to exercise flexibility in handling and protecting it. It would not be practical or cost-effective to require that all data be handled in the same manner or be subject to the same protection requirements. Without some degree of standardization, however, inconsistencies can develop that introduce risks. Formal IT security policy helps establish standards for IT resource protection by assigning program management responsibilities and providing basic rules, guidelines, and definitions for everyone in the organization. Policy thus helps prevent inconsistencies that can introduce risks, and policy serves as a basis for the enforcement of more detailed rules and procedures. Ideally, policy will be sufficiently clear and comprehensive to be accepted and followed throughout the organization yet flexible enough to accommodate a wide range of data, activities, and resources.

Policy formulation is an important step toward standardization of security activities for IT resources. IT security policy is generally formulated from the input of many members of an organization, including security officials, line managers, and IT resource specialists. However, policy is ultimately approved and issued by the organization's senior management. In environments where employees feel inundated with policies, directives, guidelines and procedures, an IT security policy should be introduced in a manner that ensures that management's unqualified support is clear. The organization's policy is management's vehicle for emphasizing the commitment to IT security and making clear the expectations for employee involvement and accountability. This study will discuss IT security policy in terms of the different types (program-level and issue-specific), components, and aspects of implementation. Potential cost and interdependencies will also be noted.

Policy Types: Program-Level and Issue-Specific

Two types of policy will typically need to be developed to meet an organization's needs: program-level and issue-specific. Program-level policy's main function is to establish the security program, assign program management responsibilities, state the organizationwide IT security goals and objectives, and provide a basis for enforcement.

Issue-specific policies also need to be developed, in order to identify and define specific areas of concern and to state the organization's position and expectations in relation to them. Following are discussions on these two basic types of policy.

Program-Level Policy

As discussed above, program-level policy is broad in scope and far-reaching in applicability. To make the subject more manageable, an effective approach to a discussion of program-level IT security policy is to break general policy into its basic components: purpose, scope, goals, responsibilities, and enforcement.

Components of Program-Level Policy

Purpose: A primary purpose of program-level policy is to establish the IT security program. This includes defining the program management structure, the reporting responsibilities, the roles of individuals and groups throughout the organization, and the organizationwide goals of the security program. (Chapter 5 provides a detailed discussion of security program management and administration.) Additionally, program-level policy should serve the purpose of emphasizing to all employees the importance of IT security and clarifying the individual employee's role and responsibilities. IT security policy may be met with a degree of skepticism unless given appropriate visibility and support by top management, and that visibility and support should be clearly and energetically reflected in the program-level policy and in its emphasis on employee participation. The program-level policy should thus firmly establish individual employee accountability. Employees should be made aware via the policy that even if they are not designated IT security program personnel, they nonetheless have significant IT security responsibilities.

Scope: Program-level policy should be of sufficient breadth of scope to include all of the organization's IT resources, including facilities, hardware, software, information, and personnel. In some instances, it may be appropriate for a policy to name specific assets, such as major sites, installations, and large systems. In addition to such specified assets, it is important to include an overview of all of the types of IT resources for which the organization is responsible, such as workstations, Local Area Networks (LANs), standalone microcomputers, etc.

Goals: According to the National Research Council's Computers at Risk, published in 1991, the three security-related needs universally most emphasized among IT resource experts and the general computer user community are integrity, availability, and confidentiality. These concepts are the focus of many discussions in this handbook as well. These concepts should be the basis of the goals established for an organization in its IT security policy. Integrity means assuring that information is kept intact, and not lost, damaged, or modified in an authorized manner. Availability means assuring that information is accessible to authorized users when needed and that, to the extent possible, IT systems are safe from accidental or intentional disablement. Confidentiality means assuring that information is accessible only as authorized and that it cannot be acquired by unauthorized personnel and/or via unauthorized means. Goals related to these concepts should be stated in meaningful ways to employees based on the given environment. It is important that the organization's program-level policy reflect goals that are applicable to the specific environment by targeting the kinds of activities, information, and terminology that employees are familiar with. For instance, in an organization responsible for maintaining large but not highly confidential databases, goals related to reduction in errors, data loss, or data corruption might be specifically stressed. In an organization responsible for maintaining much more confidential data, however, goals might emphasize increased assurance against unauthorized disclosure.

Responsibilities: As noted in the earlier discussion of Purpose, program-level policy performs the important function of establishing the IT security program and assigning program management responsibilities. In addition to the security program management responsibilities, many other responsibilities throughout the organization should also be discussed in the policy, including the role of line managers, applications owners, data users, and the computer systems security group.

In some instances, the relationships among various individuals and groups may also need to be defined in the program-level policy. Such clarification can diminish ambiguity and confusion related to areas of responsibility or authority. It might be desirable to clarify, for example, who is to be responsible for approving the security measures to be used for new systems or components being installed: Should it be the department line manager where the item will be installed? Or should it be a designated inter-departmental IT security specialist? It might even be desirable to indicate under what circumstances, if any, approval of security measures implemented would be warranted by the head of the security program.

Overall, the program-level assignment of responsibilities should cover those activities and personnel who will be integral to the implementation and continuity of the IT security policy. Without a formal, documented IT security policy, it is not possible for management to proceed with the development of enforcement standards and mechanisms. Program-level policy serves as the basis for enforcement by describing penalties and disciplinary actions that can result from failure to comply with the organization's IT security requirements. Discipline commensurate with levels and types of security infractions should be discussed. For example, serious offenses, such as theft, conspiracy, or intentional acts of sabotage, might be designated by policy as punishable by firing and prosecution. Lesser infractions, such as pirating software, might be stated as punishable by formal written reprimand. Consideration should also be given to the fact that nonconformance to policy can be unintentional on the part of employees. For example, nonconformance can often be due to a lack of knowledge or training. It can also be the result of inadequate communication and explanation of the policy. For these reasons, it is desirable that, along with enforcement, program-level policy make provisions for orientation, training, and compliance within a realistic timeframe.

Issue-Specific Policy

Whereas program-level policy is intended to address the broadest aspects of IT security and the IT security program framework, issue-specific policies need to be developed to address particular kinds of activities and, in some environments, particular systems. The types of subjects covered by issue-specific policies are areas of current relevance, concern, and, sometimes, controversy upon which the organization needs to assert a position. In this manner, issue-specific IT security policies help to standardize activities and reduce the potential risks posed by inadequate and/or inappropriate treatment of the IT resources. Issue-specific policies serve to provide guidelines for the further development of procedures and practices within the functional elements of an organization. Program-level policy is usually broad enough that it does not require much modification over time. Issue-specific policies, however, are likely to require revision and updating from time to time, as changes in technology and related activities take place. This is largely because as new technologies develop, some issues diminish in importance while new ones continually appear. A major challenge to IT security specialists has long been the fact that for every new technology there are also new associated problems and issues to be addressed. For example, the enormous increase in the use of electronic mail (E-mail) systems in recent years has introduced many new issues in communications security, which is one of the topics that will be briefly discussed later in this section. Many organizations today are developing and refining communications security policies in order to better address such questions as who should have E-mail access, how will privileges be assigned and monitored, for what types of activities and information is E-mail sufficiently secure, and what criteria should be used for the re-sending (forwarding) of messages among users. Another topic of recent notoriety impacting IT security policies is the threat posed by computer viruses. New viruses and new methods of transmitting them are making it necessary that organizations develop policies regulating activities that were once performed freely, such as exchanging floppy disks among users, accessing electronic bulletinboards, and using shareware products. As for the discussion of program-level policy, a useful approach is to first break issue-specific policy into its basic components: statement of an issue, statement of the organization's position, applicability, roles and responsibilities, and points of contact. Thereafter, some of the areas that often require issue-specific policies will be covered.

Components of Issue-specific Policy

Statement of an Issue: In order to formulate a policy on an issue, the issue must first be defined, with any relevant terms, distinctions, and conditions delineated. For example, an organization might want to develop an issue-specific policy on the use of "foreign software." "Foreign software" might be defined to mean any software, whether applications or data, not approved, purchased, screened, managed, and owned by the organization. Additionally, the applicable distinctions and conditions might then need to be included, for instance, for software privately owned by employees but approved for use at work and for software owned and used by other businesses under contract to the organization.

Statement of the Organization's Position: Once the issue is stated and related terms and conditions delineated, the organization's position or stance on the issue will need to be clearly stated. To continue the example of developing an issue-specific policy on the use of foreign software, this would mean stating whether use of foreign software as defined is strictly prohibited, whether or not there are further guidelines for approval and use, or whether case-by-case decisions will be rendered based on some defined criteria. Applicability: Issue-specific policies will also need to include statements of applicability. This means clarifying where, how, when, to whom, and to what a particular policy applies. For example, it could be that the hypothetical policy on foreign software is intended to apply only to the organization's own onsite resources and employees and is not to be applicable to contractor organizations with offices at other locations. Additionally, the policy's applicability to employees travelling among different sites and/or working at home who need to transport and use disks at multiple sites might need to be clarified. Roles and Responsibilities: Also included in issue-specific policies should be the assignment of roles and responsibilities. This would mean, to continue with the above example, that if the policy permits foreign software privately owned by employees to be used at work with the appropriate approvals, then the approval authority granting such permission would need to be stated. Likewise, it would need to be clarified who would be responsible for ensuring that only approved foreign software is used on organizational IT resources and, perhaps, for monitoring users in regard to foreign software. Related to the assignment of roles and responsibilities is the inclusion of guidelines for procedures and enforcement. The issue-specific policy on foreign-software, for example, might include procedural guidelines for checking disks used by employees at home or at other locations. It might also state what the penalties would be for using unapproved foreign software on the organization's IT systems. Points of Contact: For any issue-specific policy, the appropriate individuals in the organization to contact for further information, guidance, and enforcement should be indicated. For example, for some issues the point of contact might be a line manager; for other issues it might be a facility manager, technical support person, or system administrator. For yet other issues, the point-of-contact might be a security program representative. Using the above example once more, employees would need to know whether the point of contact for questions and procedural information would be his/her immediate superior, a system administrator, or a computer security official.

Areas Appropriate for Issue-specific Policies

Some of the areas in which management today needs to consider issue-specific IT security policies are covered in this section. These topics are intended to provide examples and serve as sources for ideas and analysis. Although many of these topics are standard to any discussion of IT security, an organization would necessarily need to tailor its policies relating to them to meet its own unique needs. Physical security: The physical protection of and access to IT resources and facilities will generally need to be addressed in one or more specific policies. In organizations with extensive IT systems and equipment, this may mean developing policies that address such issues as who has access to what sites/locations; how often risks to installations are be analyzed and by whom; what types of physical access controls and monitoring equipment are put in place; what responsibilities will be assigned to trained security officials and what activities and responsibilities will be required of all employees. Personnel Security: Depending on the types of activities being performed, degree of data sensitivity to be encountered, and sheer numbers of personnel, specific security policies related to personnel screening, requirements, hiring, training, evaluating, and firing may need to be developed and administered. It may be appropriate that a trained personnel security specialist initiate, review, approve, and perform all security-related personnel actions. Communications Security: Communications security is a complex technical specialty unto itself. In organizations where day-to-day business relies on communicating routinely with remote locations, the security of the communications transmissions and lines is usually an issue that needs to be addressed by policy.

If the data being transmitted is highly sensitive, then this concern is magnified, and issue-specific security policies may need to be developed on a number of activities. Issues associated with the use of cryptography and its related options and procedures (discussed in Chapter 19), the use of modems and dial-in lines, and precautions against wiretapping are just some of the potential issues to be addressed. Additionally, as noted earlier, the proliferation of E-mail has introduced many security- and privacy-related issues for which organizations need to document positions and policies. Administrative Security: Administrative security as it applies to IT system management and oversight activities comprises many potential security policy issues. Included are such topics as input/output controls, training and awareness, security certification/accreditation, incident reporting, system configurations and change controls, and system documentation. Risk Management: Risk management involves assessing IT resources in terms of potential threats and vulnerabilities and planning the means for counteracting those identified risks. Issues that will need to be addressed by policies include how, by whom, and when the assessments should be performed; and what type of documentation should result. Contingency Planning: Related to Risk Management, Contingency Planning means planning for the emergency actions to be taken in the event of damage, failure, and/or other disabling events that could occur to systems. Issues that need to be addressed by policies include determining which systems are most critical and therefore of highest priority in contingency planning; how the plans will be tested, how often, and by whom; and who will be responsible for approving the plans.

Policy Implementation

Policy implementation is a process. Policy cannot merely be pronounced by upper management in a one-time statement or directive with high expectations of its being readily accepted and acted upon. Rather, just as formulating and drafting policy involves a process, implementation similarly involves a process, which begins with the formal issuance of policy.

Policy Visibility

Especially high visibility should be afforded the formal issuance of IT security policy. This is due to a combination of factors, including the following:

- Nearly all employees at all levels will in some way be affected;
- Major organizational resources are being addressed;
- Many new terms, procedures, and activities will be introduced.

Providing visibility through such avenues as management presentations, panel discussions, guest speakers, question/answer forums, and newsletters can be beneficial, as resources permit. Including IT security as a regular topic at staff meetings at all levels of the organization can also be a helpful tactic. As an aspect of providing visibility for IT security policies, information should also be included regarding the applicable higher level directives and requirements to which the organization is responding. Educating employees as to the requirements specified by the Computer Security Act and related OMB circulars will help emphasize the significance and timeliness of computer security, and it will help provide a rational basis for the introduction of IT security policies.

Policy Documentation

Once IT security policy has been approved and issued, it may be initially publicized through memorandums, presentations, staff meetings, or a variety of means. As soon as possible, though, it will also need to be incorporated into formal policy documentation as well. The process of documenting policies will usually require updating existing documentation as well as creating new documentation.

Existing Documentation: IT security will need to be integrated into many existing activities and practices throughout many levels of the organization. This integration will be facilitated by revising any existing applicable documentation to reflect new procedures, rules, and requirements. Included may be the modification of various existing documents, forms, and plans at all levels of the organization to reflect the IT policy. For example, if IT equipment purchases and/or upgrades have been reviewed and approved based on documented criteria such as cost, productivity, maintainability, etc., then security considerations may need to be introduced into that criteria. Also, if it has previously been the documented policy to review the progress and status of internal IT systems under development, then security-related concerns should be introduced into that review process. New Documentation: Additionally, the development of many new documents, such as guidelines, standards, and procedures, may be required. This is often true in large organizations performing many different activities and having many levels of management. In such environments, different functional elements may have widely differing IT systems and needs to accommodate. It is therefore generally more practical, to the extent possible, to allow elements to tailor their implementations of policy to meet their unique needs. This can be accomplished through the development of documents containing more detailed procedures and practices to be used for specific kinds of systems and activities within functional elements. For example, organizations will want to issue policies to decrease the likelihood of data loss due to technology failures and/or operator errors. A program-level policy might state something to the effect that: "It is the policy of the organization to ensure against data loss due to accidents or mishaps." In an area where extensive writing and editing of lengthy documents is performed, such as a word processing or technical publications unit, security documentation might be developed on saving work in-progress much more often than would usually be done, and/or utilizing automatic "save" features on IT systems and software. In a different type of functional area, however, where, for example, databases are maintained that do not undergo significant changes very often, the security documentation might focus on procedures for the database administrator to use in performing periodic (daily, weekly, etc.) backups of the system. Appropriate visibility should be afforded the IT security policy through all applicable documentation. The more integral security policy is to all other aspects of daily routines, the more quickly the associated actions and practices will become natural to doing business. Ultimately, among the goals of policy are the assimilation of a common body of knowledge and values and the demonstration of appropriate corresponding behaviors. Those goals will be expedited by making the IT security policy integral to the organization through all avenues.

Cost Considerations

There are a number of potential costs associated with developing and implementing IT security policies. In some environments, the major costs may be those incurred through the numerous administrative and management activities required for drafting, reviewing, disseminating, and publicizing the policies. In some organizations, though, successful policy implementation may require additional staffing, training, and equipment. In general, how costly IT security policy development and implementation are to an organization will depend upon how much change needs to be accomplished in order to ensure adequate security and a basic standardization throughout the organization.

Interrelationships

IT security policy can be related to nearly every topic covered in this handbook on some level. This is because all of the topics discussed in the handbook have associated issues that organizations may need to address via policies. The topics most directly related, however, are: IT security program management and administration; risk management; personnel; security training and awareness; contingency planning; and physical and environmental security.

Conclusion

Formulating viable IT security policies is a challenge for an organization and requires communication and understanding of the organizational goals and potential benefits to be derived from policies. Through a carefully structured approach to policy development, which includes the delegation of program management responsibility and an understanding of both program-level and issue-specific policy components, a coherent set of policies - integrated into sensible practices and procedures - can be developed 6.1, para 2: IT security policy helps to provide basic standards, guidelines, and rules for everyone in an organization.

6.2, para 1: Program-level IT security policy establishes the security program and assigns program management responsibilities.

6.2.1.1, para 4: Program-level policy should be sufficiently broad in scope to include all of the organization's IT resources.

6.2.1.1, para 5: Program-level IT security policy goals should stress the universal concepts of integrity, availability, and confidentiality.

6.2.2, para 1: Issue-specific policies address particular activities, concerns, and, sometimes, systems.

6.2.2, para 4: New products, developments, and trends often require the creation of corresponding issue-specific policies.

6.2.2.2, para 1: Many activities within an organization should be considered when developing issue-specific policies, including physical security, personnel, communications, administrative security, risk management, and contingency planning.

6.3.1, para 1: IT security policy should be given especially high visibility in order to help ensure employee awareness and understanding.

6.3.2, para 4: Many existing documents of an organization will need to be revised to reflect IT security policies, and new documents may also need to be developed.

Receive All the Latest Articles by email

Get all articles delivered directly to your mailbox as and when they are released on WindowSecurity.com! Choose between receiving instant updates with the Real-Time Article Update, or a monthly summary with the Monthy Article Update.

- Real-Time Article Update
- Monthly Article Update

Network and Computer Security Tutorial Version 0.4.0 : A Case Study

This computer security tutorial is written based on my experiences with computer and network security along with my training and information I have read. The field of security is constantly changing so I cannot guarantee that information in this computer security tutorial will be current. This computer security tutorial will define some basic security issues and give insight into what causes security to be a constant issue. This computer security tutorial will help you decide what to protect and provide some basic information about attacks that may be made against your network, computer systems, or data. It will also provide computer and network security recommendations for you or your organization. Although much useful information can be derived from this document without the reader having networking knowledge, to use this document in depth, I recommend that readers of this computer security tutorial have a fundamental knowledge about networking. The information contained in The CTDP Networking Guide contains the networking documentation required to understand this computer security tutorial.

Introduction

In this computer security tutorial, the terms computer security and network security will be used often. When the term computer security is used, it specifically refers to the security of one computer, although the overall security of each individual computer is required for network security. When the term network security is used, it refers to the security of the network in general. This includes such issues as password security, network sniffing, intrusion detection, firewalls, network structure and so forth.

Security Violation Definition

Computer or network security has been violated when unauthorized access by any party occurs.

Why Security?

Computer security is required because most organizations can be damaged by hostile software or intruders. There may be several forms of damage which are obviously interrelated. These include:

- Damage or destruction of computer systems.
- Damage or destruction of internal data.
- Loss of sensitive information to hostile parties.
- Use of sensitive information to steal items of monitary value.

- Use of sensitive information against the organization's customers which may result in legal action by customers against the organization and loss of customers.
- Damage to the reputation of an organization.
- Monitary damage due to loss of sensitive information, destruction of data, hostile use of sensitie data, or damage to the organization's reputation.

The methods used to accomplish these unscrupulous objectives are many and varied depending on the circumstances. This guide will help administrators understand some of these methods and explain some countermeasures.

Security Issues

Computer security can be very complex and may be very confusing to many people. It can even be a controversial subject. Network administrators like to believe that their network is secure and those who break into networks may like to believe that they can break into any network. I believe that overconfidence plays an important role in allowing networks to be intruded upon. There are many fallacies that network administrators may fall victim to. These fallacies may allow administrators to wrongfully believe that their network is more secure than it really is.

This guide will attempt to clarify many issues related to security by doing the following:

- Help you determine what you are protecting.
- Break computer security into categories.
- Explain security terms and methods.
- Point out some common fallacies that may allow administrators to be overconfident.
- Categorize many common attacks against networks and computers.
- Explain some attack methods.
- Describe tools that can be used to help make a network more secure.

Security Interdependence

There are many different aspects to computer and network security as you will read in this document. These different areas of computer security are interdependent on each other in order for a network to be secure. If one or more areas of computer security are ignored, then the entire security integrity of the organization's network may be compromised. A clear example of this is in the area of computer virus or worm protection. Computer virus protection programs can only filter known viruses or worms. There are viruses or worms that are not yet recognized as virus programs immediately after their release. The best way to make unrecognized virus or worm programs less effective is by quickly removing the vulneribilities that they use. Some of these vulnerabilities are operating system and application program errors. When security patches are created for software, they should be quickly applied. In this way the vulnerabilty to viruses is minimized but not eliminated. There are other steps which may further reduce this vulnerability, but it can never be completely eliminated.

Security Limitations and Applications

If you are reading this document and are thinking that you can get all the information required to make your network completely secure, then you are sadly mistaken. In many ways, computer security is almost a statistical game. You can reduce but not eliminate the chance that you may be penetrated by an intruder or virus. This is mainly for one reason. No one can ever know all the software vulnerabilities of all software used on a system. This is why even those who consider themselves hackers will say that the number one computer security threat is the lack of quality in the applications and operating systems. At this point, I could talk about the various corporate entities that write software and why software lacks the quality that many of us believe that it should possess, but that subject is not only way beyond the scope of this document, but also way beyond the scope of this project. The bottom line here is that unless you can remove all the application and operating system problems that allow viruses and intruders to penetrate networks, you can never secure your network. Additionally the users on your network are potentially a greater security risk than any programs. Obviously removing all vulnerabilities is impossible and will not secure your network against user errors. I have even considered the possibility that an operating system without a network interface can be completely secure, but even this cannot be guaranteed. Unknown viruses or trojan programs can creep in with applications on CDs or floppies. This has been known to happen. Although an attacker may not be able to get data from the system, they can damage or destroy data.

Layered Security

The fact that complete security is impossible is the reason security experts recommend "layered security". The idea is to have multiple ways of preventing an intrusion to decrease the chance that intrusions will be successful. For example, you should have virus protection on your client computers. To help layer this security you should also filter viruses at your email server. To help even more, you should block the most dangerous types of email attachments to prevent unrecognized viruses and other hostile software from entering your network. Another good defense layer would also include educating your users about viruses, how they spread, and how to avoid them.

Hackers

There are many documents that attempt to define the term hacker. I believe that the term hacker is a connotative term. This means that it is more defined by people's beliefs rather than by a dictionary. Some believe that a hacker is a very skilled computer person. Others believe that hackers are those that perform unauthorized break ins to computer systems. The media and many sources have caused many uninformed people to believe that a hacker is a threat to computer and network security while this is not the case. A hacker is no more likely to break the law than anyone else. I use the more accurate descriptive term, "intruder" to describe those who intrude into networks or systems without authorization.

Physical Security

This guide will not talk about physical computer security beyond this paragraph. Your organization should be aware how physically secure every aspect of its network is because if an intruder gets physical access, they can get your data. Be sure the your organization properly secures locations and consider the following:

- Servers - Contain your data and information about how to access that data.
- Workstations - Man contain some sensitive data and can be used to attack other computers.
- Routers, switches, bridges, hubs and any other network equipment may be used as an access point to your network.
- Network wiring and media and where they pass through may be used to access your network or place a wireless access point to your network.
- External media which may be used between organizational sites or to other sites the organization does business with.
- Locations of staff who may have information that a hostile party can use.
- Some employees may take data home or may take laptops home or use laptops on the internet from home then bring them to work. Any information on these laptops should be considered to be at risk and these laptops should be secure according to proper policy when connected externally on the network (more on this later).

Some Terms

This paragaph describes some commonly used computer security terms.

- *Protocol* - Well defined specification allowing computer communication.
- *Confidentiality* - Information is available only to people with rightful access.
- *Integrity* - Information can only be changed by authorized personnel.
- *Availability* - Information is available to only those who need it.
- *Verification-nonrepudiation*- There is proof that the sender sent the message
- *Authentification* - The receiver of the message should be able to be sure of

the origin of the message. Requires a digital signature (One way hash, public key algorithm, and symmetric algorithm) or a public key algorithm.

- *Spyware* - A computer program whose purpose is to spy on your internet activities usually for marketing purposes and usually done by a shady corporate entity.
- *Malware* - A computer program with some evil intent. It may on the surface have a good or useful intent, but may be a trojan (with a hidden purpose) which can be used to gain unauthorized access to your computer.

Studies of Users of Electronic Retrieval Systems

A number of researchers have studied people using electronic retrieval systems in order to characterise the search process from a user perspective. These studies have concentrated on professional intermediaries who regularly use a system or on "end users" who may be novices or occasional users of the system. Often, these studies have been conducted using existing systems with design specifications that are typically information centered or system centered rather than user centered. Some more recent studies have taken the approach of formative evaluation in conjunction with actual system development. A few of these investigations are described here to illustrate the many factors that make up the information-seeking framework. This overview is meant to provide a context for the framework, and in subsequent chapters, we will discuss user studies in detail in light of this framework.

Fidel's work with professional online searchers is typical of the studies of expert intermediaries (Fidel, 1984). She conducted intensive case studies of intermediaries conducting searches of online bibliographic databases. Based on her observations and interviews, she defined two searching styles: operationalist and conceptualist. An operationalist searcher devotes considerable effort to manipulating the system and conducts high-precision searches. A conceptualise searcher devotes more effort to the concepts and terminology and develops subsets of results that are then combined in various ways to yield high recall. Fidel's work has been extended to address particular aspects of searching, such as how subject terms are selected and used by professional searchers in a variety of fields (Fidel, 1991). Saracevic and his colleagues (Saracevic & Kantor, 1988a, 1988b; Saracevic, Kantor, Chamis, & Trivison, 1988) conducted the largest study to date of online searching by expert intermediaries using a framework of five variable classes: users, questions, searchers, searches, and items retrieved. Their findings indicate that end-user variables have little effect on outcomes as measured by the odds of retrieved documents being at least partially relevant and that recall and precision values were generally consistent across variables. Exceptions include the following: Well-defined problems increased relevance odds; estimates of public knowledge (the end user's expectations about what information is available in the system) increased relevance and precision odds; and user-defined limits on language and currency of documents increased relevance and precision odds.

Various cognitive characteristics of searchers had mixed effects on their performance, with a preference for abstractness over concreteness as having significant positive effects on relevance and recall odds. Term selection overlap among intermediaries was low, as was overlap among retrieved document sets - reinforcing the view of online retrieval as more an art than a science. The studies reported many other results related to how searches were executed and what types of outcomes were obtained, but a key recommendation was to investigate the complex nature of the search process in context as well as in laboratory settings. In addition to the extensive portrait that these studies provide for intermediaries searching electronic data-bases, the framework for question classification and the application of quantitative and qualitative evaluation measures make these efforts seminal in the field. Studies of end users are exemplified by Borgman's investigations of the cognitive activity of college students and children using various bibliographic databases (Borgman, 1986a: Borgman, Gallagher, Krieger, & Bower, 1990). She applied the psychological theory of mental models to explain learning and errors and made a case for instructional approaches that are conceptual rather than simply procedural. Her systematic user studies also provide the basis for the continued development and redesign of an online catalog customised for elementary students (Borgman et al., 1990). Borgman's early work was the basis for some of the studies that Marchionini conducted with K-12 students searching full-text electronic encyclopedias (Marchionini, 1989b; 1989c).

In his work, elementary school children were able to use the electronic environment to conduct searches for simple subjects, and high school students had difficulties with complex queries and made mental models for the new system based on print metaphors and individual information-seeking skills and characteristics. In some cases, studies of end users were part of overall development efforts for specific electronic retrieval systems. Formative evaluation examines how users interact with system prototypes to inform the iterative design process. Egan and colleagues (1989) studied users of their SuperBook hypertext system and used the results in making substantial improvements in subsequent versions of the system. Marchionini and Shneiderman (1988) likewise used the results of user studies for subsequent versions of the Hyperties hypertext system and various Hyperties databases. Ongoing end-user evaluations of the Perseus Project system also influenced subsequent releases of this hypermedia corpus (Marchionini & Crane, 1994). Generalizable results from these studies illustrate the usefulness of high-lighted query terms, the use of tables of contents to provide content for users, and the high acceptance by users of interactive browsing.

Studies of end users concentrated on online public access catalogs in libraries. Early studies sponsored by the Council on Library Resources led to a better understanding of the types of searches that users conducted (e.g., over half of all OPAC searches were by subject rather than title or author) and identified the wide range of results that users obtained (e.g., about 10% of commands resulted in errors, except in the menu interface of MELVYL, which produced 2% error rates) (Larson, 1983; Markey, 1984;

Matthews, 1982). Studies of user error patterns (Janosky, Smith, & Hildreth, 1986) highlighted not only the interface defects of OPACs but also the fact that casual users have a poor understanding of libraries in general and exhibit naive and careless actions while searching. These results are cited as influential in the improved designs for second generation OPACs (Hi-ldreth, 1989; Larson, 1991). In sum, the results of studies of how users apply electronic retrieval systems to information-seeking problems reinforce the general theory of user-centered information seeking that focuses on highly active users with a broad range of information problems. They also illustrate the importance of task and system parameters. These results have led to new designs for retrieval systems and demonstrated the value of user testing and iterative design. More important, they have reinforced and extended the perspective of information seeking as a human-centered problem-solving activity.

Factors of Information Seeking

Information seeking depends on interactions among several factors: information seeker, task, search system, domain, setting, and search outcomes (Marchionini, 1989a; Marchionini & Shneiderman, 1988). All the factors are embedded in a setting; the domain and search system are interrelated; the information seeker perceives and interprets the setting, has mental models for the domain(s) and the search system, and turns an information problem into a task that drives his or her interactions with the search system; these interactions yield outcomes that in turn affect the information seeker and the problem. These factors are discussed in detail in the following sections.

Information Seeker

This framework for information seeking is human centered in that the information seeker defines the task, controls the interaction with the search system, examines and extracts relevant information, assesses the progress, and determines when the information-seeking process is complete. Each information seeker possesses unique mental models, experiences, abilities, and preferences. Experience with particular settings, domains, and systems generally allow more comprehensive and accurate mental models and thus more facility with these models. The information seeker's personal information infrastructure affects overall performance while solving information problems and executing tasks and continues to develop as information seekers accrue experience and knowledge. For every information problem, information seekers reinforce and extend their mental models for the various factors and subprocesses associated with information seeking.

Professional intermediaries who regularly conduct searches for others are familiar with many sources of information (search systems) and are able to apply various— information-seeking strategies. They demonstrate expertise in information seeking through their knowledge of different search systems and strategies for assisting people in articulating tasks. Experts in a Field of study have comprehensive vocabularies in the domain, know what types of sources are best applicable to problems, and are aware of alternative access points for finding information in the domain (e.g., personal, corporate, geographic). Our studies of professional intermediaries and domain experts in computer science, economics, and law suggest that although both types of experts have significant advantages over novices when conducting searches, each type of expert also exhibits specific advantages with respect to one another (Marchionini, Dwiggins, Katz, & Lin, 1993; Marchionini, Lin, & Dwiggins, 1990). Intermediaries focus on the information task as expressed in the question, on query formulation, and on the interface aspects of the system (e.g., structure of information) and are generally guided by matching questions to the database's structure. Domain experts seem to have an image of the answer and are guided by identifying possible answers in the database. Domain experts spend more time in scanning and reading text and less time formulating and modifying queries. Regardless of the specific advantages that either type of experts have, expertise clearly affects information seeking, just as it does other intellectual efforts such as chess (Newell & Simon, 1972) or medical decision making (Spiro, Feltovich, Coulson, & Anderson, 1989). Individual differences among information seekers play a role in both specific instances of information seeking and the overall development of personal information infrastructures. Egan (1988) identified age and spatial reasoning as important factors in a variety of task performance areas, including information seeking. Other researchers studied cognitive style (e.g. Bellardo, 1985) and personal variables such as academic success, reading ability, field of study, and verbal and quantitative abilities in order to determine their relationships to information seeking (e.g., Borgman, 1989; Marchionini, 1989a). Because these individual differences are not independent, no single characteristic alone can predict information-seeking performance.

However, cognitive, physical, and emotional differences between and within individual persons do influence specific behaviors and general affinities and abilities. In addition to individual differences, information seeking is part of a person's ongoing effort to understand and act in the world. Each person is situated in a context that at any given instant influences all actions, including information seeking (see Suchman, 1987, for a theory of situated human activity applied to human-machine interactions). Situational personal variables such as physical, cognitive, and emotional health affect human performance and cannot be ignored. Commitments to a work group or other persons influence performance and how people perceive themselves fitting into an organisation are part of the setting. Even more slippery is the motivation to initiate and continue information seeking. The motivation to initiate a search may be driven by external or internal needs, but the tenacity to continue the search may depend on personality factors such as perseverance and on external factors such as time and money. The most basic situational factor for information seeking, however, is the information problem that causes the user to act. Taylor (1962) defined four levels of information needs: visceral, conscious, formalised, and compromised. The visceral level is the recognition of some deficiency, although it is not cognitively defined. At the conscious level, the information seeker characterises the deficiency, places limits on it, and is able to express the problem, though not precisely. At the formalised level, the person is able to articulate the problem clearly (e.g., in English), and the compromised level refers to the formalised statement as presented in a form limited by the search system (e.g., in a database query language). The conscious and formalised levels correspond to the task in the framework presented here. Taylor's visceral and conscious levels of information need correspond to what Dervin called a *gap,* and what Belkin and his colleagues refer to as an *anomalous state of knowledge.* Using a computational metaphor, Marchionini (1989b) characterised the information problem as emerging from a defect in one's mental model for some idea, event, or object. This state initiates a search in long-term memory, and if the defect cannot be mended (either correctly or through rationalised guessing), then information seeking is initiated by activating the personal information infrastructure and passing the contextual parameters to it.

Marchionini defined the personal information infrastructure procedure by observing how people use manual and electronic encyclopedias, and he noted a significant difference in the electronic instantiations in that those systems often returned large sets of articles as outcomes rather than a single article or small set of "see also" articles in the manual case. By automatically involving the index in search, these electronic systems required additional explicit decision-making steps by users. This approach was useful in formulating the human-system interaction phases of the information-seeking process but mental model structures seemed badly suited to information needs, as they are elaborate and take time to develop. To address this deficiency, consider the knowledge state of an information seeker at some instant as a collection of noumenal clouds.

Each noumenal cloud represents a concept or idea composed of noumena (memory traces and impressions). These clouds are highly fluid; the noumena within a cloud come and go as thought progresses, as do the clouds themselves. A knowledge state consists of several noumenal clouds related by common noumena - analogous to valence bonds between atoms in a molecule. The knowledge state is well defined when the noumena within clouds are stable and the clouds have many noumena in common. In this case, new clouds are not formed, and active clouds remain active - there is relative certainty in the knowledge state. An information problem is a collection of noumenal clouds that is unstable; clouds come and go because there are not enough stable common noumena. In this case, the knowledge state has a high degree of uncertainty in the definition of noumena and clouds and thus a high potential for state change, that is, acquiring information. In the most common cases, greater numbers of noumena are needed for stabilisation (simply activating more memory traces to define a cloud). In more complex cases, overlaps of noumena across clouds are needed for stabilisation.

Information problems typically arise directly from the external world - inputs stimulate noumena and clouds. The information problem may also arise from a stable knowledge state when a cloud is deactivated or a new cloud is added to extend thought. As new clouds are activated, the knowledge state can stabilise quickly as many noumena from active clouds overlap (e.g., as one thought leads logically to the next), or the knowledge state can become less stable if noumena do not fit into active clouds. In the latter case, information is needed (e.g., finding out what one does not know may be a revelation that informs and guides one's subsequent action.). Note that each of these characterisations is based on information imparting some cognitive change, not on overt behaviors. There is a great range in the degree of cognitive change that a person may seek. For example, physicians often seek information to confirm what they believe to be the proper course of treatment. The need to confirm information does not change cognitive structure so much as reinforce it. Regardless of the terminology used and the motivation, the information problem is the trigger for information seeking and as discussed in sections ahead, it evolves and changes as the search and the overall situation progress.

Task

As used here, a *task* is the manifestation of an information seeker's problem and is what drives information-seeking actions. The task includes an articulation, usually stated as a question, and the mental and physical behaviors of interacting with search systems and reflecting on outcomes. Tasks are composed of entity-relationship states and plans for expanding those states to some goal state. Although tasks are explicitly goal driven, the human element and the interactive nature of information seeking allow the goal and therefore the task to change or evolve as the search progresses. The balance between goal-driven initiation and data-driven progress and change are one measure of the browsing. As information seekers define the information problem, they identify concepts and relationships and assign terms to the concepts in order to articulate a task. These concepts and terms vary in number (the number of noumenal clouds) and in degree of abstractness (the amount of variability possible when mapping noumena to specific objects or events), and these variations determine the complexity of the task.

In addition to complexity, tasks may be characterised according to their goals or the answers expected. A key problem in information-seeking performance and information system design is clarifying different levels of the task's goal. For example, the goal from the system's point of view is to provide a document of some sort, whereas the goal from the information seeker's point of view is to extract information (make meaning) from some document and stabilise or advance his or her knowledge state. From the information seeker's point of view, answers to questions (goals for tasks) may be characterised along three continua: specificity, quantity, and timeliness. The specificity of a goal can range from single fact to an idea to an interpretation or opinion. In the case of facts, information seekers are assured of a high level of certainty that they have accomplished the task and reached the goal. This is not to say that the answer is necessarily optimal but, rather, that there is typically a high degree of confidence in the result's validity. In the case of ideas, the certainty of attainment and therefore of terminating the search is less well defined. Such tasks may invite subsequent iterations of action and termination decisions based on factors such as time or resource constraints. In addition, these types of answers are often multiple in number, and so information seekers must choose or synthesise outcomes. Goals with very low specificity offer the greatest challenges to information seekers for they provide low levels of certainty about completing the task and require great efforts to develop confidence in the validity of one of possibly many interpretations.

Related to specificity is the volume of the answer as measured in either information bits or time for users to process the result. At one end of this continuum we have a single word, date, or image that satisfies the task. Such goals are often satisfied by ready reference services in libraries, telephone directory assistance, or traditional database management systems. Such answers can be transmitted and processed easily and quickly. Another level of volume requires one or more documents, and these answers take more time to transmit and process. Most important, these levels of goal volume traditionally require information seekers to process and extract information. This makes the information seekers' relevance judgments both more personal and difficult, with subsequent implications for evaluating the system's performance. In the most extreme case, such as the task of "keeping abreast of one's field," which we term *accretion of knowledge,* the volume of the answer reaches large subsets of a domain or domains. These goals are typically met by regular reading of periodicals, discussions and exchanges with colleagues, and participation in courses, workshops, and conferences.

Timeliness of the goal describes the expected time to completion. One of the common frustrations of information seeking is when expectations of timeliness are far out of sync with actual times to completion. Thus, regardless of how effective an information service is, if we expect the task to take 10 minutes and it actually takes 2 hours, we will be disappointed. At one end of the timeliness continuum are those answers that we expect to verify immediately or in a few minutes. We can have such immediate expectations only for high-specificity, low-quantity goals. These types of answers are not insignificant, however, because they are common and they highlight one of the distinctions between information seeking and learning. They are common in that they include things we once knew but have temporarily forgotten or things we need as an intermediate step in some larger task; thus we ask someone near us, or we quickly look them up in a reference book, dictionary, or service. In many cases, we have no intention of ever using the information again and so acquire it for immediate needs without making mental or external notes. This contrasts with learning, which always aspires to retaining the information acquired. Many tasks aim at goals that we expect will be achieved in some generally defined period such as minutes, days, or months. These tasks include most formal information retrieval such as database searching, interlibrary loan requests, and written requests to persons or institutions. At the most extreme, our expectations are that we will never fully achieve our task but will progress toward it. These accretion of knowledge tasks are part of expert learning and distinguish information seeking from information retrieval.

All these characteristics of task goals work together to define the cost of the task. The total cost is not composed simply of external costs such as connect and copying charges but also of personal costs such as time, as well as cognitive and emotional resources. Early estimates of the costs are computed by information seekers to determine whether tasks should be defined and executed. These estimates are strongly influenced by personal abilities and motivations, especially with respect to personal information infrastructures.

Search System

The *search system* is a source that represents knowledge and provides tools and rules for accessing and using that knowledge. Here a search system includes, for example, people, books, libraries, and maps, as well as a variety of electronic information systems. A search system represents knowledge in what is called a *database,* regardless of whether the search system is a book, a computer, or a person. Thus, a database refers to the knowledge potentially available to an information seeker. The representations of that knowledge and the tools, rules, and mechanisms for accessing and manipulating it is an *interface.* The search system supports information seeking by structuring knowledge and constraining access. The way that knowledge is organised and made available affects the way that information seekers are able to access this knowledge and thus their information-seeking performance. Information seekers construct and use mental models of search systems to execute information-seeking tasks. The interface serves as an intermediary between the user and the database. Conceptual elements include representations and mechanisms and physical elements include input and output devices. The database content may he in different containers (e.g., a paper and electronic version of a text), and the database and interface may be integrated or separated physically or conceptually. The interface should provide robust mappings between the database content and the conceptual representations that information seekers manipulate. In the sections that follow, we use three general types of search systems - a book, an electronic retrieval system, and an expert human - to clarify the characteristics of search systems.

Database: content and container. Information seekers are most concerned with the content of a database, which may be characterised by its topicality, aim, data type, quantity, quality, and granularity. The primary aspect of content is "aboutness," the domain represented by the database. Clearly, an information problem related to nuclear waste management will not likely be well served by a database concerning ancient Roman poetry. Books can be assigned subject headings that try to capture their primary topics; electronic retrieval systems have data dictionaries specifying what entities and relationships are included, and people develop expertise in specific domains. A second aspect of the content is whether it is primary or n-ary in nature. Secondary (e.g., bibliographic) or tertiary (e.g., a bibliography of bibliographies, database guides, directories of electronic servers) databases are important for locating primary databases, and information seekers must have clear images of the intermediate role they play. The classic disappointment in electronic environments is exemplified by students who use a CD-ROM index to conduct a search and then are dismayed that they must locate the periodical in the library. It is important that information seekers understand which level of access is most appropriate to reach the primary database relevant to their problem. Another aspect of the database content is the type of information it contains, for example, text, numeric, graphic, verbal, kinesthetic, or mixed. These types of information determine how system designers organise, index, and display information. This in turn influences the strategies that information seekers use to locate, scan, and extract information. Books often include mixed forms; electronic multi-media databases are becoming more common; and humans offer a broad range of verbal and kinesthetic information. The quantity and quality of database content also are important. It makes a great difference to an information seeker in terms of effort and expectations whether the database consists of a single book of 200 pages or an entire shelf of books on the topic.

Likewise, an electronic system of 1000 records is treated quite differently by an information seeker than is a system with a billion records. Although human memory is, for all practical purposes, infinite, different people have different degrees of experience and expertise on a topic. Experienced information seekers assess the accuracy of the content as part of search system selection and while making judgments about initiating and terminating the search. The authority of a book's author, the integrity of an electronic retrieval system, and the credibility of human experts each are taken into consideration by experienced information seekers. In addition to accuracy, the database content must be clearly organised and presented if it is to be considered a quality information source. Books can be well written or not, electronic documents can be well structured or not; and human experts can be logical and articulate or not. Finally, the granularity of the database content affects information seeking. Books, databases, and people can represent knowledge at very specific or highly general levels, with the levels of variability differing according to the needs of the information seeker. For example, a book, electronic system, or person can represent information on dogs in general or be specific to the sleeping habits of a particular family of dogs. Although experienced information seekers expect an encyclopedia to provide generic information on a variety of topics, emerging electronic environments have yet to establish specialisations and precedents for communicating granularity to users. For example, an electronic archive may indiscriminately mix highly specific commentary on minor points of an electronic forum with generic overview information on the topic.

Databases have physical attributes that affect information seeking. These at-tributes may be though of as the "container" for the contents and include the hardware, media, and physical organisation of the system. For a book, the at-tributes are related to size and weight, printing (e.g., characteristics of paper, glue, and ink), typography, and the author's physical ordering of ideas. From a computing point of view, these attributes are related to computational power, storage capacity, coding mechanisms, display characteristics, and data structures. For ex-ample, computational power determines whether graphical interfaces can be used effectively or whether sophisticated retrieval schemes will operate in a timely manner. From a human point of view, physical attributes are related to mental and verbal capabilities, and training or biases. A significant influence of the container is how it determines organisational presentation and the interface. Books generally invite sequential presentations and traversals, although there are many ways in which linearity can be disrupted. Electronic systems can use networks, webs, and arrays to invite associational traversals - the basis for hypertext. In addition, the processing and structuring of data determines whether retrieval features such as ranking and relevance feedback are available. For example, an inverted index and a primary file together facilitate rapid exact-match retrieval; a file of vector values and a primary file facilitate ranked retrieval; and both leverage the preprocessing captured in the access files to outperform a simple primary file searched sequentially. Humans can present information in free-associational or in carefully sequenced fashion, and information seekers can "traverse" these presentations in random snatches or in sequence. Whether the linear organisation and presentation of ideas is inherently more transferable by people or our culture has been conditioned by the limits of transmissional technology is a research topic that will continue to occupy generations to come.

Interface: physical and conceptual. The. interface is a communication channel between a user and a machine. Interfaces have physical and conceptual components, and the concept of interface is evolving as people use computers as intermediaries for collaborative work (e.g., Grudin, 1993). Physical input and output devices, selection and feedback mechanisms, and retrieval rules characterise an interface and serve as portals to the content. The interface determines how learnable, usable, and satisfying a search system is, and therefore, it affects information-seeking performance. The "look and feel" of a book, electronic document, or person is dependent on assumptions made about the information seeker's needs and abilities. For books, these assumptions are stable, and for humans, the assumptions are dynamic and may be personalised to each individual information seeker. For most electronic systems, these assumptions (the user model, Allen, 1990; Daniels, 1986) are, in practice, fairly stable and depend on a set of default conditions that reflect the system designer's view of typical information seekers and their information problems. Some systems have adaptable user models that can be. controlled by the user (e.g., allow information seekers to use command or menu modes), and research proposals for automatically adaptive interfaces continue to find support (e.g., Hefley, 1990). Interfaces for electronic search systems have received substantial attention, and developments in end-user interfaces have contributed to the adoption of information retrieval technology by a variety of groups and organisations.

The physical interface is composed of objects that facilitate input and output and that control interaction. For books, input to the system is limited to using separate tools such as pencils or highlighters to mark text or write notes. For electronic retrieval systems, input is typically through keyboards, although mice and touch panels are common, and speech recognisers, eye trackers, data gloves, and other devices are finding more applications (Jacob, Legget, Myers, & Pausch, 1993). Input to another person is via the entire range of the human communication spectrum, including voice, body language and gestures, and intermediated channels such as paper and chalkboards.

Output is limited by the database's container. Output from books takes the form of clear, systematic arrangements of ink on paper illuminated by a light source. Many qualitatively distinct techniques have been developed in the hundreds of years that books have been produced. Output from an electronic system is typically through a visual display unit, although printers are common, and speech synthesisers are finding wider use. Output from a human expert may come through any of the channels listed for human input. Objects that control interaction are dependent on the physical containers discussed under databases. There are physical constraints on exchange between the information seeker and the search system. Books are static in that the author makes all the decisions about what it is possible to see, and the information seeker makes all decisions about how to see it, with no exchange between the two. In electronic systems, authors can provide many alternative views of the material, and information seekers can add, modify, or delete information. Moreover, the electronic system can offer usage-sensitive help or error diagnosis that depends on the information seeker's actions. Human information systems are the most interactive, allowing control through interpersonal dynamics. Physical interfaces for electronic systems have made dramatic progress and have significantly improved the interactivity of information seeking. This trend will likely continue as alternative devices and the coordination of multiple devices evolve.

The conceptual interface of a search system limits the rules and protocols for information transfer. The main categories of the conceptual interface are interaction style, representational structure, and search mechanisms. Interaction style encompasses the mode of communication, including selection and feedback mechanisms. In the case of books, this communication is simplex, that is, the book acts exclusively as the source and the information seeker as the destination. Electronic systems have four types of interaction style: commands, form fill-ins, menus, and direct manipulation (Shneiderman, 1992).

Command-driven interfaces depend on the information seeker's knowing a specific language in order to manipulate the system. Most information retrieval systems are either strictly command driven or provide a command interface as an option. Command-driven interfaces are generally preferred by experts as they are efficient to use (once they are learned) and often can be extended to facilitate short cuts or highly specialised tasks. Command languages are so pervasive that international standards committees are working to establish a common command language for computer-to-computer communication, thus allowing information seekers to use familiar command languages available on their local machines (NISO, 1989).

Form fill-in interaction styles prompt the user with blank forms to complete. Although all the slots to fill in are defined in advance, users have wide discretion as to what they put in the slots. Form fill-ins are thus a cross between command and menu styles. Menu-driven systems have become increasingly popular and allow novice or casual users to execute information-seeking tasks without knowing a command language. Menu systems fully limit the actions an information seeker may take and thus do not allow the expressiveness of command styles. Menu-driven systems are half duplex, in that users make selections and the system provides feedback and then another menu.

Direct manipulation styles provide the information seeker with explicit map-pings between their physical activities and system responses. Direct manipulation demands rapid, reversible selections and feedback (Shneiderman, 1983). Sliding a mouse along a pad and watching the cursor slide along the screen in the same direction and at a proportional rate is an example of direct manipulation. Direct manipulation interaction styles make the system "transparent" in that users are able to focus on the task at hand rather than manipulating the system as an intermediary between themselves and the database contents. Direct manipulation is one of the key components to highly interactive, advanced information-seeking systems. Direct manipulation systems are more closely full duplex than other interaction styles are, as selections and feedback are nearly simultaneous. Another person as a search system is the ultimate in a directly manipulable interface. Although verbal language is mostly half duplex, the multiple modes of interaction that occur as humans communicate provide rapid and reversible stimulus-feedback. Direct manipulation is most obviously applicable to tasks with physical analogs, but examples of direct manipulation interfaces for abstract tasks such as information seeking have begun to emerge. Another characteristic of interaction style is the metaphor of action supported by the search system. Books emulate verbal activity, often a lecture or argument in the case of nonfiction. The metaphor of narration or thought (stream of consciousness) is often used in fiction. Electronic search systems often use the book as a metaphor, displaying screens of text or tables of data. The desktop has become a popular metaphor for today's variety of applications, and new metaphors such as agents and theater stages (Laurel, 1991) have been proposed. People do not need metaphors for other people, because other minds are ultimately the source of all information and the assumption that facilitates communication is that other people's minds work in basically the same fashion as one's own does.

The representational structure of an interface refers to the organisations of information and the physical mechanisms required to manipulate the structure. It is here that domain experts offer valuable contributions to interface design, because they know how the content should be partitioned and aggregated in order to answer the broadest range of questions. In the case of books, themes may be presented hierarchically or interwoven in webs or spirals throughout what may be a primarily linear set of physical pages. Alternative or supplemental representations such as tables or figures may be used to augment key concepts. Links among physically disparate words, phrases, and concepts are found in footnotes, tables of contents, and indexes and as anaphora within sentences or documents and as allusions and metaphors beyond documents. The physical mechanisms to manage these links depend on alphabetical-ordering principles, parentheticals, page numbers, and citations. Conceptual links are based on the reader's knowledge and experience in the domain.

Electronic search systems support linear, hierarchical, or network structures for content, as does paper, and have the potential of providing alternative representations according to users' needs. This potential for providing many levels of representation or alternative representations is an essential distinction between manual, static environments and electronic, dynamic environments. The cost of flexible representations is in the various mechanisms for controlling them. Today's systems are strictly limited to three management mechanisms: paging, scrolling, and jumping. Systems often provide scroll bars, sliders, pop-up menus, and displays in windows that may be resisted or overlapped - requiring users to develop new strategies for manipulating the information's physical structure. One result of such representational structuring is the common complaint by novices that it is difficult to know how large a specific document is. Another is the additional attention that must be given to managing multiple windows on the screen.

One approach to simplifying representation problems is to separate the representations that the information seeker manipulates in the interface from the representations that the interface manipulates in the database. In database management systems, logical and conceptual schemes serve this function. In these systems, the logical scheme for a database is distinct from the physical scheme that defines data storage. The logical scheme makes it possible for different users to have different views of the database according to their specific requirements and access privileges. The logical scheme also determines how queries must be specified (e.g., in SQL language); that is, there are explicit mappings between the conceptual inter-faces provided by the query language and the physical scheme of the stored data. This distinction between logical and physical data organisation enables end users to use database management systems. Another example is what is known as the client-server model, in which a local interface (client) can be used by an end user to access a remote system with its own logical and physical interface by means of an automatic network intermediary that transparently facilitates the exchange (Lynch, 1991).

People are capable of all types of organisational structures, although teachers and information specialists try to present information consistently and directly according to the perceived needs of the learner or information seeker. Moreover, human intelligence allows instant repairs to be made when communication breaks down. All search systems offer specific features that define and constrain search. Books provide tables of contents, section headings, citations, and indexes to support direct search for specific information, and they encourage scanning and linear reading. Electronic search systems can support these same types of search features, but they also can allow string search, Boolean logic queries, ranking of results, and relevance feedback. A grand challenge for interface designers is to create new features that take advantage of the unique characteristics of the electronic medium. People are constrained only by their knowledge and ability to articulate their ideas. Paper, electronic, and human search systems will continue to be used, and well-developed personal information infrastructures will allow information seekers to decide which features are most appropriate to the task and to select the system that best supports those features.

Domain

A *domain* is a body of knowledge (e.g., history or chemistry) composed of entities and relationships. Domains vary in complexity, number of entities and relation-ships, specificity, similarity of the entities and relationships, evolutionary status, clarity of definition of the entities and relationships, and their rate of growth and change. These characteristics determine the type and amount of information and the level of organisation for a domain. Most domains depend on textual representations of information, but some are dominated by graphical (e.g., art, architecture), audio (e.g., music), kinesthetic (e.g., dance, sports), or multiple information forms (e.g., film, journalism). The amount of information and level of organisation vary immensely across domains. Some fields have enormous and diverse bodies of rapidly growing literature that spawn dozens of subdomains (e.g., medicine), whereas others are fairly contained and growing slowly (e.g., classics). Some fields have inherent ordering relationships that provide important access points for information seeking. For example, history leverages chronology and geopolitical units; anatomy takes advantage of subsystems of the body; and the arts depend on individual artists.

The domain is important because it affects several of the subprocesses that make up the information-seeking process. For example, domains employ different mixes of search systems and search strategies. A domain like hematology offers substantial online information from various vendors in various forms, from abstracts to full texts. On the other hand, a domain like contemporary music offers little online information and limited access through such common entry points as subject headings. Differences between information in the sciences and humanities are well known. For example, information in the humanities typically does not go out of date, whereas scientific and technical information ages rapidly; humanities publications are less likely to have multiple authors; the humanities make equal use of books and journals, whereas the sciences favor journals; and abstracting standards apply more readily to technical literature than to historical literature (Corkill & Mann, 1978; Tibbo, 1989). These characteristics affect the way that search systems are organised and how information seekers access them. Scholars in all fields use a wide array of information sources, especially colleagues; however, distinct domains have sources that are frequently used. For example, business practitioners mainly use trade journals, trade associations, and word-of-mouth rather than libraries and books (Arthur Little Inc., 1967); physicians mainly use desk reference sets, textbooks, journals, and other professionals, especially colleagues (Connelly et al., 1990; Covell, Uman, & Manning, 1985). Studies of these and other professionals (e.g., clinical psychologists, Prescott & Griffith, 1970; professors, Kwasnik, 1989) agree that information seekers prefer interactive sources of information to static sources. Conversations with others who may have the information they need, conferences, workshops, and symposia are always listed as highly important sources of information in these studies, and some have expressed a desire for more active forms of information such as audiotapes and videotapes or computer programs and simulations.

Setting

The setting in which information seeking takes place limits the search process. *Setting* here is regarded as having physical and conceptual/social components, including whether the task is done in collaboration or alone and the information seeker's physical and psychological states. As such, it corresponds to the context or situation described by Suchman (1987). This perspective of situated action was applied in education by Brown, Collins, and Duguid (1989), Garner (1990), and Bransford, Sherwood, Hasselbring, Kinzer, and Williams (1990); and in human-computer interaction by Carroll (1990) and Suchman (1987). The physical setting determines physical constraints such as the amount of time allocated, physical accessibility, comfort, degree of distraction, and cost. It makes a considerable difference whether one is seeking information in a private office or in a public place with a line of impatient people nearby. Physical features such as lighting requirements for paper and electricity and hardware for electronic information are often assumed in modern environments but are basic setting characteristics nonetheless. Economic constraints such as cost and time are situational and influence whether and how tasks are initiated, executed, and terminated. The proximity of sources is a well-documented factor in information seeking, with personal collections and proximate coworkers the most commonly used information sources (e.g., Allen, 1977). Electronic networks have begun to have a significant influence on information proximity, by providing access to catalogs and primary materials from one's home or office workstation. In addition, electronic networks offer new opportunities for group collaboration on information-intensive tasks (see Grudin, 1991, for an overview). The physical setting also includes the type of access and procedures for obtaining access. Whether the information is accessed in a personal or shared work area and in paper form or electronic form affects overall information seeking. What forms must be completed, permissions secured, or identification cards shown also influence overall willingness to seek information and its costliness.

Conceptually, the setting includes the psychological and social ecology of information seeking. The cognitive aspects of this ecology were described in Dervin's (1977) situation phase of her sense-making model. These aspects may be considered to be the state of a person's working memory at any given time. Other psychological factors include a person's self-confidence in an environment. Self-confidence typically depends on familiarity with a situation or expertise in the problem area and influences how ready the information seeker is to take intellectual risks and to persevere in spite of intermittent failures. The social ecology of a situation relates an individual person to other persons or groups and to organisations. A person's role in an organisation determines his or her self-image and influences self-confidence, alertness, and, ultimately, productivity. For example, people with low status in an organisation may be less able or willing to use organisational resources to seek information. The organisational structure and procedures as described in the physical setting also influence how participants interact with the overall organisation and other people, including how they seek information. Social considerations for information seeking become increasingly important as groups use technologies to collaborate on information-intensive projects.

Outcomes

Outcomes for information seeking include both products and a process. As products, outcomes are the results of using an information system, that is, feedback from the system. Eventually, if all goes well, an outcome or set of outcomes will be attainment of the task's goal of answering a question and, on reflection, the solution to the information problem. These products range from individual words, phrases, or images provided by a source, to intermediate sets of document surrogates, to complete documents that are organised and displayed to aid the information seeker in interpretation and use. Most outcomes are intermediate stages in the information-seeking process that provide information to further the overall process. Thus, outcomes affect the task and subsequent iterations of information seeking. Out-comes affect the user as well, for they change the state of the information seeker's knowledge; that is, they impart information. Outcomes also serve as objects of evaluation to assess the search's or system's effectiveness. Typical measures of search products include assessments of relevance or utility during or after search - including such quantitative measures as recall and precision, structured or informal subjective evaluations, and examination of the resultant products or artifacts (e.g., documents or abstracts). The behavioral moves made by information seekers also help evaluate performance, because evaluators assume that searcher behaviors manifest internal information-seeking strategies, which are themselves "runs" of the searcher's mental models for the search system. Outcomes can also be viewed as mental reflections on information-seeking episodes. As such, a trace of the search process is itself an outcome, as information seekers consider the mental and physical actions taken during information seeking and adapt their personal information infrastructures accordingly. Thus, the experience itself becomes part of the searcher's knowledge for dealing with future information problems. Because of the powerful roles that outcomes play in information seeking, consistent and effective management and manipulation of outcomes are critical to the design of information systems.

Information-seeking factors are not mutually exclusive and are linked by relation-ships that vary in complexity and importance. The relationships can be considered in pairwise fashion for simplicity, but ultimately, the full interactions among the factors determine information-seeking activity. The framework is human centered, and the information seeker is responsible for integrating all the factors.

- The information seeker's problem considered in light of the personal information infrastructure manifests the task; the information seeker's mental model for the search system strongly influences performance, and the system influences this by presenting a user model that represents the designer's view of generic information seekers; the information seeker may have highly developed or novice understandings of the domain; the information seeker is influenced by the setting and may have some control over it; and outcomes are determined by the information seeker's actions and likewise themselves determine subsequent actions.
- The task influences which system is selected, and the system determines how the task can be operationalised; the task rarely influences the domain, but the domain can influence the nature and result of the task; the task and setting are weakly related in both ways; and the task determines the outcomes as they are incremental goals for the task and in turn may lead to modifications of the task.
- The search system is dependent on the domain for its content, but examples of how the search system may have an impact on the domain have just begun to emerge; the system is a part of the setting, and in extreme cases (e.g., power outages) the physical setting can influence the system; and the system is a determinant of outcomes, and given the present state of system

development, only in the case of human search systems does the system learn or change based on outcomes.

- The domain and setting have little influence on each other, and the domain has a weak influence on particular outcomes.
- Finally, the setting weakly influences the outcomes, but the outcomes only rarely and then indirectly influence the setting. These relationships are admittedly subjective but are useful to gain an overall sense of how the information-seeking factors interact. Of course, information seeking is determined by the concurrent interactions among all these factors. The main idea is that the framework is user centered and action oriented, as described in the process presented in the following section.

Evading the Log Jam

As a result of these increasing difficulties, many publishers are examining new ways of reaching the market. Clearly, direct mail remains a key alternative but works best when purchasers already know what they want to buy. In other words, it is most effective when publishers can support direct mail with a concerted marketing and publicity campaign to raise awareness and interest in the title. While direct mail remains an important avenue, however, a new distribution model is being tested which cuts out the problems of getting retail shelf space while, at the same time, giving purchasers a 'try before you buy' option. The new approach is based on the use of encryption techniques to 'cripple' access to the content of a CD title. The first consumer market example-aside from some home shopping initiatives based on CD-ROM 'catalogues'-was a title distributed in 1994 by Comptons and developed by Graphix Zone. The title had been created on behalf of the production company owned by pop star Prince (now renamed an unpronounceable symbol but for our non-hip purposes still referred to as 'Prince'). The title was ostensibly a new audio single called 'Prince Interactive' but the packaging invited purchasers who had CD-ROM drives to insert the discs into those drives in order to enjoy a special bonus. When they did so, Prince fans were presented with a playable demonstration of a Prince Interactive featuring Prince music and video clips. In order to purchase access game, the users were invited to call Comptons New Media and $40 for a unique electronic key that would release the complete game. In other words, the original CD purchased in record stores for between $6 and $8 contained an open audio 'front end' to a much more expensive but electronically crippled multimedia product. Consider, however, what has occurred as far as the retailer is concerned. The retailer has sold a product for a few dollars and gained a margin based on that price. The publisher has distributed a high price product at a low price discount and gained a revenue stream free of deep dealer discounts. Equally important, the publisher is also put in direct contact with purchasers allowing the creation of a valuable proprietary consumer database for selling upgrades and new products.

The same underlying technique has also been used in an even more radical way. In the UK in December 1994, an issue of PC *Power*-one of the growing range of consumer PC magazines flooding the market -appeared with a CD-ROM mounted on its front cover. In itself, this was nothing exceptional. Such magazines are increasingly appearing with free, cover-mounted CD-ROMs. In this case, however, the CD-ROM contained a complete game-a high profile tide from Infogrammes called 'Alone in the Dark'. The CD was described as a 'Play Before You Buy Edition' and purchasers of the magazines could play a part of the game on their multimedia personal computers (MPCs) before being presented-presumably at a suitably cliff-hanging moment-with a message telling them that if they wanted more they should call Infogrammes and purchase for £29.95 a code that would unlock the complete game.

Taken on their own, the Prince disc and the Infogrammes initiative look like isolated experiments. However, given the context of a major crisis in CD-ROM distribution in the United States and, as yet, the virtual absence of serious retail commitment in the UK, the use of crippling technology may become an important and influential new distribution model. Indeed, the Infogrammes example could be a watershed in the distribution of packaged media products and for two major reasons. First, we have hitherto always relied on a fixed pricing model based on a price defined at the moment and point of sale. By using crippling technology we can instead price at whatever level we like, whenever we like. If it had chosen, Infogrammes could have varied the price charged for the access code to the game on a daily or even moment-to-moment basis. Second, crippling fractures the link between the retailer and the retail price. In the case of the cover-mounted giveaway, of course, the retailer gives shelf space to a magazine which itself distributes a high priced media product. The Prince disc is an example of low price 'open' media products sheltering high priced but encrypted ones. The implication is serious for retailers who will have to find new ways to respond to this complex new ingredient in the distribution mix. The complexity of the situation is likely to increase as encryption is used more creatively. It is possible for a variety of new, flexible pricing models to be applied by publishers.

Encrypted CD titles, for example, can be priced on the basis of giving purchasers a fixed number of plays, unlimited plays for a limited time (with more time purchasable for additional cost), or selective access to different levels or dimensions of a product depending on the price paid. It is anyone's guess how these possibilities will eventually be commercialised but it is likely that we will see increasing experimentation during the coming years. One thing is certain, new pricing and distribution models will create major new pressures for deal-making among publishers, retailers and those-such as magazine proprietors-who can readily inject large numbers of encrypted discs into the market in some fairly targeted way. And the new deal structures will have to be founded on the back of new systems of auditing, sales in order to make sure everyone appropriate can track the revenue streams in which they may have some percentage interest.

The Web Consumer

We have already gained a sense of how quickly the Web has grown in size and significance. There are many wild estimates of how many new sites appearing. Some claim they double every few months while others with the maths and come up with at least one site every minute. The truth is, no one really knows how quickly the Web is growing. The certainty is that it is growing fast. As this book is printed, the likely of sites is probably around 200,000 and may double by the time the hands of its first readers. Anyone can come up with numbers but it is really a matter of educated guesswork. More solid numbers are available for the other end of the equation. There are plenty of sites: no doubt about it. But how many consumers are using the Web? What is the audience for this massive treasure of online experiences? A US survey conducted by FIND/SVP in late 1995 gives at least part of the answer. It revealed 9.5 million Internet users in the United States of which 7.5 million had access to the Web. Of those using the Web, 4 million (fully 53 per cent of the total) began using it in 1995. Of the newcomers, 48 per cent were using the Web exclusively from home. Out of all US Internet users, only 27 per cent were using it via a server in an academic institution, a figure that would have been closer to 100 per cent only two years earlier. Servers in business locations accounted for 28 per cent, indicating the rapid moves that corporations are making to embrace the Internet. The real surprise in the figures came when the researchers analysed the proportion of Internet users gaining access from specialist Internet service providers (ISPs), companies that had originally ridden high on the Internet boom and had been the main source of Internet provision since the crucial emergence of the first Web browsers. The results showed a significant decline in the influence of smaller ISPs and a rapid rise in the number of people accessing the Internet via proprietary networks. Why is this so remarkable? The proprietary networks had really woken up to the existence of the Internet only in late 1994 and had begun to use their own infrastructure to offer their subscribers Internet access by early 1995. This emphasises the speed with which proprietary networks have taken off as an important source of access to the Internet, driving home the message that the vast majority of newcomers to the Web were the kind of people who might subscribe to populist networks such as AOL or Prodigy and, to a lesser extent, CompuServe-in other words: mainstream consumers. The figures also tell an important story about the remarkable transformation that has taken place in the proprietary network's proposition to its customers. Without exception, proprietary consumer networks have reshaped their business models so that they are now almost exclusively defined by the influence of the Internet in general and the Web in particular.

Surfing the Web

There used to be a time when nets were used for fishing, getting wired was an activity strictly for electricians and surfing was a watersport. Today, the vocabulary has assumed a different set of meanings. The particular expression 'surfing the Web' has, in only a matter of months, become one of the worst cliches of the digital world. It was meant to imply a kind of carefree voyage of discovery which users of the Web embarked upon with every click of the mouse. Hyperlink after hyperlink would carry them through an infinite number of pathways in cyberspace. They would pause here and there to take a closer look at one offering or another but the journey was the thing: a ceaseless roaming in search of-second worst cliche-the 'coolest site' on the Web. Regular users of the Web quickly appreciate that aimless wanderings are ultimately too boring and futile for anyone to tolerate for long.

The reality of Web surfing is that surfers need to be directed, they yearn for navigational aids. In the same US Internet survey we quoted above, researchers confirmed with a single finding the fact that underpins almost every strategy for successfully commercialising the Web. Out of all the millions using the Web with its (possibly) hundreds of thousands of sites, 60 per cent of visit fewer than ten sites on a regular basis! In other words, Web surfing is not an arbitrary wandering, a voyage of discovery. Web users find the sites they like and stick to them. If they expand the number of they visit regularly they do so by being directed from a site they already know, enjoy and trust. What this means is vital for Web publishing. It means that it is possible to arbitrate how people use the Web, to influence they do and where they go. Despite the independence that the structure of the Web confers, its vastness and complexity demands the simplifying effect of navigational beacons, pointers to what is the best, most interesting and most relevant to our needs.

The idea of arbitration-expressed in different ways-is essential to strategic power over the Web and all its commercial potential. Before we look at how this works for site owners, let us consider first some models gatekeeping the Web which illustrate the potential for finding different forms of influence. The most obvious example of a gatekeeping play is Netscape Communication's effort to turn its Web browser, Netscape Navigator, into a universal and to link this with a grip on Web server supply. Although we have covered much of this ground in chapter 5, we will reprise the main in this new context. Netscape, as we saw, is the brainchild of Jim former CEO of Silicon Graphics. Clark was one of the first to spot the potential of the NCSA's Mosaic browser for revolutionising global to the Web. He realised that its 'point and click' approach to navigating the Web was exactly what was needed to transform it from an environment best suited to geeks to a wonderland of information and services for ordinary human beings. He also saw that Mosaic was merely flawed precursor of the kind of browser that would eventually dominate access to the Internet and decided that he would create a company to design the new generation of Mosaic-derived Internet tools that was needed. His of doing this was direct and uncompromising. Instead of licensing the system from its originators and upgrading it, he poached the people who had created Mosaic in the first place and paid them to start again and a much better version of the original. The result was Netscape navigator. Faster and easier to use than Mosaic, Navigator is packed with including, most significantly, a built-in security system based on Netscape encryption technology called the secure socket layer (SSL) protocol.

As soon as the first versions of Navigator emerged, Netscape began giving them away as fast as it could. The result has been a dramatic uptake the software. In January 1995, a survey of 73,000 Web users found that 77 per cent were using one version or another of Netscape's Navigator and even today most agree that Netscape has maintained a share of around 70-80 per cent despite a slew of new browsers coming to market. Competitors derided the figures saying it was easy to gain market share when you were giving your product away. But they missed the point. Clark was not initially trying to make a business selling browser software His eye was on a different ball. The importance of getting large numbers of browsers into the market was to create an effective de facto standard The reason for doing this was to sell not browsers-although Netscape having established a huge constituency of loyal and committed users, is nowadays starting to charge for updated editions of them-but Web servers. The servers are the computers used to host Web sites and services. The software they run makes them compatible with the Web and proprietary wrinkles allow vendors of servers to offer special Internet features. Most important for Netscape's range is its SSL security system. The important point about such security protocols is that they need two halves of a 'key' to work. One half resides in the server. The other, which enables secure transfers of information, resides in a compatible browser. The heart of Netscape's strategy, therefore, was to inject vast numbers of its browsers into the market and then use the existence of an effective, strong-though not impregnable-security standard based on them to sell its servers. For those looking for a secure basis to begin Internet trading, the servers would look irresistible if virtually everybody on the Internet was already using Netscape's browser.

Domination of server supply means, of course, a lucrative business but, longer term, it also implies a gatekeeping role. The reason is simple. If your browser and server together form the universal standard for Web trading, the commercialisation of the Web stands or falls on your proprietary technology. This means you can manipulate its pricing whenever you wish to control your bottomline performance. You can vary its functionality, so shaping everyone's experience of using the Web. And you can decide who and who not to do business with, so determining who gets access to the commercial opportunities of the Web. In other words, the server—browser equation is strong enough medicine to turn anyone controlling it into the Microsoft of the Internet. And that is exactly what Netscape wants to be.

In practice, of course, it is not as simple as just focusing on security because long term-as we will see later-it will be hard to resist moves to universalise an open, non-proprietary standard. The picture painted above, for example, if it was as crudely drawn in reality, would be given short shrift by US anti-trust legislation. It is not surprising therefore that Netscape has just joined with America Online, Prodigy,

CompuServe and IBM to invest in a small software security company called Terisa, which is now charged with creating a single, open security protocol for the Internet. Terisa itself has created the other major Internet security protocol known as Secure HTTP, which is based on a 'public key' cryptography scheme first devised by RSA Data Security. The idea of online and Internet majors investing in it is to merge Netscape's SSL protocol and HTTP into a single, pervasive standard for the future commercialisation of the Internet, of course, will try to ensure the final merged product looks much more like SSL than HTTP so that it can leverage its current dominant browser position even when the new security standard is established.

Gatekeeping does not have to be based on server-browser strategies. A powerful position can also be built purely on the basis of being a dominant Internet access provider. Although we have already seen what an effective proprietary networks have become by acting as access providers, major telephone companies also have a powerful position to leverage. The move in 1995 by MCI Communications-the second largest long-distance telephony carrier in the USA-to launch a nationwide dial-up Internet access service called internetMCI, is a good illustration. Although we had already seen Pacific Bell-the RBOC (Regional Bell Operating Company) serving most telephone users in California-entering access market with an initiative aimed at business users and we have subsequently seen, in February 1996, AT & T launch its WorldNet service, MCI's move was the first at the time by a US carrier with national reach. As a well-known national organisation with large numbers of exist-customers, it was uniquely placed to leverage its existing relationships with subscribers and to build a critical mass of Internet users quickly tied proprietary access provision and connection software. At the time, the only other national access providers in the United States-Uunet, Netcom, Holonet and PSI-were relatively small players compared to the financial power and commercial influence of a $13 billion corporation such MCI.

It is important to assess MCI's move to provide national access to the internet in the context of another announcement it had made. In addition to its access service, MCI announced it was launching an Internet shopping initiative called marketplaceMCI. This was a secure trading environment based on Netscape server-browser technology within which MCI hoped to gather a powerful group of traders offering an attractive range of purchasable products and services. The key point of MCI's approach was that marketplaceMCI will itself be marketed from MCI's home page-the first site customers are taken to when they log on and-more important, because home pages can be changed by users-it was also to be marketed through all MCI's existing customer links as a telephony provider to of businesses and consumers throughout the United States. By building on its existing relationships, MCI could hope to attract large of customers to market place MCI and by making it a compelling environment and by building into it good links with other Web sites, it would have a good chance of making the market-place the definitive jumping off place for Web surfers.

The AT & T initiative, WorldNet, could achieve everything MCI will gain in influence over the Web but on an even bigger scale. AT & T's offering at the time of its launch was extremely attractive to those existing AT & T customers seeking dial-up Internet access. The starting deal for them was five hours of free access per month for a year with additional hours at $2.50. Unlimited access was priced at $19.95 per month. For non-AT & T customers the deal was slightly less attractive with no free access and three hours a month available at a modest $4.95. The totally free service for existing customers was a breakthrough — the first time stand-alone Internet access had been made available at no charge. The aggressive package was all the more powerful because AT & T could immediately leverage a vast, existing customer base of 80 million subscribers. In other words, it was building instant and powerful strategic influence over the Internet in general and the Web in particular by becoming both the portal and facilitator of access for potentially tens of millions of users in the USA and — with WorldNet rolling out worldwide in 1996 — throughout AT & T's international market With its close individual billing links with every one of those subscribers, a powerhouse like AT & T is perfectly placed to promote particular Internet activities to its constituency and-if it chooses-build an effective Web commerce operation by leveraging its reach.

This is the heart of the new kind of gatekeeping which content — rather than technology-companies can also leverage. As we indicated above, the Web is a complicated and confusing place. It needs beacons to guide people on their journeys. These beacons will define the paths people take and, therefore, whose services they access. A definitive starting point for Web journeys, therefore, will be a powerful arbiter of Web usage. In other words, if MCI or other major access providers can use their success as the springboard for building their home page entry point into the regular first stop for millions of people setting out on the Web, they will have an asset of considerable strategic power and commercial potential. Other organisations, for example, will pay to have links inserted into the key home pages in order to point customers to their sites. There is money to be made and influence to be wielded.

According to a widely publicised statement by MCI's head of Internet initiatives, the Internet pioneer Vint G. Cerf, the combined moves by MCI indicate that it is 'not just a telecommunications company any more'. Since Internet provision is of course a telecommunications service, Cerf's comment indicates that MCI is seeing its future as increasingly linked to content as well as content distribution. In other words, instead of being focused on its role as a carrier, MCI is shaping a strategic future also based on what it carries and-through its influence-making added value out of its ability to shape the pathways that people follow on their journeys around the Web.

The Netscape, MCI and AT & T models add up to the same thing. The biggest game in town, as far as the Internet is concerned, is building influence over how people get access to the Web and what they do while are using it. There are different ways of playing the game but those who succeed will be the power brokers of what will eventually become the biggest and most influential trading environment the world has ever seen. It is a prize worth fighting for. In fact, in the digital media world, it is probably the only prize worth fighting for.

Home pages-the Web page that a browser starts at when it is launched by a client — are, as the MCI example demonstrates, an important influence on what people do on the Web simply because they can rely on gaining so many eyeballs. The Netscape browser, for example, when purchased Netscape, opens at the Netscape home page. Although this opening is only a default setting and can easily be changed by users, the evidence so far suggests that people do not tend to bother. Because Nets-cape is used by millions, it is not surprising that its home page is one of busiest places on the Web. It has acquired an instant, ready-made constituency of a size that Web publishers would have to struggle to achieve over months and years of expensive marketing efforts. Having such instant constituency is only part of the battle. You have to make the initial offering an attractive one or they are likely to overcome their inertia and change the default setting. Netscape has been shrewd — not just in its software strategies but in creating a home site that is dynamic, full of interest and an excellent jumping off place for Web surfers looking for initial directions to take. Netscape offers hot links to other interesting sites a direct link to key Web directories. Not surprisingly, with a big constituency of users, Netscape is also generating substantial revenues from advertisers who want the millions of eyeballs that Netscape's home page delivers.

The power of the home page has attracted many companies to buy customised versions of standard browsers which default to their home pages so that they can give these away as promotional tools. An entire division of CompuServe is dedicated to developing this kind of business. Already hundreds of companies have taken advantage of the concept. Hotel chains have placed free discs in the rooms of regular guests, for example, while in 1996 Volkswagen of America is giving away Internet software - packaged via a deal with an access provider with some free connect-time-in the glove compartment of every new car it sells and sending similar software out to 500,000 existing customers. It is a scatter gun approach but companies such as Volkswagen are obviously calculating that it makes cost-effective sense to bring traffic-hopefully, long-term traffic-to their home page and via the home page to all the retentive delights of its Web site.

The same theme of leveraging influence over how people use the Web lies at the heart of all Web publishing strategies. Most of all, of course, the central objective is to influence people to visit sites-and keep visiting them. By implication, this asks the question: what are companies really trying to achieve by building and operating Web sites? There is no single answer because objectives vary with types of companies. In some cases there is no answer because there is no objective. In other words, some companies build their sites without even thinking through their reasons for doing so.

Content companies, however, have a clear objective: they plan to commercialise some form of content asset, either leveraged out of assets they already possess in the 'real' world or via assets newly created for the online environment. The majority are seeking, more or less directly, to extend the potential of existing content and its branding. For these companies the process of Web publishing has three key phases. First, use existing brand power to build an online franchise. Second, use the franchise to create a constituency-an audience that will be loyally tied to regular use of the site. Third, commercialise the constituency. This is not rocket science-the magazine and newspaper industries have been doing it for years. What is new now, however, is the peculiar and distinctive characteristics of online environments and, most of all, how people use them.

Before we examine these issues in more detail, it is worth pausing to re-examine a word we have been using repeatedly and without qualification, as if its meaning and significance were self-evident. The word is 'content' and in the online world it needs some careful re-evaluation.

Content and Online Success

The overheated and overhyped world of the Web is putting increasing pressure on content organisations of all kinds. The issue is no longer whether to create a Web presence but to decide urgently the when, how and what of that presence. Naturally enough, many companies are snatching online strategies out of the air, deciding abruptly either to get onto the Web or do a deal with Microsoft or one of the other proprietary majors or both. Sometimes fast, tactical moves work but there is already evidence that many companies-particularly those new to network publishing-are not taking the time they need to think through the realities of the new market-place, to determine where real strategic advantage lies, what existing assets they can deploy, which new ones they will have to acquire to ensure success and, at the end of the day, what kind of business model will make serious money for them long term.

The only good online strategies begin with some simple questions. What are we trying to achieve by going online? What are our expectations? What resources and assets can we deploy? What level of commitment can we afford? Where are we weak and where are we strong? Any MBA (Master of Business Administration) graduate worth his or her salt would consider these commonplace basics but the feverish atmosphere surrounding the apparent rapid emergence of a consumer online market is in danger of sweeping away common-sense deliberations of this kind. Content companies, in particular, need to draw a deep breath before taking action. A time for cool contemplation is vital. But the pressure is growing on them to move quickly and that largely manufactured sense of urgency is pushing them to take precipitate action. It is true of course that some urgency does exist-particularly where the Web is concerned. The recent frantic pioneering activity is based on a sound policy-staking out franchises early, even before the Web can be commercialised in order to be well positioned when it is. But rushing to establish those franchises and getting it wrong could be as disastrous as thinking that the Web in particular and online in general fails the so-what test.

The worst danger for content companies is that they actually believe that-in a traditional sense-content is still really king. It is the most dangerous kind of false reassurance because it contains an element of truth. But the broader reality is that it is much more than content as we have always known it that determines online success. The real threat is that the idea of content always being the dictator of commercial advantage makes owners of content complacent and less likely to take the right action at the right time.

To illustrate this we can take a brief look at some of the major issues involved in creating an effective Web presence. There are a raft of practical and technical issues, of course, which shape the design of the site, its capabilities and-most important-the costs associated with creating and running it long term. It is clear, for example, that we must increasingly try to design our sites today with the Web technologies of tomorrow. During 1996 and 1997 the experience of using the Web will have changed beyond recognition. It will commonly offer such features as real-time audio from sites, voice communications, three-dimensional graphics and virtual reality-like experiences and-within limitations-the delivery of short, windowed video clips in more or less real time. What we can offer from these sites a year hence both in terms of an online sensation as well as basic commercial products and services will be dramatically different from the possibilities being exploited today. So we have to embrace the future in today's design and build everything we do with an easy and immediate upgrade path. In this crucial sense, the Web is and will remain a highly dynamic environment.

But to put traditional content in perspective, we need to concentrate on more general issues of site design. Here too it is vital to understand the Web as a dynamic place but in a different sense. One of the most powerful attributes of online publishing is its ability to deliver fast-changing information. In the professional and corporate market, the power of online systems to deliver volatile information, even information updated on a moment by moment basis, has been one of the key foundations of what is today a $13 billion business. Users of online systems expect and demand dynamic information. They do not want to read the same information or undergo the same experience every time they visit an online site. Going online is ultimately a communications experience and, like a conversation, what you expect to get out of it is something constantly changing. Saying or hearing the same thing over and again is simply too boring to be tolerated. In other words, Web design must embody a strategy for constantly varying, updating, upgrading the content of the site.

Communications itself is a key notion too. If using the Web is essentially a communications experience, it is largely because that is what people want it to be. While it is already evident that users of online services have a relatively few favourite things they like doing online (spending money, as we have noted, is not one of them!) the one thing that is consistently high on their priorities is sharing and exchanging information and ideas with other people. And if that is what people most like doing online, it clearly must-interpreted sensitively-be a thread of all good Web design.

So Web sites must be dynamic and communications based. But there is a third crucial ingredient. The experience of using online services is very personal. If communing with an online site is more like making a telephone call than reading a book, then users of the Web want sites to respond to them personally. This means Web design is about marketing to one person and seeing a constituency of users as a collection of well-defined and well-understood individuals. Personalising Web sites is not easy but with the right software tools and server systems it is increasingly possible to achieve. At the simplest level, customisation of this kind means that visitors to a site are welcomed with a personal message and a range of suggestions of what they may like to access based on their previous visits and the interests they showed during them. At more sophisticated levels, sites will increasingly offer fully filtered and bespoke information services.

None of this has much to do with our traditional notion of static, analogue content. And the implication is that owners of content may not be able to deploy as much of their existing content assets on the Web as they might suppose. Indeed, many are already concluding that the very idea of content on the Web-or any other network publishing environment-needs to be redefined. Building an online strategy, therefore, may well start with biting a very painful bullet indeed. We may have to accept that traditional content-important as it may be-is far from king on the Web. What really counts is understanding customers and building individual relationships with them. This is what lies at the heart of online success.

The Impact on Proprietary Networks

The idea of Web sites turning themselves into packagers of other sites may sound familiar. In fact, this emerging model for Web trade is a direct analogue of the traditional offering to subscribers of proprietary online networks. As we saw in other chapter, the essential proposition of such services to offer a low cost key which would confer access to a warehouse of people's content, licensed in by the proprietary services. Even though practice little revenue has been generated for the third party content the proposition for them was clear and apparently attractive. While network customers would have access to their content, they would have to the customers. And networks boasting millions of subscribers a very compelling carrot to offer to content companies with little other option for gaining access to online exploitation.

Ironically, the original proposition for both customers and content pro-was viable only so long as there was no consumer online market. As soon as the market emerged, the basic model began to crack under the of competitive pressure. The major proprietary services were desperate for market share—particularly since increasing the number of their subscribers was the only way they could boost their revenues. As we saw, online subscribers are reluctant to spend money online and the generated from subscriber bases was therefore largely governed by price of the subscription and how many subscriptions a network operator could sell. The battle for subscribers sent subscriptions and connect—time charges tumbling and as they tumbled-and subscriber numbers rose—the potential returns for content providers, who were usually paid percentage of connect-time charges or a slice of subscription revenues for new customers they brought to the network, began to tumble with them.

At the same time, a new and urgent element in the battle among proprietaries to win market share was the need to distinguish their offerings, particularly by including in their warehouses some highly branded crown jewel content which none of their competitors could offer. For a few content owners, therefore, Christmas had come early because, while the majority of content companies were getting next to nothing, a few were being wooed by proprietaries offering high guaranteed payments just to get hold of exclusive access to a leading brand. In an important sense, therefore, the boot was very much on the other foot. Proprietaries had originally driven a hard deal with content owners, taking everything in terms of brand value and consumer usage data and offering them little in return. This, in a curious way, was sustainable so long as there was only a small market for online services. Once the market emerged—at a gallop—content was a key factor in the battle to win customers away from competitors and content was, therefore, in a far stronger negotiating position. This is the reason why in the two years before 1994 and 1996 the original 80:20 deal in favour of the networks flipped into a 20:80 deal favouring content.

A further nail in the coffin of the traditional proprietary business model was the emergence of the Web. One very powerful reason why proprietaries were always strongly placed in negotiating with content was that content had nowhere else to go in order to gain online exploitation. The proprietaries had invested hundreds of millions of dollars building a communications and computing infrastructure that would enable them to reach the market. The huge cost of entry, therefore, meant that content owners simply had to do business with the established network because the prospect of them building their own networks was unthinkable. The emergence of the Web changed all that and it did so quickly and decisively. For the first time, content had an alternative to doing business with the proprietaries. It could invest just a few tens of thousands of dollars and instantly gain independent online access to a global market-place numbered in millions. On the face of it, the ease, autonomy and reach of the Web looks almost irresistible.

For the proprietaries, this new development made an increasingly difficult situation desperate. Not only did they now have to compete with one another for content, but also they had to compete with the lure of the Web. Their response has turned out to be a powerful one, although it implies a complete revision of their original business models. The first step in the response was to recognise that millions of consumers were seeking safe, reliable and cheap access to the Internet. Most were getting such access via independent Internet service providers (ISPs) who were buying bandwidth from telephone companies in order to gain a pipe into the backbones of the Internet. Many were small start-up, serving relatively small areas, while a few were better funded, larger entities with national god international ambitions. For the proprietary networks, the idea of also offering Internet access was a natural and inevitable step. Whether they saw the Internet as their potential nemesis or not, they had to recognise that many of their existing subscribers were interested in the Internet and that potential subscribers would be even more attracted to a proprietary if Internet access was just another part of its overall offerings. The proprietaries would probably have preferred to de-invent the Internet. But since that was hardly an option, they reckoned that people would get Internet access if they wanted it and that they might as well get it from them. Whatever their reservations about the Internet, therefore, the proprietaries determined to make Internet access another of their offerings. This first step—forced upon them by the realities of the market-place—has quickly led to a much fuller acceptance of the Internet. Within months of beginning to offer access during the early part of 1994, the proprietaries realised that they could deploy a much deeper business strategy. It became clear that offering Internet access was quickly turning into major attraction for both existing and new subscribers with literally thousands of customers signing up for it within months of access deal becoming available.

Prodigy—otherwise the laggard of the three proprietary majors—beat its competitors to the starting post, largely because it had already decided 1993 to completely revise its very poor user interface and to create a one based on HTML code, the underlying language of the Web. In 1995, Prodigy launched its first Web browser, making it available its existing customers by downloading, and also began offering Internet through its network. By March, 450,000 people had downloaded software, of whom half were new customers who signed up after the access was announced. In under two months, Prodigy had become a bigger. Web access provider than Netcom, formerly the largest ISP in the States. CompuServe launched its Web service next and AOL followed about mid-year. All found their offerings highly popular and saw in subscriber numbers — already strong — accelerate dramatically. Proprietaries quickly saw that being the point of access for such huge of Internet users gave them-like MCI, AT & T and other big and international players—a powerful influence over what people did when they used the Internet.

In particular, they could influence the use of the Web and the sites their customers were most likely to visit. Prodigy's early experience confirmed is now confirmed by subsequent more general research on Web usage: the majority of Web users pay regular visits to only a handful of sites. This immediately suggested to the proprietaries that they could add value to their access provision by including, within their own proprietary infrastructure, copies of the most popular sites. The advantages of doing this are substantial. For example, many popular Web sites can accommodate only a few hundred—or at best a very few thousand—simultaneous visitors before the server locks out any others trying to gain access. A typical site cached within a proprietary network and leveraging the powerful proprietary infrastructure can handle tens of thousands of visitors at one time. Beyond the ability to handle large numbers of visitors, caching also makes accessing sites faster and more consistent. In other words, even users with slow modems will get an acceptable experience of accessing cached sites and the speed of access will not vary with the changing overall traffic on the Internet, a frustrating phenomenon which makes general Web access fast one moment and painfully slow the next. The resulting proposition to customers was a strong one for the proprietaries and an important extension of their original positioning. In spring 1995, Ted Leonis, president of America Online services, used a striking and unusual metaphor to encapsulate the new offering. He likened the new proprietary model based on the cruise line business with the cruises being voyages of discovery on the Web.

Carnival [gives you] predictable pricing. Your fare, your activities on the boat, all your meals are included. No surprises. Your berth is going to be clean, and it's going to be safe.... When you pull into a port, Carnival plans your day for you. They say: '... for those of you who like scuba diving, here are the best places to go and here are the authorised guides. For those of you who want to go shopping, we'll take you into town. If you're looking for jewelry, we feel comfortable with these two or three chains. In fact, if you present them your berth card, you'll get a ten per cent discount.' The last point is a telling one and it relates directly to our remarks about generating strategic advantage from pointing constituencies at paid-for sites. With massive constituencies, the proprietaries can now offer chosen Web sites the prospect of huge volumes of traffic. This can be done by pointing (and otherwise promoting) from within the proprietary infrastructure to sites outside it or by mirroring external sites and making them effectively a part of the infrastructure. Either way, the proprietaries can negotiate good deals for their customers, either getting discounts or free access (with the site's reduced charge carried by the proprietary).

As this new business emerged—with proprietaries for the first time embracing content that was not proprietary to them—other signs of the shift towards a Web-centric future emerged. While retaining the idea of a proprietary environment as a part (rather than the entirety) of their offerings, proprietaries also decided to hitch their wagons to the increasing number of major content companies setting up their independent online presence on the Web. They did this by mingling two strands. One was offering services that actually helped content find its way onto the Web. These services included consultancy and the opportunity to use the proprietaries' powerful access infrastructure to speed access to sites. The other strand was to joint venture the development of such sites with content partners and so, for the first time, take a direct equity stake in content assets. In both cases, the thrust of the development was to build new and closer links with content because the proprietaries perceived deep relationships with content to be the means by which they could simultaneously leverage the power of content to generate traffic and revenue on the Web and their ability to powerfully promote selected content offerings.

At a technical level, proprietaries began to shift their user interfaces Webwards too with browsers emerging as de facto standards. Indeed newcomers to the proprietary business — especially in European outfits like UK Online and Europe Online—were effectively creating themselves as large, complex sites on the Web with content on their sites and a multitude of links to chosen external sites. Users could come and go from the strictly proprietary area—the large Web site forming the hub of their offering-and explore the further reaches of the Web or, at their choke, stick to the online a environment defined by the proprietary's strategic links. The Microsoft proprietary initiative has been reinvented by Microsoft to reflect this concept with MSN effectively becoming an influential point of access to the web and its proprietary offerings being, effectively, heavily promoted Web sites with preferential access available to its own MSN constituency. This hints at the long-term future of the proprietary business, no longer distinct from the Web but as super-sites on the Web. In other words, Internet and the Web become the defining factor with which all online providers align themselves. This is the heart of the revolution which Internet has begun.

Security and Web Payments

The commercialising of the Web depends fundamentally on being able to send messages to and from servers and clients in complete security. Much else may depend on this but being able to complete financial transactions totally governed by it. Beyond security lies the issue of how such transactions are consummated in terms of mechanisms to handle the payments themselves, particularly when those payments may come from hundreds of thousands, even millions, of geographically dispersed individuals and the size of each of the transactions can, ideally, vary from a its to very large sums. The emerging systems aimed at providing secure payment mechanisms are highly technical and commercially complex. In this section, therefore, we will not attempt to be exhaustive in our treatment but will aim to establish basic concepts and to paint the main strategic headlines. For those seeking more detail, there is plenty of material freely available on the Web itself.

Why is Internet security such a concern? The reason has to do with the way in which the Internet is organised to convey information between users. If you are a CompuServe user and you send a message via CompuServe to another user, the bits representing your message flow only through CompuServe's own computer infrastructure. If an Internet user sends a message, it may pass through hundreds of other people's computers on its way to its destination as it is switched from backbone to backbone across the globe. The fear that haunts the Internet community is that cyber fraudsters are lurking out on the networks hanging around switching points with sniffer programs that can invade other people's data and either copy or alter them. In particular, there are programs which can spot packets of data containing the configuration of digits that suggest the data are carrying, a credit card number. The reality behind this fear is far less alarming. Apart from a few well-publicised cases of such fraud, there is no serious evidence that posting your credit card number on the Internet is any more perilous than giving your card to a waiter in a restaurant. The intensity of the concern therefore is based on a perception among users that the mysterious and abstract network with all its metaphorically open doors is a dangerous place for sensitive information. Security systems, therefore, work not only in the territory of technology but also in the realm of human psychology. In other words, they must work but, even more important, they must be trusted to work.

There are three key elements to Internet security. First, the need to keep messages private. Second, the need to prevent messages being corrupted or changed in transit—a requirement known as data integrity. Third, server and client authentication so that both ends of a transaction know they are talking to who they think they are talking to.

This is a fast-moving area and anything written now-particularly at a time of particularly intense development — is bound to be quickly outdated. So, to provide some lasting value, we will examine the current security offerings as exemplars rather than a statement of any stable and lasting position. We can at least gain a sense of the issues involved in designing such systems and get insight into the strategic direction that is being followed by the main players. In early 1996, as these words are being written, there is a raft of competing security systems becoming available, all implicitly or explicitly linked to facilitating secure payments so enabling Internet commerce to get off the ground. It is important to see that security in itself while crucial to payment mechanisms is essentially a thread that needs to run through them in order to facilitate a system that can be trusted by all its users. Trust is a key issue because technological reassurance is not enough—either for vendors or customers. This suggests that the eventual systems to dominate electronic commerce will be associated with well-established brands in the field of payments. It is no surprise and a great encouragement, therefore, to see such organisations as Visa, Mastercard, Mondex and many of the major clearing banks aligning themselves with the technology gurus of IBM, Microsoft, Netscape and other technology majors.

To gain a sense of these developments, however, we will start with the key issue of security itself and look, in particular, how one powerful and immediately available system works. We have already noted how Netscape has leveraged its secure socket layer (SSL) security technology to generate influence over the market for secure servers but the mechanism by which it offers good security is instructive and worth considering as a model of-some of the more general issues important in this field. The SSL system is, of course, not the only player in the market. IBM has Internet keyed payments (iKP), Microsoft champion- secure transaction technology (STT), browser giant Spyglass has its MD5 system and the US electronic trade specialists CommerceNet utilise Secure HTTP. There is considerable consolidation taking place among these proprietary offerings — Netscape and CommerceNet and other majors are, for example, collaborating through a joint, venture called Terisa to create a single, common and open software standard to offer effective security on any server running the new software. However, Netscape's SSL is striking first because it is instantly available on hundreds, possibly thousands, of servers right now and also because it cunningly trades off inherent strength of security against other factors such as speed and cost.

The actual technology of SSL-like all security and payment systems—arcane and complex, and we will gloss over the mathematic basis of goes on for obvious reasons. With this in mind, the best way to understand how SSL operates is to imagine a real incident where a Web with a Netscape browser visits a site offering transactional activities a server running Netscape's secure server software. When the server goes into secure mode, a message is flashed on the it's screen warning that the session now beginning between the browser server will be protected by Netscape's SSL. This implies that all subsequent exchanges will be secure in the sense that the messages cannot changed or examined by any agencies between the client and the server. There is a key symbol on all Netscape browser screens which denotes exchanges are secure. Most of the time, it is a 'broken' key but when browser is communicating with a secure server, the symbol is complete unbroken. What is happening behind the scenes is technologically complex but conceptually very simple. When a secure transfer is needed, Netscape Navigator running on the client computer randomly generates a one-time token—usually a very large prime number-and this is subsequently used as the underlying mathematical basis for the encryption will then be used to protect data during the secure session. It is important to understand that this token is used only once for the particular session in hand and has no other longer-term significance. In order for the server to use the token for encryption, it has to be communicated by the browser in a secure way. To do this, the client makes automatic contact with a trusted third party server known as a Certification Authority which holds details of what are called 'public keys' owned by all Netscape secure servers. In practice, this trusted position is currently held by the major US security firm RSA Data, the original creators of public key encryption systems. The client gains the public key of the server and uses this to encrypt the token before sending it to the server that it is communicating with. The server uses its secret, private key (a counterpart of the public one) to decrypt the token. The server and client then both use the token for SSL encryption and decryption during the session. At the end of the session, the token is discarded. The whole sequence of exchanges involving the keys and the encrypted token takes seconds and is transparent to the users.

The system goes one step further and allows the client to verify that the server with which it is communicating is the server it says it is and that it is not an impostor. This verification is accomplished by the client asking the server to encrypt a short private test message using its private key. The client then asks the Certification Authority to decrypt the message using the server's public key. If it works, the server is what it says it is. If it does not, then the server is an impostor. Again, the entire process is automatic and takes seconds.

The interesting element in this picture is the way SSL trades the strength of its encryption against other important factors such as speed and cost. Partly, however, Netscape is forced to use relatively weak encryption because strong encryption algorithms are classified by the US authorities as munitions and may not be exported outside the United States. The weakness of SSL is, however, only relative and it is quite good enough to survive all but the most determined attacks. However, its sacrifice of encryption strength makes it much cheaper for users and, equally important, faster than any of its main competitors. The danger to its underlying security is cleverly minimised by ensuring that every encrypted session is based on a unique, once-only token. Even if the token is compromised by a breach in security all that is jeopardised is the single session and Netscape ensures that what is learned from decrypting the token is completely useless for decrypting any other tokens. The fraudsters would have to start all over again trying to figure out how to break the code. In other words, a single failure will contribute nothing to compromising any other secure sessions conducted by that browser-server or any other browser-server combination.

It is worth noting that SSL verifies the server's identity but does not check the client. This gap in the loop is now being closed by a digital signature technology developed by VeriSign, a spin-off company from RSA The digital signature consists of two parts: a method of signing electronically that cannot be forged and a method of verifying that the signature was generated by the person it represents. The digital signature, of course, not only is vital to confirming identity in a secure transaction of the kind just described but also leads directly to the possibility of creating effective digital contracts and, in terms of payment systems, fully digital cheques or debit and credit advices. VeriSign's technology is soon to be incorporated in both Netscape's and Microsoft's browsers but is unlikely to remain unique. The underlying concept of the digital signature will soon be widely available and its impact on Web commerce will be huge as a component within trusted mechanisms.

Full payment mechanisms go further than security. As we saw in the imaginary transaction using SSL above, the security procedures merely protect information passing between client and server. For a secure pay-process this is only the starting point. Transactions can, of course, be managed with nothing else. The server can request a credit card number, the client can send it and the server's proprietor can then manage the link with the credit card company in the same way as they might in a conventional, non-electronic transaction. The problem is that merchants hope to have hundreds of thousands of such transactions flowing through their services every day and, in some cases, the transaction value may be quite small. The costs of managing this flow of vast numbers of, potentially, low value transactions are substantial and the prospect of an end-to-end system which takes transactions from servers through to their consummation with the relevant payment agencies such as credit card companies or banks is essential to establishing Web commerce on an effective and global basis.

There is also a security concern-more perceived than real but no less important because of it. When a credit card number is sent securely to a server, the server decodes it and makes it available to those managing the server. In other words, the merchant possesses the decrypted credit card information as indeed it must in order to process the transaction. In the real world, this situation is commonplace and universally accepted. However, in the electronic world, levels of insecurity are much higher among users. Even allowing merchants access to credit card numbers and protecting them fully on their way to merchants is not considered good enough. As a result of this need to manage a perceived threat to customers, further security technologies have emerged to keep the client credit numberscard secret right up until the point they reach the credit card company. Netscape, for example, have developed software called Secure Courier which effectively seals the credit card information with a layer of encryption carried inside of SSL.

When the encrypted information reaches the SSL layer is stripped off leaving only the more deeply encrypted data. The merchant does not (cannot) decrypt this but instead adds to the encryption with further data about the sum of money involved in the transaction and the merchant's own identity. This encrypted information is then sent by the merchant the last mile to the credit card agency dealing with these transactions. The agency strips off the decrypted layers to get at both the merchant's and customer's data. Even though the examples we are giving are specific proprietary offerings, we are now beginning to see the general key elements in an end-to-end payment system. But there is a further matter of deep concern. Everything we have outlined assumes that credit cards will be used as the basis of electronic commerce.

To some extent, this is a natural and desirable way of seeing future payment systems. Credit cards are widely used, trusted and are supported by a well-developed and international infrastructure facilitating payments, customer billing and subscriber management. It would be foolish not to try to fuse electronic payment mechanisms with the world of credit cards. However, many people do not possess such cards and either prefer or are constrained by their credit ratings to deal in cash. In the record industry, for example, about 50 per cent of all products sold are sold for cash. A survey in the UK in 1995 showed that nearly 60 per cent of Britons preferred cash to cards. One way of addressing this problem would be to extend the payment systems to include direct debits of bank accounts but just as many people do not have credit cards there are also many who do not have bank accounts or would prefer not to debit them without being sure exactly what is in them to cover expenditure. Neither are credit cards or direct debits convenient for handling micropayments. Much Web commerce will want to depend on selling very high volumes of very low priced products or services. This could include the sale of access to content on a time basis measured in seconds or minutes leading to charges accumulating a few pence or cents, depending on where the server is located. All this suggests the need for something that sounds deceptively simple. As well as credit card or bank-based debit mechanisms, there is a clear need for some form of digital money. Money is an excellent basis for trade so long as those using it can rely on it being genuine and also rely on the underlying promise of those supporting monetary systems that the money tokens can be converted among currencies and ultimately redeemed in terms of the value they purportedly represent.

There are a number of electronic money initiatives already being promoted, the best known being Cyberbucks from the Amsterdam-based Cybercash. But while simple in concept, the idea founders because of lack of concerted international support by the government and financial institutions vital to giving digital cash its trusted underpinning. So far, therefore, digital cash looks like a distant prospect so far as genuinely pervasive influence is concerned and -despite their evident limitations-credit card and bank-based systems are likely to be the most widely available systems, at least until the turn of the century. At the time of writing, there are about 30 schemes either suggested or gander development to provide secure payment systems. Among the most promising are collaborations between Visa and Mastercard and moves by banking consortia in both the United States and Europe. The importance of these lies in the trusted nature of the partners. By 1997, the first of these mechanisms will be widely available and it is likely that the market will rapidly settle down into a handful of leading products all operating within a single agreed standard and all widely supported by current browser technologies. By the late 1990s, therefore, the catalyst for Web commerce will be in place and we will see an explosion in the use of the Web all kinds of trading activities.

REFERENCES

Argus Associates, Inc. "Clearinghouse: Information: Rating System." URL: http://www.clearinghouse.net/ratings.html

Beck, Susan. "The Good, the Bad, and the Ugly: or Why It's a Good Idea to Evaluate Web Sources." New Mexico State University Libraries. http://lib.nmsu.edu/staff/susabeck/eval.html

Retting, James. "Beyond Cool: Analog Models for Reviewing Digital Resources." http://www.onlineinc.com/onlinemag/SeptOL/rettig9.html

Shapiro, Jeremy and Shelley Hughes. "Information Literacy as a Liberal Art: Enlightment proposals for a new curriculum." *Educom Review*, 31(2) March/April 1996. http://www.educom.edu/web/pubs/review/reviewArticles/31231.html

Smith, Alastair (maintainer). "Evaluation of Information Sources." (Part of WWWVL-InfoQuality) http://www.vuw.ac.nz/~agsmith/evaln/evaln.htm

Smith, Alastair. "Criteria for Evaluation of Internet Information Resources." http://www.vuw.ac.nz/~agsmith/evaln/index.htm

Tillman, Hope N. "Evaluating Quality on the Net." http://www.tiac.net/users/hope/findqual.html

Treloar, Andrew. "Scholarly Publishing and the Fluid World Wide Web." http://www.csu.edu.au/special/conference/apwww95/papers95/atreloar/atreloar.html

University of Washington Libraries. "Teaching Students to Think Critically about Internet Resources: Community College Symposium on Teaching, Learning, and Technology. University of Washington, June 17-21, 1996." http://weber.u.washington.edu/~libr560/NETEVAL/index.html

Wilkinson, Gene (with Kevin Oliver and Lisa Bennett). "Evaluating the Quality of Internet Information Sources." http://itech1.coe.uga.edu/Faculty/GWilkinson/webeval.html